D1130719

The Tourist Image

The Tourist Image

MYTHS AND MYTH MAKING IN TOURISM

Edited by
Tom Selwyn

JOHN WILEY & SONS

Chichester • New York • Brisbane • Toronto • Singapore

Copyright © 1996 by John Wiley & Sons Ltd,
Baffins Lane, Chichester,
West Sussex PO19 1UD, England

National   01243 779777
International (+44) 1243 779777

Other Wiley Editorial Offices

John Wiley & Sons, Inc., 605 Third Avenue,
New York, NY 10158-0012, USA

Jacaranda Wiley Ltd, 33 Park Road, Milton,
Queensland 4064, Australia

John Wiley & Sons (Canada) Ltd, 22 Worcester Road,
Rexdale, Ontario M9W 1L1, Canada

John Wiley & Sons (Asia) Pte Ltd, 2 Clementi Loop #02-01,
Jin Xing Distripark, Singapore 0512

Library of Congress Cataloging-in-Publication Data

The Tourist Image : myths and myth making in tourism / edited by Tom
  Selwyn.
       p. cm.
    Includes bibliographical references and index.
    ISBN 0-471-96309-7 (alk. paper)
    1. Tourist trade. I. Selwyn, Tom.
  G155.A1T5984   1996
  338.4'791–dc20   95-42632
                                                                        CIP

British Library Cataloguing in Publication Data

A catalogue record for this book is available from the British Library

ISBN 0-471-96309-7

Typeset in 10/12pt Palatino by Mayhew Typesetting, Rhayader, Powys
Printed and bound in Great Britain by Biddles Ltd, Guildford

This book is printed on acid-free paper responsibly manufactured from sustainable forestation,
for which at least two trees are planted for each one used for paper production.

Contents

Contributors

Jeremy Boissevain is Emeritus Professor of Social Anthropology, University of Amsterdam. Currently a Fellow at the Amsterdam School of Social Science Research, he also works with the Med-Campus Programme for Sustainable Cultural and Ecological Tourism, University of Malta. He has published extensively on local politics, ethnic relations, small entrepreneurs, ritual change and tourism. His most recent works include *Revitalizing European Rituals* (London: Routledge, 1992) and *Coping with Tourists: European Reactions to Mass Tourism* (London: Berghahn Books, 1996).

Glenn Bowman is a social anthropologist who currently chairs the interdisciplinary programme in 'Communications and Image Studies' at the University of Kent. His primary research field has been with Palestinians in Israel and the Israeli-Occupied Territories where he has researched articulations of sectarian and nationalism identities, festivals and pilgrimage practices at local and international shrines, and the practices and politics of tourism and tour-guiding. He has also worked on questions of identity and processes of state formation in Former Yugoslavia.

David Brown is a Melanesianist, trained at the London School of Economics, with special interest in kinship and exchange. Social life in Melanesia is characterised by a sense of movement, in the ever-present exchange of things and of persons. There are parallels here with contemporary consumer society, in particular tourism, which Brown draws out in his contribution to this volume.

Graham Dann obtained his doctorate from the University of Surrey in 1975. Since then he has been lecturing in the University of the West Indies, where he is currently Reader in Sociology. He is an assistant editor of *Annals of Tourism Research*, a founder member of the *International Academy for the Study of Tourism*, and President of the Research Committee on International Tourism of the *International Sociological Association*. His latest book, published by CAB International (April 1996) is entitled *The Language of Tourism*.

Elizabeth Edwards curates photographs and archives in the Pitt Rivers Museum, University of Oxford, and teaches critical history and theory of photography in the Faculty of Anthropology. She is editor of *Anthropology* *and Photography* (Yale University Press, 1992) and has published extensively on history, photography, and anthropology as well as having curated many exhibitions of historical and contemporary photography.

Craig Fees was born in Arizona and raised in the United States. He received his doctorate in 1988 from the Institute of Dialect and Folklife Studies at the University of Leeds, and is currently an archivist developing an anthropologically-oriented research facility on "therapeutic community". He is Executive Trustee of the Guild of Handicraft Trust, Chipping Campden. Lives with wife and two noisy children in a small village at foot of the Cotswolds.

Deborah Golden is a social anthropologist with a particular interest in the anthropology of time. In addition to her work on museums, she is currently completing research on the endeavours on the part of Israelis to reconstruct the temporal perspective of immigrants from the Societ Union. She teaches at the Hebrew University of Jerusalem.

Michael Hutt is Senior Lecturer in Nepali at SOAS, where he studied for a BA in South Asian Studies (1980) and a PhD in Nepali (1984). His publications include *Himalayan voices: an introduction to modern Nepali literature* (Berkeley, University of California Press, 1991), *Nepal: a guide to the art and architecture of the Kathmandu Valley* (Gartmore, Kiscadale Publications, 1994), *Nepal in the nineties: versions of the past, visions of the future* (New Delhi, Oxford University Press, 1993) and *Bhutan: perspectives on conflict and dissent* (Gartmore, Kiscadale Publications, 1994).

DP Martinez is Lecturer in Anthropology with Reference to Japan at the School of Oriental and African Studies, London, where she also teaches a course on the anthropology of tourism. She has recently edited (with Jan van Bremen) *Ceremony and Ritual in Japan*, and is currently working on another edited volume *The Worlds of Japanese Popular Culture*.

Kevin Meethan received his doctorate in Social Anthropology from the University of Sussex, and is now Senior Lecturer in Sociology at the University of Plymouth, UK. His current research interests include tourism, place, and consumption.

Tom Selwyn is Professor of the Anthropology of Tourism at the University of North London. Trained at the LSE and SOAS, from where he obtained his doctorate following field research in Central India, he has taught at the LSE, the University of Tel-Aviv, and Roehampton Institute, from where he co-ordinated a programme of post-graduate studies in the anthropology of tourism. He presently directs one of the European Union's Med-Campus networks in the Eastern Mediterranean and is co-chair of the Royal Anthropological Institute's committee on tourism and heritage. His latest book, to be published by Prentice Hall, is entitled *Tourism and Society*.

Acknowledgements

There are many people I would like to thank for their help and encouragement during the pre-production and production of this book: those from whose work on the anthropology and sociology of tourism I have learnt a great deal of what I know of the subject – in particular David Wilson, Graham Dann, Gerry Mars, Mike Hitchcock, Monica Hanefors, Michael Ireland, Krzystof Przeclawski, and Mary Bouquet; members of the Group for the Anthropology in Policy and Practice (GAPP) as a result of whose conference on the anthropology of tourism the idea for this book first arose; colleagues at the University of Tel-Aviv, especially Emanuel Marx, whose many insights into the symbolic contours of Israeli society drew me towards an interest in that country's landscape, its visitors and the articulation of tourism and nationalism; Colleagues at the University of Alexandria with whom I have been fortunate to work, within the EU's Med-Campus framework, on matters relating to Egyptian and Mediterranean tourism and society; David Harrison for his detailed, critical and invaluable comments on the book at two of its key stages; Dean MacCannell for reading and commenting on the book's Introduction; John Eade, Shirley Eber, Andrew Garner, Dieneke Ferguson, Heba Aziz, as well as other colleagues and Masters students at Roehampton Institute; Peter Burns and Robert Cleverdon from the University of North London; Tricia Barnett and Sue Wheat of *Tourism Concern*; René Baretje, for enabling me to use the (unique) library at the Centre des Hautes Etudes Touristiques in Aix-en-Provence; Jeremy Boissevain, consistent source of inspiration and founder of the anthropology of European tourism; Michael Safier, who has taught me how to think of tourism within a much wider framework of global cultural and politico-economic relations and processes; Francesca Sylvani, for editorial skills; Linda Wilson, for secretarial help.

I would especially like to thank Iain Stevenson and Lindsay Jackson at John Wiley for their kindness and professionalism.

Finally, I would like to thank the members of my extended family, and dedicate the book to my own family – Ruth, Ben and Naomi.

1 Introduction

TOM SELWYN

ORIENTATIONS

This book is about 'tourist myths' and their settings in the world of contemporary tourism. Apart from explaining how the term 'myth' is used, and why it seems appropriate to think of a tourist as one who 'chases myths', the purpose of this introduction is to outline how the present volume contributes to current discussions in the anthropology of tourism.

Elsewhere (Selwyn, 1994) I have offered a view of the present state of the art of the anthropology of tourism, and it serves the purposes of the present introduction to recall and hold in mind some of the cardinal points made in that essay.

To start with, there seems every good reason to start off here by emphasising Crick's (1989) identification of the three main strands of enquiry within the anthropology of tourism: the semiology of tourism, tourism's political economy, tourism and social and cultural change.

Acknowledging that they overlap, what follows is underpinned by these themes. The aim is to introduce some of the ideas which have played a pivotal role not only in the anthropology of tourism in general but in the essays presented in this volume in particular. Before doing so, however, there is one further preliminary observation to be made, namely that there is a fourth line of enquiry running through the anthropology of tourism: the relationship between contemporary tourism and contemporary knowledge (cf. Crick, 1985). Much more of this in due course.

The present discussion starts off by being structured into three sections. These are concerned respectively with tourists, people living in tourist destinations and those who in one way or another (both inside and outside the tourist industry) 'observe' tourism and its works.

MAINLY ABOUT TOURISTS

Since the main focus of the present volume consists of what we are calling tourist myths, we need to start with tourists themselves. There is no better author to start with than MacCannell.

MacCannell's (1976) *The Tourist* was written, he tells us, partly in

The Tourist Image: Myths and Myth Making in Tourism. Edited by Tom Selwyn.
© 1996 John Wiley & Sons Ltd.

response to Levi-Strauss's view that structuralist interpretations of the modern world were impossible since modernity itself had destroyed the structures on which such interpretations were based. MacCannell, however, argued that modern tourists were, in fact, in many ways archetypical 'structuralists' whose motives could best be understood in terms of a desire to recover — mythologically — those senses of wholeness and structure absent from everyday contemporary life.

The sense of contemporary social fragmentation lying at the outset of *The Tourist* appears with even greater force in *Empty Meeting Grounds* 'the starting point [of which] is [the] non-controversial assumption that the cultures of the world have been radically displaced and fundamentally and forever altered by the movements of peoples' (MacCannell, 1992:3). MacCannell argues that this displacement (and the movements of the migrants, homeless people, refugees and tourists which articulate it) gives birth to two different kinds of 'displaced thought'. One of these uses the signs and artifacts of cultural difference and national boundaries imaginatively in a continuous process of formulation, reformulation and 'hybridization' of culture in a post-modern world; we are in a world where the 'heroes of these [cultural] diasporas' are travelling 'bricoleurs' (ibid.:4). The other 'consumes' cultures (in the style, for example, of tourist brochures which seek to render culture 'consumable' by tourists). At the centre of this latter process lies the subordination of local people to projects, such as tourism, which seem to depend on the mythical *reconstitution* or reconstruction of those senses of tradition uprooted by 'globalization'. Each of the cases discussed in the present volume displays evidence of both styles of thought at work in the tourist myths considered.

MacCannell builds upon ethnographic evidence from the traditional Parisian guided tour which, taking in as it did all sorts of sites including cemeteries and transport systems as well as museums and famous buildings, seemed to be based on the tourist's search for a vision of the 'whole' of the city made possible by viewing and touring around its many parts. This idea closely matches that of Barthes (1983) in his magical essay *The Eiffel Tower*.

In both his principal works, MacCannell argues that contemporary tourists habitually locate the 'Other' (frequently a pre-modern Other) encountered in the course of a holiday in a world which is in some way more whole, structured and authentic (of which more below) than the everyday world they inhabit cognitively most of the year. In short, one of the central elements of MacCannell's argument is that the tourist goes on holiday in order cognitively to create or recreate structures which modernity is felt to have demolished. It is these structures, these *mythical* structures, or tourist myths, and the imagery associated with them, which constitute the main focus of the present volume.

A word here is needed about the use of the term myth itself. The main sense employed here derives from a Levi-Straussian tradition within which myths are treated as stories which may serve the intellectual and emotional function of taking up the personal and social conundra of living in such a way that these appear 'resolved' at an intellectual and emotional level. Levi-Strauss (1986[1964]:5) approached his own studies of myth by quoting from Durkheim's observation that myths 'explain nothing [but] merely shift the difficulty elsewhere . . . [and] in so doing . . . attenuate . . . their crying illogicality'. This idea of the difficulty being shifted elsewhere (and in the present context this is taken to apply, quite simply, to difficulty, or difficulties, of life in the post-modern world) is developed by Levi-Strauss's own notion of myths as vehicles of forgetfulness and 'failures to communicate with oneself and with others' — or, conversely, as vehicles for 'overcommunication with others' (1987:186). In this vein, the myths discussed in this volume seem simultaneously to reveal and conceal, to undercommunicate and overcommunicate. Thus for example, several of the studies (very clearly exemplified in the treatment of the Shangri-La and Chipping Campden cases) are concerned with the way in which tourist perceptions, motivations and understandings about destinations are shaped by a preoccupation with harmonious social relations, ideas about community, notions of the whole. These are the preoccupations which are mythologized in the tourist's view of Nepal, the English West Country, or wherever — and which are, in this sense, 'overcommunicated'. What is concealed, however, (by the forgetfulness which mythical language permits) are the actual fractures and displacements which the more pragmatic and empirical aspects of the ethnographies in question clearly reveal.

But let me go back to MacCannell, whose thesis has come under several sorts of criticism. Of these, two are particularly relevant. The first is Cohen's (1988b, for example) objection that there is no such person as *the* tourist but, rather, many different kinds of tourist, some of whom, according to Cohen, are looking for no more than 'mere recreation'. He argues that it is simply not convincing to see *all* tourists as seekers after mythological structures and implies that the 'recreational' sort of tourist is more or less happy with 'just' building sand castles or getting laid.

The second criticism, also raised by Cohen and discussed by Crick (1989) and others, is that the notion of the tourist as a seeker after structure, authenticity and so on is based on assumptions about alienation in the modern world which are simply dated and thus of limited explanatory use. Critics have pointed out that such a view of alienation emerged directly from the sociology of the 1960s and its immediate aftermath.[1] But, in the post-modern world we now inhabit, such notions are no longer applicable. Following the absolute triumph of consumerism, individuals have become, in the penetrating words of Baudrillard (1988) 'no more than monitoring screens' . . . in the process of their thorough . . . 'indoctrination into systematic and organised consumption'. 'Monitoring screens' cannot feel alienated!

MAINLY ABOUT THE PEOPLE OF TOURIST DESTINATIONS

If one of the concerns of the anthropology of tourism is with the nature of tourists, a second is with the societies and cultures of the people living in tourist destinations. Arguably, the two authors initially responsible for founding this tradition were Smith (1977, revised 1989) and de Kadt (1979, 1990).

Smith (1977) complemented *The Tourist* in two main respects. First of all the essays in her volume moved the focus from the tourist to the people of tourist destinations (and the relation between these two) and, secondly, they brought tourism studies back from the exhilarating high seas of Franco–American structuralist speculation into the more bracing and pragmatic shores of Anglo–American empiricism and ethnographic field research. De Kadt's widely known *Tourism: Passport to Development?* (1979) was also concerned with the people of tourist destinations, the volume's authors all asking how the people of such destinations might use the tourism industry to their own economic, political and social advantage within a changing world economic order. The questions posed in that volume were taken up (over 10 years later, with Brandt and Brundtland published and a global environmental movement pointing towards Rio and beyond) by de Kadt himself in his seminal 'Making the alternative sustainable: lessons from development for tourism' (1990). The tradition of closely observed consideration of tourism development issues, stemming from the work of these authors, has found eloquent recent expression in Harrison's (1992) *Tourism and the Less Developed Countries*. But unquestionably the ethnographically richest volume in this tradition is Boissevain's *Coping With Tourists* (1996), a collection of mature studies which has effectively set a new tone and direction in the anthropology of tourism.

MAINLY ABOUT OBSERVERS

In a piece which was at once both playful and deeply serious, Crick (1985) shifted the focus yet again, this time to the *observer* of tourism and its works. Following Feyerabend's insistence that scientific research involves much ludic, not strictly methodological and even anarchistic procedures, Crick argued that scientists generally, and anthropologists in particular, play all sorts of 'games' in their research and that such games are not only justified but part of the reality of scientific processes. For Crick this is quite desirable and realistic: anthropologists should 'come clean' about their work. Indeed science itself should put an end to the pretence of methodological purity, for actual scientific procedures involve clowning. According to Crick this 'Dadaistic' or 'Derridadaistic' approach not only 'boils science down to human dimensions' but also 'returns us' (ie anthropologists) 'to the company . . . of tourists . . . who [are] our classificatory kin' (ibid.:84).

The importance of this line of thought was highlighted by Urry's (1990) argument about the changing role of those observers of tourism who are also actors in the tourism industry itself: museum curators, heritage managers, and other such professionals. According to Urry, the organization of contemporary tourism reflects a changing cultural landscape, one example of which is to be found in the way history is represented in museums. Urry argues that relatively uniform, modernist and 'auratic' historical explanations, normally structured around some form of national history, are giving way to explanations and representations which are more varied, post-modernist, vernacular and regional. Urry (in Lash and Urry, 1987 as well as 1990) links this up with the declining role of the state in economic organization (capitalist economies being increasingly organized on a multinational level) and the lessening power of classically trained élites within the educational and cultural fields of states. On a general level Urry's argument is that there is a move away from overarching scientific and other meta-narratives towards narratives of a more local and popular nature. In this intellectual landscape, a much wider variety of social groups may find it possible to represent 'their' histories. In short, singular national history, 'scientifically' represented, is giving way to multiple histories, based on locality, class, gender, ethnicity, and so on, represented in multiple ways.

This is a universe in which a museum's success is tested not so much by the ring of any overarching scientific truth but by the ring of the cash registers at the museum entrance; and it is in this universe that contemporary tourism professionals work. One of the questions underlying the work of both Urry and Crick concerns the implications — for intellectuals in general as well as for tourism professionals in particular — of the fact that the boundaries between the commercial and the scientific are shifting.

In the end, however, although both Urry's and Crick's use of tourism to comment on the state of contemporary representations of knowledge set out from similar positions, they ultimately lead to different destinations, as we shall see.

MAP READINGS

If these arguments are the landmarks against which this introduction is to be measured, it is necessary briefly to summarize exactly where we have reached and take note of the directions towards which the signposts are pointing. In short, the arguments need briefly to be evaluated.

The advantage of MacCannell's approaches to the analysis of contemporary tourism is that they start from some general theories and assumptions about the nature of modern or post-modern society. Particular aspects and examples of tourist practice are then contextualized within a broader framework and are used to advance our understanding of that broader context. In their own way (in relation to the world political economy, the production and representation of knowledge and so forth) and in the works cited here, de Kadt, Crick, and Urry do likewise, and the intention here is to follow that same route. It seems, simply, the most scenic one to take.

These observations lead directly on to Cohen and his criticism of aspects of MacCannell's work. The view adopted here is that there are two main problems with the way Cohen frames his critique. The first is methodological. While, of course, there is nothing wrong with being impatient with overarching theories and choosing instead Mertonian middle-range theories, there must remain a question about the desirability of using the latter to criticize the former. Some would say that this is to mix levels of analysis. The question is whether or not a theoretical paradigm can effectively be challenged by a classification system. The second problem is empirical. Cohen builds his classification of tourists largely on *a priori* grounds, and one is left wondering about the ethnographic justification for the various claims that are made. It is by no means clear, for example, that 'drifters' and intellectuals are necessarily 'more alienated' from their society than 'organised mass tourists', or that the former pair are more interested in encountering the 'authentic' (whatever that may mean) than the latter. After all, both 'drifters' and intellectuals have been known to become, at certain stages of their lives, establishment pillars in a variety of settings!

The great value of Cohen's work, however, lies in the attention he draws to the fact that tourism is, indeed, a multi-valent activity. Thus, for example, as Graburn (1977) has rightly pointed out, tourism grew out of and in some respects resembles pilgrimage. Some tourists may indeed be 'like' pilgrims. At the same time tourists are also, as Dann (1989) has argued, 'like' children (cf. also Selwyn, 1993 and others). This introduction takes up Cohen's challenge to interpret tourist activity and tourists in this multi-valent way. The only significant addition to Cohen's insights which might reasonably be suggested is that we acknowledge the possibility that within the same individual tourist may beat a heart which is equally pilgrim-like and child-like. Tourists seem to have, so to speak, a 'child ventricle' and a 'pilgrim ventricle': a seemingly fundamental ambivalence which, in my own view, may well be the principal characteristic of tourism in the post-modern world.

One important problem left unresolved by the work of both MacCannell and Cohen concerns the nature of authenticity. Each writer uses the term in two different senses. On the one hand there is MacCannell's assertion that the tourist, like a pilgrim, is searching for a sense (which is both Durkheimian and Turnerian) of the authentically social in order to reclaim that which has been lost by an essentially isolating and fracturing post-modern life. This sense is picked up by Cohen (1988a:35) in his assertion that *because* 'educated drifters' and intellectuals share senses of alienation they are drawn to the authentic. As he puts it, 'the greater the alienation of the tourist, the greater the search for authenticity'.

But there is a second, and quite different, sense of authenticity employed by the two writers. In MacCannell this sense is called into play in his discussions of 'staged authenticity' (1976:91–107). This expression refers to the fact that those seeking the authentic 'back stage' may encounter, in Boorstin's (1964) words (cf. also Cohen 1988b), even there, another per-formance which is staged — another 'pseudo-event'. In Cohen (1989) the same sense is picked up in his attempt to apply MacCannell's notion of authenticity to the case of alternative tourism in northern Thailand. Cohen tells us that while *in fact* the Thai Highlands have become economically, politically and socially integrated into the Lowlands and the country as a whole, they are presented to 'drifter' and 'explorer'-type tourists *as if* they were 'primitive and remote'. This time, in both writers, authenticity appears not as an alienation-smashing feeling but as a term referring to the quality of knowledge associated with the tourist experience. Here, in other words, authenticity refers to statements (for example by tour guides on whether or not people of Northern Thailand use their fingers or plastic forks to eat) which are more or less open to what we may call 'Popperian' processes and procedures.[2]

We may acknowledge that the identification of this semantic confusion owes a considerable amount to Crick's insistence that the anthropology of tourism raises questions about the character and the quality of the knowledge not only of the tourist but also of the anthropological observer. The question is whether there is any difference between the narratives of tourists and their guides and the narratives of anthropologists.

To move the argument forward it is suggested that we make a clear distinction between two different senses of the term. In the first sense, the authentic is taken to refer to those feelings, or projections of feelings, of social solidarity pursued by tourists in the several ways explored through-out this volume. In its second sense, the authentic refers to the knowledge (about, for example, the nature, culture and society of tourist destinations) which is both sought by tourists and presented to them by Cohen's 'intellectuals' — museum curators, tour guides and other 'participant observers' working in, or, like anthropologists, commenting on, the tourism industry.

We could put it like this. If we agree with MacCannell and others that tourists seek the authentic, we need to add that such authenticity has two aspects, one of which has to do with feeling, the other with knowledge. In yet other words, the tourist is after both authentic social relations and sociability (which would certainly include an authentically 'good time') as well as some sort of knowledge about the nature and society of the chosen destination. The point to make here is that statements (made by museum curators, heritage managers, sociology professors or anyone else) claiming authenticity in this second sense become, by virtue of the claim itself, subject to standard 'scientific' procedures and processes which are objectively verifiable.

Following on closely from the above, we come to Urry's (1990:132, 155, for example) arguments about the decline of the auratic, the increasing sovereignty of the consumer and the 'various kinds of accommodation and reinterpretation' (of history) which flow from these linked facts. As we have already observed, the background to this argument, promoted by several post-modernist writers, is that the very idea of statements which are held to be scientifically valid, or objectively verifiable, belongs to the failed corpus of ideas and values associates with modernity. Thus Urry chides Hewison for making an 'absolute distinction between authentic history . . . and heritage' (op. cit.:110) and quotes with approval from Lowenthal's assertion that history is not, and never was, something 'out there . . . in a foreign country' but that it is 'assimilated into ourselves, and resurrected into an ever-changing present' (Lowenthal, 1985:412; Urry, op. cit.:112). He further points to examples of groups and categories of people, such as miners in the former coal-mining areas of South Wales, who have sought to hold on to aspects of 'their history'. In this view the heritage industry has the effect of making history more accessible, popular and democratic; historians more accountable and, generally, of softening distinctions between history and heritage.

There is, it may seem at first, much that is attractive about these ideas. Urry's assertion that there is no simple route to historical authenticity is unquestionably correct, but the notion that history is socially constructed, just like heritage, is deeply problematic; and some of the reasons for it being so will be explored below.

It is now quite clear that the term 'host' is ultimately too simple a term in a complex world. Kenna's (1993) work on the island on Nisos, for example, describes a Greek island economy in which a sizeable proportion of tourist developments is organized and financed from abroad by ex-patriot Nisosians or, alternatively, by returned Nisosian migrants. Are these people hosts in Smith's (1977) sense? Another way of raising the same objection would be to point to the obvious fact that a Chinese owner of a hotel in a Malaysian tourist resort is a quite different sort of host than the peasant fisherman in the same region. That said, the seminal volumes of Smith, de Kadt, and now Boissevain (1996) serve as constant reminders, if ever we should need them, that the ethnographic study of tourism has at its heart the study of local tourist destinations, on the one hand, and wider,

Plate 1 (Eroding) Permanence: Pyramids at Giza, Egypt. Photograph: Footprints, Ian Osborn

Plate 2 Abundance for Consumption: Fish Buffet and Spanish Wine. Photograph: Footprints, Tim Montier

Plate 3 Inmates, Tourists: Royal Cliff Beach Hotel, Pattaya, Thailand (cf Bartokowski 1995). Photograph: Footprints, Nick Hannah

Plate 4 Lost Horizons: Sunbathing topless in Gambia. Photograph: Footprints, Lesley Abdela

Plate 5   Coastal Relations: Men watching surf. Photograph: Footprints, Nick Hannah

Plate 6   Enchanted City: Mont St Michel, Normandy. Photograph: Footprints, Nick Hannah

Plate 7 Servicing Shangri-la: Porter, Nepal. Photograph: Footprints, Nick Hannah

Plate 8 Beached and Unbounded: Girl lying in water, Maldives. Photograph: Footprints, Nick Hannah

including global, economic systems on the other. Each also emphasizes the fact that the understanding of the former is almost bound to remain partial without a comparable understanding of the latter.

CHARTING ROUTES

We find ourselves poised between the local and the global, conducting a three-cornered conversation among tourists, observers and those 'locals' living in tourist destinations.

In the next section we will move on to consider the context of this conversation which, it will be argued, is built on three principal foundations, at once political, economic and ideological. The first of these derives from the fact that contemporary global tourism is organized on axes of 'centres' and 'peripheries'; the second from the fact that tourism is defined by (and helps itself to define) global consumer culture; the third is derived from the fact that much of tourism seems to be concerned with the search for the authentic (in both of the senses outlined above). It is further claimed that, as well as constituting the main factors in the external world which give rise to our tourist myths, these three structures also lie at the centre of tourists' *internal* world and, thereby, also constitute the three central themes of the myths to be considered.

Before continuing, we need to draw a caveat. The triad of tourist/local/ observer is clearly no simple one, for the roles may be exchanged. Local residents of tourist destinations and observers may become tourists, tourists observers and so on. Post-modernity is unquestionably dissolving the visa controls between these terms. The position taken here, however, is that from some points of view it is important to uphold or even strengthen those controls, and what follows will explore why.

TOURIST MYTHS AND IMAGES: THEMES, FORMATIONS, SETTINGS

CENTRES AND PERIPHERIES

MacCannell (1989) has argued that the movement of tourists from the world's metropolitan centres to its peripheries, and the corresponding movement of migrant labour from peripheries to centres may usefully be understood as one event and that any semiology of tourism needs to start from this point.

Provided we bear in mind that neither centres nor peripheries are immutably fixed in a geographical or historical sense, it seems clear that tourism is one of the engines which manufacture and structure relationships between centres and peripheries. For example, two of the best historical ethnographies of tourism — of Hawaii (Kent, 1983) and Fiji (Britton, 1983) respectively — have explored the political economy of tourism in those islands in relation to histories moulded by their positions on the peripheries of spheres of influence centred, formerly, on Britain and now on the USA and Japan. The purpose of their analyses is to demonstrate the degree to which the islands have become economically, politically and culturally dependent on those political centres and how tourism has deepened that dependency.

In more general terms tourism may be said to be both an outcome and an expression of the relation between centres and peripheries (clearly in economic and political senses but also in cultural senses) for, as noted above, and following the work of several authors, one sort of tourism which anthropologists are particularly interested in is shaped by the search for the 'primitive and remote', to use Cohen's terms. As Bruner (1989) has it (ultimately too simply, perhaps, but, at first glance usefully) much of tourist activity 'reflects a world in which one segment, affluent, civilised, and industrial, projects its desires onto another segment, poorer, more primitive, less developed'.

The essays presented here concentrate on three sorts of processes in the articulation of such centre/periphery relations. These are: (a) the construction in the internal world of the tourist imagination of ideas, images, myths and fantasies about the Other (the imagined resident of those geographical and economically peripheral regions which are also tourist destinations); (b) the shaping and influencing by the tourist industry of the societies and economies of the tourist periphery; and (c) the ways in which the powerful set of forces associated with the myths and images of the Other, and the societies and cultures in which he or she is located, are challenged and resisted.

Hutt (Chapter 3) describes the construction by European travellers of the Shangri-la myth of Nepal, following the now famous novel of the 1930s by the Englishman James Hilton. The myth describes a valley of contented citizens, self-sufficient in all basic resources, ruled by a benign and democratic government. The Nepalese tourist authorities have used this myth to sell Nepal to Western tourists in search of signs of wisdom, plenty and benevolently supervised social cohesion. But Hutt also reports on a more recent novel by a Nepalese author about a search by an American tourist for Shangri-la — and the tourist's consequent encounter not with eyes of a child of the sort of Shangri-la promised by the myth but with the eyes of a child who is cold, malnourished and paralysed. Implicit in the novel, and Hutt's own essay, are questions about the interweaving of the politico-economic relations of a Northern centre with a Southern periphery and mythical perceptions by tourists from the North about the Asian Other. Edward Said (1985) seems close at hand.

Two authors, Meethan and Fees (Chapters 10 and 7) are concerned with the way British townscapes and landscapes are used as sites of fantasy and recreation by the urban middle class in ways which relegate working-class inhabitants to political, economic and social peripheries. Meethan (Chapter 10) recounts how the south coast town of Brighton enjoys a reputation as a seat of British heritage, with the added value of a certain raffish glamour associated with sexual licence, and how it has built its tourism industry on these myths. Publicity literature is based on images of Brighton as a smart and prosperous town, a centre of culture, with its music festival, and economic enterprise. Indeed so successful was the projected image of Brighton as an exemplar of 'enterprise culture' that the town was at one time removed, by the government, from its Urban Aid programme. And yet there has always been another Brighton. This town has severe social and economic problems. According to Meethan: 'The reality is that deprivation, according to the Department of the Environment's own assessment, is worse in Brighton, Hove and Hastings than in many northern industrial towns whose names are synonymous with poverty.' There is now an active political lobby in the town which is contesting the myth of 'heritage Brighton' with facts about unemployment and the needs of the unemployed and the other disadvantaged categories of the town's citizens.

Fees (Chapter 7) describes how, in the West Country town of Chipping Campden, the flow of middle-class urban incomers had the effect of relegating local residents to the periphery of the political and social stages — leaving the incomers to occupy the centre. His account is relevant to much of Britain's geographical periphery as the old economic systems give way to new ones based on tourism, ownership of second homes (by tourists who stayed) and remittances. In Campden's case the incomers have made a myth of the town as a charming pastoral seat of middle England. Some incomers have regarded the changes in the town during the 20th century as 'a record of the deterioration of the idyllic town [and] of growing urbanization, both outward and inward'. As Fees observes: 'Those who have fought to preserve the town have been people drawn from elsewhere by its beauty to live in it.' As the myth has been embellished, successive waves of incomers have found that they 'have had to fight not only against the current of modern "civilisation", but also against those Campden people themselves who have wished their town to become prosperous and modern at the expense of its unique atmosphere.' These atmospheric fantasies have fuelled political processes which seemed until recently to have rendered longer-established local residents powerless to engage effectively in local politics.

Dann (Chapter 4) builds on his own work on brochure images of Cyprus (1988) to illustrate his thesis that the underlying message of many tourist brochures is that the relationship between tourists, typically from European centres, and local Cypriot residents, in an island on the periphery of

Europe, is linguistically and photographically constructed in a way which renders the former in unequivocal control of the latter.

What these and other accounts appear to show is that: (a) tourism is organized within a framework of centres and peripheries in which the latter may have regional, class and ethnic dimensions; (b) that this external world is refracted at the level of the tourist's internal world and; (c) that this last is marked by a preoccupation with relations of power and dependence.

A picture is developing, then, in which tourism appears as a system which articulates relationships of politico–economic and cultural dependence of (predominantly tourist-receiving) peripheries upon (predominantly tourist-sending) centres. It is precisely at this point that further evidence forces us into the drawing of another important caveat. Although it can hardly be denied that peripheries are, to a large extent, indeed dependent on centres, this dependence is by no means unchallenged.

Both Boissevain and Martinez, for example, describe how the entry and activities of urban tourists into provincial localities is resisted. Martinez (Chapter 9) describes how male urban tourists at the inn at Kuzaki village are treated partly as deities, who are seen as potential benefactors in that they bring economic prosperity to the village. Deities, however, are also thought to be potentially dangerous and thus the tourists are, almost literally, kept in their place (inside the inn), where they receive excellent food and service but out of which they seldom venture to threaten the integrity of the village.

Boissevain's account (Chapter 6) of the Maltese *festi*, and tourist participation in their celebration, revolves around the distinction between the *festa ta'gewwa*, or internal feast, and the *festa ta'barra*, or external feast. Part of Boissevain's argument is that tourists and outsiders are customarily restricted to participation in parts of the latter celebrations and that other (in many cases more numerous and ritually significant) events are celebrated only by locals. Boissevain relates the symbolic construction and preservation of local residents' senses of inner and outer selves to other processes in economic and political spheres. These are observations which link up with work on Malta by Black (1996) (more of which below) who argues that notions of cultural domination of peripheries by tourists from centres may in some cases by oversimple and misleading. Both Boissevain and Martinez, then, draw attention to the way in which those in peripheries challenge the dominance of centres.

Bowman (Chapter 5) takes the argument a step further. The politics of the seduction of rich tourists by Palestinian shopkeepers in the Old City of Jerusalem is framed by the apparent, even if clearly also momentary, humbling of the economic power of Northern tourists by the physical and linguistic skills of Southern petty traders. The debates held among his informants about his own analysis provide Bowman with another dimension to his argument. Essentially these debates concern the extent to which 'fucking tourists' (and then metaphorically pissing on them) is either an act or sign of potency in any substantial sense. The idea is advanced that real potency may lie not so much with the 'image of the merchant's penis as a sign in an agonistic discourse with foreigners' but 'as an element connected with the creation of family, community and nation'. In this view sex does not appear as a substitute for effective political action: the possibility is glimpsed of sex and politics acquiring a new and mutually productive relationship which leads out of the 'closed circuit' of a competitive market-place in the midst of a hostile state. The discussion centres, then, upon the extent to which competitive sexual seduction of tourists mirrors competitive struggles between merchants caught up in an arena in which the greatest seducer of all is revealed — in all its omnipotence, omnipresence and cultural arrogance — as the market economy itself.

At this point 'fucking tourists' appears as a sign, at most, of short-term and mythical potency in a politico–economic context of long-term impotence. The prescience of Bowman's discussion, however, which owes most to his own informant's deliberations, lies in the fact that it was initially conceived just before the start of the *Intifada* (which in turn has led to more recent and monumental events in the region). What the deliberations in the street evince is the possibility of 'fucking tourists' turning out to be one stage of a process leading towards altogether more serious politics, as well as more serious sex. Perhaps the lesson being drawn in the souvenir markets of this particular tourist and pilgrimage destination is that to address questions of sexual relations and economic relations in this context is part of the same, fundamentally political, project.

Taken together, what all these data suggest is that tourism plays a significant role in the construction of relationships between centres and peripheries at the various levels and in the various forms which have been described. Although these relations are characterized by the seeming wholesale dependency of peripheries upon centres, there is considerable evidence about the ways in which tourist-related activities also play significant roles in challenging that dependency.

Indeed, it is quite possible to imagine a future in which tourism came to play a central role in the movement of tourist-receiving regions of the South away from the periphery and the dependence associated with that position. After all, the natural and cultural resources of tourist-receiving areas, including those in the Southern peripheries, are highly desirable to tourists from the Northern centres and the industries which service them. Some might even argue that, having failed to redress the imbalance of trade in raw materials and manufactured goods between North and South which has persisted through the last several hundred years, the South, in tourism, has a new opportunity to review the situation afresh. Countries of the South might start with a review of the cultural terms of trade[3] which underpin the tourist system. The extent to which the women of Kuzaki, the organizers of Maltese *festi* together with Lāmichhāne and the authors of *Brighton on the Rocks*, represent the first stirrings of a wider movement to redefine those cultural terms of trade, only time will tell.

THE CONSUMING TOURIST

Interest, within the anthropology of tourism, in processes of cultural commoditization was exemplified early on in Greenwood's (1977) well-known essay on the *Alarde* ritual in the Basque town of Fuenterrabia. Greenwood argued that under the influence of tourism this complex ritual, with its deep historical and social connotations and meanings for local people, had become part of a commoditized version of local culture sold to tourists. This line of thought has been echoed by several subsequent ethnographers of tourism. In O'Rourke's (1987) film *Cannibal Tours*, for example, European and American tourists in Papua New Guinea are shown haggling and posing with local people over cultural artifacts produced by those locals especially for tourist consumption. The inference is that here is an example of a culture undergoing a process of commoditization under the influence of tourists culturally drenched by commodity fetishism.

Following these kinds of assumptions, others have been made. Among these are the following: that commoditization is part of a general consumer culture which is itself defined by a culture of unfettered atomic individualism; that the imperative for this culture derives from the nature of advanced economic systems which produce unlimited quantities of consumer goods (Baudrillard, 1988:46); that post-modern consumers resemble either infants (ibid.:172) or schizophrenics (Jameson, 1985); that cultures defined by commoditization and consumerism are in some specific senses democratic (Eco, 1986); that the commoditization of social and ritual events leads to an erosion of their meaning and that this loss of meaning is accompanied by a parallel loss of feelings of social solidarity (Greenwood op. cit.); that tourism-induced commoditization and consumerism lead inexorably to states of dependency, including cultural dependency, in tourist-receiving regions (Erisman, 1983).

Yet these and other discussions about commoditization have turned out to be more problematic than they may have appeared at first. O'Rourke's film has a striking image of American and European tourists carefully decorating themselves with local body paints before dancing away the night as their yacht sails away from PNG following their visit there. Underscoring the point with a majestic irony, O'Rourke provides background music by Mozart for this scene. The image suggests that the tourist heroes of the film possessed, at the very least, a passing interest in dimensions of social organization other than commodity-based activity defined exclusively in terms of unfettered individualism (a form of activity for which neither Mozart nor body paints readily supply metaphorical associations). Meanwhile, Greenwood (1989) himself has reworked his view of the wholesale commoditization of ritual life in Fuenterrabia. Furthermore, the research in Malta carried out by Black (op. cit.) has led her to suggest, once again partly following Boissevain, that the existence of a sphere of cultural exchange in which culture is commoditized and sold to tourists has not prevented the persistence and, indeed, expansion of another locally autonomous sphere of cultural activity. In fact she goes further and argues that there are senses in which the causes of local cultural autonomy may actually be advanced in the interplay between these spheres. Cohen (1988b:383) has considered these themes, arguing that commoditization need not necessarily lead to loss of the meaning of cultural productions and that these may actually 'acquire new meanings . . . [while] old meanings can remain hidden for an internal public'.

Thus, in the terms in which it was posed in the 1970s, the commoditization debate seems to have run its course. Part of the reason for this stems from the partial redundancy of functionalist notions of culture, the last vestiges of which underpinned the discussion in those early days. In the course of the debate, what has been revealed is the problematic nature of the concept of commoditization itself. Perhaps the ethnographers of the 1970s were prone to their own commodity fetishism in the sense that they tended too easily to assume advance knowledge of a process which required further investigation. Cohen (ibid.) has rightly asked for more emic and comparative studies of the process of commoditization associated with tourism, and it is precisely this sort of pulling apart and examination of the process from all sorts of different angles which makes the accounts in this book pertinent. The debate needs to find new directions, and one purpose of this introduction is to suggest ways in which these might be found.

What light do our essays shed on the issues and assumptions raised above about the nature of commoditization and consumerism? The chapter most obviously concerned with consumerism, in that it is concerned with the imagery of the tourist culture of consumption, is Dann's analysis of British tourist brochures (Chapter 4). Dann follows Uzzell's (1984) claims that tourists are myth-makers and that tourist brochures are themselves myths whose ideological function is to transform ('first order') images of destinations into texts with ideologically potent ('second order') meanings for tourists. Dann's chapter is also usefully read with another of Uzzell's claims in mind: that brochures are partly 'self-images of ourselves'.

Dann's subject is the tourist image of paradise. Given the long, in many cases colonial, relationship between Britain and the countries in which many tourist destinations are found, and the present ethnically plural nature of contemporary British society, part of the chapter's significance derives from the insight provided into British tourists' conceptions of 'paradise'. Given too that the idea of paradise in the Christian tradition has a long history, it is instructive to contemplate how the idea and its associated imagery have come, in the tourist literature of the late 20th century, to be transformed to stand for idealized settings for consumption. It is interesting too that a main aspect of these settings should be the relationship between predominantly white tourist consumers and predominantly black local residents.

These observations lead directly to the chapter's central conclusion, which is that 'the projected image of a destination and its people is couched in the language and imagery of social control'. Bearing in mind that post-modern consumer culture is widely spoken and written about throughout the world's media, in language couched in the rhetoric of individual freedom, choice and democratic rights, one question arising from Dann's chapter concerns the 'deep structure', as it were, of the consumerist myth propagated in the brochures. We know, of course, that the sort of 'freedom' advertised by tourist brochures and other consumerist propaganda has little to do with the sorts of political and civil freedom discussed by Locke, Hobbes or Rousseau — or any of their contemporary followers: brochure freedoms are concerned with the fantasies of the market-place. But Dann goes further. His argument is that the language of the 'freedoms' of the brochures is reconstituted, in the very process of its articulation, into an instrument not for greater democracy but for greater social and political control. By advancing this argument Dann sets in train the idea that one of the underlying features of contemporary consumerism, as this is expressed on the world's tourist peripheries, is rooted in the orientalism of the 19th century and before — at the level both of mythology and also political economy.

Elsewhere the present writer has followed Dann in the exploration of tourist brochures (Selwyn, 1993), attempting to read them as multi-faceted texts which challenge several conventional assumptions about the nature of post-modern culture. On the one hand the brochures are on the leading edge of post-modernist styles of representation. For example, one of the brochures advertising Malaysia at the World Travel Mart in 1992 promised its readers that Malaysia is 'Dazzling Even After Dark', has 'Endless Possibilities', tourist itineraries with names such as 'City Sensations', 'Peak Excitement' and 'Wild Adventures'.[4] Potential tourists are promised meals, from every imaginable national origin, to suit tireless and gargantuan appetites. The choice — of destinations, prices, temperatures, goods, possibilities — seems limitless. In this view the brochures introduce the world as a supermarket, which, in Baudrillard's view, is one of the two 'mammary glands of the system' (1988:39).[5] It is a world in which all the connective tissues of any archaeology and architecture of meaning have been dissolved.

On the other hand, however, there is a consistent appearance of themes which are very familiar in much anthropological work, on more traditional myths, suggesting that the absolute breaks between pre-modernism and modernism (asserted, as we have seen by Levi-Strauss himself among others) and modernism and post-modernism (asserted by the post-modernist clerisy), are altogether too straightforward. There seems, furthermore, to be a fundamental ambivalence at the heart of consumerism: there are individual consumers ('clients', 'customers', and so on, in the language of contemporary management-speak) whose motivations and desires seem based upon the kind of infant/schizoid tendencies identified by Baudrillard and Jameson; there are also myth themes which seem both constructed by and are about selves who seem not to fit with this descriptive imagery at all. Some consumerist punters from the metropolitan heartlands of consumer culture seem, on the basis of data presented here and elsewhere, to pursue 'imagined communities' (to borrow from Anderson, 1983) of a very different kind from those one might expect from authors such as Baudrillard and Jameson.

Some of this ambivalence is captured by Fees' account of Chipping Campden (Chapter 7). Following a life of success in the markets of the metropolis, one favoured destination on retirement is the English Cotswolds – although it seems hardly likely that a house in a 17th-century Cotswold village is a symbol of rejection of metropolitan consumerism in favour of the harmony of the rural periphery. It seems more likely that it may be thought of in terms of appropriate reward for serving the interests of the consumerist system. In this sense it legitimates that system by appearing to embrace its opposite.

There is, of course, another aspect to this ambivalence: second-home owners and retired people in Campden purchase images of an unspoilt rural retreat, where crafts are practised in a way that stimulates incomers' imagination of what life must have been like before the industrial revolution. The families of old established craft and farm workers become part of a myth about social harmony, continuity, stability and orderliness. The paradox is that this idyll depends to a large extent on the social and political marginalization of the very families who form it.

But the fare consumed in Chipping Campden is precisely in line with MacCannell's expectations. Elderly palates jaded by the profusion of menus available in the metropolis salivate afresh in the warmth and safety of the imagined structures of middle England.

And what of the fare consumed by visitors to *Beth Hatefutsoth* or Nepal? Golden (Chapter 12) tells us that the Museum of the Jewish Diaspora offers 'nostalgia' rather than 'history', while Hutt suggests that the special appeal of Nepal as a tourist destination is that it offers the promise of instantly available wisdom: Shangri-la for the price of an air ticket. Both imply that the ease with which knowledge seems to be obtained by tourists to these sites inevitably raises questions about its value.

The evidence from the authors of our accounts suggests that whatever direction debates on commoditization and consumerism may now take, it will be away from any simplistic univocal assumptions about, or descriptions of processes recognized as complex and contradictory. There is plenty of evidence linking tourism to the consumption of kaleidoscopic dreams and fantasies, celebrations of individual choices and freedoms, promotion of the 'enterprise culture', the aestheticization of the world, the manufacture of cultural commodities lacking any use value, and so forth. But there is also considerable evidence which fits less easily into this framework. Taking the chapters by Golden, Fees and Hutt, for example, we find tourists actively pursuing the following: exhibitions involving complex historical reconstructions; images of wholeness, continuity and society; a myth about democracy and wisdom in a valley separated by high mountains from the rest of the modern world!

Finally, Dann's brochures also seem to offer a collection of wares with comparably ambivalent qualities. For example, there is the orientalism which we have already noticed; however, destination landscapes also seem to offer a version of paradise in which the tourist may not only be pampered and served but also, and arguably above all, *acknowledged as a person*.[6]

These rather surprising findings would seem to confirm, at the very least, that the processes of commoditization and consumerism are more complex than we might have recognized. One formulation might be that we live in a world which is at the same time pre-modern, modern and post-modern. If so, then any simple paradigm of contemporary culture claiming either that we had reached some sort of cultural journey's end (at a terminus named 'free market' perhaps) or that our arrival there signalled some kind of end to history, society and/or the relations between globally defined classes of oppressors and oppressed would seem partial and premature.

AUTHENTICITY

The importance of discussions concerning authenticity follow directly on from the above: as Cohen (1988b) pointed out some time ago, the place of the authentic in the tourism field needs exploration within the same framework as consideration of commoditization and consumerism. Given that the practices of contemporary tourism lie at the forefront of post-modernist cultural expression, and given also that the importance of the anthropology and sociology of tourism stems in large measure from the insights which the study of tourism promises to bring to our understanding about post-modern culture, the main questions about authenticity may be introduced approximately as follows.

The character of post-modernity is framed by cultural transformations some of which, as already observed, are usefully discussed by Urry (1990:82–103). Central among these is the collapse of the boundaries between such cultural spheres as high and popular culture, history and heritage, scientific and popular narrative, tourism and education and so forth.

Take the first of these distinctions, for example. As Urry has argued, travel and tourism were previously organized under the aegis of a politico–economic, social, cultural and intellectual framework (this latter including, among others, classically educated museum curators and tour guides) in which tourists and travellers were subject to certain overarching assumptions about the world. These assumptions were ultimately those of the carriers of a 'high culture' which exercised a hegemonic influence over cultural representations in general, including those associated with travel and tourism. However, in the contemporary post-modern age, in which tourists are daily more aware of the tremendous potential for choice (including those flowing from technologies of simulation and virtual reality), they are increasingly breaking free from the grip of high culture. Contemporary tourism thus takes place under the aegis not of high culture but of the culture of the 'high street' (ibid.:100). We may picture the post-modern tourist in the high street almost literally checking out of Sainsbury's straight into Barbados with the mere flash of a Switch card.

As far as distinctions between history and heritage are concerned, Urry argues that while contemporary tourist sites may well be subject to historical research, tourism professionals have needed to persuade new visitors to them, and have thus needed to make sites into attractive 'spectacles'. But it should not be thought, argues Urry, that such spectacles are 'inauthentic', for what the making of sites into spectacles shows is that there is no one simple 'authentic reconstruction of history . . . [for] all involve various kinds of accommodation and reinterpretation' and that one important consequence of all this is the 'democratisation of the tourist gaze' (ibid.:155–6).

With regard to this last point, it must be pointed out that there is, of course, no necessary association between post-modernity, as a feature of contemporary culture in general, and any sort of real democracy. In some contexts there is clearly a yawning gap. As Callinicos (1989:144) has put it, the 'old confidence in scientific reason' is being accompanied not by the rise of democracy but of the 'new narcissistic self . . . demanding immediate gratification' and the 'sinister, centreless chaos, in which the autonomous individual and cultural traditions are increasingly displaced by a violent, illiterate mass lobotomised by TV'. Heady stuff and illustrative of what is at issue.

Also central to the cultural transformations associated with post-modernity is the playfulness of the post-modern subject. In this cultural context Urry argues that the tourist 'knows that tourism is a game, or rather a whole series of games with multiple texts and *no single, authentic tourist experience*' (ibid.:100, emphasis mine). Thus tourists may play at being observers, 'noble savages', 'time travellers', children, and so forth, but they remain playful outsiders (loc. cit. after Fiefer 1985).

It needs to be acknowledged that Urry is too careful a writer to imply that these configurations describe *the* contemporary cultural universe. Following Lash, he observes that the post-modern is only *one* cultural 'ideal type' among others — which include the pre-modern and the modern (ibid.:86).

It is precisely at this point that discussions of authenticity fit in. Such discussions help us to remain aware of what is at stake if, as observers (museum curators, historians, heritage managers, anthropologists, or whatever), we follow the most playful (or are they the most serious?) post-modernist invitations to relax our sensitivity to the differences and distinctions between such terms as, say, history and heritage, or scholarly and popular narrative. Furthermore, it seems that the evidence from the chapters in this volume suggests that beneath the surface structures of the various tourist sites, experiences, images and myths discussed, there remains a clearly identifiable sub-structure of concern in the tourist imagination with traditional-looking themes which seem at once modern and pre-modern and to which the term 'authentic' seems all too applicable, namely the nature of the social and of the self.

In other words, paradoxically enough, the study of contemporary tourism — in several obvious senses itself a product of post-modernity — leads towards an awareness of the limits of the post-modern in contemporary culture. As far as anthropology itself goes, the limits to ethnographic playfulness are nicely indicated by Crick (1985:86): 'Dadaism involves anti-Dadaism . . . if anything goes, seriousness, better description and more demanding fieldwork are on the cards too.'

Both Urry's work and that of this volume share a concern with the post-modern although, ultimately, their overall aims are different. One of the purposes of the former is to describe how insights from the tourism world help us to describe the character of the post-modern. The present work also explores what takes place within the frontiers of the post-modern landscape. But, additionally, it is intended not only to draw attention to the frontiers themselves but also to stimulate an idea or two about what might go on outside them.

As has already been outlined above, the suggestion here is to work with two distinct senses of the term 'authentic'. A first type may be termed 'hot authenticity' and will apply to that aspect of the imagined world of tourist make-believe — that aspect of tourist myths — concerned with questions of self and society. The unashamedly modernist suggestion is that under-neath the surface structures of the post-modern tourist myths discussed in this book are modern and even pre-modern concerns with the 'authentic self' and the 'authentic other' (for which reason we may subdivide this category into two). A second type, 'cool authenticity', may be reserved for propositions which aim to be open to the kinds of procedures described by Popper and referred to earlier and which would like to claim a different kind of legitimacy from those in the former category.

'Hot authenticity': myths of the authentic other and the authentically social

By now it is widely accepted by anthropologists of tourism that much of contemporary tourism is founded upon the 'Quest for the Other', as van den Berghe (1994) has it. In the present volume Brown (Chapter 2) suggests that, pushing as they do in opposite directions, the quest for the 'authentic Other' and the quest for the 'authentic Self' constitute the 'tension which informs all tourism'. The question then becomes what does this Other stand for. On the evidence from the work presented here, the answer seems to point towards understanding the Other as the 'authentically social'.

Expressed in the terms we have been using up to now, then, Brown's observation about the Other (we will come to the Self shortly) may thus be reformulated as follows. The character of this Other derives from belonging to an imagined world which is variously pre-modern, pre-commoditized or part of a benign whole recaptured in the mind of a tourist. This is a world which is eminently and authentically social. Thus what makes a tourist destination attractive is that it is thought to have a special characteristic, a special 'spirit of place', which derives from the sociability of its residents. Or, to put it another way, in successful tourist destinations the natives are always friendly.

But how does this work in practice? There is nothing mystical about the process by which a tourist destination comes to be identified with a particular and particularly sociable spirit of place. Boissevain (1981), for example, has described how the neighbourhood *festi* came to play a significant symbolic role in post-independence Malta. He has traced the way in which the *festi* were identified by government officials, intellectuals and others as constituting an important national asset and parts of the indigenous cultural legacy. Boissevain argued that 'this heritage became particularly important to a new nation searching for its identity', a nation simultaneously attempting to stay afloat in the contemporary competitive environment of Mediterranean states vying with one another for increased market share of the tourist trade. In such a context the reputation of Malta as a tourist destination offering sun, sand, sea and sex is being down-played while the government itself has enlisted the help of the university to examine how the image of Malta might further be shaped to offer more 'cultural tourism'. Interestingly though, although the logic of this move-ment — away from organized mass tourism towards more upmarket 'cultural tourism' — has been dictated largely by the market forces engulfing islands and other tourist regions balanced between saturation and recession, it also intersects with the concerns of the growing environ-mental lobby. At any rate, in the Maltese case, the Maltese government and their supporters have decided that the *festi* are ceremonies which stand for, and may be successfully marketed as, authentic Maltese culture.[7]

Picard (1992) reports a very similar process from Indonesia. The govern-ment has drawn up a tourist plan, a central part of which is to confer upon the country's regions a special characteristic which may then be taken up as a marketing strategy by tourist agents promoting Indonesia. The particular straw drawn by the island of Bali in this process has given it the distinction of being the place of exotic religious activities and ritual procedures. In the officially determined tourist mythology of Indonesia, Bali *is* religion! In the case of Malta at least some of the tourists seem to be chasing that particular myth too.

We may place these cases beside the Shangri-la myth, dreamed up before the existence of the Nepalese Tourist Board but presently used by this and other agencies to sell tours in Nepal.

Arguably, none of these sales strategies would have worked had not religion, ritual or myths about what constituted civilization sold well. Utopian visions of good government, spirituality and its ritual expression or religiously constructed sociability have clearly not yet passed their 'sell by' date. Some might even follow such an interpretation by pointing out that these represent some of the pre-eminent concerns of Western European and North American culture. At this level their popularity with Western tourists might be taken as evidence of a kind of protest against a pre-dominantly secular post-modernist culture in which established religion and, in some versions, even society itself, had been relegated to a shadowy presence whose very existence had been questioned.

But the point to be made here follows less esoteric lines of thought. Let us take another two examples to make it. Golden concludes her chapter (Chapter 12) on *Beth Hatefutsoth* by saying that 'the lack of authentic artefacts . . . seems to me to be saying something about the inauthenticity of the life that is on display'. She argues that the museum deals more in stories such as those told by grandparents to their grandchildren than in history: more in a 'nostalgia . . . [which] assuages the fragmentary, disconcerting quality of modernity' (while itself being part of modernity) than in rigorous description. Dispersion and exile and, ironically enough, the reconstruction of Israel have placed the sense of belonging to a Jewish community at risk. Jewishness is threatened abroad by assimilation and in

Israel by secularization. Thus the original purpose of the museum was, according to its founder, to fight for the sense of belonging to a Jewish community. Golden argues that what is on offer at the museum is a mythical experience of the conquest of unity and continuity over dispersion and fragmentation — linked metaphorically to an assertion of the conquest of life over death. As she puts it, *Beth Hatefutsoth* is a 'warm' museum.

Brown (Chapter 2) starts off in the Hiroshima Peace Park at the site of an exhibition hall claiming to be the only building (albeit half destroyed) to have survived the dropping of the atom bomb. It is, however, a fake in the sense that the present structure was rebuilt by the city fathers, mindful of their cash registers over the year-long tourist season, when the original building was on the point of collapse. In short, its survival was staged, and great commercial profit has resulted from the staging. The fact is, Brown tells us, that the hall is an extremely powerful and emotionally potent symbol of shared suffering, death and its eventual defeat by a resurrected nation.

In the terms of this introduction the Hiroshima Peace Park, cold and terrifying as in other senses it must be, appears as another 'warm' attraction. It is (partly because it is my own rather than Brown's term in the context) worthwhile to spend a few sentences exploring why 'warm' seems an appropriate term to use.

In both the Israeli and the Japanese case, monuments have been set up to commemorate historical events which include exile, dispersion, defeat and death. The warmth described by both Brown and Golden lies in the capacity of these memorials to provide their visitors with the emotional coherence and potency to transform symbols of national weakness and vulnerability into symbols of national renewal. It is difficult not to link up these with the kind of totemic feelings described by Durkheim (1965[1915]) or, indeed, Kedouri's (1960) notion of nationalist 'will'. Tourist sites have always been crucibles for nationalist constructions.

In the Cotswolds tourists and prospective second-home buyers are also attracted by promises of engagements with authentic encounters in places imagined to be essentially English. In Campden the attraction amounts to the possibility of an encounter with the heartbeat of rural, pre-industrial, 'real' England. *Beth Hatefutsoth* attracts its visitors with the promise of an encounter with an authentic vision of what it means to be a Jew, Chipping Campden with what it means to be English. The *festi* become the touchstones of the authentically Maltese, and the Hiroshima Peace Park appears as an authentic symbol of Japanese national experience. In each case what is being celebrated is, in a narrow sense, a glimpse of nationhood or a sense of the authentically national. In rather simpler and broader terms, what is on offer is a sense of the authentically social. In these quite particular senses, such authenticity is, in a Durkheimian sense, eminently 'hot'.

'Hot authenticity': myths of the authentic self

For Brown, as we have seen, the tension between the twin quests by the tourist for the authentic Other and for the authentic Self forms part of the dynamic underlying tourism. But, we may ask, if tourists are chasing a myth of Self, what does this Self look like? The data suggest that it has a variety of forms and it seems plausible to suggest we find it somewhere on a continuum between two poles as follows.

On the one hand we have those Selves which are defined in terms of their proximity to, and identification with, the groups or categories of persons and communities forming the focus of their visit. One such example comes from the Museum of the Diaspora. Visitors to this museum are not merely presented with general representations of diaspora life. They themselves become its subjects. To this end they are able to use a very large electronic screen capable of plotting their own individual genealogies back through several generations. This in turn enables them to locate themselves, their family members and the towns and villages in which these lived within a wider framework of the diaspora. In a sense, therefore, the authenticity of the visitors' selves is confirmed in relation to the social life depicted by the museum.

On the other hand we have the Selves of the brochures. In these the emphasis is placed, as Dann puts it on 'individuals who can now escape the humdrum world of the masses'. According to Dann, the 'privacy' which may be purchased, at a price, in the remoter, more exclusive holiday islands may metaphorically be linked to bourgeois ideas of wealth and the privacy which flows from its possession. These ideas are in turn linked to the ability to 'take a secluded vacation when one so desires'. This Self, driven by desire and the urgent need for immediate gratification, is apparently 'free' in the sense of able to eschew any group identification as well as the social and moral constraints which that would entail and derives its authenticity from being, as it were, a Self *tout court*.

Interestingly enough both these Selves, despite their contrasting character, seem to be in vigorous pursuit of an authenticity which is staged. Thus, while Golden tells us that the history encountered in the Museum of the Diaspora is constructed without reference to a single 'authentic artefact', Brown reminds us of the obvious fact that many tourists seek out the 'authentically . . . hedonistic . . . good time'. The free Self of the brochures is eloquent testimony to this. For many tourists an authentic good time derives, precisely, from the experience of 'life as play'. Performances, spectacles, masks and make-believe are all vehicles for authentic good times: all are staged! And if, in MacCannell's terms, that makes such experiences inauthentic, then perhaps Brown's further suggestion that tourist authenticity amounts to the experience of the inauthentic is less opaque than it first appears.

Interpreted in this way, what our data show is that any post-structuralist claim that the post-modern subject, including the tourist, is locked irredeemably into 'pure' consumerism seems incomplete and unconvincing. Further claims about the death in post-modern culture of meta-narrative (Thatcher's end of society, Fukiyama's end of history, for example) seem open to further debate. In the light of our evidence, we may legitimately make the counter-claim that our data not only imply meta-narrative but demand it. Indeed we have adopted Brown's suggestion that tourism is informed by the meta-narratives of concern with Self and Other and that the latter stands, in large measure, for a sense of the social. The implication is that the sort of myths about the authenticity of Self and Other discussed here may partly be read as a popular critique of consumerism.

'Cool authenticity'

Edwards (Chapter 11) effectively brings together many of the threads of the arguments presented so far in this introduction. To start with it is written by a museum curator, but one whose tone sounds rather different from that which we might have expected to hear following Urry's contention that contemporary museum practices are evidence of a new 'accommodation' between such realms as heritage and history, scholarly and popular narrative, mythology and truth. Edwards seems to have mislaid this script when she writes that she is 'acutely aware of the cultural baggage which is brought into my own and similar institutions by a visiting public, whose images of the world . . . are formed in part by the kind of exotic imagery perpetuated in tourist postcards . . . [which] *imagery it is our job to confront*' (emphasis mine).

Edwards deals with tourist products — postcards — which are on the face of it both 'ubiquitous and ephemeral'. However, consisting as they do of photographs, they clearly promote a sense of scientific verisimilitude: as everyone knows, the camera cannot lie. On the other hand, as Edwards argues, postcard images are dislocated both temporally and spatially by being removed from any recognizable present as well as separated off from any tangible social context: we seem to be dealing with, so to speak, a 'gift-wrapped' type of authenticity. Furthermore, despite the fact that 'owning a photograph (postcard) authenticates and represents the *experience* of the possessor . . . such experience cannot ultimately be more than vicarious . . . since . . . [tourists] cannot share in the moral fabric of the visited'. Moreover postcard-induced knowledge of culture suffers from the fact that culture itself is always exoticized by being moored in the past.

Flawed as the knowledge may in the end turn out to be, the tourist appears in Edwards' chapter as one who is motivated by a 'desire to know'. The fact lends support to the claim being made here that the search for knowledge, including what is claimed to be ethnographic knowledge, is a primary motivating factor in the mind of the tourist. The question underlying her analysis, however, has to do with the quality of the knowledge being sought.

Edwards' chapter requires us to take tourist knowledge seriously. It also requires us to take the knowledge of the curator seriously — and not to confuse the two, reminding us that we are engaged in a three-cornered conversation in which observers and locals — as well as tourists themselves — are taking part. At this point we need to focus on the former pair.

Recalling Crick's comment about the close kinship between tourists and anthropologists, and Urry's suggestion that some degree of accommodation is being reached between scientific knowledge and the tourist knowledge of the High Street, Edwards encourages us to seek some different ground from which the observer may comfortably express his or her views.

There are several reasons why we may be drawn to find such ground. The first takes its lead from Edwards' concern to engage with, or even confront, the implications of some of the popular imagery which finds its way, via her postcard collection, into her museum. In order to do so it would seem necessary to reject a view of theoretical narrative — anthropological, semiological, curatorial or whatever — as essentially 'de-differentiated' (to use Urry's term) from the narratives of the visitors to her museum. As Callinicos (1989:93–4) has pointed out, if popular and scholarly narrative were indeed so 'de-differentiated', not only would 'doubts emerge about the possibility of knowledge as distinct from the various forms of narrative gratification' but also 'political critique of the status quo becomes impossible'. If, on the other hand, the distinctive character of a 'cool authenticity' is affirmed, then both knowledge and critique are possible.

The second reason follows from this and is specifically related to the nature of tourism. As well as being an arena in which myths are produced and consumed on a vast scale, it is also a very significant part of many regional and national economies and development programmes. It would be a truly extraordinary state of affairs if the myths of the tourists dovetailed with, and actually informed, decisions about real economic and social development. And yet exactly this seems to be taking place. A number of our chapters deal explicitly with the social and other consequences of policies based more on tourist-induced mythology than on clear dispassionate description. Explicit in Meethan, Fees and Dann and implicit in Hutt, for example, are the propositions that some tourist myths, nominally about social harmony, the spreading of culture, democracy and so forth, actually play a fairly decisive role in social and political processes which are quite antipathetical to the realization of these goals. Such myths have also become part of the process of political and economic marginalization of the very people who form them. Few could argue, therefore, with the proposition that it is sober and dispassionate ethnographic description, rather than mythological discourse, which is required to guide policies relating to employment, income distribution, environmental policy and so forth in countries from St Lucia to Wales in which tourism is a significant economic issue.

The third reason follows from these two. If the possibility of critique based on a meta-narrative of reason is allowed to be swept away in the heady post-modern rhetoric about High Street knowledge, then the only way in which populations of tourist-receiving localities have at their disposal to combat what they feel to be the negative politico-economic and socio-cultural consequences of tourism is through counter-narratives which have no more or no less claim to any external or objective legitimacy than any other narrative. The pattern of tourist regions becoming, first of all, arenas for tourism development and the associated development of Western consumerist values, and then, as a reaction, sites for clerical fundamentalism, is beginning to be reported by anthropologists from tourist sites in Egypt (Aziz, 1995) and Kenya (Peake, 1989).

Along with Edwards' analysis, Fees' account of Chipping Campden is an example of an observer claiming a separate (and, dare it be said, in some particular senses, 'privileged') status. Clearly demonstrating that questions of authenticity and authentication are ultimately political, Fees, like Edwards, does not hesitate to claim the authority which flows from being an observer who is also a real historian. In the sense that being such engages him in a process of evaluating the authenticity of the myths constructed about Chipping Campden by 'tourists who stayed', the claim is, of course, profoundly political.

Directly flowing from this, a fourth reason why we may follow Edwards and Fees, together with the writers of each of the other chapters come to that, in finding, or preserving, separate ground for the observer stems from Golden's worries about the possible inauthenticity of the history displayed at *Beth Hatefutsoth* and Urry's claims concerning the democratization of the tourist gaze. From one point of view Urry's claim seems born out in the way the museum has been constructed. Golden argues that the themes of the museum meet the needs of those who come to it: the museum's clients get what they want. Surely here, then, is a shining example of an accord being reached between museum curators and their visitors and of history being constructed in a way which is self-evidently popular. Is this not a good example of the democratic construction of history, of the working together or 'accommodation' of curator and tourist? Why on earth should Golden have even the slightest twinge of anxiety?

Golden tells us that the founder of the museum intended it to combat assimilation abroad and secularization at home. One way this has been achieved symbolically is to offer visitors 'experiences' (and Golden takes evident care to use this term rather than, say, 'knowledge') which, she says, set up boundaries between Jews and non-Jews and remove boundaries between 'past and present, religious and secular, Israeli and Jewish . . .' In short, the history and nostalgic feelings invoked by the museum have been constructed with a particular end in view which is much closer to popular, and indeed political, concerns than to the dry scholarship of those stiff legislators of knowledge about which Urry and others have spoken.

It would have been possible to construct another sort of museum which emphasized the continuities between Jew and non-Jew; which explored the place throughout history of intermarriage and the way in which Jews and non-Jews had co-operated in the making and remaking, forming and re-forming, of boundaries between the religious and the secular in different contexts; which described the extent to which Jewish and non-Jewish economies and societies had been, and remain, integrated; and which reflected on the discontinuities, as well as the continuities, between the categories Jew and Israeli (given, for example, that some Palestinian Arabs and Beduins hold Israeli passports).

The question is where, if anywhere, is the history between these two accounts? Difficult (if not, ultimately, impossible) question as this undoubtedly is, it would be no less than an abandonment of intellectual duty to say merely that these are examples of two different popular narratives.

Tourism is about the invention and reinvention of tradition. It is about the production and consumption of myths and staged inauthenticities. It also has far-reaching economic, political and social consequences at levels ranging from the household to the nation. It has been argued here that tourist myths have one sort of authenticity and serious historical, economic and political constructions another. The trick is to keep them apart so that consenting adults may engage in the exchange of myths without endangering those who choose, for whatever reason, not to consent. There is, therefore, a need to distinguish clearly between two types of authenticity which, in most if not quite all respects, are analytically quite separate. As we consider all this from a perspective of the traditions and myths of the tourist business, a passage from another context appears strikingly relevant:

> When it [tradition] is theatrically revived, in a kind of social inverted commas, it is revived, precisely, by disconnecting it from what is taken seriously as knowledge, and is kept alive only by this artificial insulation, by inventing special criteria and functions for it, which are carefully made distinct from serious cognition. But when serious issues are at stake, when the fate of individuals and communities is at risk, one will not fail to make use of the best available knowledge (Gellner, 1974:147).

SOME CONCLUSIONS

Although this introduction has been written principally from the point of view of the tourist and his or her myth-making proclivities, there have been three overlapping perspectives in mind throughout: tourists, those living in tourist destinations and those who observe tourism and the role of tourism in contemporary culture.

The aim, following MacCannell, has been to work towards, or within, a general theory of tourism while taking Cohen's advice to keep theory close to data which is both comparative and emic. The former's general theoretical proposition — that tourists seek out structures from which they have been alienated by daily life in the contemporary world — has provided the theoretical starting point, despite the several objections raised against it.

Starting, then, with tourists and tourist myths, it has been proposed that three settings, or contexts, may be identified in which tourist myths are constructed and that these settings themselves constitute the themes of the myths we are considering. The first consists of the relationship between centres and peripheries. The extent to which mythological constructions by tourists, from the world's political and economic centres about people on its peripheries, take part in a wider ideological frame of political domination and marginalization has been explored. The extent to which those on the periphery are increasingly combating such relations has also been traced.

The second context takes its cue from the cultural milieu in which contemporary tourism operates. To what extent are tourists driven by instincts of undiluted consumerism and the pursuit of commodities? To what extent is the post-modern tourist just another consumer junkie, infantilized, schizoid and rendered cognitively and intellectually unable to distinguish between different types of knowledge — a mere sucker for the surfaces of the tourist brochures? Surprisingly, perhaps, the evidence from the data presented here and elsewhere has suggested that were they to be made, such assumptions would be too simplistic. Indeed the evidence suggests that beneath the surface of the consumerism and the commoditization associated with tourism are structures which themselves constitute a form of opposition to those processes.

The third context takes off from the previous one and consists of the search for the authentic. Once again MacCannell's notion of the authentic being an imagined reconstruction of that which modernism has smashed was found to be useful. Data were pointed to which spoke of a persistence of myths underpinned by themes which seem clearly to be concerned with the nature of Selves and Society.

Finally, in order to make a contribution towards previous discussions about authenticity in the tourism world, it was necessary to return to insights originally posed by Crick. The question revolves around the nature of the difference between the narratives of tourists and those of observers (anthropologists, historians, intellectuals generally). Rather than join with those commentators on contemporary culture for whom post-modernism has heralded the end of meta-narrative, including that of scholarship as an *un*-differentiated activity, the presence and importance, to tourists and the people of tourist destinations as well as observers, of the notion of 'cool authenticity' was affirmed.

One reason for such an affirmation stems from the perspective of those in tourist destinations. Unless there is the ability to distinguish between the myths and fantasies of tourists (authentic in some senses as these may be), on the one hand, and politico-economic and socio-cultural processes, on the other, there may in the end, as Baudrillard (1988) has warned, be no way out of an eventual wholesale Disneyfication of one part of the world built on the wasteland of the other.

NOTES

1. Berger et al. (1973), for example, argued that modernity makes for cognitive alienation or 'mental homelessness'. It is reasonable to assume that MacCannell's notion of tourists seeking, mythologically, to avoid such alienation builds on notions such as these.
2. These ideas, which have become widely known through such works of his as *Conjectures and Refutations* (1976) and *The Logic of Scientific Discovery* (1977), on the aims and methods of the natural sciences, and the nature of knowledge and truth, were neatly summarized by the philosopher Karl Popper in a short essay with, in the present context, a most appropriate title: 'the Bucket and the Searchlight' (1972). Popper began by criticizing what he called 'the bucket theory of the mind'. This was the view (associated with Bacon and Kant, among others) in which knowledge is thought to progress as a result of accumulated sense experiences. By contrast, Popper argued that knowledge proceeds as a result of imaginative leaps and guesses (conjectures) which lead to the establishment of propositions which are then subject to the hard empirical work which eventually leads to their refutation — and so to further imaginative leaps. In our immediate context, Popper's scheme appears much closer to Crick's position than to Urry's. Thus scientists may share common kinship with tourists in their playing of imaginative games about the interpretation of the world. Inevitably, however, they part company at the stage when their imaginative propositions are put to the test. In my own view Urry is mistaken unequivocally to celebrate the end of the 'auratic'. What is needed is not so much the democratization of the gaze of the tourist or museum visitor, but the democratization of science itself.
3. I take this term from Michael Safier (personal communication) and Emanuel de Kadt (1990).
4. The similarity of these titles to those found on newsagents' upper shelves is striking. Arguably, one of the distinguishing features of the post-modern project is the erasure of boundaries between the private and the public. One manifestation is the use in advertising strategies of soft pornographic styles.
5. The other being the polling booth (ibid.).
6. This particular insight derives from a participant in Martinez's Anthropology of Travel seminar at SOAS in the spring of 1992. She reported that a female friend had confided that a holiday in luxury hotel in the Caribbean almost literally gave her back the 'sense of self' which she had lost in the hard work of raising a young family without support from a partner.

7. At Valletta's Foundation of International Studies (FIS) a lively discussion took place about the Maltese habit of dumping rubbish in the countryside and the suitability, or otherwise, of identifying this, also, as 'authentic Maltese culture'.

REFERENCES

Anderson, B. (1983) *Imagined Communities: Reflections on the Origin and Spread of Nationalism*, London: Verso.

Aziz, H. (1995) 'Understanding attacks on tourists in Egypt', *Tourism Management*, 16(2), 91–7.

Barthes, R. (1983) *The Eiffel Tower*, New York: Hill and Wang.

Bartokowski, F. (1995) *Travelers, Immigrants, Inmates*, University of Minnesota Press..

Baudrillard, J. (1988) *Selected Writings*, Cambridge: Polity.

Berger, Peter, L., Briggite Berger and Hansfried Kellner (1973) *The Homeless Mind: Modernisation and Consciousness*, Harmondsworth: Penguin.

van den Berghe, P. (1994) *The Quest for the Other*, Seattle and London: University of Washington.

Black, A. (1996) 'Negotiating the tourist gaze: the example from Malta' in J. Boissevain (ed.), *Coping with Tourists. European Reactions to Mass Tourism*, Oxford: Berghahn Books.

Boissevain, Jeremy (1981) 'Ritual escalation in Malta', mimeo, Institute of Development Studies, University of Sussex.

Boissevain, Jeremy (1991) 'Ritual, play and identity: changing patterns of celebration in Maltese villages', *Journal of Mediterranean Studies*, 1, 87–100.

Boissevain, Jeremy (1996) *Coping with Tourists: European Reactions to Mass Tourism*, Oxford: Berghahn.

Boorstin, D.J. (1964) *The Image: a Guide to Pseudo-events in America*, New York: Harper and Row.

Britton, R. (1983) *Tourism and Underdevelopment in Fiji*, Canberra: ANU Press.

Bruner, E.M. (1989) 'Cannibals, tourists and ethnographers', *Cultural Anthropology*, 4(4).

Callinicos, A. (1989) *Against Postmodernism*, Cambridge: Polity.

Cohen, E. (1988a) 'Traditions in the qualitative sociology of tourism', *Annals of Tourism Research*, 16, 30–61.

Cohen, E. (1988b) 'Authenticity and commoditisation in tourism', *Annals of Tourism Research*, 15(3).

Cohen, E. (1989) 'Primitive and remote', *Annals of Tourism Research*, 16(1).

Crick, M. (1989) 'Representations of sun, sex, sights, savings and servility: international tourism in the social sciences', *Annual Review of Anthropology*, 18, 307–344.

Dann, G. (1988) 'Images of Cyprus', *Problems of Tourism*, 3/4.

Dann, G. (1989) 'The tourist as child. Some reflections', *Cahiers du Tourisme*, Série C, 135.

Durkheim, E. (1965[1915]) *The Elementary Forms of the Religious Life*, London: Free Press.

Eco, U. (1986) *Faith in Fakes*, London: Secker and Warburg.

Erisman, (1983) 'Tourism and cultural dependence in the West Indies', *Annals of Tourism Research*, 10(3).

Fiefer, M. (1985) *Going Places*, London: Macmillan.

Graburn, M. (1977) 'Tourism: the sacred journey' in V. Smith (ed.), *Hosts and Guests: the Anthropology of Tourism*, Philadelphia: University of Pennsylvania Press.

Gellner, E. (1974) *Legitimation of Belief*, London: Cambridge University Press.

Greenwood, D. (1989[1977]) 'Culture by the pound: an anthropological perspective on tourism as cultural commoditisation' in V. Smith (ed.), *Hosts and Guests: the Anthropology of Tourism*, Philadelphia: University of Pennsylvania Press.

Harrison, D. (1992) *Tourism and the Less Developed Countries*, London: Belhaven Press.

Jameson, F. (1985) 'Post-modernism and consumer society' in H. Foster (ed.), *Post-modern Culture*, London: Pluto.

de Kadt, E. (1979) *Tourism: Passport to Development?*, Oxford: Oxford University Press.

de Kadt, E. (1990) 'Making the alternative sustainable: lessons from development for tourism', working paper, Institute for Development Studies, University of Sussex.

Kedouri, E. (1960) *Nationalism*, London: Hutchinson.

Kenna, M. (1993) 'Return migrants and tourist development; an example from the Cyclades', *Journal of Modern Greek Studies*, 11, 75–81.

Kent, N. (1983) *Hawaii: Islands Under the Influence*, New York: Monthly Review Press.

Lash, S. and Urry, J. (1987) *The End of Organised Capitalism*, Cambridge: Polity Press.

Levi-Strauss, C. (1986[1964]) *The Raw and the Cooked*, Harmondsworth: Penguin.

Levi-Strauss, C. (1987[1983]) *The View from Afar*, Harmondsworth: Penguin.

Lowenthal, D. (1985) *The Past is a Foreign Country*, Cambridge: Cambridge University Press.

MacCannell, D. (1976) *The Tourist: a New Theory of the Leisure Class*, New York: Schocken.

MacCannell, D. (1989) 'Introduction' to special edition on Semiotics of Tourism, *Annals of Tourism Research*, 16(1).

MacCannell, D. (1992) *Empty Meeting Grounds*, London: Routledge.

O'Rourke, D. (1987) *Cannibal Tours* (film) Canberra: O'Rourke and Associates.

Peake, R. (1989) 'Swahili stratification and tourism in Malindi Old Town, Kenya', *Africa*, 59(2).

Picard, M. (1992) 'Cultural tourism in Bali: national integration and regional differentiation' in M. Hitchcock, T. King, and M. Parnwell (eds), *Tourism in South-East Asia*, London: Routledge.

Popper, K.R. (1972) 'The bucket and the searchlight: two theories of knowledge' *Objective Knowledge: An Evolutionary Approach*, Oxford: Clarendon Press, 341–61.

Popper, K.R. (1976) *Conjectures and Refutations* (6th impression), London: Routledge and Kegan Paul.

Popper, K.R. (1977) *The Logic of Scientific Discovery* (9th impression), London: Hutchinson.

Said, Edward (1985) *Orientalism*, Harmondsworth: Penguin.

Selwyn, T. (1993) 'Peter Pan in Southeast Asia — views from the brochures' in M. Hitchcock, V.T. King and M.J.G. Parnwell (eds), *Tourism in Southeast Asia*, London: Routledge, 117–37.

Selwyn, T. (1994) 'The anthropology of tourism: reflections on the state of the art' in A.V. Seaton et al. (eds), *Tourism: the State of the Art*, Chichester: John Wiley.

Smith, V.L. (ed.) (1977) (revised 1989) *Hosts and Guests, the Anthropology of Tourism*, Philadelphia: University of Pennsylvania Press.

Urry, John (1990) *The Tourist Gaze: Leisure and Travel in Contemporary Societies*, London: Sage Publications.

Uzzell, D. (1984) 'An alternative structuralist approach to the psychology of marketing', *Annals of Tourism Research*, 11(1).

2 Genuine fakes

DAVID BROWN

In the city of Hiroshima there is a large open space called the Peace Park (Figure 2.1). It comes as no surprise to learn that it marks the spot where the first atom bomb fell in 1945. It not only marks the spot, but was initially cleared by the bomb. All that remained standing near the epicentre was a damaged exhibition hall, built in the 1930s, whose reinforced concrete construction saved it from complete destruction. This tangled mass of steel and concrete is a potent symbol of an awesome event. A new museum and conference centre stands nearby, containing further remains, photographs and contemporary accounts. The site is visited each year by large numbers of tourist/pilgrims from all over the world, and hosts peace rallies of widely differing political persuasion.

Potent symbol though it may be, the exhibition hall is a fake. When it threatened to collapse altogether, as weathering completed what the bomb had started, the city fathers had it reconstructed in its half-destroyed state. It was altogether too lucrative a tourist attraction, as the rest of Japan is never tired of pointing out. They contrast Hiroshima and Nagasaki, whose people never commercialized the bomb that fell on them but rebuilt their city and got on with their lives. The latter have a Peace Park, but it is small and modest. Their bomb was the second to fall not the first, of course; and Hiroshimans have claimed that the complaints against them are largely 'sour grapes'. Be that as it may, there is no mistaking the awesomeness of the Hiroshima site. Some of the attendants are (or were) themselves survivors of the bomb. While it has a fake at its centre, then, the site nevertheless arouses deep and genuine feelings. It is what I'm calling here 'a genuine fake'.

I need hardly add that Hiroshima is not unique in that respect. One is reminded of the sacred remains of certain Catholic saints — and the Protestant claim that they include sufficient bones to make up several skeletons of each. Maybe. Another example is the Finnish tree stump on which Lenin allegedly sat while awaiting the call from Moscow which used to be (if it is no longer) on the tourist circuit. The tree is particularly interesting because it is so obviously recently cut, i.e. so obviously a fake that one has to suppose collusion between the presenters of the attraction and those who visit it. The genuine fake is not just the object itself but the

The Tourist Image: Myths and Myth Making in Tourism. Edited by Tom Selwyn.
© 1996 John Wiley & Sons Ltd.

Figure 2.1   Hiroshima Peace Park

relationship between visitors and presenters which the object mediates (Figure 2.2).

Once prompted to think of tourist attractions in this way, there is hardly one that escapes. Just what, then, is the attraction for the tourist and, of course, for its presenters? What are the dynamics of their relationship? My purpose in this chapter is to examine some of the answers given by anthropologists and to offer a few more. Taking up Cohen's distinction between tourists and pilgrims, I draw different conclusions: that genuine tourists are fake pilgrims and vice versa; and that each can turn into the other with quite startling ease. They are not points on a continuum but dialectical opposites, opposing poles of the creative tension that Frow (1991) calls 'touristic shame'. This approach has the advantage that the anthropologist is firmly included as a genuine pilgrim who is also a fake tourist. It is necessary to remember that s/he may also be taken for a ride. This approach also points firmly to the relationship between tourists and locals as the focus of study, rather than either one taken separately.

Before embarking on this enterprise, let me remind the reader of Umberto Eco's *Travels in Hyper-Reality* (1987). Eco travels the USA in search of 'the real thing' or, rather, what is presented as such to the visiting public: the 'really real', ultimate experience. His search takes on a fantastic character, from the Fortress of Solitude to the Palace of Living Arts to the Enchanted Castle, and so on; all attempts in their different ways to 'improve' on reality. Thus masterpieces of European painting are

Figure 2.2   A genuine fake from Melanesia

reproduced in three-dimensional wax because, after all, three dimensions are more real than two. Or so it might seem. It might also seem that the reproduced Venus de Milo with both arms intact is more real than the one in the Louvre. The ardent pursuit of an ideal reality begets its own contradiction, in which, as Eco has it, the 'completely real' becomes identified with the 'completely fake'. It is reproduced with such attention to detail that it is evidently a fabrication. I will argue that such a sense for contradiction, in one form or another, informs the tourist/local relationship.[1]

COMMUNITAS

A common approach to tourism is epitomized by Graburn, for whom the basic motivation 'seems to be' a human need for recreation. He sees a fundamental contrast 'between the ordinary/compulsory work state spent "at home" and the non-ordinary/voluntary "away from home" sacred state' (1978:21). The structure of tourism is basically identical to that of all ritual behaviour: it first translates the tourist into a sacred world, then transforms/renews him, and finally returns him to normality. This other world is sacred because it is out of space and out of time. The normal rules are in abeyance (if not actually reversed), and replaced by Turner's close and egalitarian 'communitas'. It is evident to the tourist that this exalted state is too good to last, however, and he is returned to normality renewed in his acceptance of it. What he has experienced, then, is a classic rite of re-creation and renewal.

Or so the argument goes. Tourism is a sacred journey, the contemporary counterpart of medieval pilgrimage. It turns on a very contemporary distinction between work and play. It thereby ignores that hard work can be pleasurable and that pleasure can be hard work. It also requires that work should be 'at home', and leisure 'away from home'. Hence Graburn claims that 'doing nothing at home' is considered vaguely suspect (e.g. the proverbial layabout), while working away from home is the subject of hackneyed jokes (e.g. commercial travellers). However common statis-tically, normatively they are improper states of being.

Normative for whom, or rather, for which sectors of society? In areas of high unemployment, 'staying at home' has quite a different meaning. Among commercial travellers and the like, again, the hackneyed jokes are about 'nine-to-fivers'. This sector includes large areas of the service, media and marketing industries. Far from normatively improper, indeed, they epitomize the entrepreneurial, risk-taking spirit of a capitalist society: of the 'travelling man (or woman)'[2] for whom the next deal is going to make his (or her) fortune. And for the travelling man his family is so sacred that he prefers to worship from a safe distance. He comes home for brief joyous interludes but, as if compelled from within, 'has to' be off again in the morning. In other words, his normality is the reverse of that of Graburn's tourist. It is not that he has to travel for his job, let me add, but that he takes the job because he has to travel. If the anthropologist (among others) comes to mind at this point, that is my intention.

Graburn's analysis works better for more organized forms of tourism, but even here there are difficulties. However many rules are broken, one always remains: that the tourist 'has to' enjoy himself. If he does not join in, he is a spoil-sport. If the social pressure on him is unobtrusive, of course, he may welcome it as breaking the ice. If it fails in that, however, it readily becomes oppressive. Forced communitas is the very reverse of what it purports to be. I am not claiming that communitas is necessarily forced (that is an empirical matter) but that this very ambivalence lies at the heart of it. Here too, then, is a genuine fake.

AUTHENTICITY

This brings us to another approach which promises rather better for our purpose. I am referring to MacCannell's concept of tourism as the pursuit of staged authenticity, in conventionalized acts of respect for an authentic 'Other'. Whereas for Graburn ritual is a particular kind of event, for MacCannell it is a particular aspect of all events, which conventionalizes them. He writes that 'for moderns, reality and authenticity are thought to be elsewhere: in other historical periods and other cultures, in purer, simpler life-styles' (1976:3). It is the search for such authenticity that drives the tourist on to new and previously 'unspoilt' places and peoples. To present them as such, however, the places and people are soon transformed into 'sites' and 'attractions'. The tourist first colludes in this staging because it helps him comprehend them. His brochure provides a ceremonial agenda, which he follows more or less 'religiously' (this is Tuesday, so it must be Rome). After a while the staging becomes only too obvious, however, revealing the attraction to be inauthentic. Once again, the tourist has to look further afield for authenticity, and so on, into the ever-receding horizon. Authenticity and inauthenticity (the genuine and the fake) feed off each other in dialectical fashion, generating an ever-forward movement. Indeed for MacCannell tourism is a paradigm for modernity itself, for the sense of restlessness and inauthenticity on which (he claims) its progress depends, and which transcends the old divisions between Capitalist, Socialist and Third Worlds.

Now to my mind, it is not difficult to relativize this approach. MacCannell is referring to contemporary consumer society, in which to be seen to consume is a condition of consuming. The way to success is to invest your all in the image of success. As a Melanesianist I would claim that, their modernity notwithstanding, these attitudes were around in the Stone Age. The consumer society's paramount concern with image is readily recognizable in the systems of ceremonial exchange and warfare of High-lands New Guinea and in their 'cargo-thinking', which long pre-date colonialism and the replacement of stone axes by steel. The way to attract pigs and shells, in this system, is to create a reputation for generosity by first giving them away. The offer of a gift is a challenge to give back more in return or to fight. If a man does neither, rather than his credit, his credibility as a man is at risk. The Whole Man is involved in what is essentially a male sphere. Production is largely the responsibility of women, finally, and is comprehensively devalued. Needless to say, production is also devalued in contemporary consumer society.

Not to move forward, in consumer society, is to fall back: there is no standing still. This is what, for present purposes, MacCannell's tourists and Highlanders have in common. There are also significant differences, however, in these very same terms. While the tourists seek Wholeness elsewhere, in the authentic Other, the Highlanders seek Wholeness in unity at home, the authentic Self. Unity at home depends on creating and sustaining a credible external threat, hence the imperative to give or to fight (Brown, 1988). This points in turn to a difficulty with MacCannell's approach: the tourists' quest for authenticity can (and does) take very different (indeed, I would say, opposed) forms. In addition to authenticity in the Other, it is also sought in the Self. I am referring, quite simply, to the authentic 'Good Time': to good sand, for instance, to good sea and good sex. Graburn's approach is open to criticism but, whatever else, it does readily incorporate these well-known tourist activities.

In this view the concept of tourism as the pursuit of staged authenticity is powerful but incomplete. For the tourist, there is also the quest for the authentic Self. 'Having a good time,' runs the card, 'wish you were here.' The 'good time' may also be inauthentic, of course: as we have already seen, forced communitas is the reverse of what it purports to be. Hence the avowedly hedonistic tourist is also subject to the authentic/inauthentic dialectic. Authentic pleasure for him may lie in the very inauthenticity of a tourist attraction. The sight of jeans and trainers protruding below the 'traditional' costume reinforces his view that he is participating in a game: life as carnival, life as circus — never mind that it's an act, so long as it's a good one; life as a wrestling match, which everyone knows is fixed and need not pretend is fair but can enjoy all the more as a spectacle. You get what you pay for. Here is another instance of the genuine fake in which, in this case, the tourist seeks out the inauthentic Other in the quest for the authentic Self. At the same time, the forced 'good time' can become so inauthentic, that it is rejected in favour of the quest for the authentic Other. In this case, the sight of the jeans leads the tourist to reject the attraction as too staged and to seek out another that is more authentic. Let us now examine the relation between the two quests.

THEY ARE TOURISTS, I AM NOT

I endorse MacCannell's concern with authenticity, but hold that its quest generates opposed forms. Boorstin's opposition of travellers and tourists is particularly intriguing, in this connection, because one cannot read far into the anthropology of tourism without finding ritual denunciations of his position or what is taken to be his position. It is not altogether surprising that, in some quarters, the term 'tourist' is used as a derisive label. Stagings of 'traditional life' as a tourist attraction can be absurdly improbable, for instance, and we will all have our favourite examples.[3] This leads Boorstin to make a firm distinction between travellers and tourists, and to regret what he sees as the demise of the former. For him, 'the traveller . . . was working at something: the tourist is a pleasure-seeker. The traveller was active: he went strenuously in search of people, of adventure, of experience. The tourist is passive: he expects interesting things to happen to him. He goes sightseeing . . .' (1961:114). He goes sightseeing! It is indicative that, for Boorstin, that seems to say it all. They are tourists, one might add for him, but I (emphatically) am not.

Now the quest for the authentic Other is one of vanishing horizons. One genuine back-stage is penetrated, in Goffman's terms, only to reveal another fake front-stage: the act of observation changes that which is observed. Hence travellers do not (indeed cannot) succeed in their quest any more than tourists. That is only too clear from the accounts of the great Victorian travellers which are riddled with gross misconceptions. If they were not so serious, as with their concern (for instance) for the 'mysteries' of the Middle-Eastern harem, they would be laughable (see Kabbani, 1986). Furthermore, Boorstin's association of pleasure-seeking with passivity is most revealing. It reveals an almost patrician attitude to pleasure, that it is something for the servants. Evidently he does not recognize the quest for the 'good time', at least not as a worthy alternative.

We may think Boorstin's elitism fair game, but it is not disposed of so easily. They are tourists, for instance, but I (emphatically) am an anthropologist. Is there not an echo of Boorstin in that? MacCannell replies that Boorstin 'only expresses a long-standing touristic attitude, a pronounced dislike, bordering on hatred, for other tourists' (1976:107). For him this attitude is 'part of the problem of mass tourism, not an analytical reflection of it' (ibid.:104). Writing over 10 years later, Crick (1988) is less sanguine that we can maintain the distinction between (objective) analysis and (socially constructed) interpretation, and with it the privileged position of the anthropologist. Be this as it may (it is an issue to which we shall return), we may agree that the attitude is certainly part of the problem. Seen as a creative tension, indeed, I will argue that it is critical to understanding it.

Boorstin's failure is not to see that his travellers are also open to derision: that in their pursuit of the 'real' whatever it is, they too get taken for a ride; that in their concern not to obtrude, they don't even 'get laid' in the process; and to cap it all, they do not see the joke against themselves. In a word, his failure derives from his attitude to 'mere' pleasure. I have caricatured the travellers, but that is the point, that we are dealing with caricatures and their interplay. Even within organized tourism, there is an undoubted tension between, say, 'sex, sea and sand' tourists and their 'museum–cathedral circuit' counterparts, in which each caricatures the other. The quest for the authentic Other and for the authentic Self push in opposite directions, in other words, in a tension that informs all tourism.

TOURISTS AND PILGRIMS

If there are two quests, then, one might suppose, there are two forms of tourism. There is nothing particularly new in this, and Cohen (1979) makes a similar distinction between tourism and pilgrimage. However I would suggest that the forms are opposed aspects of a single mode (of travel) rather than empirically distinct modes on a continuum, as we shall now see.

Seeking to reconcile the opposing views of MacCannell and Boorstin, as to the authenticity of the tourist experience, Cohen argues that no single definition of 'the tourist' is possible. Moreover, we need to place tourism itself in historical context, as compared, for instance, with medieval pilgrimage. Drawing on Eliade's idea that every inhabited region has its sacred (but not necessarily geographical) Centre, Cohen (1979) contrasts travel away from the Centre and travel towards it. Medieval pilgrims travelled towards their own Centre, contemporary pilgrims travel away from it, in search of a Centre elsewhere (an elected Centre). Some of them may actually find it, in for instance, a Hindu ashram or an Israeli kibbutz. At the polar opposite are the tourists who remain firmly committed to their Centre 'back home', however far from it they may travel. Their travel is also meaningful but in confirming that 'home is best'. Towards the middle (but on the pilgrim side) are the hitch-hiking 'educated drifters' who, alienated from their own society, seek 'spontaneous experiences in the excitement of complete strangeness' (Cohen, 1973:89), take work as they may find it and would immerse themselves in the host culture. Thus Cohen erects a typology of modes of contemporary touristic experience: all tourists travel out from their own Centre, by definition, but those seeking a Centre elsewhere are also pilgrims.

It is a considerable strength of this conceptual framework that it allows a very wide range of touristic experience without ending up with a hopelessly heterodox typology. Moreover there is an analogy here with the opposed quests proposed earlier for the authentic Other and for the authentic Self. However the analogy is questionable on two principal grounds.

In the first place, what happens when Cohen's pilgrim arrives at his elected Centre? The quest of MacCannell's tourist for the Authentic Other, it will be remembered, is one of ever-receding horizons. Likewise, to my mind, an elected Centre is invested with too much potency to survive prolonged familiarity: the contemporary pilgrim either gathers strength and illumination from the experience, and moves on elsewhere in his quest for yet greener pastures, or returns disillusioned whence he came.[4] It is the quest which he values, not the pasture. If he sounds like the travelling man with whom I contrasted Graburn's tourist, well and good. It is MacCannell's tourist that he resembles rather than Cohen's pilgrim (or even less, Boorstin's traveller). By contrast Graburn's tourist values the pasture not the quest, in particular the pasture on which he makes his home. He returns to normality from travelling, renewed in his acceptance of it. In this typology of touristic experiences, then, MacCannell's tourist emerges as the contemporary pilgrim. His pilgrimage is a prime instance of the Other-centred quest and Graburn's tourism of the Self-centred form.

In the second place the two forms are opposed, not points on a continuum. This means first that either one quest would be devalued without the possibility of the other, if not lose its meaning altogether. A pilgrim is not only a pilgrim, in his own eyes, he is also and quite definitely not a tourist. Of course. But it works the other way as well: in rejecting what he sees as the élitism and hypocrisy of the pilgrim, the tourist affirms himself as tourist. To assert what they are, in other words, they have also to assert what they are not. And this means in turn that, in extremes, either one can turn into the other with quite startling ease. Genuine pilgrims are also fake tourists and quite readily turn into genuine tourists. They have only to be 'ripped off' once too often to rediscover their Centre back home and, in sudden reversal, come out with all the old discredited cultural stereotypes. Likewise, genuine tourists are fake pilgrims who can turn into the genuine article; to walk out altogether on their fellow tourists, for instance, it only needs the jollity to be forced on them once too often.

That respected weekly *The Economist* (1 August 1992) tells us that, in season, there are now queues at the summit of Everest, the ascent of which was one of the 'ultimate experiences' of the previous generation. By the end of one day in 1992, 32 climbers had stood on top of the world. Having attained this elected Centre *par excellence*, surely there is nowhere to go but retrace one's steps? But no, trend-setting climbers are now 'para-gliding' off the summit, having been dropped there by helicopter (complete with television crew). Their enterprise is thereby transformed into a spectacle, to be enjoyed as such or not at all: thus do fake pilgrims become genuine tourists. Alternatively, they remain true to their pilgrimage and seek out Centres (if only unclimbed faces) elsewhere.

Cohen is well aware of the issue of authenticity and more recently has likened tourism to play, which like all play 'has profound roots in reality, but for the success of which a great deal of make-believe, on the part of both performers and audience, is necessary. They willingly, even if often unconsciously, participate playfully in a game of "as if", pretending that a contrived product is authentic, even if deep down they are not convinced of its authenticity' (1988:383).

This is well said and brings to mind the travels of Eco (1987), but rather than bring out its contradictions Cohen (1988) attempts to incorporate the quest for authenticity within the continuum of touristic experiences. At the bottom of his continuum are the tourists 'who seek mere diversion and oblivion on their trip', and 'remain totally in equanimity and unconcerned with the problem of authenticity of their experiences'. Shades of Boorstin, with his patrician attitude to 'mere' pleasure! It is interesting that (for Cohen) these tourists are predominantly of lower social class. By contrast, the anthropologist is right off the top end of the continuum because, unlike the tourist, anthropological criteria of authenticity are not socially con-structed. Are they not? To say the least, it is open to question. My method in this chapter has been to replace the concept of points on a continuum with that of interacting opposites. The 'playful attitude of make-believe' to which Cohen refers becomes one term of an opposition, the other being the dedicated pursuit of authenticity. If nothing else, I hope thereby to exorcise the ghost of Boorstin.

EPISTEMOLOGICAL STANCE

The privileged position of the anthropologist has been questioned at several points, in the foregoing, and we are now in a position to explore the issue. As Crick expresses it,

> it may seem somewhat derogatory to speak of social science as 'collective representations' rather than 'analyses', but one of the issues that has to be raised is whether we have yet a respectable, scholarly analysis of tourism, on the one hand, and a highly evaluative and emotional 'literature', on the other, or whether the social science literature on the subject is itself substantially a part of the same powerful set of emotionally charged cultural images relating to travel and tourists. (1988:38).

Thus developmental economic studies of tourism sometimes read like industrial press-releases, as Crick points out, while some social scientific studies barely disguise contempt for the tourist as a supposed agent of deculturalization.

There has been an evident epistemological shift since MacCannell confidently distinguished between the authentic and the inauthentic tourist experience. The implication is that it is possible to know whether the tourist sight has been represented truly. The contrary position is that the sight cannot be 'seen' without the representation and is itself unknowable: to discard one representation is only to replace it by another. Thus Urry (1990:85) writes that 'as Baudrillard famously argues, what we increasingly consume are signs or representations. Social identities are constructed through the exchange of sign-values. But these are accepted in a spirit of spectacle. . . . This world of sign and spectacle is one in which there is no originality, only what Eco terms "travels in hyperreality" (1986). Everything is a copy, or a text upon a text, where what is fake seems more real than the real. This is a depthless world or, as Lash puts it, there is a "new flimsiness of reality"' (Lash, 1990:15). He summarizes this argument: *'modernism conceives of representations as being problematic whereas post-modernism problematises reality'*.

I must confess a certain impatience with post-modernist assertions of the death of meta-narrative (cf. Selwyn's Introduction to this volume): that in effect, contemporary consumer society (for instance) can only be understood in terms of itself. Cultural relativity is our stock in trade, as anthropologists, but the relativity has to be relative not absolute. Are all theories partial, inevitably, or is a unified theory possible? Are all analytical languages fallible, or does the problem lie with particular analytical languages and the methodological assumptions built into them? One such assumption is that reality (whether natural or social) consists of entities, autonomous by definition, and I have argued that this is a major obstacle to understanding. 'The problem with reification is not that it confuses model with reality, but reality with things. It would thing-ify it' (Brown,

1992:824). Thus the incompatibility of theories centred on the individual and on society, respectively, is simply a reflection of the so-called 'conflict between the individual and society', and no more enlightening. Rather we should be looking at relations, especially of class and of gender and, in our context, between tourist and locals. It is not that social entities exist but that they are brought into existence — not being but becoming. It is readily accepted that the act of observation may change that which is observed; the pursuit of truth is nevertheless directed, and this is what counts. Just to give up on it does seem a denial of responsibility.

Not to move forward is to fall back, in consumer society, for there is no standing still: this is the basis of my analogy (see above) between New Guinea Highlanders and contemporary consumerists. Movement is valued for the sake of movement. How then to construct an analytical framework, in which to 'place' these societies? In many (for instance peasant) societies, by contrast, stability is valued for the sake of stability: the paramount concern is not with image but with property. The parallel is with Durkheimian analysis in which order is valued for the sake of order in models of stable equilibrium. Like post-modernist narrative, it is implicated in that which it would narrate. Hence the opposition between these sets of values for their own sake provides a framework for contrasting consumer and (let us call it) producer society and, indeed, narratives concerning them. Since the two sets of values are opposed, moreover, one may pass into the other: genuine consumer society is also fake producer society and may transform itself from within. The dynamic here is the deepening divisions within consumer society, between those caught up in the consumerist merry-go-round and those excluded from it, in what has become known (in the UK) as the one-third/two-thirds society (Hutton, 1994). Note that this is the reverse of the 'structural de-differentiation' that post-modernists (Lash, 1990) would lead us to expect of a consumer society.[5] The argument is schematic, and here is not the place to develop it; the point is that such arguments are available, and we are not forced to give up on them.

How does this bear on the study of tourism? Frow writes that:

> The structure of the tourist experience involves a paradoxical relation at once to the cultural or ontological Other and to others of the same (tourist) culture. It is tourism itself that destroys (in the very process by which it constructs) the authenticity of the tourist object: and every tourist thus at some level denies belonging to the class of tourist. Hence a certain fantasized dissociation from the others, from the rituals of tourism, is built into almost every discourse and almost every practice of tourism. This is the phenomenon of touristic shame, a 'rhetoric of moral superiority', which accompanies both the most snobbish and the most politically radical critiques of tourism (1991:146).

There is a revealing structural homology here between the touristic experience as presented by Frow and the study of this experience as presented by Crick (1985). At the heart of both is a paradoxical relation, the phenomenon of touristic shame. Structural homologies between an analytical language and that which is under observation indicate that the analysis is worth pursuing, no more but also no less. And touristic shame is central to this chapter, let me remind the reader, in the paradoxical relation between the tourist and the pilgrim who is also a tourist. Moreover, as Frow makes clear, this relation involves the 'cultural or ontological Other' as well as other tourists. The proper focus of study is not the tourist, nor indeed the host, but the relation between them. This is already plain enough in MacCannell and Cohen, among others, and in the view expressed here, that we should be looking at relations not entities. In that view they are relations of opposition, neither complementary nor exploit-ative but uncertainly both. A potential for internal structural transformation is inherent: as social relationships they remain social facts, but they are facts that can turn themselves on their head. That 'tourism itself destroys . . . the authenticity of the tourist object' (Frow, 1991), then, gives tourist relations a powerful internal dynamic.

In the present volume this process is examined, implicitly where not explicitly, by Fees, Meethan and Selwyn among others. In other words, while tourism itself gives rise to profound social changes, tourist myths themselves are founded upon the concealing and denying of such changes and the perpetuation of the ideas and images of how things were imagined to be before tourism. My argument in this section is that the study of tourism could fruitfully proceed in this direction.

CONCLUSION

I am suggesting that tourism and pilgrimage are opposed aspects of a single mode of interaction, between the travelling tourist/pilgrim and those whom he encounters on his travels (the so-called 'guests' and 'hosts'). The terms of the opposition may differ with social and historical context (see Pfaffenberger, 1983), but not the fact of opposition. As Levi-Strauss (1967:149) puts it, 'it is not the resemblances, but the differences, which resemble each other'. Hence the mode itself may include travel for work as well as for pleasure, so long as the travel is actively sought out. Let me conclude with an illustration of some of these themes which brings out their political aspect.

In the early 1960s, Madras was a good place for Cohen's impoverished drifters. The state was dry, but foreigners could get a ration of alcohol, and this they sold to well-to-do Madrasis. The local film industry needed white extras, often as 'baddies', and this was another source of income. And most of the drifters were white. If things got bad, finally, there was always begging. The best time was outside the big offices, when the white-collar workers left for home. They saw a white sitting there at their feet, representative of the ex-imperial power, and felt marvellous. By giving him a few disdainful coins they humiliated all whites everywhere and their overbearing arrogance. And by giving five times as much they felt five times better! The drifters either professed not to care or looked upon it as a political act on their part. Either way, a few hours begging could 'see them right' for a week.

Let me say at once that it was a genuine political act. A common feature of Hindu belief systems, in contexts such as these, is that the alms-giver gains immediate spiritual merit for his act. There is no free gift and, by the same token, no freeloading or scrounging either. The beggar also pays immediately, suffering corresponding loss of merit. He is both defiled by his act and, because it allows the donor to gain merit, made 'holy' by it: their relationship is contradictory, uncertainly complementary and exploitative. These drifter–beggars, then, were genuine pilgrims; they understood they were doing their donors a favour as well, albeit seeing it primarily in political terms. At the same time they were also tourists, albeit fake ones. Their impoverishment was genuine enough, but they had Western passports in their possession or, if they had torn them up in an excess of renunciation of simply sold them, they still had the right to them. Consulates made repatriation in these circumstances as humiliating as possible but could not refuse in the end. However much the drifters begged their way, in other words, their passports distinguished them sharply from local beggars. What is more they could suddenly decide they had had more than enough and revert to genuine tourism.

In rediscovering their Centres way back home, I should add, they could never regard them in quite the same way. Nor do I mean to suggest that the pilgrim must always fail in his quest. His dilemma is that the questions interest him more than the answers, so that he must always pass on. Whatever else he is, the apocryphal anthropologist who comes back claiming 'they think I'm Quetzlcoatl' is a fake pilgrim. In the first place, he is expected (as the deity) to give answers not to ask questions; and in the second, he risks becoming a tourist attraction himself. For the genuine pilgrim (on the other hand) 'participant-observation' is not a method to be learnt and/or abandoned but a somewhat uncomfortable way of life.

I started by pointing to the prevalence of genuine fakes.[6] While contemporary pilgrims try to penetrate the mystery, tourists prefer to enjoy the joke. These are opposed aspects of a single mode of interaction: genuine pilgrims are also fake tourists and can turn into the genuine article, and genuine tourists likewise. There is a certain tension between them which, I would say, gives meaning and dignity to both. However apparently circular the process, finally, no one ever lands back quite where they started: even where they do return sadder, they are also wiser for their travels. Whether downwards or upwards, the process is not circular but spiralling.

NOTES

1. Thus Eco writes of Disneyland, in a characteristic passage, that:

   > The Main Street facades are presented to us as toy houses and invite us to enter them, but their interior is always disguised as a supermarket, where you buy obsessively, believing you are still playing. In this sense Disneyland is more hyperrealistic than the wax museum, precisely because the latter still tried to make us believe that what we are seeing reproduces reality absolutely, whereas Disneyland makes it clear that within its magic enclosure it is fantasy that is magically reproduced. The Palace of Living Arts presents its Venus de Milo as almost real, whereas Disneyland can permit itself to present its reconstructions as masterpieces of falsification, for what it sells is, indeed, goods, but genuine merchandise, not reproductions. What is falsified is our will to buy, which we take as real, and in this sense Disneyland is really the quintessence of consumer ideology (1987:43).

2. This clumsy phrase is shortened, in what follows, to 'travelling man'. No change of meaning is intended.
3. One of mine is the 'traditional' Ainu go-cart track, reached through what was presented as a 'traditional' Ainu village. The dancing bear was so obviously bored (and boring). Another is the 'traditional' grass-skirted Solomon Islanders belting out Beatles hits from car-battery powered electric guitars, deep in the 'jungle'. They keep a wary eye for the next tourist-laden minibus, upon whose arrival they revert to drums and spears. I should add that it is quite wrong to suppose that some (at least) of the tourists did not enjoy the joke as well.
4. In this view the kibbutzim can expect a tendency for second- (if not first-) generation members to move on, and to ask why they do not stay is to identify the wrong problem. They should be asking rather how to attract more new members.
5. Pursuing the analogy between contemporary consumer society and social life in the Highlands, the prevalence of exchange of like for like (in kind) indicates that exchange itself is valued. However the exchanges do not dissolve differences but create them as acts of differentiation between individuals and between groups. They bring opposing groups and sets of individuals into being. This too is the reverse of structural de-differentiation.
6. One of the most obvious instances is that of 'airport art'. To the extent that it is not the artefact it is presented to be, it is evidently a fake. To the extent that it is bought knowingly as such, however, it is genuine. As you look the vendor in the eye and complete the deal, he knows that you know it is a fake (despite his protestations), and you know that he knows that you know, and so on; that is clearly a genuine transaction. As pilgrim you would not even consider the deal, of course, but as tourist you think it a good laugh. Pilgrim and tourist may deride each other, but both are worthy of respect; indeed I would say, their attitudes are two sides of a single coin.

REFERENCES

Boorstin, D.J. (1961) *The Image: a Guide to Pseudo-events in America*, New York: Harper and Row.

Brown, D.J.J. (1988) 'Unity in opposition in the New Guinea Highlands', *Social Analysis*, 23, 89–109.

Brown, D.J.J. (1992) 'Spiralling connubia in the Highlands of Papua New Guinea', *Man* (N, S) 27, 821–42.

Cohen, E. (1973) 'Nomads from affluence: notes on the phenomenon of drifter-tourism', *International Journal of Comparative Sociology*, 14(1–2), 89–103.

Cohen, E. (1979) 'A phenomenology of tourist experiences;, *Sociology*, 13, 179–201.

Cohen, E. (1988) 'Authenticity and commoditization in tourism', *Annals of Tourism Research*, 15, 371–86.

Crick, M. (1985) '"Tracing" the anthropological self: quizzical reflections on fieldwork, tourism and the ludic', *Social Analysis*, 17, 71–92.

Crick, M. (1988) 'Sun, sex, sights, savings and servility: representations of international tourism in the social sciences', *Criticism, Heresy and Interpretation* I(1), 37–76.

Eco, U. (1986) *Faith in Fakes*, London: Secker and Warburg.

Eco, U. (1987) *Travels in Hyper-Reality*, London: Pan Books.

Frow, J. (1991) 'Tourism and the semantics of nostalgia', *October*, 57, 121–51.

Graburn, N. (1977) 'Tourism: the sacred journey' in V. Smith (ed.), *Hosts and Guests: the Anthropology of Tourism*, Oxford: Blackwell, 17–32.

Hutton, W. (1994) *The State We're In: Why Britain is in Crisis and How to Overcome it*, London: J. Cape.

Kabbani, R. (1986) *Europe's Myths of the Orient*, London: Macmillan.

Lash, S. (1990) *Sociology of Postmodernism*, London: Routledge.

Levi-Strauss, C. (1967) *Totemism*, London: Penguin Books.

MacCannell, D. (1976) *The Tourist: a New Theory of the Leisure Class*, New York: Schocken.

Pfaffenberger, B. (1983) 'Serious pilgrims and frivolous tourists', *Annals of Tourism Research*, 10, 57–74.

Urry, John (1990) *The Tourist Gaze: Leisure and Travel in Contemporary Societies*, London: Sage Publications.

3 Looking for Shangri-la: from Hilton to Lāmichhāne

MICHAEL HUTT

In the West, the most readily available representations of distant and alien cultures are those conveyed by the mass media and popular literature. Inevitably these are often simplistic, and certain clichés recur when talking about particular far-flung corners of the world — the expression 'far-flung' is a prime example. My intention in this chapter is to suggest that one particular English novel, James Hilton's *Lost Horizon*, has played at least a minor role in the shaping of Western preconceptions of one particular region: the Himalaya. The continued perception of the Himalayan countries as magical realms also feeds back into political and social processes, and the fact that many Westerners now visit this region as tourists, bringing with them their own expectations of how it will be, has led to a small-scale but interesting reaction in the local literature.

THE NOTION OF SHANGRI-LA

The phenomenon of one culture looking at another through the distorting lens of a myth which it has evolved for itself is neither new nor confined to the West. Benedict Anderson touched on this issue in his study of modern nationalisms by describing the psychological effect upon Europe of the discovery of grandiose and ancient non-European cultures during the 15th and 16th centuries. The existence of these cultures had hitherto been only dimly rumoured or even totally unknown. Their most disturbing aspect, for a Europe which was totally confident of its Christian centrality and ascendancy in the world, was the fact that most of them had developed independently of both Europe and Christianity and were thus 'outside of and unassimilable to Eden' (Anderson, 1983:67). One response to this revelation was manifested in the European literature of the period when a number of writers became famous for inventing their own versions of a perfect society. A notable feature of this was that each utopia was purportedly modelled upon a remote but contemporary society, which was implicitly compared and contrasted with the imperfect society of Europe.

The Tourist Image: Myths and Myth Making in Tourism. Edited by Tom Selwyn.
© 1996 John Wiley & Sons Ltd.

Thus, More's Utopia was in the Americas, Francis Bacon's New Atlantis was in the Pacific, Swift's Island of the Houyhnhnms was in the South Atlantic and James Hilton's (1933) more recent paradise, Shangri-la, was located in the high Himalayas.

It is important to mention that the Himalayas have possessed a mythic status since ancient times for the peoples of South Asia. Agehananda Bharati has argued that most Indians do not have a very strong geographical conception of the mountains which border their country to the north: 'to all Hindus, except those who live there, the Himalayas tend to be ascriptive rather than actual mountains' (Bharati, 1978:78). Bharati backs up this somewhat exaggerated statement (after all, many Indians do visit the Himalaya as pilgrims and as tourists) with a quote from the Hindu philosopher T.V.R. Murti: 'Existentialism says that potentiality is more important than actuality. This is true: the Himalaya of the rishis and the yogis is more important to us than the actual rocks and the miserable huts of the people there' (Bharati, 1978:78). It may be true, as Bharati argues, that an Indian Hindu who has not visited the region will consider the Himalaya largely as mythic mountains, and his/her conception of the range may well be based on the legends and myths of Hindu tradition. It may also be true to say that representations of the same region in contemporary Western literature are influenced to some extent by the currency of a much newer myth, articulated most recently by the novelist James Hilton.

Hilton's novel *Lost Horizon* was published in 1933 and won the Hawthornden Prize for fiction. In 1937, a Hollywood film version was released to general acclaim, despite one critic's remark that 'the inaccuracies must have involved tremendous research' (Halliwell, 1985:592). *Lost Horizon* begins with an evacuation of Europeans from 'Baskul', apparently following a 'native revolution'. Four evacuees board a light aeroplane: two British colonial officials are joined by a missionary and an American businessman. One of the Britons, Conway, is an educated and philosophical man who bears the emotional scars of his experiences in World War I. He is the novel's central character and was probably modelled on the mountaineer George Mallory. The plane does not follow its expected course: in fact, it heads straight for the Himalayan range, and the passengers discover that the pilot is not a British officer, as they had assumed, but an armed 'Oriental'. Evidently, they are being kidnapped. When the plane crash lands in a remote corner of Tibet, the pilot immediately dies, but his passengers are rescued by the retinue of a passing lama and taken to the valley of Blue Moon. There they are accommodated in the 'lamasery' of Shangri-la. As the story progresses, we learn that the fertile valley with its equable climate has become a storehouse of world culture, where literature, music and the arts are preserved against the eventuality of Armageddon. The 'lamas' have also discovered an elixir which enables them to live to a great age. The four people were actually brought to the valley quite deliberately, and the inhabitants do not intend them ever to leave.

Conway strikes up a relationship of unprecedented intimacy and frankness with the Grand Lama, actually a Luxemburger named Perrault, who is about 250 years old. Eventually the Lama expires, having told Conway that he must take his place as head of the monastery. By this time, all but one of the hijacked visitors have succumbed to the tranquillity of Shangri-la and are reconciled to the fact that they must remain there. The younger Briton, however, is restless to leave. Fearing for his safety, Conway escorts him from the valley but loses Shangri-la in the process. 'He was doomed', wrote Hilton, 'like millions, to flee from wisdom and be a hero' (Hilton, 1947:178). When last heard of, Conway was still desperately trying to find his way back to the valley of Blue Moon.

The success of Hilton's novel derives from the fact that its romantic theme struck a chord in popular imagination. Many Europeans before Hilton had entertained the fantasy of a paradise beyond the world's highest mountains, fuelled perhaps by apocryphal stories of 'lost valleys' where people lived to an enormous age. First Tibet, then Lhasa, became the bases for various European fantasies and aspirations, and the Himalayas and the Himalayan kingdoms subsequently became Shangri-las by default. As the sanctity of each 'forbidden' city or country was violated by travellers, the fantasy moved on from 'sacred place' to 'utopia' or from 'symbolic concentration' to 'geographical abstraction' (Bishop, 1990:216, 243). Hilton was the first writer to situate such a place off the map and to give it a name which has stuck to this day. The success and lasting appeal of his story derives partly from the fact that Shangri-la is permanently 'lost' and obviously reveals far more about the cultural context within which it was conceived than it does about the Himalayan region which is its setting. Two different endings were filmed for the original Hollywood version: the ending which showed Conway returning triumphantly to Shangri-la was deemed too happy and predictable, and so the mystical ambiguity of its alternative was chosen. It is not surprising that most of the novel's cultural assumptions and points of reference are European: the artistic and scholarly heritage which is being saved from destruction is apparently exclusively Western; indeed, the monastery itself has been founded by a Grand Lama who is not a Chinese or a Tibetan but a Luxemburger. Furthermore, the main 'oriental' characters to appear in the story are not Tibetan but Chinese, since the stereotypes of Chinese inscrutability and mysticism were conveniently familiar to the occidental mind, whereas the Tibetan character remained somewhat obscure.

Hilton's tale reflects more than anything else its author's reaction against the shortcomings of Western civilization in particular and the human condition in general. Since life at Shangri-la is extraordinarily long, none of its inhabitants hurries or exerts pressure on his fellows. Life proceeds in aesthetic and intellectual pursuits, with no competition, conflict or strife; here it is important to remember the troubled period of European history during which Hilton wrote his book and the stage Europe had reached in its imagining of Tibet. Lhasa had been 'unveiled' (Candler, 1905) and defiled, and the fantasy had moved on to a *utopia*, a 'non-place'.

The word *Shangri-la*, an invented pseudo-Tibetan place name, has now entered the English language. The *Collins English Dictionary*, for instance, defines it as 'a remote or imaginary utopia' (1982:1339). In 1942, President Roosevelt is said to have mystified the Japanese and Germans by calling the base from which American aircraft set off to bomb Tokyo 'Shangri-la' — a place they would never find (Hilton, 1947: cover-blurb). Yet the name has not become entirely divorced from the Himalayan region which originally inspired its invention and is invoked continually in Western writings on Nepal, Tibet, Bhutan and certain parts of the Indian Himalaya. By association, the popular Western conception of these countries is of romantic, mystical realms, and their expanding tourist industries do their best to perpetuate the image. This categorization of Himalayan societies as in some way other-worldly does much to obstruct objective consideration of the serious political, environmental and economic issues which affect them. Western newspaper reports on Tibet during the 1970s and 1980s, for instance, regularly referred to the tale of Shangri-la, either by refuting its validity: 'The image of a pristine Shangri-la . . . glosses over its un-enlightened past as a feudal theocracy . . .' (*International Herald Tribune*, 11 May 1983) or else by restating the myth in emotive terms. It is curious that a work of British fiction written some 60 years before was still considered to be of relevance in a discussion of contemporary Chinese rule in Tibet.

None the less, the Western mind is fickle in its application of the label. In a sense, Shangri-la is a virginal state: once defiled by foreign invasion, modernization or internal political strife, it is as if some kind of betrayal has taken place. As Said has pointed out, the Orient, in the Western mind, has generally been essentialized as feminine. Although much of its allure derived from its remoteness, Tibet was for centuries the 'navel of the world' and its capital, Lhasa, was the *axis mundi*. After an initial burst of sympathy for Tibet's exiled ruler, the Dalai Lama, a sizeable proportion of journalist coverage adopted the Chinese perception of Tibetan society as a barbaric medieval anachronism. The wooing of communist China during the 1970s encouraged many writers to portray Tibet not as a mystical realm at the northern periphery of India but as a backward, feudal society at the western periphery of China. The perception of peripheral regions thus appears to depend to some extent on what they are peripheries of and who it is that has granted the privilege of access.

Once Tibet had been sealed off to Western imaginings, the mantle of Shangri-la passed to other Himalayan realms: Nepal, Sikkim, Ladakh and Bhutan. In recent years, Nepal and Sikkim have betrayed the myth: Sikkim lost its Tibetan ruler and semi-autonomous status in the mid-1970s, while Nepal now welcomes about 300 000 Western tourists a year. Kathmandu has become a centre, and Nepal's remoter regions have become more alluring peripheries. But the excitement of engaging with the Other is diluted when the experience is shared with others. A kind of snobbery has grown up among those visitors who consider themselves 'travellers', rather than mere 'tourists' (see Shepherd, 1990, and a retort from the two 'offended travellers' in the subsequent issue of *Himal*). Moreover, Nepal parades the poverty of its people too brazenly in search of foreign aid and has developed an intellectual culture that is prone to question foreign assumptions. The physical manifestations of development and modernization in Nepal are seen as departures from the supposedly pristine nature of the authentic social and cultural order, and Shangri-la moves on.

It moves on to Ladakh, and it moves on to Bhutan. More than any other writer on the Himalaya, Andrew Harvey reminds one of Said's maxim that the Orientalist poet or scholar 'is never concerned with the Orient except as the first cause of what he says' (Said, 1985:21.) Harvey writes, 'I went to Ladakh because I wanted to go to Nepal. I found out about Ladakh because I wanted to go to Nepal' (1984:6), and quotes a young Frenchman he met in Delhi on the subject of Ladakh:

Ladakh is the last place where you can see something of what Tibet must have been like, now that Bhutan is open only to the very rich. And Ladakh is a wonderful world in its own right too. If I had a group of gangsters and a plane I would kidnap you and take you there myself. Through Ladakh I have come to see everything differently. If you have felt anything in these hours we have been together, any intensity, any trust, think that it was not just from me or from us, but from Ladakh too that they have come (ibid.:6–7).

Again, the extent to which a Himalayan region is deemed to be Shangri-la (and either Harvey or his Frenchman has evidently read *Lost Horizon*) depends on the extent to which it retains unchanged elements of the lost Tibetan authenticity. The authenticity is diluted by accessibility: the Frenchman's reference to Bhutan is significant — Ladakh is authentic now, but it will soon be spoiled by its admirers; Tibet has been ruined by the Chinese, and Nepal by tourists and by the Nepalese themselves, but Bhutan remains authentic. It is treading a 'cautious path to development', restricting the number of tourists while keeping them out of the temples. Its government has banned television antennae, and Bhutanese can be fined or even imprisoned for not wearing their traditional national costume in the prescribed places and on the prescribed occasions. All of these facts inspire universal admiration in Western writings on Bhutan, despite the fact that these and other policies have led to the flight of over 88 000 refugees from Bhutan into Nepal since 1990. Said refers to 'the truism that if the Orient could represent itself, it would; since it cannot, the representation does the job, for the West, and *faute de mieux*, for the poor Orient' (1985:21), but Bhutan has embraced its reputation wholeheartedly. According to the country's Department of Education:

> ... these make Bhutan a 'paradise' or what foreign visitors to the Kingdom like to call the 'Last Shangrila' on earth ... There are, however, many millions of people of Nepali origin living in ... the surrounding areas who are not only envious of us, the Bhutanese, enjoying so much happiness and prosperity but would like to migrate in millions so as to steal our peace, happiness and prosperity from us and our children (RGB, 1992:29–30).

LOCAL REACTIONS

There have been several local literary reactions to the Western world's idealized image of the Himalayan region. Here, I refer mainly to works by modern writers from Nepal, since this is my field of specialization. Similar sentiments might well be found in the literatures of other South Asian languages, but it is to Nepal that the vast majority of tourists come who visit the Himalayas from outside Asia. So far as I have been able to ascertain, *Lost Horizon* has not been translated into any South Asian language and is virtually unknown in Nepal outside of the tourist industry and the borrowing of the Shangri-la motif by Royal Nepal Airlines for its executive cabin. Nothing in Nepali literature addresses itself specifically to the legend of Shangri-la, but a number of interesting works do exist which are concerned with the attitudes of Western visitors to Nepal.

A Nepali poet, Ratnadev Sharmā, published a poem in the Kathmandu literary monthly, *Madhupark*, in 1971 which was entitled 'I too am a remarkable man'. This poem describes a young hippy girl in the streets of Kathmandu and expresses an interesting combination of attitudes to its subject. Sharmā, who was 43 years old at the time, evidently had some measure of insight into the mass exodus of young Westerners to the East at that time:

> How splendid you are, oh hippy,
> Now fine your tiger-teeth earrings
> And the beads and red local skirt you wear.
> On a whim you have set yourself apart
> From the spinning terrors of Science,
> From the grind and squeak of its millstone;
> You have come to stretch yourself out
> On the laps of unworried people.
> (Sharmā, 1971 in Subedī, 1982:83)

Thus, the poem begins by praising, perhaps with a modicum of sarcasm, the hippy's impressive costume. It goes on to express sympathy with her disillusionment with Science and, by association, with Western society and its values. The poet welcomes the hippy, declaring himself flattered and gratified that she has recognized something of value in his culture and way of life. Yet there is an air of bemusement about the concluding lines, where Sharmā also seems to have felt obliged to remind the hippy that he is not less interesting or flamboyant than her. 'Lifting up the sun', indeed, is the act of a deity rather than that of a mere mortal:

> So turn around once and look,
> Look closely at me:
> With my right hand I lift up the sun as I walk;
> I too am a remarkable man.
> (Sharmā, 1971 in Subedī, 1982:83)

Sharmā does not appear to object to the hippy girl's idealized view of his society. Indeed, the Nepali view of Westerners which seems to have prevailed, at least until the opening-up of the kingdom to mass tourism, is one of a technologically sophisticated, generous and egalitarian people. The anthropologist James Fisher has described what he terms a 'mutual admiration society' which grew up between the Sherpas of eastern Nepal and their foreign visitors. He suggests that a set of stereotyped images is involved, each held by one group of the other:

> the image Westerners have developed of Sherpas is extremely positive . . . This image begins on the basis of hearsay and literary evidence, which has by now assumed epic proportions, and then is reinforced . . . by personal experience . . . The reason Westerners are so enchanted with the Sherpas is that the qualities the Sherpas are thought to possess are not only those Westerners admire; they are also precisely those they feel they should have but conspicuously lack . . . So Sherpa society, or the Western image of it, represents a dramatic realisation of what Westerners would like to be themselves, hence the frequently breathless enthusiasm of the latter for the former (Fisher, 1986:46, 47).

Is there not, indeed, some tenuous psychological link between the enormous resonance and longevity of Hilton's mythical utopia and the Western tourist's admiration for Himalayan peoples? Shangri-la is everything we would wish the world to be; the Sherpas for many of their visitors are paragons of cheerful humanity. Nepalis, of course, are keenly aware of the fact that they do not live in a Shangri-la:

> It has been said that members of the Third World intelligentsia are all suckers for what the *saheb* says and does: we follow his scholarship and also his myth-making. In this particular instance, do we tend to internalise what others perceive is our culture and glamour, just as discriminated minorities in developed countries internalise negative images of themselves? The *saheb*, of course, will go back to Kansas, Kensington or Kew, but *we* have to descend

from the borrowed clouds and return to the squelch of our marketplaces (Dixit, 1990:7).

The Sherpas' initial positive image of Westerners has also been tempered by later experience: 'In addition to the original positive image, foreigners are now equally apt to be thought crude, stumbling, demanding, unpredictable and cheap' (Fisher, 1986:47). It is in the Sherpas' interests, and in the interests of the Nepali tourist industry as a whole, to foster the romantic image which foreigners hold of Nepal and its people. Kanak Mani Dixit again:

> Is life in the Himalaya on a spiritually higher plane than it is in the rest of the world? Even if it is not, does it do any harm if people across the oceans think of our mountains and their peoples as somehow exalted? Instead of pointing to the material poverty which forms a counterfoil to the Himalayas' perceived romance, should we just turn up the hype if that brings more foreign exchange laden tourists? . . . These are questions that have yet to be considered seriously in a region where the focus has been either on willy-nilly maximising tourism income (as in Nepal) or on protecting one's heritage while maximising tourist income (Bhutan) . . . Mostly, Himalayans like to bask in the world's overwhelming admiration of their region. If it doesn't bring tangible benefits, there would seem to be psychological rewards. And yet, it is bound to hurt somewhere, sometime, in some way, when people begin to believe in an outsider's well-meaning fantasy (1990:7).

The satirical Nepali poet Bhupi Sherchan exposed the contradictions inherent in the promotion of mass tourism amid mass poverty in a poem which described the comings and goings at the airfield at Pokharā, a small town in central Nepal famous for its views of the Himalayan range, and particularly of Māchhāpuchare, the 'Fishtail mountain':

> Planes are coming, planes are going,
> Coming with honeymoon couples,
> Going carrying soldiers
> Summoned to Kutch next morning.
> Planes come, bringing tourists
> To see the Fishtail mountain,
> Planes go carrying baskets and trunks,
> Ploughs and the Fishtail's children,
> Off to seek land in the plains . . .
> (Sherchan, 1969, 1983:39)

Mīnbahādur Bistha, meanwhile, jokes ironically about Nepal's reliance on foreign aid:

> Respected visitor, this is Kathmandu Valley.
> Here there are three cities:
> Kathmandu, Lalitpur, Bhaktapur.

Please cover your nose with a handkerchief,
No sewage system is possible.
The building of toilets has not been feasible.
Our next Five-Year Plan has a Clean City Campaign:
Could you make a donation?
(Bistha 1983 in Sharmā (ed.):219).

From a surprisingly early stage in the exposure of Nepal to Western thought and philosophy (Hutt 1984), some Nepali writers have reacted against visitors' preconceived notions about their land. One celebrated reaction came from Shankar Lāmichhāne, a man employed in various cultural and governmental institutions from the 1950s until his untimely death in 1975, who was also one of Nepal's most respected writers. In 1960, Lāmichhāne was employed by the Nepal–India Joint Cultural Institution in Kathmandu. While working in his office one day, he became aware of a pair of eyes which stared at him from the upstairs window of a neighbouring house. These eyes regarded him impassively all day long and later Lāmichhāne was distressed to discover that they were the eyes of a paralysed child. That same day, he received a visit from an American woman who was working on a photo-article for the *National Geographic* magazine. She asked him to accompany her to observe and photograph the colourful spectacle of a local festival, but Lāmichhāne was in the wrong frame of mind for such things, and he pointed out the eyes to her, explaining their circumstances (Lāmichhāne, 1975:63–7).

This incident became the basis for Lāmichhāne's most famous short story, 'The Half-Closed Eyes and the Setting Sun' ('Ardhamudit Nayan ra Dubna Lāgeko Ghām', translated in full in Hutt 1991:253–9), which articulates with considerable irony a Nepali's rejection of the utopian image of his society. It comprises two quite lengthy monologues; the first is that of a tourist, newly arrived in Kathmandu, and the second is a reply from the tourist's guide. The tourist describes Nepal's history and culture and shows off his extensive knowledge of Nepali legends, which he has read in the libraries of his homeland. He asserts that the spirit of Nepal is encapsulated in the smiles on the faces of its people and by the enigmatic eye motifs painted onto the Buddhist stupas which are to be found in Kathmandu Valley towns:

> It is a smile of welcome, as if our meeting were neither coincidental nor our first encounter . . . It's as if I have married the world's most beautiful woman. I am bringing her home behind me, and my mother is smiling a welcome from the door . . . This is a land of eyes, a land watched over by the half-closed eyes of the Buddha . . . Tomorrow, show me beautiful eyes, eyes without equal. Eyes whose memory will make this journey of mine unforgettable . . . (Lāmichhāne, 1979 in Aryāl (ed.):136, 137).

The guide obliges his guest the next day by taking him to a nearby village to visit a humble farmer's family. There, says the guide, he will

Figure 3.1 Bauddha Stupa, Kathmandu

show him a pair of eyes which will reveal 'the pulse of our reality'. The eyes, of course, belong to a paralysed child. He describes the child in detail and also responds ironically to the tourist's remarks about the Nepali smile. He informs him that he has lied to the child's parents, telling them that he is a foreign doctor:

> There is a child in that house who is certainly no divine incarnation. Born into a poor farmer's household and attacked by polio, he is surely incapable of spreading the holy Law, or making any contribution to this world . . . I do not intend to show him to you as any kind of symbol. Yesterday, you were swept away by waves of emotion, inspired by your 'Black and White' whisky, and you urged me to show you eyes which would forever remind you of your visit to Nepal. So I have brought you here to show you eyes like that . . . That smile you described is on their faces, as if you were their eldest son who has brought a life-restoring remedy for your brother from across the seven seas (ibid.:137–8).

Lāmichhāne denies that there is anything ugly in this spectre of a paralysed child. Indeed, the prevalence of such diseases, his guide remarks sarcastically, fosters another quality of the oriental character: 'This capacity for remaining speechless, inactive, powerless and immobile, and yet to survive without complaint: surely this can only be found in a child from the east!' (ibid.:139).

Another writer, Parashu Pradhān, has dealt with a similar theme in a brief but poignant essay which describes the thoughts of a tourist guide who has just learned of the loss of his wife.

Such a tragic thing should have made him cry, but none of it touched him at all. It seemed as ordinary as his daily life, like getting up at dawn, rinsing his mouth out hurriedly, dressing and fixing the knot of his tie, then smiling at unfamiliar faces as if he knew them well . . . He tried to forget the telegram, and to sleep. But all the tourists he had seen that day kept coming up to him in his mind and asking him questions — how old is this piece of art? What is its importance? Is woodcarving an ancient skill? And so on, and so on (Pradhān, 1984:163).

What Lāmichhāne and Pradhān wished to convey, perhaps, was their feeling that the foreigner's romance with Nepal is based on a selective view of its contemporary reality. They do not deny that their homeland possesses a cultural heritage of enormous richness but point out that there are other, less attractive features of everyday life of which visitors should be aware. The representation may continue to 'do the job' for the West but not necessarily for Said's 'poor Orient', for in Nepal it is no longer a case of *faute de mieux*. There exists a great gulf between the popular view of Nepal and the Himalayan region held by relatively uninformed visitors and the views of most of the people who live there. This is of course unsurprising: few who live in a tourist haven see their land quite as it is promoted outside. What is surprising is that it is possible for the majority of visitors to come to Nepal or Bhutan expecting a mystical utopia, to seek out the images first seen in the brochure and the picture-book (see, for instance, Frank, 1978 or Toutain, 1986) and then to return home with their preconceptions virtually intact.

REFERENCES

Anderson, B. (1983) *Imagined Communities: Reflections on the Origin and Spread of Nationalism*, London: Verso.

Bharati, Agehananda (1978) 'Actual and ideal Himalayas: Hindu views of the mountains' in James F. Fisher (ed.), *Himalayan Anthropology*, Paris and the Hague: Mouton.

Bishop, Peter (1990) *The Myth of Shangri-la*, Berkeley: University of California Press.

Candler, Edmund (1905) *The Unveiling of Lhasa*, Thomas Nelson: London.

Collins English Dictionary (1982) London and Glasgow: Collins (6th edition).

Fisher, James (1986) 'Sherpas and tourists', *Contributions to Nepalese Studies*, 14(1), Kathmandu.

Frank, Dietmar (1978) *Dreamland Nepal*, New Delhi: S. Chand and Co.

Halliwell, Leslie (1985) *Halliwell's Film Guide*, London: Granada.

Harvey, Andrew (1984) *A Journey in Ladakh*, Paladin Books: London.

Hilton, James (1947) *Lost Horizon*, London: Pan Books (1st Edition 1933).

Hutt, Michael (1984) 'Neon lights and vedic caves: European influences on the Nepali writer', *South Asia Research*, 4(2).

Hutt, Michael (1991) *Himalayan Voices, an Introduction to Modern Nepali Literature*, Berkeley: University of California Press.

Lāmichhāne, Shankar (1975) *Godhuli Samsar*, Kathmandu: Ratna.

Lāmichhāne, Shankar (1979) 'Ardhamudit Nayan ra Dubna Lāgeko Ghām' (The half-closed eyes and the setting sun) in Bhairav Aryāl (ed.), *Sajha Katha*, Kathmandu: Sajha Prakasan, 3rd edition.

Pradhan, Parashu (1984) *Pratinidhi Kathaharu*, Kathmandu: Om Prakash Agraval.

RGB (1992) Royal Government of Bhutan, Department of Education, *Eighth Quarterly Policy Guidelines and Instructions*, Thimphu, March.

Said, Edward, W. (1985[1978]) *Orientalism*, London: Peregrine Books.

Sharma, Ratnadev (1971) 'Ma Pani Euta Anautho Manche' (I too am a remarkable man), *Madhupark*, 4(7) Kathmandu.

Sharma, Taranath (ed.) (1983) *Samasamayik Sajha Kavita*, Kathmandu: Sajha Prakashan

Shepherd, Richard (1990) 'Happy tourist, unhappy traveller', *Himal*, Sept.–Oct.

Serchan, Bhupi (1983[1969]) *Ghumne Mechmathi Andho Manche* (A blind man on a revolving chair), Kathmandu: Sajha Prakasan, 4th edition.

Subedi, Abhi (ed.) (1982) *Pachhis Varshaka Nepali Kavita*, Kathmandu: Royal Nepal Academy.

Toutain, Pierre (1986) *Nepal*, London: Merehurst Press.

4 The People of Tourist Brochures

GRAHAM DANN

> It is possible that images, as perceived by individuals in the travel market, may have as much to do with an area's tourism development success as the more tangible recreation and tourism resources (John Hunt in Rosenow and Pulsipher, 1979:179).

INTRODUCTION

Considering the sheer size of the international tourism industry today, there is a remarkable lack of analysis of the many ways it is promoted. Admittedly, works such as those by MacCannell (1976), Mayo and Jarvis (1981) and Pearce (1982) make use of promotional literature in order to substantiate a number of theoretical points, but few seem willing to study in their own right the various means by which potential tourists are transformed into travellers and sojourners. Yet, without an understanding of the predispositions and motives of tourists, and how these in turn are moulded, manipulated and sometimes even created, knowledge of tourists and tourism will always be lamentably deficient. Indeed up to quite recently, there has been little interest in the various ways in which destinations and their peoples have been portrayed, packaged and presented by the cultural brokers of tourism (Adams, 1984).

There are some signs that this situation of lack of interest in promotional and other tourist-related representations is beginning to change (see below), Mellinger's (1994) and Cohen's (1993) theoretical and critical considerations of tourist representations being recent examples of this change. Nevertheless there is clearly a need for further 'semiotic ethnography' of tourist brochures and this chapter seeks to make a contribution to that emerging project by examining tourist brochures and exploring the images employed by the media-makers as they attempt to bring together on the tourism stage two sets of actors — the hosts and the guests. Before commencing this analysis, however, it is necessary to contextualize the brochure itself.

Interest in brochures has its roots in the seminal analyses of tourist guidebooks (Gritti, 1967; Laurent, 1967), including the archetypal *Guide Bleu* (Barthes, 1982, 1984 and Baudrillard, 1968, 1975, 1983). Yet apart from

The Tourist Image: Myths and Myth Making in Tourism. Edited by Tom Selwyn.
© 1996 John Wiley & Sons Ltd.

Buck (1977) on brochures themselves, it was not until the early 1980s that researchers, such as Thurot and Thurot (1983), who examined the ideology of Club Méditerranée, began to take brochures seriously. A few years previously on the British side of the Channel, Andrew (1977), under the influence of Stringer (1984), had begun to investigate brochure design and how it could influence different target audiences. Meanwhile, work by Albers and James (1983, 1988) in the United States which focused on tourist photography, in particular the postcard, could be seen as complementing more comprehensive studies by Berger (1983) and Williamson (1983) which sought to examine the whole discourse of advertising, much of which was quite applicable to brochures.

During this period there were a few more sporadic studies of brochures. Buck (1978, 1979), for instance, had extended his work to an investigation of the Amish in Pennsylvania. In nearby Canada, Papson (1981) was assembling a collection of brochures and photographs featuring Nova Scotia and Prince Edward Island. Further afield in Indonesia, Adams (1984) had enlarged her inquiry to include brochures, pamphlets and guidebooks. At the same time in the United Kingdom, Uzzell (1984) was directing his attention to the young 18–30 tourist group, while Moeran (1983) was examining Japanese images associated with overseas travel. Later, Dann (1989) began a thematic analysis of brochures by focusing on such perennial features as 'the tourist as child'. More recently there have been further contributions to the genre by Bruner (1991), Dann (1988, 1993), Selwyn (1993) and Sinclair (1995).

Theoretically speaking, a neo-Durkheimian discourse concentrated on the spuriousness/authenticity dilemma (eg Buck, 1977; Cohen, 1979; Fine and Speer, 1985; MacCannell, 1976; Moscardo and Pearce, 1986; Papson, 1981). Structuralism, after Levi-Strauss, also had its adherents (eg Uzzell, 1984), as did the parallel functionalism underpinning the Maslovian need hierarchy (Mayo and Jarvis, 1981). With the advent of semiology, however, the way lay open for a neo-Marxist interpretation, with alienation emerging as a prominent theme (eg Thurot and Thurot, 1983). Studies by Selwyn (1993) and Sinclair (1995) have sought to combine some of these approaches.

Methodologically, the different perspectives were more homogeneous, since basically they employed similar techniques. These ranged from a descriptive content analysis to an interpretative semiotic analysis and focused on visual images, written messages or a combination of both (Albers and James, 1988). The main advantage of such research was that it was unobtrusive and did not modify the behaviour of respondents. It was also extremely low budget (Stringer, 1984:163).

The present study was able to build on foundations laid by the works mentioned above. By not committing itself to any given theoretical perspective, it could enjoy the luxury of a dilettante approach, utilizing insights from a variety of frameworks which were found to be particularly illuminating. The preliminary inquiry focused on 11 representative summer-holiday brochures targeted at a cross-section of the British public, comprising some 5172 pictures featured on 1470 pages of visual and written material. The brochures were supplemented by some additional destination commentaries taken from another handful of UK brochures promoting similar foreign-holiday destinations. The data were analysed quantitatively and qualitatively.

QUANTITATIVE ANALYSIS

Given that the focus of attention was people, the normally vexed question of categorization proved to be quite unproblematic. Destination pictures were simply classified according to presence or absence of people and were sub-divided into three categories: tourists only (one, two, three or more), local residents only (one, two, three or more) and tourists and locals together. Table 4.1 provides the breakdown of the people versus absence-of-people dimension.

Table 4.1 People in brochure pictures

Category	Sub-category		% of total
No people		1257	24.3
People	Tourists only (1)	397	7.7
	Tourists only (2)	600	11.6
	Tourists only (3+)	2113	40.8
	Sub-total	3110	60.1
	Locals only (1)	149	2.9
	Locals only (2)	44	0.8
	Locals only (3+)	154	3.0
	Sub-total	347	6.7
	Locals and tourists	458	8.9
Totals		5172	100.0

It is interesting to note that almost one-quarter of the pictures featured no people at all, thereby highlighting the motif of 'getting away from it all'. However, the largest group of pictures, featuring 'tourists only', was practically nine times the size of the 'locals only' category, emphasizing advertisers' support for the normative segregation of hosts from guests. In this 'tourists only' group, pictures of three or more tourists predominated, thus endorsing the salience of the controlled package tourist community over the footloose individual. In less than 10 percent of the cases were tourists and locals shown together, an indication that, for the media-makers at least, the idea of tourism as a meeting of peoples was somehow not to be encouraged.

The data were subsequently cross-tabulated by a number of settings: beaches, transport, hotels and their surroundings, tourist sights, local scenes, entertainment, sport (excluding swimming), and animals. In this way it was possible to see how hosts and guests were distributed across a range of tourist locations. Since the direction of dependence is difficult to establish, two tables (Table 4.2 and Table 4.3) respectively present data by rows and columns. In both tables a comparison of each category of people with the overall marginal percentages quickly reveals the locations where they were overrepresented. The conclusions are similar and may be summarized as follows:

Table 4.2 (Summary)
1. No people: transport, sights, local scenes, animal scenes
2. Tourists only: beach, sport, hotel
3. Locals only: entertainment, local scenes, animal scenes
4. Locals and tourists: hotel, entertainment, local scenes

Table 4.3 (Summary)
1. beach: tourists only
2. transport: no people; locals only
3. hotel: tourists only; tourists and locals
4. sights: no people; locals only
5. local scenes: no people; locals only; tourists and locals
6. entertainment: locals only; tourists and locals
7. sport: tourists only
8. animal scenes: no people; locals only

However, Table 4.2, being more comprehensive than Table 4.3, reveals that the hotel was only overrepresented due to the strength of the three or more subcategory. Sport, by contrast, owed its importance to the overwhelming presence of individual tourists and couples. Given that the number of participants in sporting activities is often inversely related to social status, it looks as though the promoters were targeting these visual messages at an up-market audience. The fluctuations in the 'locals only' data were less dramatic than in the 'tourists only' category, except in the sphere of entertainment, where the twosome appeared as the most popular represen-tational form.

Figure 4.1 shows how the information from Tables 4.2 and 4.3 can be used to establish various 'zones' for tourists and locals: it shows that the

Table 4.2 Distribution of location by people

People category	Location								
	Beach	Transport	Hotel	Sights	Local scene	Enter-tainment	Sport	Animal scene	Total %
No people (n = 1257)	7.6	2.9	50.8	18.0	16.8	0.2	0.3	3.4	100.0
Tourists (1)	16.9	0.5	38.5	1.2	4.6	0.3	37.0	1.0	100.0
Tourists (2)	24.7	1.7	47.7	1.8	6.7	0.5	15.8	1.1	100.0
Tourists (3+)	21.5	1.4	65.3	1.4	2.9	1.7	5.4	0.3	100.0
Tourists only (n = 3110)	21.5	1.3	58.5	1.5	3.8	1.3	11.5	0.6	100.0
Locals (1)	2.7	1.3	16.8	7.4	57.7	7.4	–	6.7	100.0
Locals (2)	4.5	2.3	–	6.8	59.1	18.2	2.3	6.8	100.0
Locals (3+)	3.2	2.6	3.9	7.8	61.1	15.6	3.2	2.6	100.0
Locals only (n = 347)	3.2	2.0	8.9	7.5	59.4	12.4	1.7	4.9	100.0
Tourist & locals (n = 458)	5.0	1.1	68.6	5.4	13.1	4.6	1.3	0.9	100.0
All (n = 5172)	15.5	1.7	54.2	6.2	11.5	2.1	7.2	1.6	100.0

Table 4.3 Distribution of people by location

People category	Location								
	Beach	Transport	Hotel	Sights	Local scene	Enter-tainment	Sport	Animal scene	Total %
No people	12.0	40.4	22.8	70.0	35.3	2.8	1.1	52.4	24.3
Tourists only	83.7	46.1	64.9	14.2	20.1	37.4	95.7	22.0	60.1
Locals only	1.4	7.9	1.1	8.1	34.5	40.2	1.6	20.7	6.7
Tourists and locals	2.9	5.6	11.2	7.7	10.1	19.6	1.6	4.9	8.9
Ns	800	89	2802	323	597	107	372	82	5172
Total %s	100.0	100.0	100.0	100.0	100.0	100.0	100.0	100.0	100.0

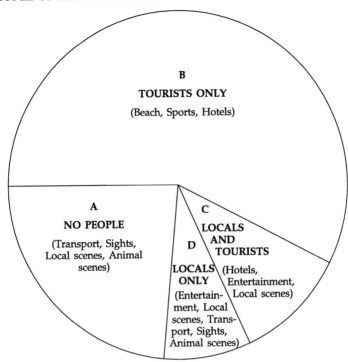

Figure 4.1 The zoning of peoples

'tourists only' group had a monopoly of the beach and sports zones. All other categories of people shared a zone with one other category, except local scenes, which were shared by three groups.

On further reflection, it emerged that four types of vacation were being promoted in the brochures and that these in turn corresponded with the four action spaces depicted in Figure 4.1. They were subsequently re-classified as the following varieties of paradise (see Figure 4.2).

A. Paradise contrived: no people; natives as scenery; natives as cultural markers
B. Paradise confined: tourists only — tourist ghetto
C. Paradise controlled: limited contact with locals: natives as servants, natives as entertainers, natives as vendors
D. Paradise confused: further contact with locals, attempt to enter locals-only zones: natives as seducers, natives as intermediaries, natives as familiar, natives as tourists, tourists as natives

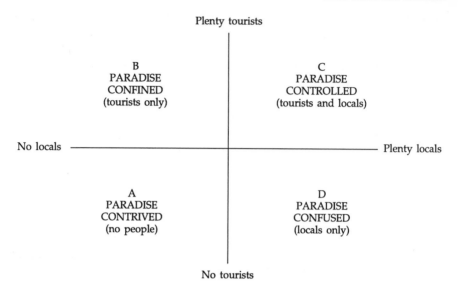

Figure 4.2   Four quadrant model of touristic paradise

Once the model was in place, it was possible to conduct a qualitative analysis of the data obtained from the brochures.

QUALITATIVE ANALYSIS

PARADISE CONTRIVED

Absence of people

Brochure pictures wishing to portray an uninhabited paradise typically showed deserted beaches on tropical islands. If there were any tourists at all, they were usually restricted to one, or two at the most, depending on whether or not sexual imagery was invoked. They were generally young and scantily clad. Their bronzed torsos were usually depicted in poses of relaxation, either lying on the sand or swinging in a hammock between two palm trees. Their single status (and hence availability) was suggested by the significant omission of children. Where hotels were featured, they were revealed as empty palaces whose luxurious interiors and bedrooms beckoned the purveyors (voyeurs?) of brochures to step inside. In so doing, they could identify with the scene and ultimately consume themselves (Williamson, 1983:70).

The following two examples are illustrative of typical accompanying texts. A Caribbean island, for instance, was described as: 'An exquisite hideaway resort . . . Petit St. Vincent offers the ultimate in privacy and seclusion in a beautiful, natural setting — your own island surrounded by superb beaches' (*Simply Caribbean*, 94–95:49). And an appeal to sample the Maldives was thus expressed: 'if in the bustle of modern day living, you yearn in vain for a getaway island of warm winds, waving palms, pure white beaches . . . take heart. That world does exist in the Maldives . . . Life is free and easy, with many areas reserved for naturism . . . we are offering you an idyllic stay in this unspoilt paradise . . . For when we say unspoilt we mean unspoilt' (*Faraway Holidays*, 1983–4:22).

Several advertising stratagems are employed here. Indeed, they occur over and over again. The first is to offer the 'natural' to replace the presumed artificiality of contemporary existence. It should be noted immediately, however, that this 'natural' is not nature in the raw (which would necessarily have to include references to mosquitoes, scorpions, skin cancer etc.) Rather, it is a sanitized transformation or 'cooking' of nature (Levi-Strauss, 1970) which has been hollowed out for the potential consumer as an acceptable commodity (Williamson, 1983:103–36). Second, the target audience is made to feel dissatisfied with its present circumstances, to the extent that the proffered alternative is shown as a glamorous solution to be envied by others (Berger, 1983:131–4). The Maldives are thus represented as unspoilt and a panacea to the alienation of urban existence. Third, and by corollary, the emphasis is placed on individuals, who can now escape the humdrum world of the masses and begin to discover themselves (Berger, 1983:138; Williamson, 1983:66). Fourth, the suggestion is made that the opportunity now exists for an increase in social status (Dann, 1977; Moeran, 1983). 'Privacy' is ego-enhancing, as is the bourgeois idea of wealth (Barthes, 1984; Thurot and Thurot, 1983), associated with being able to take a secluded vacation when one so desires, ie at a time and place which differs decidedly from that of the workers, who pack the beaches on their three-week August holiday break. Fifth, the imagery and calligraphy of advertising, knowing no present, only speaks of the future with reference to the past (Berger, 1983:130–9; Williamson, 1983:160–6). This allows viewers and readers to project themselves into new situations which often permit the carrying of personality equipment and nostalgic rewarding experiences into the future. This is the world of unrealizable daydreams and fantasy (Berger, 1983:146), the very fabric of tourism (Dann, 1976).

Natives as scenery

In spite of the attractiveness of open landscapes and seascapes, many tourists still need to be convinced that they are travelling somewhere and that destinations have identifiable characteristics. Now and then places can be highlighted simply by presenting a series of empty sights which somehow encapsulate their essence (The Acropolis in Athens or the

Colosseum in Rome, for instance). On other occasions it may be necessary to add a touch of local colour by introducing natives in national costume, so that they can represent their fellow countrymen and even replace an original sight. In both instances, objects and persons become interchangeable stereotypes (Adams, 1984; Albers and James, 1988; Williamson, 1983). Yet, despite their unreality, they tend to dominate brochure pictures, particularly those which play down the existence of local people.

In the set of brochure pictures used for analysis, typical illustrations included a group of appropriately regaled locals in the foreground of Valletta harbour in Malta and single shots of locals bearing such captions as 'Thai villager' or 'Chinese gentleman'. Where native presence was added to support the authenticity of a sight, the caption was usually bestowed on the latter, for example a picture featuring an Egyptian at the entrance to an historic monument was simply entitled: 'Temple of Karnak, Luxor'.

An example of accompanying brochure commentary also shows the use of natives as scenery: 'The Tunisians themselves are as much part of the scenery as the grand mosques and bustling cities; they provide the colour and movement that bring the landscape to life and make a second visit to any town or souk never quite the same' (Saga Worldwide, 1983–4:29).

While this description is scarcely devoid of people, the subjects are not perceived as human beings. Instead, they are displayed as stage extras, artists' models, objects which have replaced people, to be gazed at with impunity. The Tunisians are thus part of the scenery. In this respect, advertisers sometimes model their own designs on classic works of art (Berger, 1983; Uzzell, 1984). Their purpose is threefold. First, such a device affords them the opportunity to borrow from the past in order to link to the future. The paintings themselves similarly transcend time whenever they lead the observer out of the picture to an enchanted world beyond (Williamson, 1983:153). Second, the open scene and its motionless figures invite viewers to participate; they depend on their presence for fulfilment. Finally, they appeal to the connoisseur in the spectator. Just as a precious work of art denotes wealth, so too does its appreciation bestow status. Again all three themes are mutually reinforcing in the context of tourism.

Natives as cultural markers

Besides forming part of the destination decor, natives are also treated as signs, pointing to an ulterior reality. They become what MacCannell (1976) and Adams (1984) describe as 'cultural markers', signifying the host culture. In the current brochure collection there were several pictures employing this device. One showed a group of Bahia women in Candomblé attire. Above them was a map of Brazil on which the city of Salvador was encircled. Two similar shots featured a detached African dancer representing Senegal, and a woman clutching a koala bear summed up the whole of Australia. Sometimes pictures of people inside the brochure picture replaced the destination people themselves. Thus one came across a picture of a mural in Havana portraying young revolutionaries. Here the wall-painting took the place of the depicted Cubans. Even objects were able to act as substitutes for people, as in the case of a mass of colourful umbrellas standing for the inhabitants of Thailand. However, since the images were all stereotypical, tourists never interacted with them. The social distance involved never posed a serious threat to their solitude.

The commentaries were no less stereotypical. Thus: 'Rio de Janeiro has a rhythm all of its own, a city pulsating with life, reflecting the gay carefree spirit of all Brazilians' (*Speedbird Worldwide*, 1986–7:76) and: 'The fiery Costa del Sol embraces the romantic image of Spain as a land of flamenco, gypsies and fiestas' (Cosmos, *Summer Sun*, 1984:18). That the stereotyped natives were there simply to provide a backdrop of authenticity and fun for the tourist was illustrated in the following comments: 'The Portuguese were once great explorers. Today their own land has been discovered by holiday makers, who come for the scenery, the sea, the food, the wines and friendly hospitality' (*Flair*, Summer 1984:28) and: 'The Romanians themselves, as befits a nationality of Latin descent, are exuberant in their welcome to visitors' (*Saga Worldwide*, 1983–4:50).

The idea of a Samba-saturated Rio was conjured up with the image of fun-loving Cariocas. That this was a far cry from the more accurate reality of pollution, violence and favelas was glossed over. Similarly, the generalized portrayal of Spaniards as a nation of castanet players and bullfighters was not allowed to reveal the contemporary drudgery of Iberian peasantry. By means of these stereotypes tourists are thus insulated from natives, which, surveys reveal, they rarely go to see anyway (Dann and Cole, 1976). By the same token, the back regions (Goffman, 1959) of the inhabitants' world are protected from the intrusion of the tourist (Buck, 1977). As long as the natives and their transformed surroundings are not openly hostile, and provided that they give sufficient indication of welcome (as in the examples of Portugal and Romania), tourism can continue to be marketed in these terms, the terms of the brochure producer and tour operator.

PARADISE CONFINED

Travelling vertically upwards in the model (Figure 4.2) involves a substantial increase in the volume of tourists. Locals, where they occur, are kept to a minimum, since the emphasis is now very much on the encapsulated existence of the tourist ghetto. Solitude, or romantic versions of *tourisme à deux*, are now replaced with the new 'community' of tourists whose statuses have been levelled by the equalizer of conviviality. Camaraderie based on hedonistic instant gratification and immediate excitement now encourages even total strangers to reveal intimate details of their lives (Vogt, 1976:32).

Turning to the brochure pictures, those which illustrated the tourist enclave did not generally feature natives, not even as ancillary helpers. Instead, the emphasis was on the tourist group — eating together, on the beach together, relaxing by the communal pool together, enjoying themselves as one large happy family — in which home-based distinctions of wealth and class had been obliterated. Needless to say, with one notable exception, the target group for such advertising was more often than not the working class, who were temporarily permitted to be kings and queens (Gottlieb, 1982). One particular activity, in which participants were displayed at various stages of inebriation, was the 'alcoholic assembly' (Nash, 1970). Here the upper class could be aped with impunity. Furthermore, inhibitions were released, with no fear of reprisal or scandal from either employers or locals, since both were absent from the scene.

The following was a typical excerpt from a package tour to Ibiza: 'There's a host of sports available, hob-nob with the jet set, try delicious local dishes or the best international cuisine: the choice is yours . . . There's a welcome drink on arrival, to give you the chance to get to know each other' (Intasun, Summer 1984:78, 83). Among the younger set the emphasis was on: 'The camaraderie of nights under canvas, entertainment, good company and plenty of high life, living as a group' (Club 18–30, Summer 1984:8–9). For a more up-market version see Club Med (1987:back cover): 'Many of our clients like to forget the outside world altogether and are perfectly happy to spend their stay soaking up the sun, the sport and the entertainment our villages have to offer.' The last example was enclave tourism par excellence. Here special resorts ('our villages') had been created. They occupied prime beach-front property and isolated their 'gentle members' from the natives.

Although many have objected to this type of tourism, perhaps nowhere is local opposition voiced so clearly and angrily as in the words of Michael Manley, former Prime Minister of Jamaica. He supplies the missing link between the operators, their manipulated clients and the host society:

The protagonists of the industry . . . have contended that the road to success lies in the incarceration of the tourist in spectacular multi-storeyed buildings . . . within whose walls the tourist is encouraged to drink himself silly while remaining oblivious to the country beyond his hotel window. This school of thought seems to rest, at least in part, on the assumption that the rest of the country is an object of shame which the tourist could not possibly enjoy (Britton, 1980:47).

PARADISE CONTROLLED

In order to travel from quadrant B to quadrant C in the model (Figure 4.2), it is necessary to cross the line bisecting 'no locals' from 'plenty of locals'. At the same time a regular supply of tourists is guaranteed. The effect of this move is to open the ghetto and some of its expatriate management to a limited local presence.

Natives as servants

Natives who lie closest to the inner tourist domain are hotel employees — the various maids, domestics, waiters, bartenders, etc., linked to the tourist by their service roles. Typical brochure pictures revealing the asymmetrical relationship often showed tourists eating or drinking or, more accurately, about to consume food or liquor. Hovering nearby was the smiling attendant, either carrying a multi-hued cocktail, filling a glass or serving from a long buffet table. Often the tourist was seated, while the servant was standing or stooping. Where the parties were of different racial backgrounds, the tourist was usually white and the native black, thereby adding a 'massa–slave' dimension to the phenomenon. In plantocratic tourist destinations, at the table 'massa' was often mistress and the slave was male. Female attendants formerly associated with the Great House were shown to be carrying on this tradition as maids.

By contrast, written statements endorsing the host as servant were far less frequent in the commentaries, since their very blatancy would have been quite offensive. Ironically, an example was found in a Soviet operator's brochure from a supposedly egalitarian society. It spoke of Srinagar, India, as follows: 'And there can be no better way of enjoying its beauty and tranquillity than staying on board a de luxe houseboat with its traditional Victorian comfort and a cook and a servant in personal attendance' (Intourist, *Magnolia Holidays*, 1984:23).

Natives as entertainers

Locals as entertainers stand more at the periphery of the tourist's world since they are customarily brought into the hotel compound. Indeed, Nolan and Nolan (1978:7) maintain that the closest most tourists wish to get to people representing different cultures is sitting at a good table at a resort hotel floorshow featuring native dancers. Apart from dancers, often connected in the brochures with oriental destinations, there were of course other entertainers, ranging from troubadours to fire-eaters. Sometimes they were assembled collectively in the form of a cultural show, as for example in the Rose Gardens near Bangkok. That there was greater social distance involved than in the case of hotel staff could be gauged from the expressions on their faces. More often than not they did not even look at the tourist but gazed instead either at each other or else at some distant object outside the picture.

A typical commentary from St Lucia, West Indies, underlined the outsider role of entertainers: 'Entertainment at La Toc includes frequent visits from calypso groups, solo artists and steel bands, and there are also local floor shows with limbo dancers and fire-eaters' (*Pegasus Caribbean Sun*, 1985:16). That such entertainment is purported to represent indigenous culture is stereotypical in itself. However, it becomes even more explicit when supposed national characteristics are linked to entertainment, as in the case of the following excerpt featuring Tbilisi: 'The Georgians are renowned as an artistic and flamboyant race [sic] and perhaps these qualities, together with their fierce pride, are most eloquently expressed through their world famous folk dances' (Intourist, *Magnolia Summer Holidays*, 1984:35).

Natives as vendors

Finally in Paradise Controlled the tourist is likely to encounter the native as vendor, either as a salesperson attached to the hotel or as a wandering beach merchant. Included in the latter category, though not in brochures, are pedlars of drugs and beachboys, types marginal to both host and guest societies (Karch and Dann, 1981). Further afield are various store assistants and market stall-holders. Interaction with this group of residents is generally more intense than with domestics and entertainers since there is often an element of bargaining involved, and hence greater scope for misunderstanding.

The monologue of the brochures sometimes referred to such negotiation. Understandably it emphasized the perspective of the tourist. Thus in Thailand: 'Be prepared to bargain with patience and good humour and then you'll get the best from these handsome, high cheek-boned people' (*Faraway Holidays*, 1983–4:24). Nevertheless, it did not take long for the vendor to be cast in the less threatening role of entertainer or local scenery. Marrakesh was a case in point: 'Probably the most exciting and certainly the most colourful open market in Africa. Hundreds of merchants buying and selling, soothsayers, scribes and apothecaries, acrobats and snake charmers, storytellers and dancers, come one, come all to the Market of Djemaa El F'na' (*Kuoni Worldwide*, 1986–7:155).

PARADISE CONFUSED

The final quadrant shows a situation in which the locals increase while tourists decline in number. Here there is a much greater overlapping of zones. In a few cases interaction occurs where a minority of guests attempt to experience more fully the daily lives of their hosts, to go behind the touristic façade in the quest for backstage reality (Goffman, 1959). Needless to say, many such efforts prove unsuccessful, if only because there are unresolved differences in culture, language, race and education (Karch and Dann, 1981). Roles, or expectations of behaviour, require negotiation, and this process itself can lead to confusion. As will be seen presently, brochures themselves do little to reduce such confusion or to encourage sincere attempts to gain mutual understanding between peoples.

Natives as seducers

Of the various sub-categories comprising Paradise Confused, natives as seducers was certainly the most prominent brochure theme. Often a local female was shown trying to attract the gaze of the invisible male (potential tourist as voyeur). A dusky or oriental maiden beckoned her beholder to join her in anticipated pleasure. Sometimes there was a half-open door leading to a mysterious and enchanting beyond. Thus: 'Bangkok with its *dreamy* tropical scenery, glittering temples and *easy-going* beautiful people' (*Faraway Holidays*, 1983–4:11). And in Bali: 'Greeted by gentle smiling people, and surrounded by a *profusion* of hibiscus, orchids and frangipane, you will find that life's problems just seem to *drift away*' (*Kuoni Worldwide*, 1986–7:12). Or: 'In the end, the lure of Greece is as much to do with the warmth of the people as the heat of the sun . . . Don't just visit Greece, embrace the warmth of the place, *indulge in its every pleasure* and let your mind and body *switch off*' (*Go Greece*, 1995:1).

The emphasis is added to highlight the sexual innuendo and the lingo of drug culture. Perhaps this is why holidays are sometimes referred to as 'trips' (Vogt, 1976). Some brochures were less subtle: '. . . What more could you wish for? Yes, and we probably have that as well' (*Club 18–30*, Summer, 1984:9). Meanwhile in St Lucia: 'The staff, an energetic group of friendly islanders, are there as instructors, companions, guides and more' (*Speedbird Worldwide*, 1986–7:85).

Natives as intermediaries

This sub-category can sometimes be confused with the preceding one, particularly where interpretations of friendliness are left ambiguous. The term 'intermediary' has been employed to denote that section of the host community which acts as middleman, somehow cushioning the culture shock experienced by the guest. Regrettably, the touree is often regarded by the tourist with mistrust as a potential, if not actual, exploiter. The sentiment is mutual (van den Berghe, 1980).

In the brochures the intermediary was usually portrayed as a male guide, often connected with local transportation. Apparently he was there to protect mainly the young female tourist (note the sex role reversal when compared with the native as seducer). Smiling gondoliers, fishermen, camel drivers and other host macho types were typically featured as culture brokers.

In the promotional discourse middlemen were inevitable portrayed as happy people, whether or not they had come under the influence of a local smile campaign (Turner, 1976:20). Thus in Goa: 'The fishermen are friendly enough to take you out fishing with them if you ask; they are also not averse to asking you for a cigarette!' (*Inspirations India*, 1995:73). While in Barbados: 'Under the bright tropical sun no one seems to hurry and there's always a friendly face and a warm smile for visitors to the islands' (*Poundstretcher*, 1986–7:6).

At the same time it was possible to detect the marginality of the intermediary as he distanced himself from his own people in order to please the tourist: '. . . The Cuban people are definitely proud of their revolution. But what they wish to show off to visitors are aspects that have little to do with politics — the scenery, parks, ancient monuments, culture, beaches and music' (*Pegasus Caribbean Sun*, 1985:32).

Natives as familiar

Here the operator tries to persuade potential tourists that, although their holiday desire may be partially motivated by curiosity and a quest for the strange and the exotic, reality will not be so strange that they will experience disorientation or anxiety. In fact, there will be many familiar sights to remind them of the place they left behind and their need for security. By extension, it is suggested that the warm feeling of being at home can be found among the welcoming inhabitants as well.

Brochure pictures in this sub-category included a bricolage of such disembodied cultural items as fish and chip outlets, pubs, tea-places serving a brew just like mother's, double-decker London buses, red pillar boxes, English-type policemen and the odd glimpse of a fluttering Union Jack. Former colonies and locations associated with the Commonwealth were deemed particularly appropriate for this type of treatment targeted at British consumers.

The accompanying blurb was similarly reassuring. Thus describing Malta: 'Its long association with Britain certainly contributes to the pleasant familiarity British visitors feel there. English is widely spoken, shops and cafes often have English names. What you'll remember about the island is its friendly people and leisurely pace . . .' (*Cosmos, Summer Sun*, 1984:125). And Gibraltar: 'But this "island in the sun" is British through and through. You'll be made to feel right at home immediately, at the sight of British bobbys on patrol, with British beer being served in familiar pubs . . .' (*Intasun*, Summer 1984:221). Finally, there was an example which possibly went overboard with its shades of 'Rule Britannia': 'Between India and the

British exists an exceptional bond of affection which has withstood the test of Empire; the English language, the rule of law, matronly statues of the Queen Empress, the game of cricket are all reminders of our shared Imperial past . . .' The paternalism of Raj-style interaction with the natives was then spelt out more fully as the account continued: 'While new technology and modern universities point to India's future, generations of British administrators, planters and soldiers, their wives and children, look back on India as their birthplace or second home' (*Saga Worldwide*, 1983–4:72). Needless to say, the problem with familiarity is that it breeds contempt.

Natives as tourists

This sub-group of locals only adds to the confusion, since many tourists have been convinced by now that the destination belongs to them. After all, they have been led to believe that they possess the beaches, the prime real estate and all leisure facilities. Natives, where they exist, should cater to tourist desires and fit in with their free time. It may come as a surprise, therefore, to discover that locals also take holidays and even occupy the same hotels themselves.

Clearly, this rather delicate issue has to be handled carefully by the operator. Among the 5172 brochure pictures analysed it occurred only three times. One found, for instance, a shot of two Mauritian sunbathers. He was looking away out to sea, while she turned to face the observer. Then there was a group of 13 Soviet Citizens dining at a long communal table at the resort of Sochi. They appeared as young, well-dressed and serious intellectuals, possibly discussing politics. No other non-national was in sight. Finally there was a scene of the Taj Mahal featuring a number of local pilgrims going about their religious duties. Again, no other visitors were included.

Sporadic messages occasionally referred to the foregoing situation by suggesting that host–guest interaction was best ignored. Instead, as noted previously, attention could be paid to the scenery into which the locals blended: 'As the Muscovites hurry about their business, its broad modern streets present a sense of continuous activity, and yet nestled amongst them are many picturesque sites which reveal a long and colourful history' (Intourist, *Magnolia Holidays*, 1984:10). On one occasion a warning was even issued: 'On our South American panorama the itinerary is often changed due to strikes, political coups or other disruptions. Not to worry, we have never left anyone behind' (*Kuoni Worldwide*, 1986–7:158).

Tourists as natives

Finally, and in spite of the obstacles posed by the preceding types of native, there is the attempt to meet real locals on their own terms and in their own space. Some brochure pictures suggested that 'going native' could be achieved by tourists donning the same attire as locals. When in Morocco, one could sport a fez, for instance. Others indicated that a common ground could be attained by consuming the same food and drink. Thus there was a scene featuring Riviera visitors carrying enormous French loaves. In another, tourists were depicted drinking out of Spanish wine flasks on the Costa Brava. Joining in festivals, street fairs and taverna dances was yet another proposition for the tourist who wished to get closer to local reality.

The text reinforced such strategies, particularly the latter. In the Cretan town of Aghios Nikolaos, for example: 'After dark the scene changes dramatically. Tempting aromas of charcoal grilled kebabs and locally caught fish waft from the tavernas, and the waterfront is thronged with locals and visitors who've come out for a stroll, chat and drink in the cool of the evening. A lot of tavernas have live music and dancing, so many people are content to hang around the harbour all night . . .' (*Faraway Holidays*, 1983–4:114). After all: 'Life in most Greek towns revolves around its squares and tavernas. Greeks are outgoing people and love to chat over a glass of wine or ouzo . . . As the evening wears on someone starts strumming a bouzouki and few Greeks can resist the rhythm. They dance at a drop of a hat' (*Cosmos, Summer Sun*, 1984:172–3).

Other brochure advice included living in an Israeli Kibbutz in order to sample communal living (*Peltours*, 1983:27), rubbing shoulders with locals at a night market in Singapore (*Kuoni Worldwide*, 1986–7:12), trekking through the Amazon jungle to meet the Yagua Indians, who still hunt with poisoned arrows (Kuoni Worldwide, 1986–7:18), learning how to paint beetles in Bali (*Club Méditerranée*, 1987:112) or even watching road sweepers at work in Beijing (*Jet Set Tours, Orient* 1984–5:12).

Yet at the end of the day, 'going native', the bane of anthropologists, is still largely a problematic exercise in fostering international understanding since the two parties involved are still represented as stereotypes. Even the native that the tourist seeks to emulate is a caricature, and no amount of dressing up, dancing or drinking is going to alter the mundane and often harsher realities of the everyday host society.

CONCLUSION

This analysis has demonstrated that in less than 10 percent of all brochure pictures surveyed were tourists shown mixing with members of local populations. Furthermore, in most of these cases indigenous people were featured either as ancillary hotel staff, vendors or entertainers. In the remaining few cases the less attainable host society was portrayed as comprising persons in national costume forming part of the scenery, stereotypical cultural markers, middlemen, smilers or else as tourists themselves.

At the same time, by means of well-known advertising devices, the operator attempted to persuade potential tourists to leave their unsatisfying homes and routines and travel to exotic destinations. In spite of the occasional unobtrusive presence of locals, there they would be able to discover themselves and their fellow sojourners. If tourists still wished to pursue the indigenous, that was their business; the remaining 90 percent of the trade still belonged to the operator.

Of course, the story, just like the foregoing analysis, is far from over, and is in many senses incomplete. The promotional stage is only the first in a series of communication patterns which extends along the route to the destination itself and back home again (Rosenow and Pulsipher, 1979:186). The projected image of a destination and its people, while couched in the language and imagery of social control, remains to be confirmed or invalidated by experience. The trip in turn can lead to conversational promotions by tourists themselves and lead to further decisions and choices (Albers and James, 1988; Stringer, 1984). Thus, how tourists react to the visual and written messages of the media is every bit as important as the iconography and discourse which seek to mould them (Chalfen, 1985).

Nevertheless, without the first stage there will be no others. Hence its significance in understanding modern tourism. Tourism is not a product since it cannot be sampled in advance. It is a collection of projected images which establishes the boundaries of experience (Papson, 1981). The images define what is beautiful, what should be experienced and with whom one should interact. Understanding the people of tourism is thus, above all else, an analysis of images.

NOTE

An early version of this chapter was originally presented as a paper at the conference 'Tourism: A Vital Force for Peace', Vancouver, 1988. While the examples provided are typical of that time, from more recent material there is little evidence to suggest that the verbal and iconographical language of brochures has changed in any significant way.

REFERENCES

Adams, K. (1984) 'Come to Tana Toraja, land of the heavenly kings. Travel agents as brokers in ethnicity', *Annals of Tourism Research*, 11, 460–85.
Albers, P. and W. James (1983) 'The changing image of the Great Lakes Indians', *Annals of Tourism Research*, 10, 123–48.

Albers, P. and W. James (1988) 'Travel photography: a methodological approach', *Annals of Tourism Research*, 15, 134–58.

Andrew, C. (1977) An Investigation into Holiday Brochure Design, unpublished MSc thesis, University of Surrey.

Barthes, R. (1982) *Image-Music-Text*, London: Fontana.

Barthes, R. (1984) *Mythologies*, London: Paladin.

Baudrillard, J. (1968) *Le Système des Objets*, Paris: Gallimard.

Baudrillard, J. (1975) *The Mirror of Production*, St Louis: Telos Press.

Baudrillard, J. (1983) *Simulations*, New York: Semiotext, Foreign Agent Press.

Berger, J. (1983) *Ways of Seeing*, London: BBC and Penguin.

van den Berghe, P. (1980) 'Tourism as ethnic relations: a case study of Cuzeo, Peru', *Ethnic and Racial Studies*, 3(4), 375–91.

Britton, R. (1980) 'Let us handle everything: the travel industry and the manipulation of the travel experience', *USA Today*, May, 45–7.

Bruner, E. (1991) 'Transformation of self in tourism', *Annals of Tourism Research*, 18, 238–50.

Buck, R. (1977) 'The ubiquitous tourist brochure, explorations in its intended and unintended use', *Annals of Tourism Research*, 4, 195–207.

Buck, R. (1978) 'Boundary maintenance revisited: tourist experience in an old order Amish community revisited', *Rural Sociology*, 43(2), 221–34.

Buck, R. (1979) 'Bloodless theater: images of the old order Amish in tourism literature', *Pennsylvania Mennonite Heritage*, 2(3), 2–11.

Chalfen, R. (1979) 'Comment on Uzzell', *Annals of Tourism Research*, 12, 123–6.

Club 18–30, Summer 1984 brochure.

Club Méditerranée 1987 brichure.

Cohen, E. (1979) 'A phenomenology of tourist experiences', *Sociology*, 13, 179–201.

Cohen, E. (1993) 'The study of touristic images of native people. Mitigating the stereotype of the stereotype' in D. Pearce and R. Butler (eds), *Tourism Research. Critiques and Challenges*, London: Routledge, pp. 36–69.

Cosmos, Summer Sun 1984 brichure.

Dann, G. (1976) 'The holiday was simply fantastic', *Revue de Tourisme*, 3, 19–23.

Dann, G. (1977) 'Anomie, ego-enhancement and tourism', *Annals of Tourism Research*, 4, 184–94.

Dann, G. (1988) 'Images of Cyprus projected by tour operators', *Problems of Tourism*, XI(3), 43–70.

Dann, G. (1985) 'The tourist as child. Some reflections', *Cahiers du Tourisme*, Série C, no. 135.

Dann, G. (1993) 'Advertising in tourism and travel: tourism brochures' in M. Khan, M. Olsen and T. Var (eds), *VNR's Encyclopedia of Hospitality and Tourism*, New York: Van Nostrand Reinhold, pp. 893–901.

Dann, G. and J. Cole, (1976) 'The tourist in Barbados: stranger and friend', *Caribbean Issues*, 2(1), 3–13.

Faraway Holidays 1983 brochure.

Fine, E. and J. Speer, (1985) 'Tour guide performances and sight sacralisation', *Annals of Tourism Research*, 12, 73–95.

Flair, Summer 1984 brochure.

Goffman, E. (1959) *The Presentation of Self in Everyday Life*, New York: Doubleday.

Go Greece 1995 brochure.

Gottlieb, A. (1982) 'Americans' vacations', *Annals of Tourism Research*, 9, 165–87.

Gritti, J. (1967) 'Les contenus culturels du Guide Bleu: monuments et sites a voir', *Communications*, 10, 51–64.

Inspirations India 1995 brochure.

Intasun, Summer 1984 brochure.

Intourist, *Magnolia Holidays* 1984 brochure.

Karch, C. and G. Dann, (1981) 'Close encounters of the Third World', *Human Relations*, 34(4), 249–68.

Kuoni Worldwide 1986 brochure.

Laurent, A. (1967) 'Le thème du soleil dans la publicité des organismes des vacances', *Communications*, 10, 35–50.

Lévi-Strauss, C. (1970) *The Raw and the Cooked*, London: Jonathan Cape.

MacCannell, D. (1976) *The Tourist: a New Theory of the Leisure Class*, New York: Schocken.

Mayo, E. and L. Jarvis (1981) *The Psychology of Leisure Travel, Effective Marketing and Selling of Travel Services*, Boston: CBI.

Mellinger, W. (1994) 'Toward a critical analysis of tourism representations', *Annals of Tourism Research*, 21, 756–79.

Moeran, B. (1983) 'The language of Japanese tourism', *Annals of Tourism Research*, 10, 93–108.

Moscardo, G. and P. Pearce (1986) 'Historic theme parks: an Australian experience in authenticity', *Annals of Tourism Research*, 13, 467–79.

Nash, D. (1970) *A Community in Limbo, an Anthropological Study of an American Community Abroad*, Bloomington: Indiana University Press.

Nolan, S. and M. Nolan (1978) 'Variations in travel behaviour and the cultural impact on tourism' in V. Smith (ed.), *Tourism and Behavior*, Studies in Third World Societies, No. 5, Williamsburg: College of William and Mary. pp. 1–15.

Papson, S. (1981) 'Spuriousness and tourism', *Annals of Tourism Research*, 8, 220–35.

Pearce, P. (1982) *The Social Psychology of Tourist Behaviour*, Oxford: Pergamon.

Pegasus, Caribbean Sun 1985 brochure.

Peltours 1983 brochure.

Poundstretcher 1986 brochure.

Rosenow, J. and G. Pulsipher (1979) *Tourism — the Good, the Bad and the Ugly*, Lincoln, Neb.: Media Production Marketing

Saga Worldwide 1983 brochure.

Selwyn, T. (1993) 'Peter Pan in South-East Asia. Views from the brochures' in M. Hitchcock, V. King and M. Parnwell (eds), *Tourism in South-East Asia*, London: Routledge, pp. 117–37.

Simply Caribbean 1994–95 brochure.

Sinclair, D. (1995) Tourism in Guyana: a Semiotic Analysis, unpublished MPhil thesis, University of the West Indies, Barbados.

Speedbird Worldwide 1986 brochure.

Stringer, P. (1984) 'Studies in the socio-environmental psychology of tourism', *Annals of Tourism Research*, 11, 147–66.

Thurot, J. and G. Thurot (1983) 'The ideology of class and tourism: confronting the discourse of advertising', *Annals of Tourism Research*, 10, 173–89.

Turner, L. (1976) 'The international division of leisure: tourism and the Third World', *Annals of Tourism Research*, 4, 12–24.

Uzzell, D. (1984) 'An alternative structuralist approach to the psychology of marketing', *Annals of Tourism Research*, 11: 79–99.

Vogt, J. (1976) 'Wandering: youth and travel behaviour', *Annals of Tourism Research*, 4, 25–41.

Williamson, J. (1983) *Decoding Advertisements. Ideology and Meaning in Advertising*, London: Marion Boyars.

5 Passion, Power and Politics in a Palestinian Tourist Market

GLENN BOWMAN

Sex tourism has become a central icon in a liberal Western discourse condemning the tourism industry. In this discourse sex tourism is figured as a machinery of desire constructed and programmed in the 'First World' to sate the jaded appetites of the rich and powerful with the lives and labours of socially and economically disadvantaged 'Third World' victims. The category of sex tourism, which assimilates phenomena ranging from southeast Asian brothels run for foreign men by international crime cartels with the covert support of national governments (see Hall, 1992 and Truong, 1990) to the 'sugar mummie' phenomenon wherein older women tourists travel to tourist centres in order to enjoy sexual encounters with local youths,[1] is well suited to represent the exploitative character of much of the tourism trade between the developed and less-developed countries in so far as it foregrounds the destructive playing out of empowereds' irresponsible desires on the bodies of those immobilized by poverty and lack of alternative opportunities. Critiques of sex tourism thus condemn not only the sexual exploitation they analyse but also the structure of international tourism which, as a form of neo-imperialism (Nash, 1977), 'mines' the host society for commodities to be enjoyed by First World tourists with a blithe disregard for the effect of extraction on the social and economic fabric of the tourist-receiving culture.

The metonym is appropriate; the various forms of sex tourism do in fact make corporeally manifest the gross inequalities of power upon which the entire dynamics of both contemporary international tourism and the current world market depend (Ong, 1985). However, the simple, if compelling, opposition of oppressor and victim in a relationship which looks more like rape than intercourse partakes of a dualism which shares more with the discourse of colonization than it does with one of liberation. To see the object of the tourist's desire as a passive entity subjected to the overpowering will of another is to reproduce in representation precisely the structure of domination one claims to criticize. By presenting the 'host' as a victim to whom the 'guest' does things, one perpetuates the modernist assumption that non-Western peoples are objects upon which Western

The Tourist Image: Myths and Myth Making in Tourism. Edited by Tom Selwyn.
© 1996 John Wiley & Sons Ltd.

projects are inscribed and consequently suggests that the only way they will be rescued from the dire situations in which tourist projects place them will be through the promulgation in the West of more enlightened tourist attitudes and activities.

'Green' tourism manifests this 'orientalist' attitude in its assumption that we can make things better for the host societies not by entering into discussion with local communities about what they want from tourism but by unilaterally redefining the character, and the goals, of the tourism we feel we 'should' practise in, and on, those communities. 'Green' tourism, which strives to allow host cultures to retain their 'authenticity' by intruding as little as possible on the infrastructure of the societies, has in fact generated complaints in the host societies that this more enlightened tourism deprives people of work and of the capital generated by their participation in more 'exploitative' forms of tourism. Third World peoples may not want to be allowed to remain 'noble savages'. Valene Smith, in a study of touristization on the small Philippines island of Boracay, points out that:

> the people of Boracay, like all rural Filipinos, would enjoy having the infra-structure that is needed to support tourism, because it would make their lives easier, pleasanter and safer. And they certainly *want* the income generated by tourism, in the form of cash with which to buy goods and services including better education for their children. They appreciate the employment that is enabling their young people to stay on the island, or to return home to Boracay from the squalor of big cities, and be with their families. In the eyes of most villagers, tourism has been very positive — and the sins of the 'drifter' tourists can be temporarily overlooked in the face of their largesse (Smith, 1988 cited in Harrison, 1992:11).

Spokespersons for 'moral' tourism, which protects these people — against their will — from the 'sins' of touristic largesse, pay as little attention to local peoples' definitions of their needs and desires as did apologists for earlier forms of touristic practice who assumed, without inquiring into local perceptions, that everyone wanted the 'passport to development' that large-scale touristic development was believed to provide (see de Kadt, 1979). Thus the obverse of the modernist assumption that it is legitimate and desirable for the 'developed' world to transform the 'underdeveloped' world into an image of itself is the belief that development is illegitimate and undesirable and that Third World peoples will be much happier if we can take what we want from their environments without implicating them in the business. In both instances the political issue, which pertains to the perceptions of and relations between the parties of a collusion or confrontation, is subordinated to and effectively rendered extraneous by the moral issue, which concerns the way our practices coincide with or contradict our images of ourselves. The 'others' in each case exist only as mirrors which return our own self-imagings to us.

I am not here taking a partisan role towards either touristic development or underdevelopment but am pointing out that there is a substantial flaw in the models we use to analyse tourism and its impact on non-Western cultures. Our perspectives on host societies are, I argue, informed by a basic narcissism which prevents us from examining the responses of their populations to our various interventions. We ceaselessly scrutinize our own moral *cum* aesthetic categories without attempting to open a dialogue between our modes of evaluation and those of the people with whom tourism brings us into contact. The history of the concept of 'authenticity' in tourism studies, summarized by Selwyn in his introduction to this volume, seems precisely to illustrate the shortcomings of our analytical chauvinism in so far as the telling criterion in debates on authenticity is not whether the cultures concerned see their practices and possessions as 'belonging to themselves' but whether those cultural manifestations confirm or conflict with our images of what those cultures and their constructions should be.

Social and cultural anthropologies, which claim to examine other cultural systems from 'within' and subsequently to translate those world views into terms which render indigenous interpretations comprehensible to the 'outside' without effacing their alterity, should generate anthropologies of tourism which allow students to 'see' what tourism and its effects look like to the people who host and accommodate it. None the less, perhaps because anthropologists are discomfited by an approach to other cultures which is a bit too close to their own, there has been a tendency to draw analytic categories for the study of tourism from sociology, and these 'empirical' devices are deeply implicated in the same modernist faith in the universalism of our particular cultural categories which I have criticized above (see Crick, 1985; Crick, 1988; and Peacock, 1986). The alternative is to delve much more deeply into what members of host communities have to say about tourism and how it affects their worlds. As Crick saliently points out:

> Without close attention to the local voice (indeed, we must be careful here, local *voices*, for tourism produces a range of very different local reactions), our social scientific work risks being descriptively poor and ethnocentric . . . . We need to know the local perceptions and understandings of tourism, we need to know the local perceptions of change and continuity, and we need to recognize that any culture is likely to have contradictory things to say about both. If international tourism is about *our* culture rather than the destination country (Thurot and Thurot, 1983), an anthropological approach to international tourism that cannot accord a crucial status to the full range of local voices risks putting itself in the same position (Crick, 1988:68).

If we attend to these local voices we find that the members of host societies are involved in their own politics of accommodation with or resistance to the development of international tourism; they interpret the consequences of touristic development in 'their own' terms (terms which themselves are likely already to reflect previous acts of accommodation and resistance to other forms of Western incursion) and they act according to those interpretations (Scott, 1990). Such actions may prove ineffectual or even counter-productive since, as I suggested in my opening, the power of the developed nations far outweighs that of the developing or undeveloped countries. None the less, if we do not consider what local peoples think of what is being done to them and what strategies they devise to resist such encroachments or render them bearable, we will continue to see them as mere objects of our aggression or beneficence and thus remain committed to forms of cultural imperialism which force our wills, and our images, on peoples who want to create their own lives in accordance with identities they choose for themselves.

Erik Cohen's writing on sex tourism provides exemplars of how one can acknowledge that persons caught in difficult and demeaning situations are victims of forces beyond their control without simultaneously denying them the right to struggle according to their own strategies to accommodate themselves to or overcome those forces. In 'Lovelorn Farangs: the correspondence between foreign men and Thai girls' (Cohen, 1986), Cohen examines the postal dialogue which takes place between Thai prostitutes and men who have returned to their home countries after extended relationships with the women. He discusses the dependency which expresses itself in the mix of sexual fantasy and romantic longing in the men's letters and contrasts this to the opportunism which informs the pleas for money and duplicitous vows of fidelity the women return. Cohen, against the grain, concludes that 'sex-tourism may indeed engender the sexual exploitation of local women on the macro-social level; but on the micro-level of interpersonal relationships, the state of affairs may often be inverted — the local women actually exploiting the foreigners' (Cohen 1986:124).

This simultaneity of weakness on the 'macro-social level' and power on the 'micro-level' is mirrored in his study of the way short-term Palestinian labourers in Acre in Israel talk about their relationships (actual or invented) with foreign tourist women (Cohen, 1971). Although the paper in large part emphasizes the investment of Palestinian youths in unrealistic fantasies of escaping from the miseries of their marginal lives through marrying tourist women and emigrating from Israel, it also points out that such shared fantasies about affairs with tourist women create an arena in which a struggle for status can successfully be played out between men whose marginal positions in wider Israeli society allow them little access to any other status. In exchanging stories of sexual conquests, in parading a succession of foreign 'lovers' in front of other Palestinians who consider such capital prestigious, and in flaunting foreign addresses and perfume-scented letters from Canada and Scandinavia, young men with no future and little in the way of a present are able to show themselves as more successful than their peers who, like them, have no access to any other forms of success or status. Whereas in the global context these men can be seen as manipulated by comparatively well-off tourists who use them as the raw material of 'holiday romances', in the local context within which the men live they show themselves able to salvage 'symbolic capital' (Bourdieu, 1977:171–83) from the affairs, capital which they invest in circuits of exchange they see as satisfying and empowering. In 'Arab Boys and Tourist Girls in a Mixed Jewish Arab Community', as in his study of tourist–prostitute correspondence, Cohen is less concerned with quantifiable positivist data than he is with texts — stories, letters, comments — in which he can read the way members of the host community interpret the contacts they have with tourists and with the tourism machinery which generates those contacts. Through focusing on discourse, Cohen is able to demonstrate that power not only devolves from 'the top' or 'centre' but that it also rises up from 'beneath' in acts of 'deviant' interpretation which shift the parameters of evaluation so as to render the weak as strong and the strong as weak.

In the following essay, a study of narratives told of sex with foreign women by Palestinian men in a Jerusalem tourist market, I intend to engage the issue of power in a more explicit way than does Cohen. This is in part because of a choice to foreground issues of domination and submission which are only implicit in Cohen's work but more signally because merchants in tourist markets compete fiercely with each other to attract and sell to tourists in whose largely arbitrary decisions rest the success or failure of the merchants' personal and financial investments. Their relative powerlessness in the face of the vacillating demands of groups of foreigners endowed with economic and social superiority was counterbalanced, in the particular setting of the Jerusalem *suq* (market), by the development of an aggressive sexuality focused on the women of the tourist populations. Sex with tourists in Jerusalem was not a means of escaping or fantasizing escape to another world but was, more complexly, a means of imagining and acting out a power that, in objective terms, the merchants did not have. The tourist merchants' obsessive interest in having sex with, and in stories of having sex with, foreign women served a dual purpose: it provided merchants with a field in which to play out scenarios of vengeance against foreigners who, in their eyes, oppressed them both economically and socially, while at the same time constructing an arena in which the merchants, all of whom were similarly at the mercy of economic demands over which they had no real control, could compete for the status of being one of those few able to master the masters. It is this motive of mastering or, to phrase it differently, of overpowering, which marks the significant difference between the ways the lumpenproletariat of Acre and the petit bourgeoisie of Jerusalem conceived of sexual relations with foreign women. While the 'Arab boys' observed by Cohen dreamed that their foreign girlfriends would save them from the lives they were living and transport them to fairer shores, the Palestinians with whom I spent two years expected nothing from tourists but a contest for cash and conquest. Encounters were brief and in many ways brutal, and all that was desired from tourists was money and the material for narratives of sexual conquest to reinvest in a closed world of selling and seduction from which the merchants had no intention of escaping.

Furthermore, the situation of Palestinians in the Occupied Territories when I did my fieldwork (just prior to the outbreak of the *intifada* 'the Palestinian Uprising') was different from that of 'Arabs' in Israel proper just after the disastrous defeat of the 1967 war. Whereas Palestinian Acre in the late sixties was marked by a quiescent despair, the Old City of Jerusalem in the mid-eighties hummed with debates on the ways Palestinians could rise up and overthrow Israeli dominion. As I will show in the closing pages of this chapter, such debates could not but influence the ways tourist merchants interpreted their relations with outsiders whom they came to see as implicated in the political oppression they suffered.

Jerusalem, despite the sordidness of some of the scenarios I will recount below and the political struggle which simmered beneath its glittering surface, is the focus of Christian Holy Land pilgrimage and is dense with the shrines and holy places which make Jerusalem sacred to Christians throughout the world. Before the outbreak of the *intifada* a bright halo of religious and secular souvenir shops (many now abandoned) owned and staffed by Palestinians bore testimony both to the attraction to foreigners of shrines like the 'Holy Sepulchre', the 'Lithostratus' and the 'Stations' of the Via Dolorosa and to the assumptions of local peoples that such attraction should generate substantial economic benefits for those who knew how to exploit it. In the vicinity of the holy places and along the crowded streets which connect them lay scores of shops — some only the size of a small sitting room and others nearly that of a typical British corner grocery store — filled with items arranged to catch the eyes of passing pilgrims and tourists. From the street each of these would appear as a single door, always open when the metal security shutters were unlocked, flanked by display windows. Inside the windows, and often suspended as well from boards and wires above the doors and outside the windows, would be dozens of often dusty articles for the tourist trade — pieces of what appeared to be local jewellery (much of it made in Taiwan), swathes of embroidered cloth, small brightly coloured cotton throw rugs, candles with transfers of Jesus or Mary stuck on them, reproduction icons, olive wood carvings of holy figures (both Judaic and Christian), T-shirts emblazoned with 'Israel is Real' or 'Israel We Love You', small metal castings of the word 'Shalom' and so forth. In case the baubles on display were not adequate to catch the attentions of passing tourists, or simply because there was nothing else to do, a Palestinian youth would either stand in the doorway watching the tourists go by or sit within smoking a *nargilah* (water pipe), talking with friends, or telling beads while attentively watching to see whether a tourist passing by might be lured in. Within the shop, and depending on the space allowed by the shop, the visitor would find at least one sofa and one chair, a small table, a mirror, and a tape deck playing anything from Michael Jackson to Um-Khalsum. These furnishings would typically be surrounded by trappings (hung cloth, incense sticks, brass coffee pots, etc.) designed to provide an air of the Orient. There would as well almost inevitably be a private space, usually another room behind the first with its entrance hidden by hanging cloths, sometimes even an attic or loft reached by climbing up a spindly ladder and through a trap door, or, in the case of the smaller and poorer shops, the shop interior itself sealed off from the street by closing the iron shutters at opportune moments. Whatever form the hidden room took, there would always be a place within where one — or two — could lie down.

Sitting in the back of these shops with men who in the course of time became my friends I would, time and time again, watch tourists, alone or in small groups, guardedly enter to look at the items displayed. These tourists, themselves informed by an attitude promulgated by their Israeli guides and by Ministry of Tourism handouts (see Bowman, 1992), would studiously ignore the welcome offered them by the merchants, handle the goods, and discuss them in hushed voices with their companions, should they be accompanied, before breaking silence to ask the price. The shopkeepers would then testify at length to the fine quality of the merchandise and to its superiority over identical items being sold in all the other shops up and down the street before offering an often inflated price. In most instances the tourists would put the item down and walk out or laugh and offer anything between one-tenth and one-quarter of the price asked. Sales were — occasionally — made, but usually negotiations ended with the tourists walking out and the shopkeepers muttering 'fucking tourists'.

This drama was, for the most part, scripted by the nature of the tourist market. The shops of the traditional *suk*, although retreating steadily in the face of rapidly escalating municipal taxes and the expanding tourist market, still sold food, clothing and household items to a local clientele. This local market, like the Sefrou *suk* described by Clifford Geertz (1979), was made up of a multitude of shops, each of which, while selling commodities similar to those of the surrounding shops, depended on a fixed clientele. Established networks linking particular shops with particular customers guaranteed merchants a number of clients who would — as long as goods remained adequate and reputations untarnished — come to them rather than going to the shops of their neighbours.

The merchants of the tourist market, on the other hand, strove to sell nearly identical items — mementoes with little if any use value — to a transient population which was only vaguely desirous of souvenirs. The merchants neither sold the sorts of goods which ensured demand, nor provided the sort of specialization which made one shop different from the next. Nor could they depend on a flow of established customers (although the struggle to 'corner' a tourist guide and his clientele was constant, as was the effort to get 'good' customers to refer friends from abroad). In consequence, the tourist *suk*, unlike the traditional market, was fully, often cut-throatedly, competitive and was, to a rather brutal degree, a buyer's market.

The only thing ensuring survival in a market where shops opened and closed down with dizzying speed was a merchant's style in selling (Khuri, 1968). The nature of competition in the largely undifferentiated market determined that appearance was all and that economic and personal success depended on the merchant's success in selling himself to usually indifferent if not openly hostile customers. Street merchants prided themselves on chameleon-like qualities, being able to shift language, religion, politics and even their national identity to suit what they perceived to be the tastes of potential customers. Most of the merchants whose businesses had survived for more than a year or two were capable of speaking five to six languages with a surprising proficiency. Muslim merchants could be good Christians for Christian tourists and pilgrims, and many Muslims and Christians played at being Jews for foreigners delighted with the success of the state of Israel. Often shopkeepers would listen carefully to the conversations of tourists in the shops or on the streets in order to judge their political inclinations. Having evaluated the terrain, the dealers would then present themselves as Zionists, Palestinian victims of the establishment of the Israeli state or even Cypriot nationalists in exile. Others, like the Ibrahims turned 'Avis' or the Dauouds become 'Davids', would deny being Palestinian and claim to be Israeli if they thought their customers might not like Arabs. More subtly, there were constant shifts in styles of solicitation manifest not only in what clothing was worn in what manner but also in the degree of deference, aggressiveness or seductiveness in the approach chosen to draw a customer to oneself and away from others.

When people find themselves wanting nothing in particular in a place where so many merchants are so adept at forming themselves to fit the whims of their elusive customers, the tourists' choice of where to buy is largely arbitrary. This essential arbitrariness is not comfortably embraced by the dealer who depends on sales to make a living. Consequently, in Palestinian tourist markets as in, I suspect, any saturated tourist market, there develops the concept of a near-magical 'method' of mercantile efficacy which can, it is believed, counter the structural inefficacy of the merchants' efforts. When merchants were not engaged in discussing their own and others' sexual exploits, they were often redesigning their shop displays, debating why particular merchants were bad salesmen and why others were successful, and evaluating the positive and negative points of their own encounters with tourist purchasers. One consequence of this continuous struggle to discover the 'method' of drawing tourists was that any innovation in the market that seemed temporarily successful was immediately copied by the other merchants so that the edge an innovator might gain was lost as soon as it became apparent to his neighbours. Thus the chimera of market power proved as elusive as its pursuit was passionate.

The shopkeepers in the Jerusalem tourist market depended for the survival of their businesses and the esteem of their neighbours on precisely that which the market, because of its structure of supply and demand, could not provide, namely prolific custom. The inherent weakness of the merchants' situation was not, however, interpreted in terms of the economic structure of the market but instead, as one would expect of the petit bourgeoisie, in personal terms. Each merchant saw his difficulties in appropriating a sufficient share of the market as, first of all, a consequence of his inability to overcome the reticence of tourists about buying in his shop and, secondly, the result of unfair trade practices — lying, underselling, deprecation — by his neighbours. It was consequently believed that if the merchant were better able to attract tourists and overcome their hesitancy he would not only succeed in making a decent living but also, through mastering a substantial share of the market, succeed in defeating the machinations of his competitors and gain their respect. It is not surprising, when one considers the obstacles the nature of the market throws in the way of the successful sales on which economic survival depended, that the Palestinian merchants' conceptions of themselves and their powers were very closely tied to their abilities to seduce customers into their shops and tourist moneys into their tills. It is also not surprising that a tremendous amount of resentment was felt towards those persons, the tourists, who somehow always seemed to succeed in resisting and rejecting these efforts at economic seduction.

Considering the way these men passed their daylight hours and made their living, it is not surprising to find that by night they continued to play at attraction and seduction with tourists. In the early months of my fieldwork I was struck by the fact that men who spent their days muttering 'fucking tourists' at customers who failed to buy would spend their evenings obsessively absorbed in either talk of, or the actual game of, fucking tourists. Those men able to arrange liaisons with tourist women during daylight hours would spend their evenings buying them dinner and drinks in a sustained effort to take them to bed. Others would gather in the bars of the many cheap hostels of the Old City staring at the women who came in, attempting to talk to them and speculating about having sex with them. The owner of a local hostel *cum* bar told me that he did not make money from providing rooms to the men and women tourists who passed through but from selling drinks to the crowds of young local men who, drawn by the presence of foreign women lodgers, would hang about for hours drinking, watching and waiting in the basement bar.

This time and effort, much of it wasted but some rewarded, was relived, embellished and transformed through the long dull hours spent on the following day or days waiting in the shops for customers. When I was with my friends in their shops and there were no customers to be seduced, conversation turned to which men had had sex with which tourist women and which had strived but failed. For the most part, the successful seducers in these tales were the tales' tellers or their close friends, and stories which featured successful seducers who were not close to the teller inevitably told of how the woman who had been seduced was 'easy' and had already slept with several other men. Clearly, status investment in these stories was quite high and, as one might suspect from constantly hearing of the successes of self and friends and the failures or easy wins of persons more distant, the veracity was correspondingly low.

To a large degree, the value of the sexual act was in its telling, since that could be circulated among peers, and not in its enactment, since that — when it did occur — was shared only between the self and a stranger. As in the many places where male sexual fantasizing serves to compensate for felt insecurities or impotencies in sexual and other domains, the woman in the narrative was a set piece, and her imagined investment in the scenario was itself a construction designed to further the enhancement of the teller's status. The act (or imagined act) of intercourse was performed and narrated by males for males. I found it difficult, while in Jerusalem, to inquire into the motives of those tourist women who went out with, and sometimes had sex with, the Palestinian merchants: to them I was, I suspect, just another male predator on the street. Women with whom I have subsequently spoken off tourist ground have told me that in situations like those which arise in Greece (Zinovieff, 1991), Israel/Palestine and other heavily touristed nations, the woman traveller finds herself so intensely harassed by local men that she may, for relief, take up with one of them simply to get the others to leave her alone.

Such a rationale did not, however, find a place in the stories I heard narrated by the men. Those stories were structured to celebrate the power of individual merchants over women and, through that overpowering, over other men. Consequently, their narrative strategies would disallow state-ments which exposed the successful seducer as a man fairly arbitrarily chosen from an undifferentiated mob of would-be seducers. The situation rendered in the women's interpretations would come all too close to mirroring, and thus reasserting, the contingency of the market situation by exposing behind the tale of seduction the same structure of arbitrariness which causes the tourist to buy an item from one shop rather than another. The male stories sought to deny this arbitrariness.

Remaining within the domain of male tales, one finds that the graphic detail of these stories of sexual encounters does more than give an air of authenticity to the narratives. A close examination of a typical story of tourist sex reveals a complicated terrain of resentment, power, anger and, somewhat surprisingly, failure. I'd like, in what follows, to retell a tale told to me by Salim,[2] a young man in his late teens, about his encounter with an older foreign woman. Salim's narrative is only exceptional in its rehearsal of so many of the themes informing the many tales of sex with tourists. I will attempt to correlate Salim's tale not only to the stories of others but also to a shared perception of the world which those stories articulate.

Salim told me one morning that the previous day a woman, alone, had walked into his shop to look at bedouin dresses. He described her as 'a motherfucker' and 'a real bitch' who was rich and beautiful and who looked 22 despite being 31. The woman was a New Yorker, elegantly dressed and married to an older man who was 'foolish enough' to leave her to wander alone in the market. Salim 'courted' her successfully, keeping her in the shop for a couple of hours, giving her cups of *kawa* (Turkish coffee) and *chi* (mint tea), telling in his faintly accented but quite fluent English of his (imaginary) years in America, his disdain for the other men in the market, and the exotic provenance and antique excellence of his bedouin dresses. The consequence, reiterated several times as the story grew more tawdry, was that she bought from him for $400 a dress he claimed was worth no more than $200 which she thought was a great bargain because she had managed to talk him down from $450.

Having succeeded in the significant financial seduction Salim proceeded to 'ice the cake' by asking the woman to meet him later in the evening so that he could show her the city. She was, according to Salim, as adamant in her refusals as she was clearly drawn by his charm and his virility. When she left his shop Salim told her, 'I will be in the lobby of the King David hotel at 10 pm and I hope I will see you there'. Salim went on to tell of arriving at 10:20 and of finding the woman waiting there, dressed exquisitely and looking very anxious at the possibility that her date might not show. Salim, aware that he had already 'won', asked her to accompany him to a friend's house. She refused, and yet it was quite clear that she was incapable of really refusing. In spite of her wealth, her nationality and her often mentioned (by Salim) husband asleep upstairs in the $120 a night hotel room, she could not resist his seductiveness. The upshot was that Salim took her from the King David's opulence to 'a dirty little room' where 'he fucked her till 5 am'. She, allegedly, was ecstatic about both the size of his 'Palestinian cock' and his technique, and was carried to heights of sexual fulfilment. He, on the other hand, was dropped into disgust and depression by the whole experience. Looking down on her, supposedly flushed by orgasm, he told her she was 'just a slut' and that he was sure 'she fucked with everyone in all the countries she'd been in'. She was, he said, deeply offended, but he claimed that saying this 'made him feel good afterwards'. The story closed with a retelling of Salim's success not only at 'fucking' this woman but also at overcharging her on the dress he sold her. 'I figure I got a good deal with the profit and the fuck thrown in.'

Interestingly the story was closed by Salim's telling of his sorrow that a Palestinian woman whom he'd long loved was marrying another man because Salim wouldn't marry her. Salim claimed he couldn't marry his true love 'because the involvement would be too great'.[3] None the less he swore that if he did marry 'a Palestinian virgin' he'd be faithful to her and 'would go out on the street, take out [his] cock and piss on all the foreign women, even if one of them was the Queen of Sheba'.

Several themes arise in Salim's story. The first, and most embellished, is that of the helplessness of the woman in the face of Salim's charm, despite her possession of all that Western society could give — freedom, beauty, cosmopolitanism and a rich husband. In the early parts of the story the seduction is a strictly 'hands off' affair which operates through Salim's success at marketing both his goods and his self. Sexual violence was strongly frowned upon in the market, and two young boys who, in another circumstance, took liberties which had not been offered (touching the breasts of two Finnish women, for whom they had bought drinks, despite the women's protests) were shamed up and down the street by being told that 'men don't take what is not given'. In Salim's story the course of the in-shop seduction is lovingly narrated — the details of conversation, Salim's small gifts of 50-cent earrings and cups of tea and coffee, the displaying of his own goods and the denigration of those of others — to suggest that the woman, despite her multitudinous advantages, walked into a situation she could not handle. In Salim's narrative, as in so many others, she who is seen as representative of the empowered, when forced to deal with the weak face-to-face, one-on-one, is incapable of defending either her economic or her bodily integrity. The narrative logic of these tales reveals that after one strips away the structural inequalities built into the relationship between tourist and tourist merchant by economic inequality and the hostility of the Israeli-run tourist industry, the merchant is exposed as inherently more powerful. The woman's helplessness before Salim and her willingness to leave the opulence of the King David hotel and the security provided by her wealthy husband stand as testimony to his power over and superiority to the personal representatives of the impersonal forces which would destroy him.

The compounding of the economic and the sexual in the woman's surrender serves to prove Salim's power in both valued domains of the world of the street merchant. The fact that these two motifs — of selling and of seducing — are interwoven with such complexity in the story suggests that it is the act of overcoming which is significant rather than that of making profit or enjoying the sex. That it is power in general rather than financial or sexual power which is being discussed is revealed by the fact that throughout the story the woman's imagined power, both in getting a good deal and in controlling her body and her will, is shown to be a sham. Another shopkeeper told me that when he seduces tourist women the 'game is over when she takes off her underpants'. From that moment on he loses interest and feels disgusted. I found myself several times in situations where merchants who had made it clear to me that they had had sex with women who were still in the neighbourhood offered me a woman (in her absence or in Arabic) as though, having 'had' them, they were theirs to pass on. the women became tokens testifying to the sexual capital accumulated by the merchants, and by offering these foreign women to me they were suggesting that I, though empowered like the women by my origins, was poorer than they in the personal powers that mattered.

This story then, like dozens of other similar stories, was about the potency of the individual in a situation where impotence was structured into the social situation by political and economic forces. Its theme of seduction reveals how these individuals imagined themselves able to manipulate a world which appeared designed to suppress or destroy them. Salim's power is doubly asserted in his story in that his ability to take the woman's money in a sale reinforces and is reinforced by his ability to take her body in a scenario which reverses their structural positions. In the 'dirty little room' she sheds all her powers — her freedom of will and mobility, her wealthy husband, her luxurious locale and her elegant clothing — in exchange for five hours of intercourse with a man who, despite having none of her privileges, treats her with disdain. The fact that a significant player in the story, the husband, is absent in body but constantly present in reference, suggests that, as in all the most satisfying stories of sex with tourists, the victory over the woman is at the same time a victory over the man whose identity, and whose power, is seen as being tied up with her. Just as offering me their sexual hand-me-downs and claiming that the 'easiest' women were British asserted the merchants' superiority over me as a foreigner, so too did 'taking' the woman of a foreign man. Juliette Minces, in The House of Obedience, writes of 'a well known phenomenon, the desire of the colonially dominated to revenge himself upon the woman of the dominator' (Minces, 1982:38), and in these stories, where the sexual act is described in the terminology of violence, we see a symbolic displacement of a struggle that the dominated cannot, in fact, win. The men, like the women, can be taken on. Another form of narrative favoured by Jerusalem merchants tells of fights with foreign men which, despite the odds against the Palestinians, the Palestinians always win. What cannot be taken on is the imbalance of power that sets up these oppositions in the first place.

Sexual tales relate how the structurally 'fucked' become the 'fuckers'; they tell, in other words, of the way a group of persons 'feminized' (Brandes, 1980:206 and Herzfeld, 1985) by their economic and political positions are able, through sexually dominating the women of the dominators, to retake a 'masculine' position both in relation to the women and, through a triangular struggle in which they prove more masculine than the women's men, in relation to those men as well.[4] Thus in a domain which I can only refer to as mythological, the slaves become the masters of those who, in the real world, appeared in positions of dominance.

Interestingly, though foreign women played such a central role in the scenarios of these narratives, the treatment of Israeli women was completely different. I cannot recall hearing a merchant tell of seducing an Israeli who'd come to buy in the market, although more than half of the tourist market's trade was with Israeli domestic tourists or Israeli Jerusalemites who would stroll through the market on the Sabbath when West Jerusalem was closed. When I asked about this absence of tales about seducing Israelis, I was told that Israeli women 'didn't count' because seducing them took neither skill nor effort. Clearly implicit in such statements — solicited by and directed towards a foreigner rather than by and towards another merchant — is the assertion of the sexual superiority of Palestinian men over their Israeli rivals. Another story, which I heard several times in different shops, suggests another, perhaps more substantial, reason for the street merchants' hesitancy at attempting to accrue status by narrating tales of the sexual conquest of Israeli women. This told of an Israeli woman who frequently came to the Old City on Saturdays to wander through the shops looking for goods which attracted her. She consistently brushed aside the flashy rubbish and well-crafted imitations offered her and inevitably discovered the best items that the shops held. Having found these she would signal to the merchant (she was always represented as refusing to speak Arabic and speaking only in Hebrew or with gestures) that she would have sex with him in exchange for the goods. In the stories the merchants always succumbed to the 'seduction' despite their knowledge that they were being 'had'. She always, after passionless sex, would wordlessly stand up and walk out of the shop with the merchants' most cherished articles. The tale suggests that Israeli power was too imminent to be denied even in a displacing language so far as of sexual politics. The Israeli woman was able without even compromising to use the language of the merchants, to outseduce the seducers. In the domain of sexual representations of economic and political power it is she who played the successful businessperson and the merchants who were analogous to the tourists in losing both their valuables and their bodily integrity.

The way that more typical sexual stories displace and yet represent political and economic inequalities shows up quite saliently in stories of the failure of sexual forays. One afternoon Masim, a merchant devoted to body-building who frequently attempted to provoke fights with foreigners, came to my room in a surly mood and told me he had earlier in the day been entertaining an English woman behind the closed metal doors of his shop. In the course of 'heavy petting' she inserted a finger in his anus and he ejaculated. He claimed that he had immediately jumped up, thrown open the metal doors and forced her, half-dressed, out into the street.

To understand what lay behind his anger one must relate his story to the term *manioc* with which Palestinian youths in the streets frequently greet friends — but never anyone who is not a friend. *Manioc* translates as 'the one who takes his pleasure in the ass'. By addressing a friend as *manioc* one playfully demasculinizes him in suggesting that he, though a man, enjoys sex passively 'like a woman' (compare Brandes, 1980:92–6). The term is also used to describe perjoratively persons who, in one way or another, surrender face. Thus someone walking in the street holding hands with a foreign woman, dancing Western style in a pub or simply talking too much or too loudly in the street is described as a *manioc*. Masim's anger was about being figuratively feminized while he was attempting — literally and in terms of a discourse on social intercourse — to assert his dominant, 'masculine' role over a tourist woman. His anger and dismay, both strong enough to allow him, just *ex post facto*, to tell me (an 'outsider' to the circuit of status accrual) the story, was not because the woman had seemed to try to feminize him by inserting her phallic finger in his vaginal anus but because he, subject to this symbolic reversal, seemed, by having an orgasm, to legitimate the inversion.

This rare, but succinct, story of failure enables us to see more in Salim's much more typical narrative of success. At the moment of Salim's sexual victory, when he dispassionately stares down on the body of a woman allegedly still caught up in the passion of their intercourse, that victory turns to ashes. Salim's statement that the woman has sex with all the men of all the countries through which she passes did more, I suspect, than manifest a desire to add insult to injury. Salim's statement was more strategic; he did not say that she sleeps with other men in Palestine/Israel but that she sleeps with other men in other countries. He was able still to accrue status on the street since she, in Palestine/Israel, chose to sleep with, and to buy from, him. He was not able, however, to convince himself that his sexual exploit provided him with any power over her since she, in the global situation, was recognized as the consumer. He was successful over his neighbours in the market, but that success could not provide him, or any other merchant, with any real power over the world that made him a passive supplier of goods to active consumers of goods. He finally acknowledged both to himself and to the people to whom he told his tale that he had been chosen from among the other available bodies in the market in the same way his dress had been chosen over others that other merchants had had on display. He may have, through his ability to present his commodities with greater style than his compatriots, succeeded where they failed, but finally, in the stories of the bedroom as in those of the shop, the person and the people with the significant power are represented as those foreigners who wander from nation to nation purchasing the most attractive commodities and picking up the prettiest boys.[5]

I suspect that the woman's story would not validate Salim's interpretation either of her motives or her promiscuity. Her view of the incident was not, however, pertinent to Salim's story or to the interpretations of those to whom he told it because the story told not of the world seen by foreigners but of the world experienced by the street merchants. The tail of Salim's tale is particularly interesting to an interpretation of the narrative as a failed attempt to overcome a structural inequity. His story of his unwillingness to marry a Palestinian woman suggests the degree to which the street merchants, having chosen to deal with the impoverishment of their situation through the economic and sexual seduction of tourists, had isolated themselves from the wider, and potentially more fulfilling, domains of Palestinian life. Salim gave up the Palestinian woman he claimed to love because he could not disinvest himself from the struggle on the street. His compulsive desire to re-engage constantly in a competition which he, and his fellow merchants, already knew was unwinnable separated Salim, and those others, from the wider world of domestic reproduction and political recuperation. The symbolic economy of the tourist market, which linked personal identity and integrity to success in selling to foreigners, required that all the merchant had would be invested in that seduction and that nothing would be left for investment elsewhere. This was manifest in the prodigality of the merchants who would spend most of what they earned on entertainment and other forms of conspicuous consumption and were willing to throw the little they had saved into highly speculative and generally untenable schemes for making rapid profits. It was also manifest in the number of street merchants who remained unmarried at 35 despite being members of a wider Palestinian community which considers an unmarried man to be a failure. The merchant's exclusive investment of his person in the market revealed itself in the closing section of Salim's narrative. Salim dreamed, as did most of the men with whom I talked, of eventually marrying a Palestinian virgin who was, unlike the tourist women, uncorrupted. Nevertheless, according to his narrative, even after having done so his penis would be invested in the struggle with foreigners rather than in his relationship with his wife: 'After I marry her I will be faithful to her and I will go out on the street, take out my cock, and piss on all the foreign women, even if one of them was the Queen of Sheba.'

Salim's closing image of the merchant's penis as a sign in an agonistic discourse with foreigners rather than as an element connected with the creation of family, community and nation enables us to picture the alienation of the tourist market, and of its indigenous participants, from the community in which it is set up and which it commodifies. The engrossment of tourist merchants in the market was nearly total, and Palestinians within Jerusalem and in the surrounding towns and villages who were not involved in that market looked upon it and its shopkeepers with scorn. It was assumed that men who became tourist merchants gave up on their responsibilities to the wider Palestinian community in order to make money quickly by dealing with Israelis and foreigners. The fact that few in the market did make money, and that those who did did not make it quickly, was no more recognized by their critics than it was acknowledged by the merchants themselves. For each group the tourist market was seen as a rapid route to riches. While for those persons outside its 'charmed circle' the process of gaining those riches was seen to involve degradation if not outright betrayal of the Palestinian people, for those shopkeepers who were caught up in it the failure to get rich quick fuelled their compulsive engagement in its economic and extra-economic circuits. Their failure to make money increased their aggressiveness towards the tourists they saw as denying them their just deserts and intensified the competition between them for mastery over the tourists. Each augmentation bore fruit in an escalated investment in the mythic economy of 'fucking tourists'.

Such a closed circuit can, however, only remain integral for as long as its logic serves to explain the world of its participants. The tourist market separated shopkeeper from shopkeeper by forcing them to compete for the scarce resource of tourist customers. As long as they could see their competitors as their chief enemies and their own inabilities to grasp the 'magic' of economic seduction as the chief impediment to their mastering of the market and those competitors, the tourist merchants remained indifferent to the encompassing political and economic framework which determined the workings of the market. Instead they fully invested in mythologies which asserted that the individual could overcome customers and competitors. However, by the time I returned to Jerusalem in 1987, six months before the outbreak of the *intifada*, the efficacy of that mythology had been undermined by what was perceived to be active intervention by the Israeli state. Taxes on the shops in the Old City had increased several times between 1983 and 1987 and so too had the previously lax state surveillance of who was and who was not paying them. At the same time, international tourism to the entire area of Palestine/Israel had plummeted — in part because of developments in the Lebanon — and fewer customers were being seen in the market. The merchants, faced with vastly increased overheads and diminished incomes, and conscious of the presence of tax collectors and of Israeli guides who prevented tourists from entering Palestinian shops, interpreted what was going on as part of what they came to define as an Israeli project to drive Palestinian merchants out of the Old City. The adoption of a political discourse on the workings of the market had begun, by the time I visited, to undermine the previous mythology. The lament that 'the situation is very bad; there is no money, the women are hard to find and it is very hard to live' was formulaicly repeated in 1987 just as it had been earlier in the decade, but in 1987, unlike between 1983 and 1985, the onus for this paucity was shifting from tourists who would not buy and other merchants who lied and cheated to the state itself and 'the political situation'.

This reinterpretation led to the integration of the Palestinian tourist merchants into the nationalist mainstream. Their participation in the strikes which were a major part of the *intifada* was comprehensive despite the economic deprivation entailed in that participation (Tamari, 1989 and 1991). Such a transformation in interpretation and strategy suggests that host communities in underdeveloped regions are not passive and power-less recipients of whatever, be it good or bad, the developed world deems to impose upon them but are instead made up of persons con-tinually assessing their situations and capable of changing their responses to those situations when previous strategies of empowerment prove ineffectual. I will close with a field report which, while illustrating this point, also serves to undermine the entire opposition of First World/ Third World, developed/underdeveloped which structures liberal dis-course. In 1989 I sent an early draft of this chapter to a Palestinian academic I knew from the West Bank who was, at that time, a visiting lecturer at a university in the United States. Two weeks later I returned to Jerusalem to follow up on some fieldwork and was approached by two tourist merchants who told me 'we want to talk to you about your paper'. That evening I met with half a dozen merchants who had either read the paper, or been given detailed summaries of its argument by friends who had read copies of the draft. It turned out that the paper had been faxed to Birzeit (a West Bank University) where it was photocopied by a member of the academic staff who had close ties with the 'street' and had distributed copies among merchant friends. What was more surprising than the speed with which the paper had reached the 'field' was the fact that the merchants with whom I discussed the paper were sympathetic to the argument and claimed they were using it as a means of 'thinking through' an obsession with sex with tourists they claimed to want to overcome.

The situation was, however, even more complex. The merchants' encounter with the paper came at the end of a process of reassessment which had been initiated when, in the midst of the politicization mentioned above, one of the former merchants returned to the Old City from Paris where, through the patronage of the Jerusalem Franciscan monastery, he had achieved his doctorate in psychoanalysis in a Lacanian department. Despite his qualifications the psychoanalyst had been unable to get employment in Israeli hospitals because he was Palestinian. A short stint of work in a Palestinian hospital had resulted in his being fired because his insistence on practising 'the talking cure' offered him access to domains of family life which, in traditional Palestinian communities, were considered inviolate. In consequence, he spent two years without work sitting in shops with his friends and former colleagues introducing them to basic concepts of psychoanalysis and offering them ways of using them to make sense of their lives. Access to that material, at the same time that the worsening political situation was leading them to look for ways of escaping from their isolation from the wider, and increasingly more politicized, Palestinian community, gave them the means of understanding their previous incarceration within the closed circuit of 'fucking tourists' as well as ideas of how to escape it. My paper was merely another contribution to a radical melange of political, sociological and psychoanalytic theories which these 'victims' were using to make sense of their situation so that they could devise more effectual ways of dealing with the impacts of tourism, economic peripheralization and military occupation on their lives.

None the less, it must be recognized that understanding a situation and devising strategies of empowerment within it is often not a sufficient defence against the overwhelming powers of hostile states and exploitative international economies. In Israel/Palestine at present the *intifada* has given way to a 'peace process' which may hold out prospects for an improvement in the political situation. It remains to be seen whether a political settlement will substantially improve the economic situation of merchants and former merchants in Jerusalem's Old City. The backdrop to the political wars of 'Jews' and 'Arabs', as to many of the political struggles which have marred the past two hundred years of world history, is a more perdurable antagonism between those who have the power to collect and disperse an economic surplus and those who struggle against the odds to lay hands on one. This is a war which continued in spite of the fact that borders are labile and antagonists change sides. What this paper has described in Israel/Palestine in the 1980s is one of many skirmishes in this war, and whatever the resolution of that skirmish it does not mark the end of the war. It is important however that we as anthropologists attend carefully to the character of the conflict; the Palestinian merchants described in this paper, like so many other communities struggling against the structural inequities of international tourism and other modalities of colonial domination, are certainly not helpless – they are merely outgunned.

NOTES

The materials for this article were gathered during field research funded by grants from the Palestine Exploration Fund, the Lady Davis Foundation, the Deya Mediterranean Area Research Centre, Oxford University and the University of Kent at Canterbury. The Sociology and Social Anthropology Department of Hebrew University generously provided office space and library access during the early stages of research. I would like especially to thank the men whose lives and stories provide the basis for this analysis and with whom I discussed an earlier version of the paper (published as 'Fucking Tourists: Sexual Relations and Tourism in Jerusalem's Old City' in *Critique of Anthropology* IX:2, Autumn 1989, pp. 77–93) for their friendship, assistance and comments. That this chapter addresses only male merchants and their relations with women tourists is not to suggest this is a more important issue than the problems of identity for Palestinian women, especially for the mothers, sisters and future wives of these merchants. Rather, it is that as a man I had access only to the merchants' street lives and the stories they told of those lives.

1. It seems apposite that a Sunday *Observer* article reporting on the papers dealing with sex tourism in the Anthropology of Tourism held in 1988 at the Roehampton Institute was entitled 'Sugar Mummies and their Prey' (Hale, 1988:35).
2. The names in the recountings that follow are pseudonyms.
3. An older merchant told me 'I want to be a good Muslim, but I cannot because I cannot go to the mosque to pray. To sell things to tourists I have to lie, and because of that I am too impure to pray.'
4. The politics of 'triangular desire' are convincingly set out in René Girard's work (1965) and are useful in the analysis of this situation if it is seen that the merchant does not simply want to become the man whose partner he seduces but wants to take the position of power occupied by that man in both the sexual relation with the woman and in the wider field of social and economic power.
5. The knowledge which surfaces through the cracks in these stories that the Palestinian 'fucker' is always, at base, 'fucked' by the rest of the world may have been behind one informant's statement that 'one should never fuck in a shop; sex and money don't mix'. The strategic purpose of sex with tourists seems here to be recognized as always already thwarted. It is seen, through the same metonymic logic that represented sexual empowerment as an extension of economic power, that the inevitable failure in the sexual domain will turn and curse ventures in the economic.

REFERENCES

Bourdieu, P. (1977) *Outline of a Theory of Practice*, Cambridge: Cambridge University Press.

Bowman, G. (1992) 'The politics of tour guiding: Israeli and Palestinian guides in Israel and the Occupied Territories', in D. Harrison (ed.), *Tourism and the Less Developed Countries*, London: Belhaven Press, pp. 121–34.

Brandes, S. (1980) *Metaphors of Masculinity: Sex and Status in Andalusian Folklore*, Philadelphia: University of Pennsylvania Press.

Cohen, E. (1971) 'Arab boys and tourist girls in a mixed Jewish Arab community,' *International Journal of Comparative Sociology*, XII, 4:217–33.

Cohen, E. (1986) 'Lovelorn farangs: the correspondence between foreign men and Thai girls,' *Anthropological Quarterly*, LIX, 3:115–27.

Crick, M. (1985) '"Tracing" the anthropological self: quizzical reflections on field work, Tourism and the Ludic,' *Social Analysis*, XVII:71–92.

Crick, M. (1988) 'Sun, sex, sights, savings and servility: representations of international tourism in the social sciences', *Criticism, Heresy and Interpretation*, I, 1:37–76.

de Kadt, E. (1979) *Tourism: Passport to Development?*, Oxford: Oxford University Press.

Geertz, C. (1979) 'Suq: the bazaar economy in Sefrou' in C. Geertz, H. Geertz and L. Rosen (eds), *Meaning and Order in Moroccan Society: Three Essays in Cultural Analysis*, Cambridge: Cambridge University Press, pp. 123–276.

Girard, R. (1965) '"Triangular" desire' in R. Girard (ed.), *Deceit, Desire and the Novel: Self and Other in Literary Structure*, Baltimore: Johns Hopkins Press, pp. 1–52.

Hale, S. (1988) 'Sugar mummies and their prey', *The Observer*, 30 October: 35.

Hall, C.M. (1992) 'Sex Tourism in South-east Asia' in D. Harrison (ed.), *Tourism in the Less Developed Countries*, London: Belhaven Press, pp. 64–74.

Harrison, D. (1992) 'International tourism and the less developed countries: the background' in D. Harrison (ed.), *Tourism and the Less Developed Countries*, London: Belhaven Press, pp. 1–18.

Herzfeld, M. (1985) *The Poetics of Manhood: Contest and Identity in a Cretan Mountain Village*, Princeton: Princeton University Press.

Khuri, F. (1968) 'The etiquette of bargaining in the Middle East', *American Anthropologist*, LXX:698–706.

Minces, J. (1982) *The House of Obedience: Women in Arab Society*, London: Zed Press.

Nash, D. (1977) 'Tourism as a form of imperialism' in V. Smith (ed.), *Hosts and Guests: the Anthropology of Tourism*, Oxford: Basil Blackwell, pp. 33–47.

Ong, A. (1985) 'Industrialisation and prostitution in southeast Asia', *Southeast Asia Chronicle*, LXXXXVI:2–6.

Peacock, J. (1986) *The Anthropological Lens: Harsh Light, Soft Focus*, Cambridge: Cambridge University Press.

Scott, J.C. (1990) *Domination and the Arts of Resistance: Hidden Transcripts*, New Haven: Yale University Press.

Smith, V. (1988) 'Geographical implications of "drifter" tourism: Borocay, Philippines' in *Symposium on Tourism*, International Geographical Union, 13–20 August, Christchurch, New Zealand.

Tamari, S. (1989) 'The revolt of the petite bourgeoisie', paper read at Georgetown University, Washington, DC, 26 April.

Tamari, S. (1991) 'The Palestinian movement in transition: historical reversals and the uprising', *Journal of Palestine Studies*, XX, 2:57–70.

Thurot, J. and G. Thurot (1983) 'The ideology of class and tourism: confronting the discourse of advertising', *Annals of Tourism Research*, X:173–89.

Truong, T. (1990) *Sex, Money and Morality: Prostitution and Tourism in Southeast Asia*, London: Zed Books.

Zinovieff, S. (1991) 'Hunters and hunted: *Kamaki* and the ambiguities of sexual predation in a Greek town' in P. Loizos and E. Papataxiarchis (eds), *Contested Identities: Gender and Kinship in Modern Greece*, Princeton: Princeton University Press, pp. 203–20.

6 Ritual, Tourism and Cultural Commoditization in Malta: Culture by the Pound?[1]

JEREMY BOISSEVAIN

> Between May and October every town and village . . . celebrates the feast day or 'festa' of its patron saint . . . no holidaymaker to Malta should leave the Island without experiencing one. (1992 NTO brochure)

> Commoditisation of culture in effect robs people of the very meanings by which they organise their lives. (Greenwood, 1989:179)

For some time now I have been trying to understand the apparent growth in the scale of public rituals, both in Malta and elsewhere in Europe, since the early 1970s. Carnival, neighbourhood feasts, traditional rural weddings and fairs have been revitalized in the Netherlands and Germany. In Spain, Italy and Malta there has been a general increase in carnival, festas and Holy Week celebrations. Even Swedes are organizing carnival-type 'samba-festivals', complete with samba schools, costumes and processions (Boissevain, 1984, 1991, 1992, 1996; Koster et al. 1983; Weber-Kellerman, 1985; also see Manning, 1983).

One set of explanations that keeps cropping up attributes this expansion to the growth of leisure time, commercialization and tourism (Werdmölder, 1979; Manning, 1983; Weber-Kellerman, 1985). In this chapter I explore to what extent commercialization of culture to attract tourists is taking place, and, if so, what effect it has had on parish celebrations in Malta.

CULTURE BY THE POUND

The argument about the influence of commercialization runs roughly like this. People in tourist destinations commoditize their culture for gain. Celebrations are increased to maximize profit. This commoditization has a detrimental effect on the rituals celebrated.

Greenwood, who coined the expression 'culture by the pound' (1989), described the effects of the commoditization of a public ritual, the *Alarde*, in

The Tourist Image: Myths and Myth Making in Tourism. Edited by Tom Selwyn.
© 1996 John Wiley & Sons Ltd.

the Basque community of Fuenterrabia. The Spanish tourism ministry and private tourist entrepreneurs promoted this colourful event to attract tourists to the town. The municipal government then decided that the *Alarde* should be performed twice on the same day to enable more onlookers to see it. From being a performance for the participants, it was transformed into a public show for outsiders. Greenwood argued that this had disastrous consequences: 'By making it part of the tourism package, it is turned into an explicit and paid performance and no longer can be believed in the way it was before. Thus commoditization of culture in effect robs people of the very meanings by which they organise their lives' (ibid.:179).

The view that certain celebrations have been commercialized, and that this has degraded traditional culture, has also been voiced by Maltese intellectuals. Sociologist Mario Vassallo argued that the persistence of the Maltese *festa* is due to the

> opposition by conservative elites in the different parishes, and the demand to exploit the past as a commodity with which to lure tourists, combined to preserve the traditional *festa*. But even this festivity, and such other previously purely religious activities as the Good Friday processions . . . became regarded less as coherent elements in everyday activity, less as essential features of the community's symbolic universe, and more as isolated, saleable artifacts of culture, to be produced and performed 'to order' for outsiders for whom they bore no intrinsic meaning but only qualities of spectacle . . . What was once sacred, jealously guarded and good-in-itself, had become another item to be put into the balance of payments as a credit-earning product (Vassallo, 1979:207; also see 1981).

Paul Xuereb supported this interpretation when he reviewed Vassallo's book for the influential *Sunday Times* (of Malta):

> The mass servant ethos engendered by tourism has artificially prolonged the life of much of our religious pageantry but it has also secularised it by transforming it into something picturesque merely to be exploited and sold. Most notably, our Good Friday processions have become gaudier, more vulgarly elaborate, mainly a spectacle for the amused or patronising tourist and largely divorced from the solemnities that originally gave them birth. (Xuereb, 1979)

In short, the persistence, if not the increase, of celebrations is seen as a consequence of the commercialization of culture for touristic purposes and this commoditization is regarded as fundamentally destructive of the meanings by which people organize their lives. This pessimism provides the central focus of this discussion. Is it warranted?

MALTA AND TOURISM

Malta is located in the middle of the world's oldest and most crowded tourist area. The Maltese Islands measure only 120 square miles (310 km^2) and, with 350 000 inhabitants, Malta is the most densely populated country in Europe. There are more than 50 villages and towns which form discrete parishes and residential areas. The Maltese are intensely devout Roman Catholics. Since Malta became independent in 1964, the economy has grown considerably. Tourism has played a major role in this.

In 1992, just under one million tourists visited Malta, each staying an average of 10 days. The Malta National Tourist Organization has been successful in promoting travel to Malta in the off-peak season. In 1985, 70 percent of tourist arrivals were between June and September. By 1992, annual arrivals had nearly doubled but only 40 percent were in the high season. Malta's NTO has increasingly shifted its imaging away from swimming and pleasure to history and culture.

In 1976, Malta Government Tourist Board brochures stressed sun, sea and monuments. The 16-page, 1400-word English brochure was coyly aimed at the middle of the road mass tourist. It had this to say about the country's history: 'Malta's history is pre-historic history, is ancient history, is modern history. But most of all, Malta's history is a history of foreign rulers and invaders. They came from just about everywhere in Western Europe and Northern Africa . . .' Its mention of parish celebrations was equally lightweight, if not simple-minded: '. . . Or partying. (In Malta a party is called a Festa. And they happen all year round.) Singing, laughing, dancing in the streets. Fireworks that light the night like day. Which next thing you know it is . . .'

NTO priorities began to change in the 1980s. Malta's image as a seaside resort was by then well established (some would say too well, for it has been called 'Blackpool in the sun'). The government sought a different type of tourist, a 'quality tourist', and one who would also come in the off-peak season. The current (1992) NTO brochure is aimed at the tourist who is interested in more than swimming and night life. Its 4000-word text provides a sound overview of the Island's geography, history, people and culture. It sets out in some detail the advantages of a winter visit. Beaches, swimming and night clubs are not mentioned. Instead of sun, monuments and pleasure, the NTO now promotes culture and learning: 'The intelligent visitor is never satisfied with just skimming the surface of his holiday destination. His appetite for learning urges him to delve deeper into the origins and history of the country and people he is visiting.'

Popular culture, for the first time, is prominently featured. Parish celebrations in particular are discussed seriously, and in some detail: 'The festa is the most important event in each village's annual calendar and the villagers eagerly look forward to this very special day . . . There is a three-day build-up to the feast and the atmosphere throughout is one of gaiety and merriment . . . no holiday maker to Malta should leave the Island without experiencing one.'

It is clear from the above that parish celebrations have been commoditized. What effect has this had on these traditional festivities? To answer this I will describe developments in the village of Naxxar, with which I have been in contact for 30 years, and where my wife and I now live.

NAXXAR

Naxxar is an inland village. It has grown from a population of approximately 5000 in 1960, when we first lived there, to its present population of just under 8000. The village is focused on the enormous parish church and the square in front of it, from which the principal streets radiate, and on which are located (or lie within a few minutes' walk) the principle associations, band clubs and offices of the authorities — police, political parties, parish priest, post office and health centre.

The old core of the village consists of several neighbourhoods, each of which is centred on a chapel. One of these, the small Chapel of St John, located at the western edge of the village, forms the focal point of the poorest neighbourhood. This is connected to the main parish square by St Lucy Street, one of the oldest and longest streets in the village. Much of the parish's ritual activity takes place along this street.

A large belt of new housing, constructed bit by bit during the past two decades, surrounds the old core. Much of it has been built by and for the many outsiders who have moved into the village. Many Naxxarin have also built modern houses there and moved out of the core. Many of the vacated traditional houses in the St John and St Lucy neighbourhoods have been acquired by foreigners who have retired to Malta or have plans to do so. These stone 'houses of character', with their arches, wooden beams and large interior courtyards, are now also being bought by well-off young Maltese couples from urban middle-class areas. They then convert them, often at great expense, to their conception of a 'traditional' rural house. They chip off the stucco, plaster and paint applied by previous generations, often adorning the bared walls with old farming implements and other icons of a rural past which neither they nor their parents experienced, and which, less than two decades ago, they abhorred. They also install modern plumbing and kitchens. Thus Naxxar's core is slowly being abandoned by natives and reoccupied and gentrified by wealthy outsiders.

CELEBRATIONS

Naxxar, like other Maltese villages, celebrates an annual cycle of religious festivities. There are two ceremonial high points, the annual *festa* and Holy Week. The *festa* of the parish patron saint, the Nativity of Our Lady, celebrated on 8 September, involves two weeks of religious preparation, band marches and firework displays. These build up to a three-day climax. Three days before the feast, on the Eve-of-the-Eve, (mostly) unmarried village young men and (increasingly) some of the wilder girls stage a boisterous evening parade to mark the end of the Triduum, the three-day period of prayer that precedes the feast. On the Eve of the feast, the decorated village and its church are on show. Band marches, concerts and firework displays entertain the crowd made up of residents, visitors from all over the island and tourists. The following day, the principal feast is celebrated with a solemn high mass in the morning and, at roughly the same time, another wild parade of village youths — the morning march. That evening the village and church are again on show, and a religious procession and bands accompany the statue of the patron, *Marija Bambina*, through the village. Villagers, visitors and tourists are again entertained with more parades and music by hired bands. At about 10:30pm there is a final firework salute to the patron, and the statue is then returned to the church for another year.

The other major series of celebrations takes place during Holy Week. These include devotional exercises, rituals and pageants held in the parish church. The high points are the devotional processions commemorating Our Lady of Sorrows in which hundreds of villagers take part: Palm Sunday, Good Friday and the Resurrection on Easter Sunday.

Besides these major events, a number of lesser rituals are celebrated publicly. These include the *festi* of the neighbourhood chapels, Christmas and the Eucharistic celebrations in June of Our Lady of Doctrine, Corpus Christi and the Sacred Heart of Jesus.

INSIDE, OUTSIDE, BACK AND FRONT

The Maltese make an interesting linguistic distinction between the devotional rituals of a feast that take place inside the church, the *festa ta'gewwa* or 'internal feast', and the often exuberant celebrations that take place, frequently at the same time, outside the church, the *festa ta'barra*, or 'external feast'. The former is organized by the clergy and conforms fairly strictly to the prescribed liturgy. The latter is generally organized by one of the parish priests with a committee and a group of volunteers who arrange for street decorations, music, fireworks and much of the fundraising. The internal feast is characterized by ritual and formal rules and maintains its traditional aspects. The external feast is more playful and open to improvization and thus more prone to change.

Another internal–external distinction can be made. This is the differentiation between 'insider' and 'outsider' events, between celebrations that are attended primarily by Naxxarin and those which are open to outsiders — visitors from other villages and foreign tourists. Only the evening events of the Eve and day of the *festa* and the Good Friday procession are attended by outsiders. All other events are normally celebrated only by Naxxarin. These include all the ceremonies of the *festa ta'gewwa*, the processions of Our Lady of Sorrows and Palm Sunday, and the Resurrection on Easter Sunday and such *festa ta'barra* events as the band marches during the two weeks preceding the *festa* and the wild parades on the Eve-of-the-Eve and the morning of the *festa*.

What I have called 'inside and outside spheres', to a certain extent parallel what MacCannell, following Goffman, has called 'back' and 'front' regions: 'The front is the meeting place of hosts and guests or customers and service persons, and the back is the place where members of the home team retire between performances to relax and to prepare' (MacCannell, 1976:92). MacCannell's back regions are normally closed to outsiders, and for him their mere existence implies their possible violation. His back region is somehow more 'intimate and real', as against the front region's 'show', and consequently more 'truthful', thus more authentic (ibid.:94–9).

The differences between MacCannell's backstage events and what I have called insider events are that the latter are also performances and they are not closed to outsiders, whether Maltese or foreign.[2] There is no overt feeling — at least at present[3] — that outside spectators violate the insider events noted above. Since these celebrations are also staged, spectators are generally much appreciated. But outsiders just do not come. Maltese outsiders are uninterested. Tourists, who might well be interested, are simply not told about them by Maltese cultural commoditizers and guides. They assume tourists share their own disinterest in village back regions.

DECLINE

In the 30 years that we have been in touch with Naxxar, a period which coincides with the development of tourism in Malta, these public celebrations have undergone a number of changes. Some celebrations have declined or disappeared, others have greatly increased. Since 1961 several processions have disappeared completely. Except for Holy Week events and the celebration of parish and chapel patron saints, all other processions have decreased considerably. For example, the number of participants and observers of the processions of Our Lady of Doctrine, Corpus Christi and the Sacred Heart of Jesus are down by a half to two-thirds compared to 25 years ago (cf. Boissevain, 1991).

The pattern of the decline noted in Naxxar is general in villages throughout Malta. The feasts that have declined in importance are, as in Naxxar, the celebrations of secondary saints and the Eucharist. These are festivities that are not identified with any particular parish. They are celebrated simultaneously throughout Malta. Several reasons were offered to account for their decline. Contrasting Eucharistic celebrations with those of Holy Week, for example, people said that the former were much more difficult to identify with. They were too abstract, it was difficult to conceptualize them. Eucharistic celebrations were no longer able to hold the attention of parishioners as once they had when there were few other entertainments, and transportation out of the village was difficult. Since many feasts are celebrated at weekends, the Saturdays and Sundays from June through August have become ever more hectic as *festa* organizers compete for the same public. Patronal feasts, with their band marches and firework displays, draw crowds from all over the island, upstaging less spectacular devotional rituals such as the Naxxar Corpus procession.

There is another contributing factor to the decline in popularity of the feasts of secondary saints. In the past, religious confraternities organized the celebrations of the saints. For example, the procession for the feast of St Joseph, which is no longer held, used to be partly organized by the confraternity of St Joseph, the Our Lady of the Rosary procession by the confraternity of the Holy Rosary and that of Corpus Christi by the confraternity of the Blessed Sacrament. During the past 25 years these religious brotherhoods for laymen have all but died out. Members who are too old to take part in processions or who die are not replaced. Young men find the confraternities dull and old-fashioned. Some parish priests, faced with the total absence of confraternity members willing or able to participate, have had to resort to hiring men from other parishes in order to preserve the traditional form of the processions. The archpriest of Naxxar, for example, has been obliged to hire confraternity members from other villages to take part in the liturgical procession of the annual *festa*. Naxxarin refuse to take part as they wish to join the *festa* crowd and enjoy themselves. Although Naxxar volunteers still carried the statue of *Marija Bambina* in 1992, their numbers are dwindling year by year. Parish priests no longer have the power to oblige persons to take part in these processions.

In view of MacCannell's (1976) discussion on staged authenticity for tourists, it must be noted that outsiders are hired to ensure that the procession retains its traditional form and conforms to liturgical norms. This staging is done not for the benefit of tourists searching for authenticity, as MacCannell suggests, but to meet the expectations of the Naxxarin themselves and, especially, to keep the parish from losing face before the hordes of critical visitors from other villages. In short, declining interest, competition from other events and a growing manpower shortage caused by the demise of the confraternities are responsible for the decline of many of the traditional rituals.

INCREASE

Parallel with this decline, two sets of rituals have grown in popularity: those celebrating Easter and those celebrating community patron saints. Since 1961 the Good Friday procession has grown from 420 to around 550 participants. The increase includes persons who now participate wearing biblical costumes, a second band to play funeral music and more penitents dragging heavy chains tied to their ankles. The procession accompanying the statue of the Risen Christ on Easter morning has grown from a ragged band of 17 youths and a few musicians to a procession of 130 costumed participants accompanied by a band. Naxxarin now also perform a theatrical pageant of the Passion in the parish church on Holy Wednesday.

The annual *festa* of the Nativity of Our Lady has also increased in scale since 1960. By 1992 it had acquired a noisy demonstrative morning march, the traditional triumphant Eve-of-the-Eve demonstration down St Lucy Street had grown and it now ends with a spectacular firework display. The number of band marches during the *festa* has increased from eight to twelve. In 1986, the *festa* committee, chaired by the parish priest, decided to move the traditional Eve-of-the-Eve parade from St Lucy Street to the wider 21st of September Avenue. The reason given was that the village's Peace Band refused to accompany the parade because it had become 'too wild' and it felt threatened in the narrow confines of St Lucy Street. The residents of St Lucy Street were furious. A group of men and youths from the St Lucy Street area resolved to defy the local authorities and do something about it. They raised funds, hired a band and jubilantly staged their traditional parade. Their defiance of the local establishment gained momentum, and by 1988 they had founded a second band club, located in St Lucy Street.[4] This episode was, in part, a rebellion against Naxxar's establishment by St Lucy Street neighbours who have increasingly been marginalized by both wealthier Naxxarin who have been able to move to the outskirts and by affluent outsiders who have been gentrifying their neighbourhood.

In short, the last quarter of the century has seen an increase in participants, events and the general theatricality of many of the religious events celebrated in Naxxar. There has been a decrease in organized devotional aspects of public religious rituals but an increase in popular festive manifestations such as costumes, theatre, bands, fireworks and boisterous parades. All the celebrations that have grown, except for the Good Friday processions, are insider events that are celebrated chiefly by Naxxarin. As noted, visitors from other villages and foreign tourists are absent during the wild demonstrations. 'Ritual' seems to be giving way to 'play'. Organized devotional processions are giving way to costumed events, band marches and spontaneous happenings.

What is behind these developments? Have Naxxarin retained parish pageantry and expanded it in response to pressure from 'conservative elites' or from a desire to earn money from tourists? Conservative elites have certainly not promoted the expansion of *festa* exuberance. Quite the contrary. Naxxar's conservative elite tried its best to reduce *festa* effervescence. Those intent on protecting traditions and expanding the celebrations were working-class youths and men from the St Lucy Street neighbourhood. Class-based tension between local establishment and opposition interests lies at the root of most factional conflict and the divisions present in so many Maltese villages (cf. Boissevain 1965, 1978, 1988). The growth of the *festa* exuberance has not taken place because Naxxarin are selling their *festa* to tourists. The elements of the *festa* that have expanded — notably the wild parades — take place when tourists are not present. As already noted, these are insider events.

CONTEXT

The chief factor behind the growth of celebrations is a desire to combat the social distance created between erstwhile neighbours by the rapid changes that have occurred since independence. Interdependence of, and thus contact between, neighbours has been reduced by developments related to Malta's rising prosperity. Expanding work opportunities in industry and tourism have meant that most men and unmarried women work outside their place of residence. Villages have become dormitory communities. Most families now own a car (in 1992 there was one vehicle for every two inhabitants) and can leave the village when they wish and return long after 10pm, when the bus service stops for the day. Comfortable government welfare and health benefits have sharply reduced or eliminated dependence on family and neighbours for help. Driven by rampant consumerism to take on a second (untaxed) job, particularly in the booming construction tourist industries, many are also too busy and/or tired to socialize with neighbours. Affluence has created independence but has reduced interdependence, and thus interaction between neighbours.

Increased wealth has also brought about a housing boom that monopolizes free time and keeps people tied to their houses. As old neighbourhoods are broken up, new neighbours stare suspiciously at each other. Because of these developments, Naxxarin no longer spend as much time socializing in the streets, buses, shops, clubs and wineshops as they did in the early sixties. In short, since independence there has been a marked reduction in the interaction between neighbours.

The increase in the celebrations of parish and neighbourhood patron saints and Holy Week is a comment on and a reaction to the increasing isolation of Naxxarin from each other. It is a manifestation of a desire to do something together. People who have grown up together in poverty and are now separated by prosperity try to recapture, for a few moments, the feeling of belonging, or togetherness, of being part of a community. They achieve this by celebrating together. Naxxarin are expanding their celebrations for themselves, not for tourists.

TOURISM

Tourism does affect these popular celebrations. Its role is neither as crude nor as spectacular as the critics of cultural commoditization have suggested. The influence of tourism has been complex. Those who supervise and participate in spectacles such as Holy Week events do not sell themselves. Naxxarin earn little or nothing from their Good Friday pageant. Occasionally the Peace Band Club makes a few pounds renting chairs to tourists. All food and wine shops are closed. In fact, it costs many hundreds of pounds to stage such processions. This money is collected laboriously by the clergy and others organizing the procession.

It is also incorrect to suggest that all tourists are 'amused' or 'patronizing'. Most are fascinated by the solemn pageantry, and many are moved by the devotion displayed by those who take part. Some, of course, are indeed patronizing if not amused. Several years ago I stood behind a Dutch couple watching the Naxxar Good Friday procession emerge from the church. The man, who had been avidly videoing the event, leaned over to his partner and exclaimed in Dutch, 'Jesus! What a heathen business.' Obviously a Protestant of the old school. Certainly, the presence of many tourists during the final two evenings of the *festa* is good for street vendors and club barmen. But, except for fireworks and denser crowds, the scale of celebration during this phase of the *festa* has not really grown.

Tourism is indirectly related to the revitalization of some Maltese celebrations. Rather than merely watch, tourists can actually participate in much the same way as the Maltese do: by mingling with the crowd, eating, listening to music and watching fireworks as the procession slowly winds its way through the decorated streets. Many tourists come from anonymous urban areas in northern Europe. In Malta they become welcome participants in traditional community celebrations. This enables them to share a sense of togetherness, to experience a feeling of solidarity and oneness that transcends their personas as foreigner or outsider (roles that most tourists seek to shed). They momentarily become part of a celebrating community. For many this is a unique experience, and in part it accounts for the growing popularity of Malta's parish celebrations among tourists.

Tourists, through their interest in what are basically traditional working-class village events, have helped to make them more acceptable to the urbanized middle-class elite who previously denigrated many parochial pageants. As was usual in colonies, this class identified with the culture of its foreign masters. Recitals by British Council musicians and Shakespeare's plays were legitimate cultural events; Good Friday village processions and *festi* were not. Yet these events formed part of the indigenous cultural legacy. This heritage has become important to a new nation searching for its cultural identity after imitating much of the culture of its foreign masters for more than 450 years. Thus religious pageantry is beginning to play a new role. It is being accepted by many young intellectuals and, somewhat more grudgingly, by some members of the Anglicized urban middle classes as an important cultural resource. Government interest in the village *festa* and Holy Week celebrations gave them new meaning. Along with sun, sea, prehistoric temples and monuments built by the Knights of Malta, parish rituals are now considered assets that attract tourists. This, in turn, has provided the organizers with a new sense of purpose, stimulating them to expand the celebrations, especially the fireworks. Naxxarin, like the inhabitants of other villages, want a high public presence at their celebrations.

PLAY AND COMMUNITAS

We are still left with the paradox of why most growth has taken place in the ludic, improvised celebrations that are not attended by, though not closed to, tourists, whether Maltese or foreign. The explanation lies in two aspects intrinsic to every celebration: 'ritual' and 'play'. These two modes correspond crudely to the distinction the Maltese themselves make between the 'internal' feast, the celebrations organized by the clergy according to a rigid scenario, and the 'external' feast, the popular festivities that take place outside the church, organized by laymen. The ritual mode has been related to an elite concerned with ritualizing, and so legitimizing, its superordinate position (Manning, 1983:7). Ritual confirms the social order and structure. The ritual mode depends on traditional authority, it reflects and projects what should and ought to be (Turner, 1982:82).

In contrast, the play mode of a celebration is associated with those in socially subordinate positions. It often negates, reverses, challenges and questions hierarchy and rules. In Naxxar, ceremonies that are characterized more by ritual than by play, such as the Eucharistic celebrations, have declined. The ritual dimensions of Good Friday and the various patronal celebrations have remained constant or increased slightly during the same period. But their play dimensions — the theatre, costumes, band marches and wild spontaneous demonstrations — have increased markedly. The increase in the play mode may be seen as a comment on the nature of ordinary life (Handelman, 1977:186). Elements of the 'nature of ordinary life' on which this increase appears to comment include the increasing erosion of interdependence as a consequence of industrialization and the expanding activities of the welfare state as well as the general increase in anonymity and individualism due to industrialization combined with the influx of outsiders (Boissevain, 1991).

The increase in play is more than just a comment on the social order. Play also has instrumental attributes (Handelman, 1987:363). The play mode is instrumental in two ways. It promotes both a sense of identity and a sense of *communitas*. Festive celebrations promote: *individual identity* by providing scope for people to dress up, to be on stage, to take part as individuals in a public event; *neighbourhood identity* by celebrating patron saints and so creating a Durkheimian sense of segmentary solidarity around local symbols; *village identity* via the elaboration of Good Friday and *festa* activities performed for outsiders; and *national identity* by consciously celebrating aspects of Malta's public ceremonial cultural heritage in front of outsiders.

Playful celebrations in which, quite literally, participants let their hair down, put on special clothes, dance and kick up their heels or watch their neighbours doing so promote a sense of community solidarity. Much of the ordinary structure of daily hierarchy disappears as neighbours meet each other in the street or square, invite each other to a club and/or home for a drink. The playfulness creates, for a few hours each year, a sense of what Turner has called existential or spontaneous communitas: 'the direct, immediate, and total confrontation of human identities which tends to make those experiencing it think of mankind as a homogeneous, unstructured and free community' (Turner, 1974:169). Since, as I have argued above, there is a growing sense of isolation, of estrangement due to rapid industrial and social development, it is not surprising that especially the playful dimensions of the celebrations have grown.

COMMODITIZATION RECONSIDERED

The celebrations of the Maltese have not increased because they sell their 'culture by the pound'. The growth of Holy Week and *festa* celebrations represents a conscious attempt by Maltese villagers to renegotiate their social boundaries. These celebrations have become less religious, less concerned with the transcendental and more instrumental (Vassallo 1981:57–8).

While Malta is indeed now selling its colourful rituals to tourists, this commoditization is not destroying them. On the contrary, it has imbued them with new meaning. On the other hand, critics of commoditization, like Greenwood, Vassallo and Xuereb, are correct in pointing out that these celebrations have in part become separated from 'the solemnities that originally gave them birth'. The celebrations perform these new instrumental tasks, *in addition to* the religious and entertainment tasks of yesteryear.

First of all, parish celebrations now serve to define the boundary between self — we Naxxarin — and the new Others, the outsiders who have moved into the village and the foreign tourists. Second, they are used to recapture the sense of community for people who have less and less contact with each other as neighbours or who have moved elsewhere but were once closely knit. They also serve as vehicles for expressing Maltese culture to visitors from abroad. They are also occasions used by the modernized urban (mostly young and educated) elite to explore and take part in events that are part of their cultural heritage. Finally, they provide neutral occasions for neighbours divided by politics to meet.

In spite of the overt commoditization of some religious pageantry, the religious rituals of which these form a part are very much alive. Commoditization of outdoor celebrations is accepted and even encouraged by organizers. The tourists increase the sought-after audience for the main events on the Eve and the day of the *festa* and on Good Friday. The number of tourist buses parked at the edge of a celebrating parish, like the quantity and quality of the fireworks, have become markers in the competition between parishes.

To sum up, the commoditization of culture to attract tourists does not necessarily have the destructive effect postulated by Greenwood. The observation is not new (McKean, 1989; Stott, 1979), nor is it surprising. But it is worth restating in view of the increasing interest in, and promotion of, cultural tourism (Urry, 1990).

This discussion should not be interpreted as a signal to stop guarding against the encroachment/intrusion/incursion of tourists. Over the past 30 years, Maltese authorities have extended the definition of culture beyond the domain of archaeologists, art historians and folklorists to include that of anthropologists: 'the way of life of a people' (Hatch, 1985:178). This is modifying the tourist industry's past lack of interest in Malta's back regions. Some agencies have recently organized tours to 'Malta's Forgotten Villages'. In one village, Qormi (a town of 19 000!), tourists are taken to visit a bakery and a band club bar, where they are served cheese cakes and drink their tea out of glasses like the locals do. Both bakery and band club welcome tourist interest. Because tourists are unaware of this, and cannot find their way there, such areas can be marketed as back regions and evoke a frisson of 'violation', of penetration into an authentic, intimate area.

Cultural tourists, increasingly bold, are also setting out on their own to look at what has been sold to them: the way of life of the Maltese. In

September 1993, friends celebrating the *festa* of St Leonard in Kirkop discovered two Germans peering about inside their house. The curious couple, in the village with a *festa* tour, had simply walked through the half-opened glass inner door into their brightly lit front room. Our friends politely showed them out. They then closed the heavy wooden outer door that is always left open during the *festa* so that the festive decorations can be seen from the street.

Other anthropologists have recently reported the stumbling about of tourists in domestic back regions in Sardinia, Austria, the Lofoten Islands (Odermatt, 1991; Droog, 1991; Puijk, 1996). Such episodes will multiply as cultural tourism is marketed to the masses. 'That is the perversity. The commoditization of culture does not require the consent of the participants' (Greenwood, 1989:180).

NOTES

1. With thanks to Inga Boissevain, Vicki Ann Cremona, Tony Ellul, Godwin and Maryanne Ellul, Maria Farrugia and Anna Zammit for their help.
2. There is one exception. The procession of Our Lady of Sorrows has no audience; villagers either take part or conceal themselves out of a sense of shame for not joining it.
3. But this feeling may change when villages are actually confronted with numbers of tourists during insider events. On Gozo, Malta's sister island, the villagers of Nadur reacted to the growing number of expensively costumed Maltese tourists whose presence was destroying the essence of their central carnival activity; non-recognition by fellow villagers during the ludic costumed parade. They now only don their masks on Shrove Tuesday, after the weekend visitors have taken the ferry back to Malta. Though Nadur villagers were initially pleased with the Maltese attention, they came to realize that outsiders spoiled the intimacy of their celebration. Hence they redefined the boundaries of their carnival. Tuesday has now become a 'back region' protected by the fact that visitors from Malta by then have returned to work and thus are sure not to come (personal communication from Vicki Ann Cremona). It is evident that front and back regions are fluid concepts that can change over time. (See Boissevain, 1992:12–13 for further discussion of the emergence of back regions as a reaction to tourist attention).
4. Three years previously, a group in the neighbouring town of Mosta, Naxxar's arch rival, intent on expanding the wild demonstrative parades of the *festa*, also against the wishes of their parish priest, had established a second band club.

REFERENCES

Boissevain, Jeremy (1965) *Saints and Fireworks, Religion and Politics in Rural Malta*, London: Athlone Press.
Boissevain, Jeremy (1978) 'Of men and marbles: notes towards a reconsideration of

factionalism' in M. Silverman and R.F. Salisbury (eds), *A House Divided? Anthropological Studies of Factionalism*, : Memorial University of Newfoundland, pp. 99–110.

Boissevain, Jeremy (1984) 'Ritual escalation in Malta' in E.R. Wolf (ed.), *Religion, Power, and Protest in Local Communities*, New York: Mouton, pp. 163–83.

Boissevain, Jeremy (1988) 'Festa Partiti and the British: exploding a myth' in V. Malia-Milanes (ed.), *The British Colonial Experience 1800–1964: the Impact on Maltese Society*, Malta: Mireva Publications, 215–29.

Boissevain, Jeremy (1991) 'Ritual, play and identity: changing patterns of celebrations in Maltese villages', *Journal of Mediterranean Studies*, 1, 87–100.

Boissevain, Jeremy (1992) 'Introduction' in J. Boissevain (ed.), *Revitalizing European Rituals*, London: Routledge.

Boissevain, Jeremy (ed.) (1996) *Coping With Tourists: European Reactions to Mass Tourism*, Oxford: Berghahn Books.

Droog, Marjolijn (1991) 'En dan wordt je weer gewoon mens' Het opleven van feesten in een Oostenrijke dorp, unpublished MA thesis, Department of Anthropology, University of Amsterdam.

Greenwood, Davydd J. (1989) 'Culture by the pound: an anthropological perspective on tourism' in V. Smith (ed.), *Hosts and Guests, the Anthropology of Tourism*, 2nd edition, Philadelphia: University of Pennsylvania Press, pp. 171–85.

Handelman, Don (1977) 'Play and ritual: complementary frames of meta-communication' in A.J. Chapman and H. Foot (eds), *It's a Funny Thing, Humour*, London: Pergamon Press.

Handelman, Don (1987) 'Play' in Mircea Eliade (ed.), *The Encyclopedia of Religion*, Vol. 2, New York: William Pith, 363–8.

Hatch, Elvin (1985) 'Culture' in Adam Kuper and Jessica Kuper (eds), *The Social Science Encyclopedia*, London: Routledge and Kegan Paul, 178–9.

Koster, Adrianus, Yme Kuiper and Jojada Verrips (eds) (1983) *Feest en ritueel in Europa, antropologische essays*, Amsterdam: VU boekhandel/Uitgeverij.

MacCannell, D. (1976) *The Tourist: a New Theory of the Leisure Class*, New York: Schocken.

Manning, Frank E. (1983) 'Cosmos and chaos: celebrating the modern world' in Frank E. Manning (ed.), *The Celebration of Society: Perspectives on Contemporary Cultural Performances*, Bowling Green, Ohio: Bowling Green University Press.

McKean, Philip Frick (1989) 'Towards a theoretical analysis of tourism: economic dualism and cultural involution in Bali' in V. Smith (ed.), *Hosts and Guests, the Anthropology of Tourism*, Philadelphia: University of Pennsylvania Press, 119–38.

Odermatt, Peter (1991) Over de nuraghen en wat verder over de zee kwam! Een onderzoek naar het tourisme in Sardinë, unpublished MA thesis, Department of Anthropology, University of Amsterdam.

Puijk, Roel (1996) 'Dealing with fish and tourists. A case study from Northern Norway in J. Boissevain (ed.), *Coping With Tourists: European Reactions to Mass Tourism*, Oxford: Berghahn Books.

Stott, Margaret (1979) 'Tourism in Mykonos: some social and cultural responses', *Mediterranean Studies*, 1, 72–90.

Turner, Victor (ed.) (1982) *Celebration: Studies in Festivity and Ritual*, Washington DC: Smithsonian Institution Press.

Vassallo, Mario (1979) *From Lordship to Stewardship: Religion and Social Change in Malta*, The Hague: Mouton.

Vassallo, Mario (1981) 'Pageantry and secularisation — the Malta case' *Melita Theologica*, 32, 50–8.

Weber-Kellerman, Ingeborg (1985) *Saure Wochen Frohe Feste. Fest und Alltag in der Sparache der Bräuche*, Munich and Luzern: Bucher.

Werdmolder, H. (1979) 'Karnaval anders bezien. Een studie naar het organisatorische aspect van het karnaval te Venlo', *Volkskundig Bulletin*, 5, 1–20.

Xuereb, Paul (1979) 'Review' of Mario Vassallo, *From Lordship to Stewardship: Religion and Social Change in Malta*, *Sunday Times* (Malta), 16 September, 10.

7 Tourism and the Politics of Authenticity in a North Cotswold Town[1]

CRAIG FEES

One of the forms that tourism takes is the resident tourist: the immigrant for whom the locale is a leisure backdrop to a 'real' life lived primarily elsewhere — in the past, in the case of retired persons; in the present, in terms of commuters and of holiday/second-home owners. These leisured immigrants, for whom leisure is the primary function of the locale, present a challenge to the rest of the population which can be characterized in the questions: who and what is the place for? Is it for people from outside, who wish to experience its beauty (for example)? Or is it for people who live and work there and whose children muddy grassy banks with their bikes?

The dilemmas thrown up when two populations attempt to live in the same place while holding radically different answers to these and similar questions — and the constructive role that an anthropologist might play in their resolution — are discussed in this chapter in the context of the recent history and development of an English town which discovered its own potential as a tourist venue at the end of the last century and has been 'discovered' continuously since. This is set against the backdrop of the question of 'authenticity', with particular attention to the role of narrative traditions and discourse in the definition of authenticity, 'belonging' and identity.

There are a number of British TV programmes concerned with the evaluation of the antiques people discover in their lofts and back rooms. Typically, a panel of experts which travels Britain, takes a local hall and provides expert analysis (and usually a valuation) of the objects in question. Someone might bring in a particularly attractive flower pot which their mother bought years before at a car boot sale for five shillings and be told that it is, in fact, a particularly fine and rare example of a sought-after potter's work and therefore worth five or six hundred pounds. Another will arrive with a prized painting which has hung proudly in the family dining room for generations, only to be told that it is a 19th-century

The Tourist Image: Myths and Myth Making in Tourism. Edited by Tom Selwyn.
© 1996 John Wiley & Sons Ltd.

reproduction and therefore, effectively, worthless. What was formerly a utensil on the kitchen window-sill suddenly becomes an object of art which must be insured and put on display, and what was a source of family pride is just as suddenly relegated to the spare room or perhaps taken to a car boot sale and sold. In neither case is the object itself changed — what changes is the meaning ascribed to it and the world it evokes.

This illustrates several points. First of all, it shows that 'authenticity' is not a quality of objects in themselves but is something which is ascribed to them; second, that objects are authentic because someone with the authority to do so says they are; and third, that the experience of an object as authentic or otherwise has practical consequences.

One of those consequences has to do with the nature of objects themselves, which are never 'alone', so to speak, but are always part of a world which they evoke and invoke. For example:

> I am in Wyoming, in the United States, and, walking through a field with my brother. I kick up what appears to be an arrowhead and, yes, on examining it I find that the shape and flaking rule out natural causation: I determine that it is authentically an arrowhead and — based on what I know of Wyoming and American Indian culture — that it is an authentic American Indian arrowhead. It becomes a potent artefact of a bygone era to which I belong as an American, and I show it to my brother. He points to a tumbledown building in the neighbouring field and tells me that it is the remains of a Japanese–American internment camp, set up here during World War II. He then tells me that these Japanese–Americans made thousands of arrowheads to sell during the war. What I found was almost certainly one of these. The arrowhead itself is unchanged. But what is evoked by it now is an entirely different world: of native Californians packed off to the hostile and cold plains of Wyoming, their businesses sold at knock-down prices, lives and careers ruined because of their ancestry. The arrowhead's meaning and value change.[2]

Transpose this now to contemporary Britain, where a piece of wasteland scheduled to be bulldozed for a new motorway is redefined as a Site of Special Scientific Interest. That designation, that authentication, brings a whole machinery into play. The world evoked by the motorway — of cars, cities and transport-sector special interests — crashes up against the world evoked by the SSSI — of a vanishing Britain, fragile eco-cultures and green activism. A legal machinery is set in motion, as is a political machinery and a social and economic machinery. The object itself — the land — has not changed. But because it has to be authentically something, whether that something is authentic wasteland or an authentic reserve of rare and endangered species — it becomes the object of a social, cultural and economic contest. What is at issue is where the authority ultimately resides to determine the meaning, value and use of the land. It must be authentically *something* — even, to paraphrase Brown (Chapter 2), authentically fake.

Figure 7.1 Campden cyclist, circa 1910. Reproduced by permission of The Guild of Handicraft Trust, Chipping Campden

The question is: where does the authority to ascribe that authenticity lie? The answer is: at the Centre. The 'Centre', of which Selwyn speaks (Chapter 1), is where the authority to ascribe authenticity resides. The 'Periphery' is that which accepts the authority, or, to look at it in less consensual terms, the Periphery is where the authority of the Centre holds sway, where its definition of what things are and mean holds.

Authentication is the province of authority. It is what authority does, and it is through authentication that authority (and all it represents in terms of power and capacity to move in and effect the world) is. But 'authority' is complex. There are different kinds of authority, which may or may not conflict, coincide or compete; and the same kinds of authority may have different domains. An expert, like those in the TV programmes about antiques, is *an* authority (and only in one particular field), but there are also people *with* authority (charismatic leaders, for example, who can authenticate through their presence the truth of a particular vision); people *in* authority (the minister or civil servant whose decision will eventually determine the fate of the motorway vs the SSSI); and there is the *authority of tradition*, for which certain people have the right to speak (the owner, for example, before the painting is shown to be a reproduction).

Figure 7.2 Campden Market, early 1900s. Reproduced by permission of
The Guild of Handicraft Trust, Chipping Campden

By the definition of 'authority' all of these can claim to be at the Centre
or to be Centre. But what happens when two or more Centres attempt to
occupy the same space? For example, what happens if the owner of the
painting refuses to jettison family tradition and accept the authentication
of his painting as a reproduction? The expert insists. The owner asserts
his authority and the authenticity of family tradition against the authority
of the expert, countering assertions of inauthenticity ('crank', 'trouble-
maker', 'ignorant amateur') by asserting the inauthenticity of his oppo-
nent ('quack', 'pompous self-serving know-nothing', 'snob'). The authority
of 'family tradition' is attacked by the art historian; the authority of
'art historian' is attacked by the owner. There is the struggle for the
authority to define and thereby to determine the nature and outcome
of things (heirloom or fake/motorway or nature reserve). There is the
drive to inauthenticate, to trivialize, to extend one's authority to authenticate, to peripheralize the Other. There is the politics of authenticity, in
full cry.

Because it involves the assertion of authority to authenticate others — to
define who and what they are and therefore what should happen to them
— the politics of authenticity is also the politics of identity; and where
distinct cultures are in competition for the Centre from which their mutual
identities and relationships will be determined, it becomes the politics of

Figure 7.3 Maypole dancers, Campden, 1905. Reproduced by permission of The Guild of Handicraft Trust, Chipping Campden

ethnicity as well. Transpose all of this now to the rural English town of Chipping Campden, Gloucestershire.

THE DEVELOPMENT OF TOURISM IN CAMPDEN

Chipping Campden (or Campden) is a small rural town and parish in northern Gloucestershire, England, 12 miles southwest of Stratford-on-Avon in the North Cotswolds. During the past century the principle industry of the area has shifted from agriculture to tourism.

The origins of the modern tourist industry in Campden can be traced to events of the late 1870s. At that time Campden was the administrative, market and political centre of the North Cotswolds, and it had what, in contemporary terms, were various urban features, including slums, dense housing and overcrowding. While agriculture and its ancillary industries and businesses (basket-making, cartwrighting, blacksmithing, land and property management) were at the centre of the local economy, the local middle class indulged the urban rural idyll, taking picnics and holidays in the 'country' and kept up with and contributed to the latest fads and fashions of the city. The town as a public body was characterized by a self-conscious sense of progress and growing prosperity within the

Figure 7.4 Campden Morrismen, circa 1965. Reproduced by permission of The Guild of Handicraft Trust, Chipping Campden

context of the Empire, as evidenced in new public buildings and civic amenities.

In the late 1870s, however, Campden was hit by the Agricultural Depression. Between the censuses of 1870 and 1901, in the crippling economic conditions of a depression which went on and on, the population of Campden fell by nearly a quarter. Houses fell empty, businesses closed and Chipping Campden faced the dilemma that British mining and ship-building communities are facing today: to diversify, to attract new invest-ment and new industries, to provide opportunities for the young and to hold onto the skilled work-force, or to become an economic, social and political backwater. In Campden this meant, among other things, attracting inward investment in the form of new middle-class residents, each house-hold of which employed numerous maids and help of various kinds, increased local trade, paid rates and perhaps rent. It also meant attracting shorter-term residents, who brought many of the same benefits, mainly during the summers; visitors, resident for a few days or weeks; and people visiting Campden for the day or as a brief stop during a tour. In short it meant developing the tourism industry, transforming Chipping Campden into a retirement and tourist venue and actively identifying, promoting and enhancing features which would attract people to the town.

Conceptualizing Chipping Campden as a tourist attraction required a fundamental cognitive shift in which the working political, social and economic centre for the local agricultural industry was recognized and authenticated as a desirable and marketable entity in its own right. Prior to the Agricultural Depression there was simply no need to regard Campden in this way; it was visited and admired, but there was no great motive to transform that admiration into an active tourism industry. In the 1880s and 1890s and concurrent with a shift in the local balance of social and political power from agriculture to trade, the necessary cognitive shift took place. 'Campden' was explicitly recognized as a marketable entity, with qualities such as 'beauty' and 'antiquity' which could be singled out, developed, advertised and sold. It was argued that in developing 'Campden' in this way all parts of the community would benefit, from farmers and traders, to working men and landlords, to members of the gentry who would benefit from the enhanced social life which would follow.

Initially it was not primarily the beauty and antiquity of the town but its possibilities as a health resort which were publicly recognized:

> We have, I say, in that copious flow of excellent water, and in the natural gifts around us, undeveloped stores waiting to be worked for the good of this town, and of thousands of our neighbours, for whom a retirement (temporary or permanent) from city life is an absolute necessity.[3]

It soon became clear, however that the major attractions for the contemporary tourist were the town's antiquity, its historical associations, (Civil War ruins; Robert Dover's Games; 'The Campden Wonder') and its beauty and the beauty of its setting. Efforts were made to develop these. In order to enhance the setting, for example, trees were planted along the High Street. New buildings, such as the Catholic Church, were intentionally designed and constructed using recycled stone and/or local and compatible materials in order to blend in with the extant architecture. The Town Trust made an order prohibiting the storage of farm carts in the Market Hall in the centre of the High Street, on the grounds that they disfigured the picturesque old building. The first history of the town was written. The self-conscious theme of 'Ye Olde Campden' emerged in local entertainments for the first time and in a series of elaborate Whitsun celebrations in the late 1880s designed to promote the town and its trade, 'Campden' was reframed for public consumption in images of Merrie Englande drawn from the antiquarian repertoire of the day: Robin Hood and his Merry Men walked the streets alongside May Queens, floral carts, Yeomen of the Guard, morris and maypole dancing. The campaign to promote visitors was a success: the only industry which definitely grew in the 1880s and 1890s was tourism.[4]

The real coup in the campaign to promote Campden as such, however, came in 1902, when 150 men, women and children came *en masse* to establish the London-based arts and crafts firm, the Guild of Handicraft, in Campden. The Guild was in the *avant garde* of the international Arts and Crafts Movement, and its well publicized move to Campden — attracted by the town's image and setting and by the availability of premises within convenient distance of the railway — was a radical and unique realization of back-to-the-land Guild Socialism. As such, as an ambitious socio-industrial experiment, the Guild itself became an object of considerable tourism; indeed, the volume of visitors to the new Guild workshops was such that visiting times and visiting charges had to be established to help keep the numbers from interfering too much with the craftsmen's work. Until the business failed in 1907–8 the Guild was a major Campden attraction, akin to a modern heritage centre, such as Ironbridge or the Black Country Museum in England ('I have seen the past, and it works'). Indeed, even after its winding up, the Guild continued to play an important role in promoting tourism to Campden, and may be on the verge of playing a greater role still.[5]

Tourism slowed during World War I, but afterwards there was a dramatic boom. Cars and charabancs brought increasing numbers of day-trippers, while overnight visitors, certainly in the years immediately after the war, occasionally over-saturated the commercial capacity to house them and could be found knocking on the doors of private houses trying to find someone who would take them in. The town's fame as a tourist venue grew steadily, abetted by broadcasts and publications which pictured it as a reservoir of an agricultural way of life and an honesty and depth of an unspoiled rural character which was rapidly disappearing elsewhere. Along with 'beauty' and 'antiquity' tourists therefore came to Campden in order to discover and engage with the authenticity of the rural 'character', the farmer or farm labourer who carried the wisdom of the soil in his bones and the untutored eloquence of a past era in his speech. It was a period in which labourers and other local people could and literally did play a part in the local tourist industry.

Following World War II (the massive military tourism of which has paid and repaid dividends in the form of returning ex-soldiers) this inter-war style of tourism temporarily re-emerged. Gradually, however, has come the demand that Campden be rural in a different way: that it cease to be a working, boisterous and earthy agricultural community and become instead a quiet gentle place of rest and respite from the cares and worries of the city. During this period the Cotswolds have been set aside by Parliament as an 'Area of Outstanding Natural Beauty', and the centre of Campden itself designated a conservation area. It has thereby been authenticated by the state and declared as a site of outstanding aesthetic and historic merit and officially bracketed off from the urges and pressures of modern develop-ment. Within the current tourist industry Campden, in common with the

Cotswolds generally, is primarily promoted as a beautiful and peaceful retreat.

THE PERIPHERALIZATION OF CAMPDEN

The development of tourism in Campden has been paralleled by its economic and political peripheralization, a process familiar throughout Britain. In 1870 Campden, for most purposes, was its own unit of government. National legislation was implemented largely through the vicar, the farmers, the traders and the other prominent residents who lived in and around the town. It was they who, for the most part, took local decisions concerning roads, water, sanitation, education, the welfare of the poor and so on. Crown and County offices — Inland Revenue, police — were manned in the town by people who lived there. The centre of daily life, on the background of national imperial life, was therefore local. Local political life was vigorous; religious and social life were intense; the locus of the politics of authenticity was very much and for the most part focused on people one lived among and knew.

This has largely changed. Administratively, a succession of government acts has shifted authority over most areas of public life from Campden to increasingly distant District offices, to the County, to London, and now, more and more, to Brussels. The shift in Centre is reflected in most areas of life: against protests from local farmers and warnings from local working-men, successive Education Acts have imposed urban-oriented structures and curricula which prepare local children for urban, not rural-centred lives and industries; and of course to pursue their personal development such children have tended to move from Campden. Individual wells gave way to a town water system, which was appropriated to a district system, which was taken into the national system, and is now, through sale by the national government, in dispersed private ownership. The local train service, postal sorting station, telephone exchange and, recently, the magistrate's court have gone. Alongside this have been the technological developments — the telephone, car, radio, television — which have dispersed the cultural and communication centres of everyday life and tended to place them elsewhere.

All of this reflects the receding of the Centre from Campden. This means, in lived terms, that for most practical and governmental purposes the authority to authenticate Campden has been withdrawn from the town and lodged with people who live in suburbs and cities, who work in offices and for whom the daily life of an agricultural district has little reality. Campden has become a satellite, firmly in the Periphery, of a Centre which has effectively moved, as it were, from Campden to London, whence significant elements of it have been dispersed in the national and

international culture of bureaucracy and business. Campden, in that sense
— and as experienced by local people — no longer belongs to Campden.

LOCAL VS INCOMER

My introduction to Chipping Campden came through the back door. When
I arrived in England from the United States in the autumn of 1981, my
intention was to focus my research and energies on a defunct mumming
custom in Yorkshire, mumming being a perambulatory Christmas custom
historically performed by working men. My tutor suggested going up to
Campden, which still supported a living mumming, to ask its leader
whether he would be bringing the custom out that year, and if so whether
I might come back and see it; and with that in mind I was walking towards
Campden with a backpack full of camping and recording equipment when
the blizzard of December 1981 set in. I sought refuge in a smallholding just
outside the town and explained myself to my accidental host. He took me
in hand, and by the time the snow had thawed sufficiently for public
transport to take me back to the University of Leeds his energetic intro-
ductions and facilitations had entrenched me in fieldwork and engaged my
commitment to Campden.

The way in which I came into it meant that all of my fieldwork at that
point and for some time after was among 'locals'. It was therefore from this
perspective that I became aware of a rupture at the core of everyday life
down or around which every local complaint and conflict seemed to run.
What I was introduced to was the notion that there were two populations
in the town. On the one hand were 'incomers', resident outsiders as it
were, who were relatively wealthy, had moved into Campden from cities
and suburbs, who bought up local properties at outrageously high prices,
formed and joined various Societies from which Campden people were
excluded, were on all important local committees, who pulled strings and
had contacts in high places which made it possible to impose their ideas on
the place, and who were for the most part retired people, second-home
owners or commuters. Furthermore, they came and went. After a few years
in Campden they died or sold their properties at a profit to new wealthy
incomers and went elsewhere. It is for this population that I have used the
term 'resident tourist'.

'Local people', on the other hand, among whom were native
Campdonians, were the ordinary people of the town. (The term 'local' is
unfortunately an ambiguous one, which I shall in this chapter be using as
defined here. I was momentarily set on the wrong track recently when,
speaking with an 'incomer', he said 'We really must keep local people
informed of this.' He then went on to define 'local people' in terms of
members of the local amenity society and the local historical society — in

the membership of which local/native people form a distinct minority). I am using the term 'local people' to apply to those largely working people, who could not afford the high property prices created by the Incomers and whose children therefore had little if any prospect of being able to stay in Campden once they left home. Those young people who could live at home faced unemployment or poor career prospects because restrictions on change and development insisted upon by Incomers and outside organizations (such as the Council for the Protection of Rural England) virtually precluded the development of any new industries apart from those which were tourist or service oriented.

These restrictions were intended to 'preserve' Campden. The effect, however (I was told), was that 'Campden' was dying. The town was being turned into a museum, from which real Campden people were being forced to emigrate, and in which they were not even wanted. During a spate of Welsh nationalist burnings of English holiday homes in the 1980s an elderly informant in Campden shocked me with the vehemence of her support; but hers was simply an extreme version of what other people were saying to me.

THE INCOMERS' MYTH

Because of the backward way in which I came into fieldwork it was some time before I began to read the standard historical literature on Campden, written almost exclusively by immigrants and outsiders. When I did so it was with eyes already conditioned by local informants and by the search I had begun through the primary sources — the local newspaper (first published in 1860) and so on. Against this background the narrative I encountered in the standard secondary literature appeared strange and distorted. It was written as history, but it did not reflect the world presented in oral and contemporary sources, and indeed the Campden of the secondary literature seemed sometimes altogether detached from the place described by the newspaper reports and letters to the editor, government reports, petty sessions records, diaries, school logbooks and the rest of the primary record. I began to realize that what was presented almost universally in books and magazines, television and radio programmes, tourist guides and journals as the history of modern Campden was in fact a Myth. It also became clear that this Myth was based on the traditions of a particular group of immigrants: the Guild of Handicraft and those most closely associated with it. What was treated as history was in fact tradition, with the sense given by Martin Heidegger (1978:43) that tradition 'takes what has come down to us and delivers it over to self-evidence . . . and makes us suppose that the necessity of going back to these sources is something which we need not even understand'. The narrative had been so self-evidently true for so long that virtually no writer — immigrant or outsider — had felt it necessary to go beyond the Guild-based story to the local historical record. It also became clear that one needn't previously have been aware of the detail of the Campden narrative to have shared essential elements of it. The Campden narrative is a local variant of a national urban-centred view of the countryside, which is itself an introspected form of the British myth of Empire, which in itself gives power to the self-evidence of the narrative.

The Myth goes basically as follows: in 1902 the Guild of Handicraft, led by C.R. Ashbee, moved to Campden from the East End of London. At that time Campden was a morally and physically decaying village, with a feudal social structure dedicated to resisting any improvement in the lot of the labourer.

Beneath the contemporary surface decay, however, was a 'little forgotten Cotswold town of the Age of Arts and Crafts which industrialism had never touched, where there was an old silk mill and empty cottages ready to hand, left almost as when the Arts and Crafts ended in the 18th century (Ashbee, 1908:42). The Guild set about sweeping the corrupt old order out and bringing new order in: creating productive commercial workshops in healthy arcadian surroundings, while simultaneously restoring genuine life and traditions to the countryside.

Passive and peaceful, grave with the weight of antiquity, Campden 'was like the Sleeping Beauty waiting to be awakened by Prince Charming in the person of Mr Ashbee' (letter from H.T. Osborn to Fiona MacCarthy, 1.5.81; cf. Fees, 1986), and under his touch sprang to life. A swimming bath was built so that the children of Campden could grow up healthy and strong. A School of Arts and Crafts was opened in the face of entrenched opposition from the Earl of Gainsborough (the lord of the manor and principal landowner), local farmers and the governors of the Grammar School: 'not because they wanted to hurt the Guild or its enterprise, but because they considered that anything in the nature of educating the labourer would endanger the local labour market'.[6] Areas of local farm workers' culture were reborn, thanks to the Guild. For example, 'The Brass Band was reinvigorated by new blood and was provided with uniforms. The Morris Dancers and the Christmas Mummers' Play were revived and reinvigorated.'[7]

In 1907–8 the Guild broke up, but a dedicated core of Guildsmen remained and formed the nucleus for new generations of aesthetically aware and sensitive immigrants, similarly dedicated to Campden and the effort to preserve and save it from the 'follies and futilities', the 'bad and ugly work of the great towns'.[8] Pre-eminent among these was F.L. Griggs, RA, Campden's 'most distinguished inhabitant during the years from 1904 to 1938' (according to his friend Christopher Whitfield (1958:237) who himself immigrated to Campden in 1924). Among his many achievements for Campden, Griggs persuaded the Post Office to run its telephone lines into Campden underground, thus leaving the skyline unspoiled by wires.

Whitfield observed:

> It is remarkable that *all those* who have fought to preserve the town have been people drawn from elsewhere by its beauty to live in it. Often they have had to fight not only against the current of modern 'civilisation', but also against those Campden people who have wished their town to become prosperous and modern at the expense of its unique atmosphere.[9] (emphasis added).

Whitfield also remarked that the history of Campden in the 20th century has been 'a record of the deterioration of the idyllic town . . . a growing urbanisation, both outward and inward . . .'[10]

The Myth is one of discovery, rebirth and decay, in which local people and the modern world conspire against the principles of new life and beauty represented by the Guild and since taken up by others. The fountainhead of the Myth is C.R. Ashbee, leader of the Guild, whose articles, books, manuscript *Journals* and typescript *Memoirs* create a persuasive foundation. Ashbee had a private income and a Cambridge education, and he was a Morris and Ruskin-inspired Guild Socialist reformer who made no pretence of needing, liking or accepting the social order in Campden. He spent most of each working week in London — an archetypal commuter — and took his holidays elsewhere. He was resident in Campden, but his centre was not its centre. In Campden terms he was an urban eccentric, and had he been on his own he would perhaps have been isolated and made harmless, inauthenticated as a crank; but he was surrounded by a small group of similarly liberal and artistically minded people within the Guild and was one of a number of artistically oriented immigrants attracted to Campden both before the Guild's coming and after. Furthermore, as a member of the Art Workers Guild and of the broad Socialist liberal reform movement of the day, Ashbee drew support from many well-known and well-connected people, many of whom visited him and were introduced to Campden through him. Consequently, from the point of view of the outside world, or of a literate and influential part of it, Ashbee became and for the most part remains the authoritative spokesman for life and society in early 20th-century Campden.

Before the move to Campden Ashbee held the firm view that rural life in the industrialized West had become pale and lifeless in the wake and shadow of industrialism and that the health of society needed to be revitalized. He imported this personal myth to Campden, and publicly and privately inauthenticated the daily life of Campden and its customs as fake. For example, in the Christmas 1903 entry in his unpublished *Journals*, held in the Modern Archives of King's College, Cambridge, Ashbee characterizes the locally eminent chairman of the Parish Council and Campden public life generally in these terms:

Farmer Stanley is a splendid type of do-nothing . . . On the days when he is really at work, for one can hardly call public business of Campden work, he wears a white overall, or as they call it here the milking slop. That is a misnomer, for I'm sure he never milks, and he is much too friendly and gracious with everybody to devote much time to any real occupation . . . Farmer Stanley plays at reform; he likes to pretend that he means it; he knows that he does not mean it at all . . . (Quoted with kind permission of Felicity Ashbee.)

This string of negations, or inauthentications, echoes throughout Ashbee's *Journals*, as, for example, in his June 1906 entry, where he epitomizes modern rural celebration in his description of the Viscount Campden's coming of age party: 'I think everybody except perhaps Hodge and I would have been convinced by today's pageantry. It seemed so very real and everybody was made so happy.' He simultaneously authenticated the architecture — the shops and cottages built in an earlier era — as forgotten jewels from the great pre-industrial tradition of craft building. 'Campden' as a living society he declared corrupt and fake; 'Campden' as architecture and setting he declared real. In so doing he laid out the fundamental terms in which the history of Campden has since been written.

The Myth arising from this eliminates the 'Campden' of Campden people — social and cultural 'Campden' — and authenticates the town in terms of its architecture and setting, as a beautiful wasteland open to immigration and development. The fact that it was a lively town at the turn of the century and that it was through local work and publicity that the Guild was ultimately attracted to Campden are lost. The fact that cottages were not 'ready to hand', but that labourers had to be evicted to make room for the higher-paid Guildsmen is lost. Local contemporary sources show that Campden people can not be characterized *en bloc* as passive or opposed to the education of the labourers — indeed, I have shown (among other things) that it was only after Ashbee was forced to accept local farmers on to the Board of the School of Arts and Crafts that its classes really became popular among labourers — a high proportion of students beforehand would appear to have been persons of leisure, dilettantes and hobbyists. I have also shown that those farmers most castigated by Ashbee for their resistance had a long history of promoting technical education, better conditions and higher wages for farmworkers (Fees, 1988a). The Guild never had anything to do with the Mummers, and it did not revive the morris, both quintessentially 'Campden' customs. The town band was a going concern, the creation of the swimming bath can be seen by reference to its history as the clever exploitation of a wealthy new resident to achieve a desired but expensive local amenity without cost to the parish. The record shows that local people were very involved in the beauty and preservation of Campden before the Guild came and that it was local people who met and negotiated with the Post Office to have telephone lines run underground. The record also shows that Campden people spoke up in the inter-war period when F.L. Griggs flourished but were denied a voice or were consistently ignored. Having been peripheralized, and having been inauthenticated, they became invisible.

The Myth is a narrative of, by and for Outsiders, some of whom have settled in Campden, and it is believed because it is part of a tradition and mythology to which they belong. It is one version of a national myth, the roots of which lie in the mythology of the Empire, the central concern of which is the nature of the Periphery and its relation to the Centre. It is a myth of foundation — the foundation of 20th-century Campden and the coming of outsiders to save it. It is an authenticating myth, authenticating a particular tradition as history. It is teleological, providing that tradition and the people who take it up with a foundation of meaning and purpose within Campden. And it is a myth of appropriation, arrogating 'Campden' to those people.

As 'history' written by immigrants or outsiders, the Myth gives immigrants authority at the centre of local culture and history. Where natives appear they are placed firmly in the periphery: as innocents, 'characters', eccentrics, incompetents or in some way corrupted by that impure world outside of Campden which is intent on destroying it. As history, it establishes the right of immigrants, or incomers, to authority in and over Campden; it displaces those who were born there or who have merged with it to become 'local', and it makes the local invisible in the politics of authenticity. Incomers/resident tourists fill the place, and thereby its centre, and there is no room left for Campden people. Along with the peripheralization *of* Campden, there is an extended peripheralization *within* Campden.

PERIPHERALIZATION, LOSS AND THE POLITICS OF IDENTITY

Though one can find elements of localism and the politics of identity in Campden prior to World War I, the first public expression of 'Campden' as an ethno-political position dates from 1921. At that time the Town Trust, which had been formed by the Charity Commissioners in 1886 to look after town property, decided to send Campden's two town maces to London for safekeeping. The maces dated from the time of James I, and had lain safely, if unseen, for some years under a local bed, but the Trust took the decision to make a long-term loan of them to the Victoria and Albert Museum and to replace them in Campden with exact replicas for display. The immigrant chairman of the Trust at the time was the internationally known stained-glass artist Paul Woodroffe, and although there were 'Campden' people on the Trust, and immigrants among the opposition, when the plan became unexpectedly known in the town, the unprecedented protest which blew up characterized it as a contest between 'Old Campdonians' and 'new-comers', between 'local' and 'London'. To these opposing centres were attached the authenticating/inauthenticating pairs: 'elected' vs 'appointed'; 'public' vs 'secret'; 'open' vs 'conspiring'; 'forthright' vs 'innuendo'; 'courage' vs 'fear'; 'fair/just/popular' vs 'autocratic/austere'; real objects of Campden history vs fake replacements.[11]

Prior to this the politics of authenticity had been waged in conventional political terms of class and political affiliation, of 'old order' against 'new order', Liberal against Tory. But over the course of World War I there had been a massive change in Campden, and in wrestling with this change, another significant cognitive shift took place. 'Campden', as the world in which local people lived and discovered self and belonging, was explicitly posited and formally recognized as such: as a particular 'place', a world, an intangible object which was filled with cherished meanings and value. The mechanism behind this was straightforward: one in five Campden men found themselves serving in the war and being absent from Campden had the chance to experience it as an explicit world of people and things which they missed. One in five of those who served was killed, which heightened for their survivors the experience of the world which had been evoked and invoked in Campden by them. For the better conduct of the war central government imposed regulations, many of which were aimed at industrial cities and did not make sense in a rural setting, were arbitrary or incompetent, which offended local autonomy and which highlighted the familiar local world which such things attacked and changed. The 'Campden' of local people and their local life and heritage, which Ashbee and those around him had declared fake, became intensely real and precious in its absence and loss and in the face of changes imposed and supported by outsiders.

In short, during the course of World War I the people of Campden discovered that what they had taken for granted and used everyday as if it were a common and inexhaustible resource was actually an object of rare and priceless value. This was discovered, moreover, in the context not only of its loss through the war but through its theft and appropriation by people who were not part of it, had no legitimate birth-claim to it and indeed did not understand it. This fundamentally altered the politics of authenticity in Campden which emerged as the politics of localism, in which the authenticating pole of 'Campden' was opposed for the first time to the inauthenticating pole of 'Not-Campden' ('newcomer', 'London'). Within this process the ongoing peripheralization of Campden acquired a new dimension in which the two centres or positions of authority which were 'not-Campden' — Incomers and Outsiders/Government — appeared to be working together to the exclusion of the third, the Local or Campden position.

The working of this latter pattern can be seen as early as 1892 in the nearby town of Broadway, Worcestershire, where a group of influential

Birmingham people (Birmingham being some 30 to 40 miles away as the crow flies and the principal commercial and industrial centre in the region) intervened with Worcestershire County Council and stopped it repaving the streets of Broadway with blue bricks because, as one of the group said:

> Broadway is essentially an old English village, almost unique in having for the most part escaped the desecrating hand of the 'improver' and the avarice of the jerry-builder. It is in this that its attractiveness to the outsider and the visitor chiefly consists, and no surer means of driving him away can be devised than levelling the place up or down to a standard of suburban trimness.

He suggested that a 'Defence Association' be formed 'for which I am sure many outsiders would subscribe, *to protect themselves from the encroachment of this sham and shoddy age of "improvement"*'[12] (emphasis added). To which a local resident responded:

> ... because certain private individuals in Birmingham, occasional visitors to Broadway in fine summer weather, 'don't like the look of blue bricks', the work is stopped! Whom should the County Council consider in the matter? The inhabitants of Broadway and their convenience and comfort in all sorts of weather, or the fads and would-be antiquarians of Birmingham or elsewhere?[13]

In almost identical terms the local (but by no means 'local') secretary of the Gloucestershire Society of Antiquaries (and others) argued successfully in 1934 against plans for a practical replacement of the town hall in Campden, a scheme supported by local people because it would have meant a parish hall large enough for full-scale parish meetings, large-scale dances, even a cinema:

> Here in Campden our duties are plain [said the Secretary]. We are custodians of a very beautiful town and it's up to everyone to see to it that first of all the town is not harmed ...

> I should like you to remember that it is not only the people who come into this building who have to be considered; *it is perhaps more the people who stand outside and look at it* (emphasis added).[14]

The appropriative 'we' of the outsider/incomer (a local farmer had asked in vain, 'Would it not be possible to have some real Campden people on the Committee — Campden-born and bred?' and was answered: 'This is not the time and place for these distinctions. I think with any proposal of this kind Campden is in need of the help of every one of her sons and daughters whether they were born here or adopted')[15] reflects back to the Myth of the Incomer, to the fact that, within that Myth, 'Campden' consists of its architecture and setting, Campden exists for those who can appreciate it from outside; and in the end, where the other 'Campden' of local life and society is a consideration, it is at best secondary.

It also reflects the gradual exclusion of 'Campden' people from the determination of Campden. Although the 'local' position won in the town maces affair in 1921–22, and the maces stayed in Campden, the indications are that those who had 'adopted' Campden were progressively occupying its centre. By the 1930s, one sees local people appealing to be heard (as the farmer, above) but left out of organizations and committees. A local tradesman recounted in 1983 how he and other local tradesmen lost their traditional role in putting together local celebrations when immigrants appropriated the organization of the 1935 Jubilee and 1937 Coronation celebrations.[16] Elsewhere (Fees, 1988a), I have discussed various areas and instances of appropriation.

This external authentication of 'Campden' as its architecture and setting has become increasingly statutory in post-war legislation: Campden has become part of the Cotswolds Area of Outstanding Natural Beauty, and the town centre as a whole has been designated a conservation area, effectively transforming the town and its setting into the heritage and beauty equivalent of an SSSI. Following the National Parks and Access to the Countryside Act 1949, the Historic Buildings and Ancient Monument Act 1953 and the Town and Country Planning Act 1968, for example, fields, field-dividers and woodlands which before had been private property used in farming became statutory objects of beauty. Their 'beauty' became a legal entity, an officially recognized property, the ownership of which was appropriated to the Nation. Buildings which, before legislation, had been either a house in which people lived, or a shop or a town hall in which public meetings were held likewise became objects of outstanding beauty and historical interest. Their 'beauty' and their 'historical interest' became entities, and these were similarly nationalized. The woodlands, the fields, the buildings were not changed — indeed, that is the whole point. But what can be done to them, and who may determine that, has changed, and the power has gone out of local hands. They no longer belong simply to Campden or to the people who live and work in the town. They belong — through peripheralization, reconceptualization and appropriation — to the 'us' of the nation, or indeed, of the world, and their meaning is to be there on call for when 'we' should want to come and appreciate them.

DISCUSSION

The politics of authenticity arise when two or more competing claims are made to the authority to determine what a thing is and what (and who) it is for, and for the most part the politics are waged in terms of inauthentication

GREETINGS from Chipping Campden

Figure 7.5 Christmas card, circa 1955. Reproduced by permission of The Guild of Handicraft Trust, Chipping Campden

and periphalization. The latter is to do with power, with the assertion of and acquiescence to or acceptance of authority. The former is to do with negation, a denial of the other's right to a place in or to a positive relation to the Centre. To say that something is not real, for example, or is not really what it claims to be — to say that it is a 'fake'; to call a person's argument 'nonsense'; or to say that a person or thing is decayed or corrupt (or criminal) — is to state that it has no standing *vis-à-vis* authenticity and the claim and counter-claim in the politics of authenticity.

In Campden, the two main competing centres in the politics of authenticity can be referred to as 'locals' and 'incomers'. Being 'local', in this sense, means belonging to the world of symbols and narrative structures which are recognizably local, as founded in people whose centre is firmly there and not outside, whose sense of self exists in the people of the place, in their discourse and in the place itself. At the core is the 'native', the Campdonian 'Campden-born and bred'. Because it is a phenomenological 'place' the boundaries of the local constantly change, depending on speaker and context. There are variable dimensions (of class and so on), and the boundaries themselves are capable, for example, of variously including and excluding people who could technically be called 'immigrants':

While I am talking to the leader of the Mummers an old man goes by who lays a family-based counter-claim to the custom. On this occasion the leader of the Mummers seeks to inauthenticate the other by telling me that he's a 'moonman', ie crazy. On a later occasion he says that the 'moonman' is not actually from Campden, the he was born in the nearby village of Willersey. This means that he can have no real claim to Mumming, the essence of which is that it is thoroughly of, by and for 'Campden'.

On still another occasion, however, when we are discussing incomers I put my foot in it by assuming that the elderly man (despite having spent his entire life there) is still not 'Campden'. I am brought up short by the forceful assertion that he certainly is, and the leader of the Mummers shows no sense of recognition that he ever said otherwise. Though rivals when it comes to authority *vis-à-vis* the Mumming, in the context of discussing incomers with me, both are authentically 'Campden'.[17]

The local life of Campden is rich in the discourse of authenticity, with 'local' people contesting authority among themselves over certain customs or in respect of certain historical facts and events. It is in belonging to this and its many levels and subtleties that one is 'local'.

Incomers, on the other hand, however much they would like to appropriate it, do not belong to the local discourse. That is the sense of the term 'incomer', which is a locally devised, inauthenticating one, with a slightly derogatory tone. In practice it indicates people who are wealthy enough to move into the town, who come from a different, urban-centred culture, who do not take the 'local' as centre and do not allow themselves to be drawn into its orbit, who instead import a centre around which they expect the local to gather, who adopt and who belong to the narrative tradition based on the Guild which firmly places the incomer at the centre of modern Campden history. Immigrants who assimilate to the local, and who do not attempt to appropriate, override or dictate to it do not necessarily become 'local', but they also do not tend to fall into the category of 'incomer'.

While the term 'incomer' is that used in Campden, I have used the term 'resident tourist' at different points in this chapter in an attempt to underline the real and phenomenological relationship between the 'incomer' and the tourist. The migration of the one and the immigration of the other are manifestations of a single social and cultural process, the roots of which are in the peripheralization and appropriation of Campden. Both tourist and incomer have their origin outside Campden in a world for which Campden is peripheral, firmly and safely tucked out of the way, a centre of retreat, respite, retirement: the contrary pole to their authenticating Centre, which is, speaking abstractly, the City. To put it another way, incomers and tourists belong to the Modern, the cognitive Centre whose characteristics have been delineated by Heidegger (1977, 1978, 1985), Berger et al. (1973), Baudrillard (1988) and others. On to Campden, as the archetypal old English village, is projected the opposite of the Modern — with its underlying alienation, its break-up of belonging, its ceaseless reorganization, its change, its destruction of the past and its flight from the present, its tilt towards the maximum yield at the minimum expense, its proliferation of containing and defining structures and therefore of bureaucracy and ramified uniformity, the avarice of the jerry-builder and the sham and shoddy age of 'improvement', to quote the Birmingham defenders of turn of the century Broadway. It brings to Campden its relentless framing and re-creation as a picture, as a place to be set aside and as an object on hold and on call for whenever its use by the City may be called for.[18] It brings to Campden the concept that it belongs not to itself, but to Others; and that in becoming a commodity it belongs to whoever can afford it, or whoever has the power to appropriate it.

The politics of authenticity operate on many dimensions and on some of these — eg on the level of straight economic self-interest ('not in my backyard') or where ethnic or social division are explicit and entrenched — the anthropologist can't really expect to have a major impact. But where, as in Campden, there are dimensions which owe more to taken-for-granted cultural stereotype, tradition and myth, and impoverished knowledge of and communication among protagonists, the anthropologist can have an impact, can help to bridge or heal the rupture and can contribute in however small a way to happier solutions to local distress. To do that, however, one must have a clear idea of the source and nature of the rupture; and in Campden, at any rate, that brings us back to the question of 'authenticity'.

'Authenticity' is not only a characteristic ascribed to objects (as discussed earlier) but is also, to use Selwyn's phrase, an '"alienation-smashing" feeling'. 'Authenticity' in this sense is an *experience* — an authenticating experience — where what is authenticated is one's Self, in and through one's experience of an object as authentic. This experience does not relate to the *actual* authenticity of an object, but to an individual's perception of the object as authentic, and in itself has an alienation-smashing quality of wholeness and fullness and of 'timelessness' which makes it much sought after, particularly where the lived world is alienated, fragmented and situated in the hurly-burly of commercial/industrial time. 'Authenticity' in this sense becomes a commodity in its own right, and the possibility of obtaining it is projected into (ec)-Centric objects and places (bringing a whole world of myth and expectation with it), which are thereby filled up to the exclusion of whatever might have already been there in the way of local or competing claims or understandings.

What we experience in the 'discovery' of 'authentic' objects is the discovery of our own authenticity. Having discovered it, we become reluctant to lose it or let it go and may well return for it again and again, ultimately taking up residence. The Modern seeking authenticity becomes a tourist; becomes a resident tourist; and driven by the sense of an impending loss of something which, having been lost once (wholeness, beauty, sense of purpose), must not be lost again, establishes societies and associations to preserve things as they are. But as their experience of their own authenticity is mediated through *things*, and is experienced as a quality or characteristic of places or objects outside themselves, it is those *things* which they feel must not, at all costs, be allowed to change; the culture in which those things were formerly embedded and which lodges a counter-claim to those things is inauthenticated, made invisible, peripheralized.

Change, in this sense, is seen as what is negative in what the City in its alienation has become — but which the 'village' has not yet become, though pointed towards it. This is one source of the rupture between Outside and Local: what is 'present' for the local is 'past' for the tourist; what is participation in the national economy for the local is a race towards a present from which the resident tourist has fled, viewing it with dread or at least with the dis-ease characteristic of the Modern, and as a threat to the sense of their authenticity.

Another source of rupture lies in the nature of the local. For those born and brought up in a place, it has the character of always having been, and of always having been the way it is. It, and any processes of change from within, is taken for granted as part of what it is. Being the world in which one has grown up, it acts as a holding-place of memory, it gives a continuous and taken-for-granted reflection of the Self, wherein one's Self is continuously unfolding. Whereas the incomer discovers a 'forgotten' self in the 'forgottenness' of the countryside, and is self-conscious in that discovery, the native dwells in an already-discovered world in which the Self is constantly developed and encountered and in which meaning and understanding of the Self are constantly given back by encounters with and in this world. Change which comes abruptly, unexpectedly and imposed from Outside is not simply 'change', therefore, but is experienced as a catastrophe, a deprivation and loss of Self, of identity.

Historically, the 'discovery' of Campden by the City (by the Guild of Handicraft and its successors) came as a wresting of Campden away from local people, who shared a broadly common culture and were already developing Campden's potential as a tourist and residential venue. Outsiders and immigrants who were determined to save Campden from the City allied with one another and, in the consequent proliferation of organization, regulation and securing which are characteristic of the Modern, and in the attempt to 'save' Campden, they overwhelmed it. Local ways of doing, of seeing and meeting situations, of organizing fêtes and customs were either not perceived at all or were perceived as already corrupted by the City — in decay, defunct, degenerate. In the logic of Modernization, in the ironic flight of the Modern from itself, the authentically rural culture and society of Campden were overridden by Modern solutions and conceptualizations at an increasing rate and with the consequence that locals were increasingly denied access to themselves *qua* 'Campden': to the Campden not simply of architecture and setting but to the Campden of countless formative experiences and encounters, of Self, of the local grammar of discourse and change.

Heidegger speaks of the 'phenomenon in which surroundings, especially the most familiar ones, become a compelling presence when something is missing in them'.[19] World War I created a great and continuous 'missing' which firmly propelled 'Campden' into the forefront of local consciousness as a compelling presence, as that which had been lost and was also continuously threatened. Tourism, resident tourists and the actions of the government and other outside organizations have ensured that this 'compelling presence' has remained in the forefront of local consciousness as that which is continuously on view and threatened. To be 'Campden', to be locally born and bred, became an ethnic position — and it consequently became and remains an explicit pole in the politics of authenticity.

This ethnicity, this discovery of Self and identity in belonging to the locality and its people, has found itself and its expression in fewer and fewer elements of local life as greater dimensions of this have either been seized and reserved for the use of incomers or have lost significance in the diffusion of general contemporary culture. These remaining elements have therefore taken on greater significance. However hidden or unvalued an item or a custom may have been in the everyday world before the centre of culture slipped away from the local, this deprivation has isolated it and brought it to the fore as a sign. However insignificant it might have been beforehand, the item now becomes an icon and celebration of 'Campden' — and therefore acquires an especial value as that which brings 'Campden' into being, which continually revives and renews it and which thereby asserts 'Campden' against the claims of Outsiders and Incomers who would try to inauthenticate or appropriate it. It becomes a badge of 'Campden' and a pole in the politics of authenticity.

We see this heightened significance displayed particularly in customs: either in a greater or more intense awareness which brings a custom into unprecedented prominence; by a proliferation of occasions on which a particular ritual is publicly performed; or by the revival and creation of customs (see Fees, 1988b), all of which have ramifications not only locally but in terms of the tourist industry. Through what is invested in them, customs become an assertion of possession, of belonging, of the authority and of the authenticity of the 'local'. With access to most of the effective economic, social and political sources of authority in Campden denied to locals, the assertion of the 'local' is increasingly displayed in performance, in the symbolic discourse through which the local is defined.

The anthropologist is peculiarly situated to understand this symbolic discourse and to speak it in a way that the Modern can and perhaps will hear, understand and reflect on. By listening and recording, and by the seriousness of his or her research, the anthropologist can also affirm the local in its sense of its own authenticity and broaden its understanding of the processes in which it is involved. Through the privileged position of belonging to both and neither, and on the fulcrum of authority of the 'expert', the anthropologist can help bring about a change not in the things themselves but in the way they are viewed. And in the end, if that change of view is rooted in the authenticity of the situation, and in the way that things authentically are, then this is a considerable and practical power. It is the power of transforming a politics based in the self- and ethno-centric disregard of others immanent in inauthentication and peripheralization into a politics based on mutual recognition of one another's authentic-ness, out of which flows a new basis of communication, resolution and unexpected possibilities of change.[20]

NOTES

1. This study builds on field, archive and library research carried out from 1981–8. A detailed description of that work, with full citation and support, is available in Fees (1988a).
2. Personal experience, March/April 1989. My brother is Dr Paul Fees, Senior Curator at the Buffalo Bill Historical Center in Cody, Wyoming.
3. *Evesham Journal* (1887), 28 May: 3.
4. Based on commercial listings in *Kelly's Directory*. See Fees (1988a: appendix B).
5. With the creation in Chipping Campden of the Guild of Handicraft Trust, dedicated to the creation of an archive and study centre on art, craft and design as such, with particular reference to their history and practice in the North Cotswolds.
6. C.R. Ashbee, *Memoirs*, Vol. 2, 'Introduction 1938', Part II, Sept. 1903–Dec. 1906: p. 215. The unpublished *Memoirs* are held in the Modern Archives of King's College, Cambridge.
7. Christopher Whitfield (1958) *A History of Chipping Campden*, Eton: Windsor Shakespeare Head Press, p. 237.
8. C.R. Ashbee (1903), quoted in 'Campden's Beautiful Houses', *Evesham Journal*, 4 April: 6.
9. Ibid.: 238.
10. Ibid.
11. The continuity of the tradition is apparent in the rhetoric of localism since World War II, in which 'Native' is contrasted with 'Incomer'; 'real Campden people, working People' with 'snobs, toffs, hoteliers, tradesmen': elected representatives with the self-appointed members of the local amenity society; 'socially oriented/native industry' with 'tourist-related industry'; 'living/ working environment' with 'museum/preserved quality'. See Fees (1988a:489).
12. *Evesham Journal* (1892), 3 December: 5.
13. *Evesham Journal* (1892), 'A Disgusted Ratepayer', 12 December: 7.
14. *Evesham Journal* (1934), 24 March: 11.
15. Ibid. For the appropriative 'we', see, for example, F.L. Griggs, 'The Foreword Read to the General Meeting March 20th 1925 written by F.L. Griggs', *Campden Society Minutes*, Gloucestershire Record Office D2857 1/1: 'we resent anything that is not of Campden . . . In Campden we call it "Campden".' Broadcaster Georgie Henschel, who lived for a brief time in Campden in the early 1950s, adopted the appropriative 'we' for the benefit of interviews about the place: see, eg BBC Written Archives Centre; Scripts; Holt, William and Georgie Henschel: *Festival in Britain*, broadcast on General Overseas Service

18.9.1951, 1700–1715 hours. The original Campden Society was a short-lived 'Defence Association' as was called for in Broadway in 1892 (see below), created by immigrants and outsiders to 'save' Campden.

16. Lionel Ellis, Ellis family tape, Cassette 79. Mr Ellis concluded: 'That was the start of Campden people not bothering. I'm sure of it.' Quoted with kind permission of Dorrie Ellis.

17. Fees, Field notebook 2:20.2.1982. Personal experience.

18. Heidegger, in Heidegger (1977), p. 130 remarks: 'The world does not change from an earlier medieval one, but the fact that the world becomes picture at all is what distinguishes the essence of the modern age.' This reminds one of C.E.M. Joad's comments (as related in R.I. Wolfe (1966), 'Recreational Travel: The New Migration', *Canadian Geographer* 10:6. 'That it would be said of his generation that they found England a land of beauty and left it a land of beauty spots.' Heidegger also (1977), pp. 16–17, in discussing the nature of modern technology remarks that, 'Everywhere everything is ordered to stand by, to be immediately on hand, indeed to stand there just so that it may be on call for further ordering. Whatever is ordered about in this way has its own standing. We call it the standing reserve.' Tom Selwyn, in a personal communication, draws attention to the similarity of Marx's conception of a 'standing reserve army' of the unemployed.

19. Heidegger (1985:189).

20. It would be unrealistic to expect wonderfully dramatic changes all the time, and it is part of the sorrow of anthropology to see destructive forces going forward in front of one's eyes. But I am aware through my own work, for example, of a greater respect for the integrity and authenticity of a custom previously considered by many in the town to be disreputable and right for appropriation, and a more critical approach to the absolute authority of C.R. Ashbee and the Guild-based tradition of the town's history, with a greater understanding among some, at least, of the dynamics surrounding appropriation and the fear of appropriation. These are small things, but not inconsequential, and can be seen as part of a national and global shift in the understating of our impact as tourists and immigrants on a world which exists before we come into it, and hopefully endures after.

REFERENCES

Ashbee, C.R. (1908) *Craftsmanship in Competitive Industry*, Campden and London: Essex House Press.

Baudrillard, J. (1988) *Selected Writings*, Cambridge: Polity.

Berger, Peter, L., Briggite Berger and Hansfried Kellner (1973) *The Homeless Mind: Modernisation and Consciousness*, Harmondsworth: Penguin.

Fees, Craig (ed.) (1986) *A Child in Arcadia: The Chipping Campden Boyhood of H.T. Osborn 1902–1907)*, Chipping Campden: Campden and District Historical and Archaeological Society,

Fees, Craig (1988a) Christmas Mumming in a North Cotswold Town: With Special Reference to Tourism, Urbanisation and Immigration-Related Social Change, PhD thesis, Institute of Dialect and Folk Life Studies, University of Leeds.

Fees, Craig (1988b) 'Maypole dance in the twentieth century: further studies of a north Cotswold town', *Traditional Dance* 5/6, 97–134.

Heidegger, Martin (1977) *The Question Concerning Technology and Other Essays*, trans. William Lovitt, New York: Harper Torchbooks.

Heidegger, Martin (1978) *Being and Time,* trans. John Macquarrie and Edward Robinson, Oxford: Blackwell.

Heidegger, Martin (1985) *History of the Concept of Time,* trans. Theodore Kisiel, Bloomington: Indiana University Press.

Whitfield, Christopher (1958) *A History of Chipping Campden,* Eton, Windsor: Shakespeare Head Press.

8 Atmospheric Notes from the Fields: Reflections on Myth-collecting Tours

TOM SELWYN

The purpose of this chapter is to explore several features of walking tours (*tiyoulim*) in the Israeli countryside organized by the *Society for the Protection of Nature in Israel* (hereafter SPNI). The present account complements an examination of the centrality of the landscape to Israeli ideas of nationhood which appears elsewhere (Selwyn, 1995). The two pieces might fruitfully be read together. It is also hoped that the present chapter will be read alongside those in this volume by Bowman and Golden and that all three will be taken as contributions to an understanding of the symbolic architecture in a corner of the Eastern Mediterranean which has, arguably, provided the richest imaginable seam of religious, nationalist and tourist mythology.

CONTEXTS

Most of the material presented here is taken from participant observation in some 30 walking tours in Israel over a period of about a decade from the early 1980s to the early 1990s. These were, for the most part, organized by the SPNI although a small amount of data derives from similar tours organized by another Israeli tour company, Neot Hakikar. Apart from written diaries on the tours themselves, the data is also drawn from extensive taped interviews with travellers and the management of both companies.

The tours, parts of which are described here, are characteristic of a kind of approach to Israeli geography, history and society known as *Yediat Ha-aretz* or 'knowledge of the country', and the main intention is to give some insight into the process through which such knowledge is constructed in the process of tourism in the Israeli countryside.

Following some very brief and general remarks on nationalism, excerpts from field notes taken during actual tours will be presented. A conclusion

The Tourist Image: Myths and Myth Making in Tourism. Edited by Tom Selwyn.
© 1996 John Wiley & Sons Ltd.

reflects on the way in which the myth themes upon which the tours appear to be structured might also find their way into larger projects concerned with weaving a tapestry of nationalist mythologies.

Underlying the present chapter are a set of widely known ideas about nationalism. These include Gellner's (1983) and Hobsbawm's (1983:263–307) observations that nations and nationalist traditions are invented rather than given and Anderson's (1983:14–16) idea of the nation as an 'imagined community'. Because of the self-evident fact that such inventive imagination needs to be transformed into active nationalist *will* if it is to bear practical results, Kedouri's (1960:81) assertion that 'Nationalism is, in the first place, a method of teaching the right determination of the will' is also taken as axiomatic.

One of the most vital of the ingredients which make up any programme of nationalist invention is that bundle of symbols which link a people with a territory. Terms such as 'motherland' create feelings of natural and fundamental ties between land and people and serve nationalist rhetoric well for that reason. And it is, indeed, the landscape itself, as Smith (1983:185) has pointed out in relation to Russian landscape painting, which often provides the most potent imagery for the nationalist imagination.

But it is not a matter merely of the inculcation of feelings of attachment of people to land. Beyond that, as Barthes (1973) has pointed out in the case of the *Guide Bleu*'s instructions to the European bourgeois traveller about how to view Alpine landscape, lies the association of land and landscape with particular values. The value systems are substantially different in each case, but Barthes' notion of mountain walks as expressions of what he calls 'Helvetico–Protestant morality' (which includes 'regeneration through clean air . . . summit climbing as civic virtue' and so forth) serves as a model here for an interpretation of Israeli *tiyoulim* as expressions of virtues of a definitively Israeli kind.

It will become apparent that MacCannell's notion of the tourist as one seeking holistic visions of society and history (cf. Chapter 1 of this volume) plays a significant role in the present chapter. So do the notions of such writers as Wright (1985) and Frow (1991) regarding the attractiveness of nostalgia in historical moments of conflict and uncertainty. The former discusses the appeal of institutions such as the National Trust in contemporary Britain in terms which are not dissimilar from MacCannell's. For an urban tourist — fresh from an environment of inner-city decay, unemployment, public-service cuts and racial tension — rural manor houses, which have become the centres of the Trust's concern, appear as representative of the authentic and powerful heart of the national heritage. They are attractive because the symbolism surrounding them suggests answers to fundamental questions about 'where we have come from, where we are and where we are going' which are at once simpler, grander and more readily comprehensible than those suggested by the experiences of everyday life in the city. In the Trust's domain, among the lavender bags, embroidered cushions and rolling parklands, one may encounter, Wright (1985:24) argues, 'the nation [working] to re-enchant a disenchanted everyday life'. As he observes, nostalgia beckons most beguilingly at moments of dislocation.

It is hoped that the relevance of these ideas will become clear shortly. It will be argued that, for an Israeli, the experience of the *tiyoul* provides precisely those conditions under which the imagined community of the nation, as a pure totality as it were, may be recovered from the more complex and fragmented experience of everyday life in a modern plural society.

In a now widely known article on the historical roots of *tiyoulim* and the guiding traditions associated with them, Katz (1985) makes the following points. *Tiyoulim*, Katz argues, quoting from Mark Twain's *The Innocents Abroad*, have their origins in the Holy Land tours conducted in the 19th century, by companies such as Thomas Cook, for European travellers 'seeking evidences', as Mark Twain put it 'in support of their particular creed'. As Twain wryly observed, tour guides helped 'Presbyterians [find] a presbyterian Palestine . . . Baptists a Baptist Palestine . . . Catholics, Methodists and Episcopalians a Catholic, Methodist and Episcopalian Palestine'.

Later on, in the late 19th and early 20th century, Jewish immigrants adapted this tradition of touring the country in order, says Katz, to 're-establish links with the biblical territories' and to 'concretise earlier religious links with the land of Israel'. At the same time these trips, some of which, following contemporary German education traditions, were organized by High Schools and were designed to acquaint pupils with the geology, geography, botany and zoology of the country. It is this combination of scientific and biblical studies which came to be known as *Yediat Ha-aretz*.

In 1920, the Histadrut, the labour federation, was founded and a Committee of Culture set up under its aegis. The function of this committee was to establish and supervise adult education classes for newly arrived immigrant workers. Many of these had previously had experience of Jewish Youth movements in Central and Eastern Europe (movements which in turn had been influenced by the European Boy Scout and German *Wandervogel* movements). Walks and tours were organized by these classes as part of a general programme of *Yediat Ha-aretz* study. A sizeable number of workers participated in such *tiyoulim* and they became a widely popular form of leisure pursuit. *Yediat Ha-aretz* courses developed and expanded through the thirties and forties until in 1953 an institute near Tel-Aviv was established for the sole purpose of developing this programme of study.

Katz's account ends with a description of how, in the changing social and political atmosphere of the mid-fifties, which was marked by the declining role of the *Histadrut* in Israel's cultural life, the SPNI arose and from then on, soon with the active support of the government, carried forward the banner of *Yediat Ha-aretz* study.

There is just one point, adding to Katz's authoritative account, worth emphasizing here. (In making the point, the help is acknowledged of several colleagues, friends and informants. These include Dan Rabinowitz, Asaria Alon and Tuvia Gelblum — the latter two were members of the Palmach, the élite commando unit of the pre-state army, the *Hagana*.) The suggestion is that we should not only treat with some care Katz's view of the early 20th-century *tiyoulim* as 'concretising earlier religious links with the land of Israel' but also give slightly fuller recognition to the fundamentally secular tradition underlying *tiyoulim* throughout the first half of the century. It may be useful to recall Eisenstadt's (1985:115) conclusion that: 'As for the reconstruction of a new collective identity, the religious component was not very active in the period of the Yishuv, nor in the first stage of the State of Israel, and the more secular orientations were much stronger.'

Furthermore, as Eisenstadt (op. cit.) points out, the various socialist pioneer and youth movements were not only, as Katz himself says, connected closely with the workers' education movements but also, later on, with the 'upper echelon of the *Hagana* . . . and *Palmach*'. In other words it seems sensible to emphasize strongly that part of the touring tradition derives, first, from Marxist and revolutionary rather than biblical thought and, second, from those state-building fighting units which were located firmly within that tradition. I will return to this point later, and here simply emphasize Katz's main thesis: that *tiyoulim* began with 19th-century Christian pilgrimages to the 'Holy Land' and developed in the *Yishuv* period primarily under the *Histadrut* and labour ideology.

The SPNI was founded in 1950 by a group of academic biologists whose background lay in the kibbutz movement and the *Palmach*. In the early years the society was not concerned with organizing *tiyoulim*; their main effort was directed towards lobbying the government to set up nature reserves. In 1965 the government set up the Nature Reserves Authority which now operates some 80 reserves. The touring side of the society's activities began modestly in the mid-fifties and expanded steadily through the sixties, by the end of which they had established about 10 field schools and had also attracted support from the army, which allowed a certain number of women soldiers to work for the society as tour guides from these field schools. The SPNI's touring activities expanded after 1970, when the Ministry of Education decided to subsidize the society's *Yediat Ha-aretz* course, the backbone of which was their field trips. Nowadays the SPNI runs a large number of tours for Israeli adults and families. Most tours last from one to eight days and are conducted in Hebrew, but there is also an extensive programme of tours for English speakers. The SPNI also has nearly 30 field schools. Each of these host some 60–70 groups per year for school children, with about 120 children in each group. As a consequence, half the SPNI's budget comes in subsidy from the government. A considerable number of women soldiers work for the SPNI as guides and it has a substantial full-time and part-time staff.

In short, the SPNI was started by scientists whose principal interest lay in nature conservation and is now a very large organization whose main activity is arranging tours and operating field schools around which these tours are based.

FRAGMENTS FROM A TOURIST'S DIARY

The following are selected excerpts from the diary of the present writer from accounts of tours in which (with the exception of the final one) he participated.

SUN AND WATER

Much of the trip to the Zaki tributary of the River Jordan consists of a five-hour walk and swim down the river. We entered the stream from a glade of trees and bushes which, the guide explained, contained the seven natural products identified in the Book of Deuteronomy as being representative of Israel (wheat, barley, grapes, figs, pomegranates, olives and honey). Part of the Golan region, before the 1967 war the glade had been an orchard belonging to Syrian farmers.

From there we alternately walked and swam down the stream. The stones under foot were slippery and people fell over from time to time. Clothes got wet, but quickly dried off in the sun. The water, coming from the mountains, was cold while the outside temperature was contrastingly hot. Periodically we stopped to pick and smell flowers and other plants growing on the side of the stream. Many of these had biblical names. Towards midday the journey became more difficult and several people experienced real difficulty in negotiating the now wider and deeper stream. The guide offered an easier route across dry land, but no one accepted it.

CLIMBING AND FALLING

A comparable tour is the one to the Yehudia canyon, although this tour is longer and more difficult and involves considerably more physical skill as we had two steep downward rock climbs (both in the path of waterfalls) and a steep climb up the canyon, all at the conclusion of the trip. Our guide told us that an average of two people per year suffered fatal falls in this area. We were advised to follow his lead very closely. The main part of the trip consisted of walking, swimming and picking wild fruit. We also saw flocks of birds of prey riding on the thermal currents far above our heads; we had been given a scientific lecture on these birds the previous evening. At the end of the trip our guide told us about the plans of the Israeli water authority to draw water from the Yehudia to ease the perennial water problems in the country.

MAGICAL BEETLES

On the first day of the six-day tour to the Eilat region we were taken up to a spot in one of the mountains which cluster around the town from where we could see, not just neighbouring peaks, but the Red Sea and across into Jordan and Saudi Arabia. At this point we were given pieces of differently coloured transparent paper and told to look at the view through them. The effect of this was intended to be 'magical'. The magical power of colour was emphasized by our guide shortly after this multicoloured viewing. We were shown a black beetle on our path. Our guide explained that not only did his colour keep him warm on cold winter mornings but that the colour black helped male and female to see each other clearly before mating; it was said that if one placed a piece of black paper in front of the beetle, the effect on him was so powerful that he would attempt to mate with it.

JOKES AND DANGER

Wherever possible the tours include an element of physical danger. On a trip to another mountain near Eilat our tour was conducted down a canyon wall by way of a route which at one place passed through a small hole between two boulders with sheer drops down from narrow ledges on the boulders' far sides. An easier route around the boulders enabled the less adventurous to avoid the danger and discomfort of the main way, while the 'real men' of the party had an opportunity to demonstrate their skills and bravery in taking the harder path. There was an amount of physical tension and excitement. People made jokes in the face of shared danger. On a safer spot at the base of the canyon, the guide explained the history of the rock formations in the region.

ROMANS, SYRIANS AND UNITED NATIONS' RESOLUTIONS

On the way to Mount Hermon our bus passed along a road on the eastern shore of the Lake of Galilee. Eucalyptus trees had been planted along the right-hand side of the road and the guide explained that these had served, during the Syrian control of the Golan, to hide their view of the road. We passed buildings still marked by Syrian gunfire and were told that before 1967 this area had been extremely dangerous for the residents of the Israeli settlements. We then drove up the mountain road to the new settlement of Gamla. Our guide explained that this hamlet (now a successful farming co-operative) had been built quite deliberately following a 1975 United Nations General Assembly Resolution that Zionism was racist. From a vantage point in new Gamla our guide pointed to the site of ancient Gamla, a settlement described by the Jewish Roman historian Josephus Flavius, whose inhabitants, rather as the Maccabees had resisted on another occasion, had heroically resisted the Roman conquest of their town for a considerable length of time. (The message here, at least, seemed very plain. As old Gamla was to the Romans, so new Gamla is to the United Nations. Both stand as powerful symbols of Jewish independence and solidarity against the forces of imperialism or external interference.)

IN AND OUT OF THE DESERT

In the Eilat field school, where the SPNI tourists stay, the pictures on the wall remind tourists of the geographical and historical features of the place. There are framed biblical sayings. One says: 'The children of Israel were travelling from the Red Sea through the desert. Three months after leaving Egypt they arrived at Sinai.' Another says: 'We were slaves and God delivered us [from Egypt].' In another frame is a picture of a Beduin woman herding her goats. Particularly at Passover, of course, when tourist families in the field school celebrate the *Seder* night, but at other times of the year too, the proximity of the Sinai desert and the Egyptian border is emphasized. Daily and nightly trips into the hills and desert around the field school combine with pictures and photographs of local Beduin, bringing to mind the appearance of ancient nomadic figures. All of this combines to produce a strong sense of shared experience and solidarity with the biblical children of Israel.

One of the features of the natural landscape, which plays a dominant role in the tours from the Eilat Field School, is the Syrian–African Rift Valley. Attention is drawn, for example, with particular emphasis, to species of flora and fauna which, originating in Africa, have migrated along the path of the rift valley, northwards to the area around the field school.

This rift valley is a fissure in the earth's crust which makes a natural 'corridor', stretching from Ethiopia to Southern Turkey. Up and down this corridor have travelled birds, animals and species of plants. SPNI guides consider such species to be especially worthy of mention in their explanations of the natural surroundings. Indeed, it might not be going too far to suggest that the Syrian–African Rift Valley constitutes a powerful symbol — of both natural universality and mobility — the flora and fauna that pass along its route recognize no boundaries. In a sense — quite *unlike* the White Cliffs of Dover or the countryside around Granchester which are inescapably and narrowly 'English' — the species inhabiting this biological niche are true 'citizens of the world'. Any yet at the same time as these international and universal features of Israeli natural history are emphasized by the SPNI guides, the tours they lead in this area include quite detailed and lengthy visits to the frontiers between Israel and Jordan to the east, and Israel and Egypt to the west. Sentry points are visited and border guards are photographed. In this way frontiers appear naturally permeable but culturally impermeable. Arguably, the symbolic purpose of the SPNI is to draw attention to the idea that the possibility of the former is made possible by emphasis on the latter.

MOBILE CEMETERIES

The night tour of Jerusalem starts at 10 pm from Mount Scopus and proceeds, via a long walk down, to the Mount of Olives and through the Kidron Valley, entering the Old City at around 1.00 am. On the way the tour passes several Christian churches and the spot where the High Priest customarily made his sacrificial 'sin offering' on the Day of Atonement before entering the temple on that day. Attention is drawn to three cemeteries.

The first cemetery, on the Mount of Olives, is an ancient one from the time of the 2nd Temple. The second one is more modern and had been a Jewish cemetery before 1948 when it became part of the Jordanian-occupied area of Jerusalem. Following the Israeli victory in the war of 1967, the cemetery passed back into Israeli hands. The remains of soldiers who died in the War of Independence were then moved from a cemetery in West Jerusalem to this one. The third cemetery consists of the Kidron valley itself. This was a pre-Temple cemetery and contains the tomb of David's son, Absalom. Explaining the significance of these cemeteries the guide told us that Muslims, Christians and Jews each viewed Jerusalem in a different way. Muslims regard the city as a place to live; Christians see it as a place to pray; Jews as a place to die. One could remember this with the mnemonic '*Dira, Tfila, Kvora*', the Hebrew words for apartment, prayer and burial respectively.

THE CONTINUOUS AND THE DISCONTINUOUS

The eighth trip is the tour organized to Egypt by Neot Hakikar. This trip starts by crossing the north of Sinai, past Yamit, the settlement given back under much public protest to Egypt as a result of Camp David, and scenes of Egyptian–Israeli battles in the recent past. There is intense excitement.

From this point the bus soon enters the fertile cultivated area of the Nile delta and reaches Cairo in time for the travellers to rest there overnight. The following day they visit the sites, with the pyramids and the sphinx of Giza, of the ancient Pharaonic civilizations at Memphis and Sakar.

At these sites attention is focused, by Israeli and Egyptian guides alike, upon the frescos on tomb walls portraying everyday life in the area, and an attempt is made to point out and explain to the travellers the continuity existing between those depictions and the actual scenes of peasant farming that they can see in the fields around them. Comparisons are also made between facial features of the men and women of the frescos and the Egyptian guides' features. Signs of Pharaonic architectural styles are looked for upon the houses of contemporary villagers, and a papyrus shop is visited. The next four days are spent in the Upper Nile, in the Valley of the Kings, at Aswan and at Abu Simbel. During this time explanations are made about the importance of the River Nile in Egyptian history, about the consequent necessity for controlled irrigation and, thus, a centralized political system. For some of the travellers one of the high points of the tour is the Temple of Abu Simbel, which was built by Ramses II, the King ruling at the time of the Exodus of the ancient Hebrews from Egypt. Stories are told of the conquest, by Ramses II, of the Nubians, who are, indeed, much in evidence in this region. It is said that good relations exist between the Israeli tourists and the Nubians.

The last full day of the tour, the travellers having returned from Aswan overnight, is spent in Cairo, where time is spent in the Egyptian museum. A little of modern Cairo is also seen. The following day the return bus journey to Israel is undertaken during which most people sleep. We may notice one point, above all, about this trip: it is clearly designed to introduce travellers to the Pharaonic period rather than to more recent ones. Only about half a day out of six is spent in the streets of modern Cairo. In a sense, therefore, Ramses II appears to the tourists as a dominating figure in Egyptian history, while Nasser, for example, hardly appears at all.

MYTHICAL CLUSTERS

My intention in the foregoing has been to give some idea of the atmosphere engendered during SPNI tours. I would like to summarize what seem to be their main features by extracting from them four clusters of significant ideas.

PRESERVING THE UNIVERSAL BY DEFENDING THE PARTICULAR

Smith (op. cit.:183) observes the tendency for some nationalistic ideologies to 'evoke community and a sense of solidarity from the symbolism of unusual natural features'. In rather the same vein Wright (1985:128) focuses upon the symbolic uses of nature in British nationalist thought. He discerns in the preoccupations of the British middle class with natural features (such as the 'greenness' of authentic British turf) which are perceived as 'essentially', 'exclusively' or even 'secretly' British, evidence of a 'national consciousness' which is above all *particularistic*. British bourgeois particularism, in this context, appropriates features of the landscape and makes them into particularly British and, at the same time, particularly middle-class entities. Such an attitude, suggests Wright, at once derives from and reflects political values which are also particularistic in the sense that they are 'not guided by potentially universalistic [notions] such as freedom or equality'.

These observations provide a good background against which to identify the first cluster of ideas associated with the type of tour described above: they contain a fundamentally ambivalent mixture of universalism and particularism. One of the founding members of the SPNI argues that the organization rests upon two principal foundations. The first consists of a natural history which combines the natural history of three continents and several different climatic zones. Because of these facts, he explains, there are at least 470 species of migratory birds and 2500 species of plants, many of which derive from Africa, Asia or northern Europe. There is, in short, 'an unbelievable variety of natural species'. There is also a constant flow of species in and out of the country; some species have been lost, but at least one hundred new species have taken their place, many from America. The country, he argues, has been the origin of scores of plants cultivated elsewhere: wheat, barley, radishes, carrots and so on. The other principal foundation on which the society is based is 'keeping the landscape, the phenomena, the nature, animals, plants — which means also keeping the Hebrew culture, language and literature'. There is a tension here between visions which at the same time encompass a natural universe which is truly universal and a cultural universe which is contrastingly particular (and exclusive). This is one of the tensions upon which the tours under discussion are grounded. A good example of this is provided by the symbolic use made in them of the Syrian–African Rift Valley, described above. In short the SPNI tours contain a dual and profoundly ambivalent stress on natural universalism, on the one hand, and cultural particularism on the other. The metaphorical associations that this ambivalence has with the question of what it means to be an Israeli (a citizen both of the world and of a small heavily bounded and fortified state) seem quite striking.

BOUNDARY HOPPING

A second cluster of ideas has to do with the mixture of 'scientific' and 'magical' experiences which the tours involve. The traveller is propelled, so to speak, backwards and forwards, with exhilarating speed and force-fulness, between a scientific looking plane, where he or she learns about birds of prey or the Israeli Water Board, to a more lyrical, enchanted and magical plane, where he or she is encouraged to look through half-closed eyes at the moonlit shapes of the roof tops of the Arab village of Silwan and imagine that the scene is the City of David. Such stirring oscillation calls to mind one of Gellner's (1974:163) arguments: that the achievement of empiricism has been to inculcate sensitivity to the existence of a boundary between the 'cold field of the empirically testable' and the 'transcendent' and to 'discourage systematic boundary-hopping'. The achievement of *tiyoulim*, by contrast, lies quite precisely in their positive encouragement of systematic boundary-hopping. Guides and officials of the SPNI express their feelings about this oscillation in different ways. One guide instructor, for example, told of his growing awareness, as he became older, of his need to see and experience *mystery* in the landscape. As a student and young instructor he had seen himself as a pure geologist whose aim was simply to teach his guide-students to understand the landscape in an exclusively scientific way. One of the earliest members of the SPNI uses another idiom. He explains that: 'Wherever I go, whenever I open an eye, wherever I look there is a chapter of the Bible. I go with it; my children go with it; you can't go anywhere in this country without connecting it with thousands of years of history . . . It's not only in the Bible, it's in geology.' On the other hand he takes considerable care to emphasize not only that he is 'anti-religious', as he puts it, but that when the society was founded its members had a purely scientific interest in the Israeli landscape.

According to Katz the 'modification of diachronic sequences' charac-teristic of the *tiyoulim* and other *Yediat Ha-aretz* material consists of 'shrinking' some time sequences such that 'the feeling is of witnessing scenes and heroes of the past as if they were taking place here and now' (1985). The examples presented hardly need further elaboration, except to make the obvious point that the erasure of temporal boundaries applies only to particular historical sequences and not others.

Thus the boundaries between the times of Moses, David and the kings, the heroes of Massada and Gamla, the settlers of the first *aliya*, the great Zionist pioneers of the twenties and thirties, the fighters of the war of Israeli independence are all abolished — effectively giving the impression of a seamless, boundaryless web of time which encompasses the past in the present. But other historical boundaries are by contrast emphasized. Moses and Absalom may seem to belong almost to the present. The Canaanites, Greeks, Persians, Romans, Crusaders, Turks and British all belong to the past and are projected in the tours as if they are separated from the present by almost unbridgeable boundaries.

The history reconstructed in the *tiyoulim* is simultaneously embedded in nature so that cultural and natural evolution appear closely interdependent and subject to the same kind of laws. Thus Egyptian peasants become the sons and daughters of Pharaonic farm servants, modern Israelis the children of the ancient Hebrews and, as one Neot Hakikar officer put it: 'In order to explain what the military government in Turkey is doing today, you have to understand what the Hittites were doing three and a half thousand years ago.'

As he says:

> Our approach is to take a region as a complex, to understand the concrete structure of the land, mountains, beaches — the general morphology — and then to understand the climate, and then the workings of the flora and fauna of the region. When you understand all this it is possible to understand how many years ago cultures got started and how they then progressed. With this background you can understand what is going on today. Basically it doesn't matter where you go in the world, you always have links between these elements.

This view of history seems based upon a conception of independent nations which were each separately established early on, soon after the natural world itself, and of their unfolding through time in much the same way as, say, rock formations. There is a clear and strong feeling of permanence and historical continuity. We may place this view beside an actual history of much suffering resulting from repeated dispersal, dislocation, degrees of assimilation and intermarriage and the emergence of the modern Israeli state in only the very recent past.

The SPNI tours thus specialize in hopping, or leaping, across at least two identifiable kinds of boundaries: between the scientific and the religious and between the present and the past. It is likely that tour guides and tour managers might concur that such heady processes conspire to raise the internal temperatures of their tourists to match the external heat in which the tours often take place.

THE GUIDE AS HERO

There are several senses in which the SPNI guides are 'heroic' figures. Only those who have completed army service are hired in this capacity (effectively ruling out the possibility of Arab guides). For the 'difficult' tours, as the society terms them, which include rock climbing or long treks across the desert, the skills of former commandos are manifestly useful. Apart from these physical attributes, however, and possibly more important, are the wide range of scientific skills invariably assumed to be possessed by the guides. Tour members listen to their explanations about the environment, treating these with considerable respect. Furthermore, the guides habitually assert their roles as charismatic leaders (with tourism followers) quite emphatically. I have referred to a trip to the Yehudia Canyon, the memorials in that canyon to the two kibbutz members who died while walking in it without proper guidance and to the reference to periodic deaths there every year. This is just one example (out of very many which could be given) of the tour leader's use of powerful images of the possible malevolent consequences that could follow from acting independently of the guide/leader.

All these points are made forcefully and sharply by an SPNI guide-informant:

> Even if there is a disparity between the evidence of scientific books and the guide's opinion, then the guide's opinion holds — this is really a very important aspect of the whole thing. The guide represents something bigger than himself; something they can believe in. They need the guide to be right — to be somebody to follow — in fact to represent the aura of the land of Israel, the beautiful land of Israel, to represent the great Zionist value of an uprooted Israel coming back to the land. It's true for each group of tourists as they go through the desert — including Americans. They are going there the first time — they are the pioneers at that particular moment. The guide is Berl Katsenelson or Alef Gordon or Moses who leads them. They feel helpless without him or her; he represents leadership.

THE *TIYOUL* AS NATION

In various ways *tiyoulim* are designed to heighten a sense of group solidarity among the tourists themselves. In the examples above we may count the following as aids to the production of group solidarity: the shared experience of travelling over difficult terrain; shared emotions produced by heightened awareness of colours, smells, viscosity, heat and cold, and so forth; awareness of 'danger' on the margins — whether this be expressed in terms of getting lost or falling off the side of a canyon or the past experience of Syrian bombardment; terrorist infiltration; a preoccupation with social and national boundaries and so on.

Much of this group solidarity is achieved through a broader affirmation of solidarity with the Israeli nation as a whole. In a sense the tour group 'becomes' the nation for the duration of the tour. The experiences of the group are consciously organized to recreate at the level of the tour the experiences of the nation itself.

Furthermore the solidarity induced by the tour has both a synchronic and diachronic dimension. Whether expressed in terms of the generations of dead in the Jerusalem cemeteries, the attention paid to places such as Gamla (or Massada or any other of the many sites of ancient Jewish settlements), a deep sense of solidarity with past generations of Jews is established.

CONCLUSION

Israeli *tiyoulim* provide us with particularly luminous examples of a kind of tourism dedicated to the production and consumption of myths. The first great Exodus of the Jewish people out of the desert from slavery in Egypt has provided the modern State of Israel with the cornerstone of its political legitimacy and is called to mind with each celebration of the Passover meal. Arguably, journeys undertaken on weekends and other days by modern Israelis, with the SPNI as their guides, into the desert and countryside from residential and cultural centres such as Tel-Aviv and Jerusalem complete, complement and refresh that process by offering another.

Distilling the clusters of ideas explored above, we may suggest that the mythology woven by the SPNI tours is to be found in the articulation of three themes located in the relationships between six terms, the first of which is part of the society's own name. It is, after all, the Society for the *Defence (hagana)* of Nature. Such defence is clearly linked in several senses to associated ideas of *danger* and threat — to which the style and atmosphere of the tours offer a riposte.

The first theme of the myth, therefore, is to be found in the relation between danger and defence. In this context it is concerned with threatened species of fauna and flora which are being defended by the SPNI.

The relationship between two further terms gives us the second theme of the myth. The first of these is rooted in the fact that one of the SPNI's foremost aims is to defend species of flora and fauna which belong to a *universal* natural order (including birds, for example, which migrate across Israel from Africa and Asia to Europe). On the other hand, however, in the sense that *tiyoulim* are not only journeys of exploration but also encounters with the deep sense of safety that only immersion in that which is truly known and truly ours can bring, it is clearly the effervescent *particularism* of their tours which lends the SPNI its appeal. This sense is induced by a cluster of features characteristic of *tiyoulim*: the heroic guide, heightened physical sensations associated with enhanced feelings of heat and cold, with laughter, with the sight of magical black beetles and so on; and the exhilarating opportunities that the tours give to transgress playfully the normal parameters of all manner of boundaries, including that between the earnest scientism of the SPNI's early founders and the biblical visions suggested by many of their tours.

From these two pairs of relations we are ineluctably drawn towards a third. The terms of this third pair are generated metaphorically from the former pairs but, in turn, not only give these their social and cultural meaning but also serve to locate them geographically and politically. If, as we have just seen, the first underlying theme of the SPNI *tiyoulim* concerns the way in which the dangers to Israeli flora and fauna are addressed by the organisation's protective measures, and the second is concerned with the particular (and particularly beneficial) methods and approaches of the organisation towards the protection of a substantial part of the universal natural heritage, the third theme – which also happens to be the subject of the final chapter of the present volume – appears as one of the most central of all contemporary Jewish and Israeli concerns, namely the relation between the Jewish *diaspora* and the Israeli *state*. Our homologue thus turns out to have a tripartite structure as follows:

danger:defence::universalism:particularism::diaspora:state

SPNI tours are truly mythical adventures!

REFERENCES

Anderson, B. (1983) *Imagined Communities: Reflections on the Origin and Spread of Nationalism*, London: Verso.
Barthes, R. (1973) *Mythologies*, London: Paladin.
Eisenstadt, S.N. (1985) *The Transformation of Israeli Society*, London: Weidenfeld and Nicolson.
Frow, J. (1991) 'Tourism and the semiotics of nostalgia', October, 123–51.
Gellner, E. (1974) *Legitimation of Belief*, Cambridge: Cambridge University Press.
Gellner, E. (1983) *Nations and Nationalism*, Oxford: Blackwell.
Hobsbawm, E. and Ranger, T. (eds) (1983) *The Invention of Tradition*, Cambridge: Cambridge University Press.
Katz, S. (1985) 'The Israeli teacher-guide', *Annals of Tourism Research*, 12, 49–72.
Kedouri, E. (1960) *Nationalism*, London: Hutchinson.
Selwyn, T. (1995) 'Landscapes of liberation and imprisonment: towards an anthropology of the Israeli landscape' in E. Hirsch and M. O'Hanlon (eds), *The Anthropology of the Landscape*, Oxford: Oxford University Press.
Smith, A. (1991) *National Identity*, London: Penguin.
Wright, P. (1985) *On Living in an Old Country: the National Past in Contemporary Britain*, London: Verso.

9 The Tourist as Deity: Ancient Continuities in Modern Japan

D.P. MARTINEZ

This chapter continues the work of an earlier article (Martinez, 1990) in which I examined the tourist image of the *ama* (diving women) of Japan. The argument there was that the modern image of the 'sexy' diving woman was based on older romantic images of the *ama*, as well as on the sexual symbolism of the ocean and water which is so prevalent in Japan. The article concluded that, for economic reasons, the *ama* of the village in which I did fieldwork were content to manipulate — rather than to reject — their tourist image. In short, they had a certain amount of control over the 'tourist gaze' and directed this gaze to meet their own ends. It was not until after I wrote that article that I began to ponder the question of why it was so easy for the villagers to adjust to tourism. By that I do not mean just adjusting to the economic fact of tourism but to all the implications of what it meant to become a host in the tourist industry.

In writing the chapter on tourism for my doctoral thesis, I recalled an article by the Japanese anthropologist Yoshida which offered an explanation of the Japanese attitude towards foreigners (in Japanese: *gaijin*, literally 'outside person') and it seemed to me that this explanation could apply generally to tourism in Japan. Thus this chapter has grown out of the idea that tourists, whether foreign or domestic, fall into the category of strangers and that, since the Japanese have very specific ideas about strangers, the treatment of tourists can be linked to older traditions.

THE STRANGER

Of course, the Japanese are not the only people with very specific notions about and attitudes towards strangers. In his succinct and elegant article, 'The Stranger', Georg Simmel pointed to the essential ambiguity of the stranger in any society. As described in his essay, the stranger is an outsider

> fixed within a particular spatial circle, or within a group whose boundaries are similar to spatial boundaries. But his position in this group is determined,

The Tourist Image: Myths and Myth Making in Tourism. Edited by Tom Selwyn.

Figure 9.1 A visiting photographers' club photographing *ama*. The two young girls in the picture fit touristic descriptions of divers, but never dived in real life. Photo by D.P. Martinez

essentially, by the fact that he has not belonged to it from the beginning, that he imports qualities into it which do not, and cannot, stem from the group itself (Simmel 1950:402).

This seminal idea of an ambiguous person who imports qualities into a group 'which do not and cannot stem from the group itself' has been labelled ambiguous. Simmel insists on the 'unity and remoteness' inherent in the phenomenon of the stranger, for 'to be a stranger is naturally a very positive relation; it is a specific form of interaction'. (1950:402)

The fact that the article is discussing the position of the Jew in Europe is essential to the understanding of Simmel's definition. The stranger is not an outsider who happens to pass through, nor someone who is quickly incorporated or assimilated into society:[1] the stranger is someone who dwells side-by-side with the 'natives', who is never accepted by them but who never leaves. For these reasons, the stranger is 'near and far *at the same time*'; he is not really conceived as an individual but as a type (1950:407). In the post-modernist anthropology of the 1990s we would probably call this stranger 'the other'.

The Japanese anthropologist Teigo Yoshida added a new dimension to Simmel's model: that of the stranger as god,[2] the bearer of ambiguous qualities which could be interpreted both as dangerous and beneficial to the group (Yoshida, 1981:87–99). Although he does not refer to Simmel's article, Yoshida's strangers and deities *do* fall into the category of beings who are strange yet dwell, if not within, at least on the margins of society. Yoshida's article is a structural analysis of the role of the stranger in Japanese folk religion and asserts that:

> strangers, visitors, and flotsam not only represent the mystical 'other world', but they are also the marginal, 'liminal' figure or things which mediate between the world of *uchi* (inside) and the world of *yoso* (outside), between men and gods, between the *ke* (secular) and the *hare* (sacred), or between 'this world' and the 'other world' (ibid.:96).

Yoshida uses material from the traditional Japanese 'village' to demonstrate how the modern attitude towards foreigners stems from the ancient symbolic and ambiguous position of the stranger. The village is capable of both hospitality towards strangers, who, like the Shinto deities, can bring good fortune and good luck and, on the other hand, of remaining essentially closed to the outsider because he/she is essentially polluting. What he does not mention, but what any student of Japan will be quick to point out, is that his article is rooted in the fact that foreign strangers can no longer be ignored in Japan. The country may have closed its doors to outsiders for two centuries during the Tokugawa era (1600–1867), but now the doors are open and the 'foreign devils' can no longer be dismissed. Indeed, they are now part of the world which Japan must inhabit as an international power. They travel in the country as tourists, they sometimes dwell there permanently and they appear constantly on television and in films.

Although I will discuss the foreigner as stranger in Japan, the core of this chapter is about a different category of stranger: the domestic tourist now found in innumerable Japanese coastal villages. Like Yoshida's foreign strangers and Simmel's archetypal stranger, they too have become a permanent category. From season to season, the individuals may change, but the fact of the strangers' presence remains. For a village which survives on tourism there can be no denial of the existence of these outsiders, but as Simmel noted 'the relation to [them] is a non-relation' (1950:407). In order to understand this attitude towards strangers, a brief look at the nature of the Shinto deities and strangers in Japan is in order.

THE NATURE OF THE DEITY IN JAPAN

The Shinto deity in Japan, *kami*, is also an ambiguous concept. As defined by Sokyo Ono, a lecturer at the National Shinto University in Ise, the 'term is an honorific for noble, sacred spirits which implies a sense of adoration for their virtues and authority. All beings have such spirits, *so in a sense all beings can be called kami or be regarded as potential kami*' (Ono, 1962:6) (emphasis added).

Examples of the various things which can be regarded as *kami* in Japan abound in my fieldnotes: the 'body' of the deity in a Shinto shrine, unusual rock formations, newly cut trees and the anthropologist herself. All these were left (or treated to) offerings of rice, sake and sweets. The general attitude towards all *kami* was that one could leave offerings and pray in order to have a request or two answered.[3] I was told that to demand too much of a deity was to ask for punishment, the *kami* did not like greedy people. Clearly, deities are seen as having a dual nature. They are both *ara-tama* (violent spirit) and *nigi-tama* (peaceful spirit). The sea is an excellent example of this idea of a *kami*: as the source of their livelihood, the sea-deity was seen as potentially bountiful as well as dangerous, a place where a diver might easily be hurt or killed. Accordingly, offerings to the sea where the women dived were frequent and generous.

It is important to understand that for the Japanese a deity is a type of power. In general, deities are powers tied to specific locations or objects. Deities may dwell on the top of mountains or be manifest in unusual natural features which are then marked by gates and surrounded by sacred rope. Most frequently, the deity is located in the 'deity's body' (*shintai*), which is kept locked inside a small shrine usually found in the innermost section of a Shinto shrine that is located in a carefully marked-off area approached by a winding path and through various sacred gates. In short, all deities may dwell *in* Japan, but, like strangers, they are confined to separate spaces of their own which must be especially marked and cautiously approached.[4] Most deities become dangerous, or manifest in their *ara-tama* form, when they come visiting out of season.

In Japan there were various times of the year when the deities and other 'mysterious strangers' came visiting. These occasions traditionally fell between the harvest and New Year (cf. Hori, 1963:76–103). At such times, the visiting stranger was considered not only beneficial but necessary to the continued well-being of the village. For the deity or stranger to come at a different time or to stay a long time could be disastrous, and special precautions and purifications had to be undertaken (cf. Ogura, 1963:133–44). Worse, to deny a visiting stranger hospitality could lead to calamity.

Yoshida gives various examples which indicate that strangers should be treated well, in the hope of reaping benefits, but should be sent on their way quickly for fear of incurring pollution. Thus,

in Japanese villages strangers known as '*tabi*' or '*tabihito*'[5] are much more feared and treated with great caution. They do not share the basic values and assumptions of the village concerned. . . . While the people belonging to the inside are classified into various categories, outsiders and strangers are un-differentiated. They are unknown and unclassified. How they fit in is not determined. Therefore, when they enter *uchi* (inside) space they are considered potentially dangerous, both in a physical and mystical sense (Yoshida, 1981:95).

Thus, another aspect of the *kami* is the very ambiguity of its duality. The strange, the unknown, the mysterious outsider — all things which might be dangerous and polluting can be *kami*. This is reminiscent of Douglas's (1970) ideas on purity and danger: the idea that those things which fall out of the norm, outside established social categories, are dangerous and polluting is clearly there in these Japanese examples. Yet, the analogy must be made with caution, for even the *kami* who are strangers are just as capable of bringing good luck and fortune to the village as they are of bringing bad. Yoshida's notion of the stranger as mediator between the inside and outside, this world and the other world, the secular and sacred and, thus, partaking of the nature of both is important.

Other anthropologists of Japan have discussed the concepts of the stranger, danger, marginality and pollution. Yamaguchi has written two articles on the Emperor (who is or was a deity), an essential symbol of Japanese society, who, like Simmel's stranger, can never be a member of that society (Yamaguchi, 1977 and 1987). Namihira considers the ideas of pollution in relation to outsiders in another brief article (Namihira, 1987), while Picone points out that the duties of dealing with the deities of the household are left to the daughter-in-law, the stranger in the family, and examines some of the implications of this practice (Picone, 1984:248–9, 317–20). Hendry gives various examples of how modern urban Japanese continue to deal with the pollution of the outside world (Hendry, 1984) and Goodman shows how even native Japanese can be seen as 'dangerous' if they return after having lived outside the country for a long period (Goodman, 1987). No article, to my knowledge, elaborates these ideas in order to examine domestic Japanese tourism and this is what I shall attempt to do here.

While no villagers ever referred to a tourist as '*kami-sama*' (honourable deity) — and indeed, if asked, any villager would have laughed at the notion — all guests *should be treated like kami* as Ashkenazi has noted in passing (1983:87, fn 3). Yet, on a concrete level, very unusual strangers can still be referred to as deities, as I was (see Note 4). Thus the relationship between domestic tourists and deities is more distant than the relationship between foreigners and deities. In order to elucidate this abstract relationship, I will try to describe the relations between the Japanese villagers and their weekend or summer guests. My main purpose, however, is not merely to describe this tourist–host relationship but to demonstrate how it is possible to see a continuity between the older Japanese attitude towards outsiders and the way in which modern tourists are treated.[6]

In a larger sphere, I am also unaware of any studies in the anthropology of tourism which have explored the way in which the attitudes towards strangers traditionally held by the host society might affect the way in which that group treats their tourist guests. I hope that this look at Japan might lead to an examination of this area by anthropologists of other societies.

THE SETTING, SHIMA PENINSULA AND KUZAKI VILLAGE

South of the industrial city Nagoya is Shima Peninsula where the association between pearls and women divers (*ama*) is inescapable. One of the main tourist attractions in this peninsula is located in Toba City where, daily, Japanese and foreign tourists visit the museum island called Mikimoto Pearl Island. The Mikimoto exhibits and brochures always make clear that the *ama* dived for various things, not just the pearl oysters which Kokichi Mikimoto would buy for his experiments in the creation of the cultured pearl, but no tourist, foreign or Japanese, ever seems to take in this fact. Thus, since the perfection of the cultured pearl in 1893, the image of *ama* as pearl divers has developed so forcefully that it is almost impossible to convince people it is a recent creation.

Toba City is in a National Park which was established in 1946. This large area of Shima Peninsula was made a park in order to protect the ancient, once sacred, domain of Ise Shrine, the Shinto shrine where Amaterasu, the sun goddess and ancestress of the imperial family, is housed. Until the Meiji Restoration in 1868, Toba City and all the surrounding villages were part of the Ise Domain. Among these villages, Kuzaki (where I did my fieldwork in 1984–5 and 1986) was a fishing and diving village which made a sacred tribute of *noshi awabi*[7] to Ise Shrine rather than paying taxes. Although the creation of the National Park was, I suspect, an attempt to protect a sacred place from the secularizing force of MacArthur's new constitution for Japan, the end result was that the area became a tourist attraction — and remained a pilgrimage attraction — long before the tourism boom of the 1960s increased domestic tourism all over Japan.

The inhabitants of Shima Peninsula were ready to take advantage of this tourist boom. Although the peninsula is protected from industrialization, pollution from nearby Japanese industry affects the sea there, adding to the problem of overfishing created by the high market prices of the 1950s. With no major industry other than that of cultured pearls, the villages of Shima were losing people to the big cities in the north. That trend is now being reversed: tourism ensures employment in various areas. Villagers dive and fish for the catches which are served in hotels and restaurants; many men do construction work widening roads for tourist traffic and building hotels for the increased tourism; and most of the young women of the area work as tour-guides, in shops which cater to tourists or in the hotels of Toba City.

Kuzaki, just 20 minutes from Toba City, is typical of many coastal villages. Squeezed between the mountains and the sea, it has a long scenic coast with seven wide beaches and two harbours. Nineteen of its 116 households run inns and most of the other households are involved in work in the village. Most of the fish and shellfish caught in Kuzaki waters is sold to the village innkeepers and most of the people who work outside the village in Toba are engaged in the sorts of tourist-related jobs described above.

Diving as a way of life is becoming less and less lucrative in Kuzaki. The co-operative[8] which acts as the village government and oversees all farming and fishing in the area also enforces the national laws designed to prevent overfishing in the Pacific Ocean. This means that divers now only dive for an hour daily, or at the very most, two hours, rather than spending a whole day in the sea. In Kuzaki, with all its restrictions on diving but with diving continuing all year around for various seaweed and shellfish, I have estimated that a diver now brings in around £4500 per year. In a community where in the past the wife's contribution to the household income was quite large, £4500 a year is very little, and so the divers have turned to various part-time jobs to fill the gaps.

Pollution and overfishing have also caused a decrease in the number of village fishermen. Before World War II, about 96 percent of village men fished either in Kuzaki or outside the village in large fishing fleets. Nowadays, less than 15 percent of village men fish. Fishermen who were especially successful in the years after the war have opened inns, and they constitute 10 percent of village households. Another 55 percent of households are supported by men who work outside Kuzaki, particularly in Toba City, and 20 percent are headed by retired men or widowed women. This is a shift in the traditional mode of production. In the past, young couples did migrant labour (either separately or together), middle-aged couples fished and dived locally, while grandparents farmed. Yet, as Kim also noted in her article on mountain resort tourism in northern Japan (1986), contemporary tourism is accepted by the villages as a way in which the traditional household can continue to work together. In inn-owning households, the entire family runs the business, while in other households the men commute to work, the grandparents farm and the wife of the household generally dives and works part time.

The most popular part-time job is as geisha[9] in the village inns, that is, acting as hostesses to the tourists who come to Kuzaki to see the diving women and to enjoy the food. Thus, most of the village is involved in some way with tourism, but the increase since 1965 of inn-owning households, from two to 19, means that there are now tourists *in the village* who are entertained by village women, a pattern rather different from the immediate post-war period when the villagers worked in the tourist trade outside Kuzaki and could leave the strangers behind when they returned home.

Who, then, are these tourists and how are they treated?

THE TOURISTS

With the growing economic success of Japan, taking a holiday has become more and more popular. According to Tokushima (1980), domestic tourism has been increasing steadily in Japan since the 1960s. The idea of leisure in its modern secular sense is new, as is a Japanese middle class with time for pleasure. Yet, as Plath noted in his study of the 'after hours' (1964), in Japan even leisure time is often very structured. Graburn noted in his monograph *To Pray, Pay and Play* (1983) that it is only recently that the Japanese tourist has taken up the idea of a recreational holiday.

Domestic tourism in Japan can be divided into three main types: group tourism which consists of friends or company employees travelling together for a few days; family tourism which consists of a family spending a week or two together at the seaside or at some other resort; and a very small number of repeat tourists, who buy or rent a small villa near the tourist resort and return to it yearly. The favourite activities of group tours are sightseeing, visiting temples, drinking and eating and shopping for gifts for family and friends.

As the tourist brochures note, all these activities can be found on the Shima Peninsula. The younger Japanese are becoming more and more interested in holidays which involve sea, sun, surfing and sex, and Shima Peninsula can provide these activities as well.

In Kuzaki, groups of businessmen were the favourite type of inn guests; they would come for one night of rest after a visit to Ise Shrine and Mikimoto Pearl Island and spend this time in the inn, rarely venturing out. In 1984, one evening in a *ryokan* with a geisha, dinner, breakfast and all the alcohol during meals included came to ¥10 000 per person (£41.66). These were often groups of five men who needed two geishas. Out of the ¥50 000 paid by the group, the two women would be paid ¥3000 each, the excellent seafood meal would be worth about ¥10 000, another ¥5000 would go towards the costs of cleaning linen. Since the other work in the inn was done by the owner's immediate family, this left a profit of ¥29 000 (£120) per night per group of tourists. Depending on the size of the inn, this figure could be multiplied by four to 20. In deep winter, an inn might have had only one group of guests on Friday and another on Saturday night. In the summer, the inns might have been full every night of the week. Thus one could say that the businessman tourist is like the stranger deity who visits at a set time, leaves at a specific time after being sheltered and entertained by the villagers and bestows tangible benefits (cash). Knowing their place and having a 'relation' which is in fact a 'non-relation', these tourists are the villagers' favourites.

In contrast, the summer tourists, family or student groups who came only for the beach and who ate in the two or three cafes which would open only in the summer, did not bring as much business. Frequently, these groups would camp near the beach and were called the 'summer people'. As for the third type of guest, there were two locations within the village's boundaries but outside the immediate village area where summer villas had been built by big conglomerates. To the villagers' immense relief, neither location ever became popular. Outsiders did not buy the villas which therefore remained closed and empty throughout the year, and the villagers were spared the stranger who would *always* be there, who might threaten to establish some sort of permanent relationship.

This situation, which might change at any time, suits the people of Kuzaki. The worst time of year was the summer season when the place was full of outsiders who shopped in village shops, drank in village pubs, and who sometimes tried to strike up conversations with working fishermen or divers. Far better, as I have described, is the businessman tourist who came even in the winter when the sea is rough and who rarely ventured into the village itself. Given that the group tourist was the predominant type in Kuzaki, it is easy for the villagers to claim, as I was first told when I arrived: 'There are no relations between villagers and guests. None at all'.[10] The fact that there is an economic relation is important, but this is not what the villagers understand by 'relation'. A relation would imply something of an intimate nature and that is not how the villagers see their association with the tourists. They were willing to treat the guests 'well' as guests deserved, especially guests who brought a certain amount of prosperity to the village, but they always harboured a feeling of fear towards tourists.

RELATIONS BETWEEN HOSTS AND GUESTS IN KUZAKI

As I have already mentioned, a stranger, in Japanese tradition, could be both special and sacred or dangerous and polluting. A stranger was treated with respect, as if he/she were a deity with the power to bring good or ill to a place. So too with the tourists to Kuzaki. They were treated with great respect, they were fed the best of seafood, received wonderful service from the *ama* and were taken to fish in the best spots if they were interested in fishing. If these tourists wandered through the village and stopped to ask a question of someone cleaning or making nets, the replies were always cheerful and polite. People would say that one must always be *yasashii* (gentle) when talking to outsiders. In practice, however, although responding politely as they saw it, the villagers often bellowed out directions to tourists much in the manner adopted by those people who, when speaking to foreigners, shout in the hope that shouting will solve the language problem.

At the same time, tourists are seen as dangerous and dirty. Messy beaches, typical of all tourist beaches in Japan, are always blamed on guests. In the summer, when the tourist season is at its height, the village hires a nightwatchman to make sure that the outsiders do not harm people's homes. Women who work constantly as geisha in the inns did not hesitate to tell me that tourists could be bad and dangerous for the village and that the children needed this nightwatchman to keep them safe. No one was very clear on what the dangers might be: it was just the presence of outsiders that was threatening. Fishermen take the tourists to the best spots for fishing and then sit back and wait for the amateur to get seasick. When drinking in the pub, the fisherman would ignore the guests, sometimes leaving one place to go to another if there were too many outsiders in his regular drinking place. Some husbands were jealous of the attention the outsiders paid their wives and would go out drinking with their friends on the nights the wife was at work in an inn. It happened more than once that a working wife would encounter her husband at a pub. In such situations, the husband and wife would ignore each other. However, the man might be heard to complain about 'outsiders' until his friends suggested leaving for another place.

Some families would be openly disapproving of some of the women who did work as geisha and would lecture me about the ambiguous dangers of going to the inns. The blunt query, 'why is it bad or dangerous?' would bring the reply, 'it just is, bad things can happen'. I learnt that disapproval was strongest for women who were under 40 and who had children still at school; grandmothers in their forties were not so disapproved of. No one was ever clear on 'bad things', but from hints I learned that there was a general feeling that the tourists were only interested in sex and that that was not good.

Other villagers and the geisha themselves were aware that sex was part of the tourist image. As one informant put it: 'There is a lot of PR to bring the tourists here and 50 percent of PR is lies.' Since sex has to do with images and not reality, these people are not bothered by the tourists' expectations. They know that the sexual atmosphere of the inns is mostly jokes and innuendo and little else. If that is what tourists come for, fine. Most stay less than 24 hours and leave. What harm can it do to exploit the image a little? In short, attitudes towards the tourists vary but all rest on one basic fact: tourism is important if Kuzaki is to continue as a functioning village. Most importantly, the economic success of tourism meant that the traditional household could continue, as all members of the household could now find employment in or close to the village.

Thus, in order to encourage and increase tourism, especially summer tourism, the villagers voted to allow the co-operative to set aside one beach for tourists in 1986. The inns paid the village a fee for use of this beach which was run by two grandfathers who were paid a small salary. For ¥1000 (£4.15) a day, guests had mats, cabanas, showers and toilets at their disposal. The beach was cleaned daily and a long row of a dozen food and drink stands was there to provide anything a sunbather and swimmer might like. These stands were run by relations of village innowners, the concession belonged to an inn; these were given (for a fee) to close kin. The beach was named Diana Beach in honour of the Princess of Wales who had visited Japan that spring.[11]

Villagers liked the idea of Diana Beach. Guests, chauffeured to and from the beach hourly by hotel vans, were out of the way in an area which was cleaned regularly. So, the dangerous outsiders were both confined and yet honoured as they should be; and, importantly, the beach provided a new way of earning money. In 1986, teenagers and diving women ran the concession stands, and found the job great fun because it gave them a chance to sit and gossip while working.

CONCLUSIONS

I hope that this brief description of host–guest relations in Kuzaki and of the economic importance of the tourist industry for the village clearly demonstrates how the model of Japanese tourism fits the models developed by other anthropologists of tourism. The economic importance of tourism for small villages has been an important theme in various articles, notably in discussions of Germany (Melghy et al., 1985:181–99), and Portugal (Mendosa, 1983:213–38). The ways in which tourist and host relations are based on stereotypes have also been discussed for Spain (Pi-Sunyer, 1978:149–56) and Mexico (Passariello, 1983:109–22 and Brewer, 1984:487–501). My description of the situation in Kuzaki has been an attempt to go beyond all of these external models to the internal structure which gives meaning and coherence for the Japanese.

The importance of language in host–guest relations has been very carefully examined in an article by Cohen and Cooper (1986:533–63). Although the tourists in Kuzaki are Japanese, they are still considered outsiders. While they are not referred to as *gaijin* as foreigners are, they are addressed by the honorific term for guest (*okyaku-sama*) and this very use of polite language is a way of distinguishing between villagers and outsiders. In the village, as I was told, there was no need for polite language, all villagers were spoken to as if they were kin. The levels of polite language used by the innowners and geisha also indicated a separation between guests and villagers: when addressing the guests, people tried to use standard Tokyo Japanese rather than the village dialect which was a mixture of Osaka dialect and words particular to the area. The notions that these guests were dirty (messing up beaches) and dangerous (requiring a nightwatchman in the summer) were held in conjunction with the idea that guests must be well treated, fed with good food and addressed politely. On one level, of course, this is only good business, but at a deeper level this ambiguity is fuelled by older ideas of the power of the stranger.

In Japanese folk religion, strangers are unknowns, they are dangerous and yet they bring benefits which cannot be ignored. Tourists are like the ancient strangers who were both honoured and feared. Like the deities of Yoshida's article, they should be well treated but quickly sent on their way before they bring trouble. The new tourists are economically powerful and it is economic well-being that they bring to Kuzaki, though few villagers claimed to like them. The guests are middle-class Japanese and the villagers believe themselves to be middle-class as well. They too go on group holidays to resort areas, but the tourists to Kuzaki are urban Japanese, and Kuzaki people have definite feelings about the meanness and unfriendliness of city people. In the sense that the village is still on the margin of modern Japanese society, the tourists to the village can be seen as mediators between the traditional fishing and diving life of the old days and the new modern successful life of urban Japan. Like the mystical strangers of old, tourists mediate between this world (village Japan) and the other (city Japan), while their power to benefit and pollute is now seen in very literal terms. Most importantly, these tourists are part of the very society, Japan, in which the villagers dwell.

This model can be expanded to include the Western tourist in Japan, the visitor who is offered — as the anthropologist Joy Hendry puts it — a 'gift-wrapped' Japan (Hendry, 1988). The Western tourist, generally well-to-do, travels through the Japan of Tokyo, Kyoto and Nara where there are first-class Western hotels, people who speak English, romanized restaurant menus and underground signs and where the tour guides to the 'must-see' sights will also speak a variety of foreign languages. Service is excellent and journeys into the 'real' Japan include travelling on the smoothest, fastest railway in the world; Kabuki theatre (with English tapes of the dialogue); geisha (with interpreter); sumo wrestling; tea ceremonies; and guided trips to see the 'pearl divers'. As described so brilliantly by Alan Booth (1985), to divert from this path is to encounter a Japan where children chase after one shouting 'gaijin, gaijin', where no one speaks English, where the signs are no longer romanized; where the 'typical' inns will not accept a foreigner ('we don't speak English') and where food must be obtained by pointing at plastic food in the restaurant window. Even those people who think they have penetrated into the 'real' Japan will — from time to time — be reminded that they are essentially and forever strangers by people who will not understand their Japanese no matter how fluent it is. They have entered a Japan where there is no way of handling the potentially dangerous stranger who, unfortunately, refuses to go away. The best example I have is of an incident which occurred not to me but to a good friend.

This friend, an anthropologist of Japan, was travelling on a domestic airline to Okinawa for a break from fieldwork. A non-smoker, he had a seat in the no-smoking section. Just after take-off, a stewardess came up to him and asked him — in English — to change to the smoking area: the stewardess in the no-smoking section did not speak English but she, the smoking-section stewardess, did. In Japanese, he told her that he was quite happy to be served by someone speaking only Japanese. In Japanese, the stewardess explained once more that the stewardess in his section spoke no English but she did; would he kindly change seats? This argument went on for about 20 minutes, entirely in Japanese. In the end, he acquiesced and moved to the other section.

The airline wanted his custom and wanted to provide the best of service in return for this, but that could only be done by someone who spoke his language. Conceptually, it is too much to ask a Japanese to believe that a foreigner might speak the language well. That would be too close to the stranger becoming not a stranger: a great confusion of categories. The fact that Asians, among others, are learning Japanese and causing great confusion in this manner has led to the reinforcement of Japanese nationalism through the growth of a literature called *nihonujinron* or 'theories of Japaneseness'. This literature describes in minute detail how different the Japanese are from everyone else in terms of culture, language, the development of the brain and blood types.

Westerners often see this as racist, but from a Japanese perspective it can be seen as the natural reaction of a people whose belief in the danger and polluting qualities of the ambiguous stranger who should be kept separate is still strong. These reactions may very well have been reinforced by both the progress and the destruction which followed the forced opening of Japan to the West in the 19th century. If one examines the 'cycles' of receptiveness and hostility to outsiders which have occurred during the last century, it becomes clear that the model of the foreigner as stranger is not static. While the domestic tourist, the Japanese outsider, can be both beneficial and dangerous at the same time, the modern *gaijin* seems to be an even more ambiguous figure in which one aspect or another of his ambiguity is emphasized at different times. Which aspect of the model will be emphasized depends on all sorts of factors, too complex to describe here: these include fashion as well as the political and economic situations.

Thus, if the domestic tourist should be treated like a *kami*, the foreign tourist is perceived to be more like the *kami*: sometimes threatening and sometimes the bearer of good fortune. Whereas the former appears to the Japanese as complex, ambiguous and timeless, attitudes towards the *gaijin* oscillate diachronically between the two poles which are contained within the concept of the stranger as both sacred and polluting. This may explain how a frequent traveller to Japan can find it possible to say: 'a few years ago everyone was so friendly and Western things were greatly admired, but now the Japanese have turned inwards'. Once the foreigner represented the novelties of the outside world, then he represented all the dangers of the Western world. Soon, since the foreigners are not going to disappear, the attitude may change again. Truly, the tourist in modern Japan is close to the deities of old.

NOTES

1. For a discussion of the way in which some sociologists believe that Simmel's ideas about the stranger have been misinterpreted and used to describe either the passing outsider or the immigrant, see William A. Shack's 'Introduction' to *Strangers in African Societies* (1979:1–17) as well as Donald N. Levine's *Simmel at a Distance* in the same collection (1979:21–36).
2. Yoshida translated the Japanese Shinto term *kami* as 'god' since he wanted to draw parallels with the notion of the stranger as god in Greece, Mexico and Ethiopia. However, I prefer the term 'deity' as the translation of *kami* for it holds fewer associations with the Western notion of an all-powerful patriarchical figure. The Japanese deities are, indeed, closer to the ancient Greek deities of nature than they are to the Judeo–Christian notion of god.
3. While I was not prayed to, I certainly was continually offered food, drink and, after my host household brought in the largest shrimp catch of the year, I was nicknamed *'dairyō kami-sama'* (deity of the large catches). Soon after, the rumour went around the village that those *ama* diving in the same general area as I did always had large catches.
4. There is, in general folklore of Japan, a bit of confusion about where the deities dwell: they can be in more than one place at the same time (Amaterasu is both in the village shrine and Ise Shrine, as well as in numerous other shrines); and they can dwell in the heavens which can be either a mountain top or a land across the sea. This confusion does not negate the fact that the deities dwell in a separate space which is still part of Japan.
5. Yoshida does not define these terms, but here *tabi* and *tabihito* mean, respectively 'journey' and 'journeying person'.
6. For more empirical data on the villagers' attitudes towards tourism, see Martinez, 1990.
7. Dried and cut strips of abalone or ear shell.
8. The village Farming and Fishing Co-operative in Kuzaki (*gyogyō kyōdō kumi-ai*) has existed since 1903 and is the nearest thing to a village governing body. It administers the village as a ward of Toba City as well as overseeing all aspects of village economic life, deciding when to fish, when to dive, when to take in any harvest, negotiating sales for the households, organizing village festivals and overseeing the increasing tourism in the area through its subsidiary, the Kuzaki Tourism Co-operative. The village seacoast belongs to the co-operative and village fishermen must be licensed to fish in it. The co-operative takes funds from fishing households for National Fishermen's Aid and Insurance, buys petrol for the boats, as well as nets, weights, bins, tackle and other gear to sell to the fishermen. It communicates with other villages over fishing territories, settles disputes and monitors the weather most carefully. Since the co-operative's role in diving and fishing is so large, its head and the other five executive officers are usually fishermen. Kuzaki's co-operative is unusual in that the office of co-operative head and village head are merged. All households in the village belong to the co-operative and have the power to vote on all decisions made by it.

9. The women who work in the inns serving the meals and entertaining the guests always refer to themselves as 'geisha'. However, more properly, the term is used to describe the highly skilled women who train for years as entertainers and singers in order to earn the title of 'geisha'. The *ama* do not use the more appropriate term 'hostess' because this word is often used to refer to the women who work in bars and sometimes provide sexual favours. To make clear that they do not do this, the women of Kuzaki call themselves 'geisha'. The visitors tend to refer to them either as *'ama-san'* or address them by their name.

10. I later learned that the wife of the man who told me this worked as often as she could in inns, that the man himself took tourists out fishing in his motorboat and that their eldest daughter did summer work as a maid in one of the inns. After I left the village, this family finally put the funds together to build their own inn and, when I returned in 1986, had a thriving business.

11. I find the naming of this beach highly suggestive for two reasons. The first includes both the association of domestic tourism with an outsider as foreign as the Princess of Wales and the attempt to appeal to trendy urban Japanese by the use of a foreign word (cf. Moeran 1983:93–108). The other is the hope, occasionally expressed by the villagers, that Westerners might discover Kuzaki as a resort. I imagine that they might well regret the fulfilment of the latter, for reasons I discuss below.

REFERENCES

Ashkenazi, Michael (1983) Festival Change and Continuity in a Japanese Town, unpublished PhD thesis, Faculty of the Graduate School of Yale University.

Booth, Alan (1985) *The Roads to Sata*, New York, Tokyo: Weatherhill.

Brewer, Jeffrey P. (1984) 'Tourism and ethnic stereotypes, variations in a Mexican town', *Annals of Tourism Research*, 11, 487–501.

Cohen, Eric and Robert L. Cooper (1986) 'Language and tourism', *Annals of Tourism Research*, 13, 553–63.

Douglas, Mary (1970) *Purity and Danger*, Harmondsworth: Penguin

Goodman, Roger (1987) A Study of the Kikokushijo Phenomenon: Returnee Schoolchildren in Contemporary Japan, unpublished PhD thesis, Faculty of Social Anthropology and Geography, University of Oxford.

Graburn, Nelson H.H. (1983) To Pray, Pay and Play: the Cultural Structure of Japanese Domestic Tourism, *Les Cahiers du Tourisme*, serie no 26, Centre des Haute Etudes Touristiques, Université de Droit, d'Economie et des Sciences, Aix-en-Provence: Centre des Hautes Etudes Touristiques.

Hendry, Joy (1984) 'Shoes, the early learning of an important distinction in Japanese society', in Gordon Daniels (ed.), *Europe Interprets Japan*, Tenterden, Kent: Paul Norbury Publications.

Hori, Ichiro (1963) 'Mysterious visitors from the harvest to the new year' in Richard Dorson (ed.), *Studies in Japanese Folklore*, Bloomington: Indiana University Press.

Levine, Donald N. (1979) 'Simmel at a distance: on the history and systematics of the sociology of the stranger' in William A. Shack and Elliot P. Skinner (eds), *Strangers in African Societies*.

Kim Moon, Ok-Pyo (1986) 'Is the ie disappearing in rural Japan? The impact of tourism on a traditional Japanese village' in Joy Hendry (ed.), *Interpreting Japanese Society*, Oxford: JASO.

Martinez, D.P. (1990) 'Tourism and the Ama, the search for a real Japan' in Eyal Ben-Ari, Brian Moeran and James Valentine (eds), *Unwrapping Japan*.

Meleghy, Tamas, Max Preglau and Alois Tafertshafer (1985) 'Tourism development and value change', *Annals of Tourism Research*, 12, 181–99.

Mendosa, Eugene L. (1983) 'Tourism and income strategies in Nazare, Portugal', *Annals of Tourism Research*, 10, 213–38.

Moeran, B. (1983) 'The language of Japanese tourism', *Annals of Tourism Research*, 10(1), 93–108.

Ogura, Manabu (1963) 'Drifted deities in the Noto Peninsula' in Richard Dorson (ed.), *Studies in Japanese Folklore*, Bloomington: Indiana University Press.

Ono, Sokyo in collaboration with William P. Woodward (1962) *Shinto, the Kami Way*, Tokyo: Charles E. Tuttle.

Passariello, Phyllis (1983) 'Never on Sunday? Mexican tourists at the beach', *Annals of Tourism Research*, 10, 109–22.

Picone, Mary J. (1984) Rites and Symbols of Death in Japan, unpublished PhD thesis, Faculty of Social Anthropology and Geography, University of Oxford.

Pi-Sunyer, Oriol (1977) 'Through native eyes: tourists and tourism in a Catalan maritime community' in V. Smith (ed.), *Host and Guests: the Anthropology of Tourism*, Oxford: Blackwell.

Plath, David W. (1964) *The After Hours, Modern Japan and the Search for Enjoyment*, Berkeley: University of California Press.

Shack, William A. and Elliott P. Skinner (eds) (1979) *Strangers in African Societies*, Berkeley and Los Angeles: University of California Press.

Simmel, Georg (1950) 'The Stranger' in *The Sociology of Georg Simmel*, trans. and edited by K.H. Wolff, New York: Free Press.

Tokushima, Tomao (1980) 'Tourism within, from and to Japan', *International Social Science Journal*, 32, 128–50.

Yamaguchi, Masao (1977) 'Kingship theatricality and marginal reality in Japan' in R.K. Jain (ed.), *Text and Context, the Social Anthropology of Tradition*, Philadelphia: Institute for the Study of Social Issues.

Yamaguchi, Masao (1987) 'The dual structure of Japanese emperorship', *Current Anthropology*, 28(4) (supplement), 5–11.

Yoshida, Teigo (1981) 'Stranger as God, the place of the outsider in Japanese folk religion', *Ethnology*, 202, 87–99.

10 Place, Image and Power: Brighton as a Resort

KEVIN MEETHAN

Struggles over the appropriation of economic or cultural goods are, simultaneously, symbolic struggles to appropriate distinctive signs in the form of classified, classifying goods or practices (Bourdieu, 1984:249).

INTRODUCTION

This chapter is concerned with the social production and reproduction of places as objects of tourist consumption. Tourism, as the other contributors to this volume make clear, is a simple label for a complex phenomena, encompassing different activities in different forms. Despite this variety, tourism can be typified in some respects as the experience and consumption of place. Tourist destinations — resorts, sights, heritage centres and even entire countries — are all places removed from the everyday concerns that revolve around the home, the family and work, at least as far as the visitors are concerned. The tourist experience is thus marked as distinct in both spatio–temporal terms and also in the kinds of behaviour both expected and indulged in. Time is not spent in productive activity but in the conspicuous consumption of leisure. This formulation is similar to that used by Urry (1990) when he talks of the 'tourist gaze' involving the production and consumption of signs. Irreducibly associated with such a process are issues of power (Harvey, 1993; Robins, 1993; Rotenberg and McDonogh, 1993). For places to achieve the distinctiveness which is the necessary condition of their symbolic status, as places to go to, to be seen in, they have to be created as such (Kearns and Philo, 1993). The process involved is one whereby space, in the generic sense, is appropriated and constituted as specific places; how symbolic value is ascribed to and derived from the environment. As Lefebvre states, space is 'a *stake*, the locus of projects and actions deployed as specific strategies, and hence the object of *wagers* on the future' (1991:142–3, emphasis in original). It is to these stakes and wagers, the players, and the game they are involved in that I now turn.

The Tourist Image: Myths and Myth Making in Tourism. Edited by Tom Selwyn.
© 1996 John Wiley & Sons Ltd.

PAST TO PRESENT

The role of tourism in Brighton — and by extension, the status of the 'traditional' seaside resorts of Britain — needs to be set in an historical context. Not only does this inform us of the long-term changes that have occurred in the patterns of leisure consumption but also because the issue of history itself, in the guise of heritage, is a significant factor in the ways in which spatial forms are conceptualized and appropriated (Ashworth and Larkham, 1994; Ashworth and Tunbridge, 1990; Corner and Harvey, 1991; Hewison, 1987; Wright, 1985).

By the 18th century, it had become established medical orthodoxy that bathing and drinking water — of a particular kind — was both a cure and a palliative for a variety of ailments. Increasing numbers of the rising merchant classes began to patronize both inland and seaside spas (Walton, 1983). It was the patronage of such activities by the then highly fashionable Prince Regent that led to the establishment of Brighton as the premier resort in the country.

Having purchased land on what was then the fringes of a fishing town, the prince commissioned the building of a 'marine pavilion', which during the early years of the 19th century was remodelled and extended, resulting in the building which today is known as the Royal Pavilion. Following the prince came the world of regency fashion. The consumption of sea air and water was not only accepted medical practice but also a conspicuous show of wealth and privilege. The influence of the Prince Regent and his court was to have profound effects on the fortunes of the town. Brighton began to acquire a reputation as a place given over wholly to the pursuit of pleasure, personified by the prince's 'raffish' behaviour (Musgrave, 1970).

The growth of the town was rapid: along the sea front, imposing terraces were built facing the sea, while behind, a jumble of cheap and squalid terraces sprang up to house those who served the gentry. A new attraction, the Chain Pier was built in 1823. Originally intended as a landing stage for passenger and goods traffic, the pier soon became the place to be seen taking the air.

Until the mid-19th century then, Brighton was a town for the privileged, a town whose existence owed nothing to the manufacture of goods, and everything to the consumption of leisure by the élite. The arrival of the railway from London in 1853, and the subsequent introduction of cheap excursion fares meant that the town of privilege became available to the urban working classes of the capital. The accession of Queen Victoria to the throne ended the direct connection between the town and the monarchy. The Royal Pavilion was allowed to fall into disuse and was only saved from demolition by the Town Commissioners, the fore-runners of the borough council — who negotiated the purchase of the building from the Crown in 1850.

Figure 10.1   Overlooking the seafront promenade the Grand Hotel
epitomizes wealth and privilege. Photograph G. Selwyn

The growth of leisure time during the Victorian age led to further
expansion of the town. Following the prevailing pattern of urban
development this led to the creation of high-status areas on the fringes of
the town, so that the houses of those who serviced the tourist trade,
originally isolated behind the seafront terraces, became an inner town area
noted for its overcrowding and slum conditions. It was also at this time
that the neighbouring borough of Hove began to expand, quickly acquiring
a reputation for select charm and elegance, in contrast to the vulgar
amusements that could be found in Brighton (Musgrave, 1970).

The increasing provision of leisure amenities continued through the 19th
century. The West Pier was built in 1866, to be followed by the Palace Pier
in the closing decade of the 19th century, while the original Chain Pier was
destroyed by a storm in 1895. Other attractions were added: an aquarium
and Volks's Electric Railway. In common with the two piers, all these were

Figure 10.2 Consuming sun, sea and air on the Palace Pier. Photograph
G. Selwyn

financed by private capital. Despite the influx of working-class day-trippers
and holidaymakers, and competition from neighbouring Hove, the town
still managed to retain the patronage of the rich élite, a trend which
continued into the 20th century.

Although the beach itself may have been neutral territory where both
high and low consumption of sea air and water co-existed side by side,
other areas of the town were marked by their symbolic status into places
for the upper class and places for the working class, with the emphasis
changing from the consumption of air and water to the consumption of
amusements and novelties in the form of penny arcades, souvenir shops
and other places of entertainment.

The pattern of demand and consumption of leisure had been met
through the use of private capital until the 1920s and 1930s, when Brighton
Council began to take over what were then loss-making ventures like the
aquarium and Volks's Railway, as well as investing in new attractions such
as an athletics stadium and an open-air swimming pool. In order to attract
the still buoyant domestic tourist market, the council also invested in
publicity campaigns, publishing official guidebooks and even making a
film entitled *Playground of the Kings* to be shown to audiences in Canada
and the USA.

The existence of such material served to attract holidaymakers by
differentiating the town not only from the world of work but also from
other rival seaside resorts. Brighton was portrayed not only as a town

boasting modern — and municipally funded — attractions but also as a place of history. The handbook for 1938/9 for example, contains a whimsical tale in which the ghost of the Prince Regent, found wandering in the town centre, is given a tour of Brighton by the author, so he can marvel at the changes and benefits of modernity. The literary connections and the romance of the town, from Jane Austen to Arnold Bennett, are stressed: 'It is a "romantic name" to people all over the country. Outside the country too. Its reputation is international. No one who reads English books can help hearing of it. It has a secure place in literature' (Musgrave, 1970:18).

It is ironic that the most secure place was to be that provided by Grahame Greene, whose novel *Brighton Rock*, originally published in 1938, depicts the other side of Brighton in less than flattering terms

> The streets narrowed above the Steyne [sic]; the shabby secret behind the bright corsage . . . the children played about the steep slope of rubble; a piece of fireplace showed houses had once been there, and a municipal notice announced new flats on a post stuck in the torn gravel and asphalt facing the little dingy damaged row, all that was left of Paradise Piece (1975:140–1).

Both the book, and the film (shot on location in 1947) were condemned by the council and the local press as having created an unfavourable image of the town which might damage the tourist trade.

The earlier associations of the town with the raffish behaviour of the Prince Regent took on a new dimension in the inter-war years when Brighton acquired the reputation of the town of the 'dirty weekend', where those cheating on their spouses would meet their lovers for illicit liaisons. The existence of this widespread but rather erroneous view (Shields, 1990) was not confined only to Brighton but rather reflects the point that inasmuch as tourism removes the distinction of work — home — family, it also removes (or is presumed to remove) the accepted constraints of conventional behaviour (Bowman, 1992).

The post-war years witnessed the start of the decline in the home tourist industry. In order to diversify the economic base of the town, the council encouraged the development of light industry and discussed ways of invigorating the tourist trade, including one proposal to remove the 'cafes, fish stalls and small shops in the arches under the seafront; the removal of the "dodge-'em" car track from the beach opposite the aquarium; and the creation of a continental atmosphere on the front by the provision of colour, flowers and music' (Musgrave, 1970:411).

The restoration of the Royal Pavilion also began at this time. The Victorian interior decor and additions were removed and much of the original furniture, on loan from the Crown, was returned. Attitudes towards the pavilion and the architecture of the town in general were, however, far

Figure 10.3 The seafront mansions are now subject to the tourist gaze.
Photograph G. Selwyn

removed from the current vogue of dewy-eyed heritage nostalgia, at least as
far as the official guidebooks were concerned: 'In one respect the slick,
streamlined up to the minute Brighton is unique. It preserves, not as a
museum piece but at the thriving centre of its life today a set of building
begun by a Prince's whim in 1787' (Brighton Borough Council, 1951:8).

The emphasis throughout the immediate post-war years, and into the
1960s was on the virtues of the sea, the sun and the variety of amenities
and entertainments that the town could offer, as this example, produced by
both Brighton and Hove councils, shows: '"Sunshine holidays are best". So
these pictures show what sunshine happiness can mean . . . Lovely girls on
holiday in high spirits, contented folk, sunshine, dozing' (Brighton and
Hove Publicity Committee, 1954:5).

As long as the domestic tourist market remained buoyant, the town
could offer different kinds of attractions to different sections of society,
with each confined to its appropriate place, both physically and symbolically, but the focus was still on the seafront. In 1952, a development
plan for the borough was prepared, in which it was stated, with what now
seems like foresight, that

> So long as the principle attractions of Brighton consist of the sea, and its
> proximity to the capital, this part [the seafront] must remain the town centre.
> This could only be altered by the emergence of a greater social magnet than
> the sea (Brighton Borough Council, 1952:70).

THE PRESENT PAST

The advent of cheap air travel and the package holiday meant that Brighton could no longer compete in the mass tourist market. When trade declined, the council invested heavily in the Brighton Centre, in order to encourage conference business to the town, or, to paraphrase Lefebvre (1991), began making wagers on the future. The growth of this sector throughout the past 20 years can be gauged by the fact that in 1973, 220 conferences had been held in the town; by 1984, the total had risen to 1100 (Brighton Borough Council, 1986:139), a figure which since has grown only marginally to 1200 in 1994 (Department of the Environment, 1994:143). In addition, it is estimated that the conference trade generates revenue of £63M annually (ibid.).

In common with other resort towns, the council also took a proactive role in encouraging service industries to relocate. Between the years of 1971 and 1984, occupied office floor space increased by 1.2M square feet, and many large organizations such as American Express and Trustcard established large offices in the town. Higher education also expanded with the establishment of the University of Sussex in 1963 and the later establishment of the University of Brighton, formerly Brighton Polytechnic. The consequent influx of white-collar jobs altered the composition of the work-force.

Other changes in both attitude and legislation towards the urban environment were also to have a big impact. The slum clearance schemes that transformed the urban landscape of Britain during the 1960s and early 1970s also left their mark on Brighton. Large sections of poor quality housing were cleared and were replaced with tower blocks and offices. Protests against such building and the slum clearances that it entailed began to be voiced by an increasingly influential environmental lobby. With the passing of central government legislation, local councils were allowed, in 1976, to designate groups of buildings of historical and architectural interest as conservation areas, within which development was to be controlled. In Brighton, seven such areas were designated in 1976 which have since been increased to 27, with some 1900 listed buildings (Department of the Environment, 1994:143).

The appropriation of these areas, with the official designations changing in some instances from slums to conservation areas, together with the increasing number of service-sector jobs in the town, created the conditions whereby parts of the town underwent a process of gentrification (cf. Smith and Williams, 1986). Such appropriation of space, or elevating the mundane to the special, confers on such places a form of symbolic capital, resulting in what Zukin has termed a 'coherent space of consumption' (1990:41) in which the environment itself becomes not the location of production but the object of consumption, offering a spatial narrative complete with a legitimizing myth of historical origin and significance subsumed under the rubric of heritage.

In its broadest sense, heritage not only provides a visible and tangible link to history but also implies that it is a commodity in danger (Hewison, 1987; Wright, 1985). Threatened by development and slum clearance, heritage needs to be isolated at both a material and symbolic level from the processes of change and confined to specific areas. Incomers to such areas can use their economic capital to acquire the added symbolic capital that is conferred by the past.

In the case of Brighton, the incomers to one particular inner-town area constructed a common identity — a 'community' in their own words — by acting as self-appointed guardians of the area's heritage, by using the same set of symbolic associations, the same signs of distinction that objectify status, that the town in general was thought to possess. The most common reasons given by these incomers for choosing that particular area were its character, heritage and style (Meethan, 1990:126). Similarly, Fees (Chapter 7) describes how, in Chipping Campden, the new incomers appropriated the town as a place of heritage and the consumption of privilege.

Such changes in status, however, were only made possible by the active intervention of the local council. The widespread nature and importance of this power of local authorities, to designate areas as possessing historical significance, thus commodifying the environment, should not be underestimated. Ashworth and Tunbridge (1990) note that it is now exceptional for any town or city not to have at least their central area covered by such protective legislation. Such a change in the values that are ascribed to, and derived from, the environment can also have significant consequences in attracting inward investment. Ashworth and Voogd (1990), for example, point out that an appreciation of the quality of life in urban areas can be a crucial component in the location of economic activity (Bagguley et al., 1990; Cooke, 1989, 1990; Harloe et al., 1990; Kearns and Philo, 1993; Urry, 1990). In short, the image of place, the symbolic capital that places of history possess is itself a significant factor in decisions which might appear to be made on the basis of economic criteria alone.

As the elements of the town were being objectified as places set apart, of historical importance by both council officials and sections of the population, the images produced for the tourist trade were also undergoing a similar change. A focus on the benefits of the sea air and the seaside amenities of the town changed to a concern with the appearance of selected areas of the urban landscape cast in terms of heritage, an appropriation of the past and a disavowal of the modern, as the 1984 handbook makes clear:

> The rich history of Brighton and Hove stems from that handsome, wayward, gifted and spendthrift prince known as 'Prinny', George, Prince of Wales . . . In addition to the unique Royal Pavilion, many fine examples of Regency

Figure 10.4   Below the promenade, tradition becomes nostalgia.
Photograph G. Selwyn

buildings are to be found . . . being a worthy reminder of one of Brighton's
most colourful periods (Brighton Borough Council, 1984:13).

Out goes the 'streamlined up to the minute town', to be replaced by a
town of history, a key factor in recent tourist developments (Ashworth and
Voogd, 1990). As the English Tourist Board's survey of the town in 1983
was to comment:

> Tourism reinforces endeavours to conserve Brighton's heritage of old
> buildings because history and architecture and the environment generally are
> among the top attractions. Furthermore, a minority of visitors were vocal
> about the need for further renovation . . . Priority for future action should be
> given to putting right the dilapidation of the most prominent and visible sites
> . . . Apart from its outstanding architecture, Brighton is quite exceptionally
> rich in characterful history (ibid:78–9).

The creation of place, of Brighton as a resort that was linked to and
focused on the sea and its attendant attractions, had been displaced by a
new focus — a new social magnet — that sought to create a 'characterful
history'. In terms of the townscape itself, this is manifest not only by
attention to the prominent façades of buildings but also to the changes that
were recently made to the Old Town (commonly known as 'The Lanes')
conservation area. Here, streets have been closed to traffic, paving slabs

replaced with more picturesque red bricks; cast-iron pillars whose function is to mark the pedestrian areas have been added as well as cast-iron signposts, litterbins and benches, painted black with gold lettering; new shopfronts are designed to look old. The process is thus one of obliterating the immediate and modern past by the creation of a townscape that is decked out in the street furniture of an imagined bygone era — cast iron displaces plastic, concrete and galvanised steel; modernist design is consigned to the scrapheap, resulting in the creation of a townscape which idealizes an imaginary past.

The links with history are also manifested by the large number of antique shops and traders in the town. Here, heritage becomes tangible, a consumable take-away history where even the most banal household artefacts and bric-à-brac acquire value by virtue of their age. If the town is perceived as having a characterful history — and is hence a place of characters — then this too can be provided. One attempt to capitalize on this image of Brighton as a town inhabited by a colourful and flamboyant population was the promotion of the annual Brighton Festival.

Although established in 1966, the Brighton Festival was regarded by many in the town as a low-key, élitist event. In 1985, with the appointment of a new festival director and an increase in funding from both the borough and county councils, the festival began to assume the character of a large-scale event. Held annually in May, the start of the tourist season, the festival involves music, theatre, performance and art exhibitions and is seen as a way to attract the high-spending cultural tourists to the town.

In 1986, the director commissioned a report, submitted to the county council arts committee, which reiterated some of the 1983 tourist board recommendations:

> The colourful and flamboyant population is an ongoing spectacle that makes Brighton stand out from other towns . . . The Palace Pier should get rid of its casino games, expensive fast food and plastic chairs which turn it into a 'teen hangout'. Instead, quality activities should make visits to both piers a memorable experience . . . It should be called 'Brighton International Festival' (*Evening Argus*: 10 October 1986).

The festival director, when asked what the attraction of Brighton was, told me that it consisted of 'the historical and heritage aspects, plus a sense of fun, a young person's place, raffish, but with a feeling for progressive style'. In terms of the tourist potential, I was informed that 'cultural tourism is a key national development area. With the advances made at Glasgow, Bradford, Birmingham, Bristol etc. (areas with little in the way of 'traditional' tourist attractions), Brighton is in danger of slipping behind, even in terms of attracting the conference trade. The festival can help to project the town's individuality and validity'. As the festival duly turned international in the following year, the *Independent* described the town as follows:

famous watering hole — a favourite of kings, princes, characters in farces
who are cheating on their wives, and Londoners in need of a glimpse of the
sea . . . The tree lined Old Steine and Royal Pavilion area is a must . . . The
Palace Pier is all candy floss and bingo, and Brighton at its most garish and
vulgar (2 May 1987).

While disavowing the vulgar, the festival also began to incorporate some
more arguably traditional elements such as maypole dancing outside the
pavilion to mark the start of the festival. Local community groups were
encouraged to participate, and their contribution took the form of small
plays, performed in the Old Town conservation area. The festival director
was to write that 'I floated the idea of a revival of the mystery plays, where
the craftspeople of a town would be organised into guilds . . . Brighton's
version of this medieval custom will deal with the town itself . . . We are
allowing a tradition to start in Brighton' (Brighton Borough Council, 1987a).

As the festival became international and invented new traditions, the
Borough Council also added their contribution. As well as appointing a
town crier to act as an official character, the council began to subsidize the
arts in the town, since 'the richness of the arts in Brighton makes the town
an exciting place' (Brighton Borough Council, 1987b).

A five-year plan was also launched to boost the tourist trade. The Resort
Services Department described the town in the following terms: 'A combination of heritage and stylish elegance, a sophisticated London by the sea
with a reputation for good food, good fun, first class accommodation and a
good natured acceptance of the cosmopolitan lifestyle the town attracts'
(personal communication).

The central idea behind the strategy was to attract the higher-spending,
long-stay tourists, as a member of the Tourism and Marketing Department
told me:

> Brighton is a resort that epitomizes, and therefore attracts, stylish elegance. Its
> appeal will be extended beyond the present young ABCs into the maturer AB
> as this market segment increases. Brighton will endeavour to provide and
> anticipate the requirements of an increasingly demanding and sophisticated
> customer whilst at the same time increasing its appeal to the long-haul (and
> therefore long-stay) overseas market by offering itself as an alternative to
> London as an attractive and exciting tourist base for both the south-east and
> the rest of the country (personal communication).

What is of significance here is the explicit codification of cultural values
(Watson and Kopachevsky, 1994) in the way that the seaside and its
attendant attractions, the original *raison d'être* of the town, are associated
with 'vulgar', 'low' culture, while the more refined consumption of high
culture is associated with the town's festival and architectural heritage.
Such a reversal of values can be seen in the contrasting fortunes of the
West Pier and the Pavilion. The West Pier was closed in 1974, due to the

poor repair, and has been partly dismantled and left to decay. Although some limited restoration work has been carried out, the main structure, now cut off from the land, stands as a stark reminder of the declining fortunes of Brighton as a seaside resort. In contrast, the Pavilion has recently undergone an extensive programme of renovation costing millions and taking many years. A council handbook of the mid-1980s simply states that the West Pier 'has been closed since 1974' while the Pavilion is 'renowned throughout the world and is one of Brighton's key tourist attractions, and of great importance to the town's economy' (Brighton Borough Council, 1984:12).

In order to promote this aspect of the town, the high cultural reading of the urban townscape, the low cultural pursuits epitomized by the seafront entertainments have to take a less prominent role, as the Council's Borough Plan made clear.

> boisterous seaside entertainment uses are not allowed to spread into the more sensitive areas where their presence would not only harm the function and character, but also prejudice other aims of conservation . . . the perception [of Brighton] as an historic town falls seriously behind other areas and a dilapidated appearance of some seafront buildings and the existence of derelict sites have not improved its image (Brighton Borough Council, 1986:114–15).

Here, the appropriation of spaces for the traditional and boisterous, and for the more sensitive cultural pursuits, reveals that one tradition — the seaside holiday — is being superseded by the creation of another tradition — that of heritage and architectural conservation. The boisterous nature of the seaside holiday is marked by the consumption of trivia, absurd hats, ice cream, fish and chips and Brighton rock, goods and pastimes set against the aggressively modern background of amusement arcades — flashing lights, plastic, chrome and noise — which become the outward signs that distinguish one group of tourists from residents and one group of tourists from another.

The consumption of heritage, the high cultural reading of the town, is an altogether more discrete affair. Within the Pavilion, the tourists file past the exhibits in a quiet reverence, while the shop, in common with many of the more upmarket retail outlets, markets heritage in the form of reproduction wallpaper and furnishing fabrics, reproduction Victorian jewellery, history books of the town and, for those whose incomes are more modest, 'Regency Preserves' — the market equivalent of Brighton rock. The class dimension, the downplaying of the vulgar and the elevation of the tourist experience to an aesthetic one, becomes cast in the form of a historicity in which fragments of the past are made visible, where a visit to the Pavilion becomes a Regency experience, where culture is commodified for the AB market segment.

BEHIND THE FAÇADE

The existence of a dominant image of the town that emphasizes the virtues of high culture, over those of low culture, relates to the need to generate sufficient numbers of the right kind of visitors to support the tourist sector of the local economy. It also relates to wider processes of economic change and the consumption of culture. In turn, this symbolic appropriation of place was reinforced by certain groups of recent incomers to the town. In short, these elements act as a system of distinction and exclusion, in which attributes of the urban form are selected and taken to be the authentic town — the real Brighton.

There is, however, also an image of the town that stands in direct opposition to the preferred high culture model, in which an attention to the character of the town is nothing more than an empty sham and a charade. In 1984, when the Conservative Party held their ill-fated annual conference, the local press reported that one local Conservative councillor had written to the prime minister, inviting her to see at first hand the social problems that lay behind the façade: 'Behind our elegant regency façades there lurks too frequently a seedy side of life which we are not anxious for our visitors to see' (*Brighton and Hove Leader*, 5 October 1984).

More recently, a Labour councillor also used the image of the façade to describe the problems that existed in the town: 'Behind its Regency façade, Brighton has severe social and economic problems' (*Evening Argus*, 5 October 1985). One of the ironies is that the image of Brighton as a rich, successful and prosperous town was so successful that in 1985 the government of the day removed Brighton from the list of areas that qualified for the then Urban Aid programme. The rationale for this decision was that as Brighton had a presumed higher than average number of pensioners, the indicators of social deprivation used to calculate urban aid were being 'distorted'. Even by the Department of the Environment's own estimation this was somewhat short of the mark, for with most of the indicators used, Brighton ranked in the top 10 percent. As the local press was to comment, under the headline 'Behind the Façade': 'Brighton's pensioners have been blamed for a number of things in the past . . . But a government minister, Sir George Young, has come up with a novel accusation. He says the large number of old people is distorting official figures on poverty' (*Evening Argus*, 17 September 1985).

At the same time, the (Conservative) MP for the constituency of Kemptown, the eastern half of Brighton, made a statement to the press condemning the decision: 'All the politicians see when they visit Brighton is the glamour and the expensive restaurants, the seafront and the posh hotels' (*Brighton and Hove Leader*, 19 September 1985). As the arguments continued in the local press, it was clearly the mistaken perceptions of the government that were to blame: 'Ministers probably have the idea that

Sussex seaside towns are rich and ritzy, full of well heeled retired people. The reality is that deprivation, according to the Department of the Environment's own assessment, is worse in Brighton, Hove and Hastings then in many northern towns whose names are synonymous with poverty' (*Evening Argus*, 2 December 1985).

In terms of local politics, members of all parties were aware of the social problems that existed behind the façade. This counter-image was not, however, confined to the council chamber or the local press. As an example, in 1986, the Brighton Council for Voluntary Service, a local development agency for the voluntary sector, published a booklet entitled *Behind the Façade? Social Need and the Voluntary Sector* in which it is stated that 'This booklet is about Brighton; it is an area of the affluent south east which has consistently sought recognition for its special needs. . . . [this] recounts a number of features of the town, so well known to us residents but little known to those in Whitehall, whose perception of the town is marred by images of bygone days' (Farleigh, 1986:1).

This counter-image, of Brighton as a town whose essence is one of deprivation (the shabby secret that Greene described uses the same set of signs) has the Regency terraces and their associated glamour as the dominant image. One further example comes from a press report of 1985: 'it was reported last week that there are 93 people living in one building in Oriental Place, Brighton . . . this is only one of the problems in a street which has an exotic name and an elegant façade' (*West Sussex Gazette*, 28 November 1985). The image of Brighton as a town whose gritty authentic reality is hidden behind a façade did not only apply to the local press. In 1987, for example, Cowan wrote in the *Architect's Journal* that 'many of the crowded rabbit warrens lie behind elegant regency façades, regularly painted by their landlords with the aid of grants designed to make the town look salubrious for tourists' (Cowan 1987:42).

While many of the reports are couched in terms that refer to the reality of deprivation behind the façade of elegance, others use the Pavilion — the epitome of Regency style. A newsletter produced by a housing action group on one of the peripheral — in more than one sense — council estates, criticized the cost of restoration work.

> Has your house been modernised? Is it expensive and hard to heat? I'm sure you would like to do something about it. So would I, but when the council is asked to do it, what do we get? 'Sorry, but we haven't the money for things like that.' Yet £6,000,000 has been spent renovating the largest council house of all — the Royal Pavilion which is just a tourist attraction, but which is considered to be more important than the houses in which people live (East Moulsecoomb Residents Association, 1985).

In fact, some of this was paid for by sources other than the council.

This image of a town suffering from hidden social problems was to be further cast in terms of the north–south divide. In 1987, the local newspaper, the *Evening Argus*, exchanged reporters with the *Liverpool Echo*, each producing an article about the other's town. Brighton was typified as a place of contrasts:

> Brighton is a confusion of facts. There is the contradiction of the very rich, the not so rich, and those who know the full reality of Mrs Thatcher's Britain, those on the dole. For Brighton has over 18,000 of these. And there are some facts to shock: Brighton has hovered between 35 and 37 on the list of socially deprived areas of Britain. It now has a Labour Council. They have been rate capped by 20 percent. The Labour Council is short by £46 million. And this is Brighton (*Evening Argus*, 10 March 1987).

As with other representations of the town, it is the Pavilion that stands for and encapsulates the whole.

> And [as] you walk round the Pavilion, Brighton's most famous of landmarks, you can see by the sheer eccentric madness of it all that the town has suffered from this all along. In recent years it has been falling about their ears and is now shrouded in sheets of blue plastic and looks like a sad old lady in need of repair and that is costing the council more than it cares to think about just to restore (ibid.).

Whereas the dominant representation of the town can be located in a body of literature, in histories of the town, in the local press, in council policy and documents and publicity booklets, the inversion of the dominant themes outlined above is less well documented. One exception to this general rule was the publication in 1982 of book entitled *Brighton on the Rocks* which sets out with the specific aim of representing the 'other' Brighton. Few positive aspects of the town are mentioned. Rather than the glossy photographs of the Pavilion and the festival, used by the council, the reader is offered instead grainy black and white photographs of children playing in a desolate wasteland, piles of rubble, refuse collectors and the unemployed — the world of *Brighton Rock* indeed. As for the Palace Pier: 'In winter it shelters those who come south to sleep rough. In summer there are still buckets and spades, some small, others larger, to dig bait (£6 for a hundred worms) — now part of the informal economy of Brighton's unemployed (Queenspark, 1982).

To many of the residents on the peripheral estates of the town, the attention paid to the tourist trade and the attraction of the town centre was indeed a sham. 'We are the real Brighton people' was a phrase I often encountered, used to distinguish the estate dwellers from the 'newcomers' of the gentrified central areas. Yet even within the centre, for those who lived in the bedsit accommodation of the seafront terraces, buildings whose exteriors are maintained but whose interiors are often squalid, phrases such as 'glamour of the Regency era', 'stylish London by the sea', 'a young person's place' bore little relation to their lives.

In some respects, the opposing representations outlined above can be seen as attempts to provide a legitimizing myth, with each claiming to represent the authentic Brighton. However, simply to state that these are the only representations to be found would be overstating the case and would be denying the multiplicity and value of those images of the town held by other discrete groups of residents who also have a stake such as pensioners, students and the substantial gay population.

PLACE, POWER AND IMAGE

The spatial manifestations of certain forms of cultural consumption act as tangible and visible symbols of power. Control over space, the appropriation that creates distinctive places, imposes ways of perceiving and acting by precluding the articulation of alternatives. In the case of Brighton this can be seen in the ways in which the 'boisterous' and hence 'vulgar' elements of the tourist trade were to be confined to selected areas of the town in order that they might not impinge on the high-status cultural image that was considered necessary for the continued success of the town not only as a resort but also as a town of enterprise.

The appropriation of space that created the seaside town, that typified Brighton as a place of pleasure, resulted in the creation of an image of the town as a place given over to 'raffish' behaviour, peopled by characters who are 'colourful', 'flamboyant' and so on. This was linked to the economic necessity of maximizing the available resources, itself the result of competition between localities as they strive to encourage the investment of capital and tourism by creating a sense of distinctiveness. Therefore, both the councillors and the council officials, faced with the need to bolster the tourist and conference trade, had little choice but to act in a way that would maximize the resources of the built environment, to imbue the spatial form with values of heritage and culture by creating an image of the town that marked it as distinct.

This image of distinctiveness is constructed from selected aspects of Brighton's urban form and architecture associated with certain social and behavioural attributes, a mixture of high and low culture which in turn is derived from historical antecedents in the kinds of leisure and mixture of social classes that the town attracted. Both high and low culture could exist side by side, as long as they were clearly delineated and recognized as such. However, the need to turn from the seafront to the architecture of the town itself as the 'new social magnet' meant that controls over the spatial form of the town were necessary; the vulgar amusements had to be contained and isolated, precluded from the town of heritage by both legislative and symbolic means.

The consumption of place is a spatial manifestation not only of power relations but also of the distinction between the space of work and the space of leisure. The problems of the town that lead to the existence of a counter-image are well known to the residents, the councillors and council officials, as well as those working with the poor and unemployed. But the dominance of the image of Brighton as a town that is colourful, cultural and enterprising is reinforced rather than negated by the existence of this counter-image. Those who are prevented from articulating a different image have no choice but to enter the game on the same terms — and by doing so become part of it — to use the same symbolic associations of the Pavilion, the seafront and the Regency architecture but to assign to it a negative valuation.

By accepting the same set of symbols of distinctiveness, such attempts to portray Brighton as town of deprivation behind the façade — the truth behind the sham — indicate not that tourism is a charade, that somehow it involves 'unreal' and 'inauthentic' elements, but rather that the production and consumption of tourist space is inherently ambiguous. Although tourist places are those given over to leisure, removed from the world of work for the visitors, they are also the places of work, the locus of productive activity for its inhabitants.

The analysis of tourism needs to closely examine the power relations that are inherent in the work–leisure divide, their realization as specific places, the strategies of inclusion and exclusion that they involve and their articulation through the symbolic and economic appropriation of space.

REFERENCES

Ashworth, G.J. and P.J. Larkham (eds) (1994) *Building a New Heritage: Tourism, Culture and Identity in the New Europe*, London: Routledge.

Ashworth, G.J. and J.E. Tunbridge (1990) *The Tourist — Historic City*, London: Belhaven Press.

Ashworth, G.J. and H. Voogd (1990) *Selling the City: Marketing Approaches in Public Sector Urban Planning*, London: Belhaven Press.

Bagguley, P., J. Mark-Lawson, D. Shapiro, J. Urry, S. Walby and A. Wardle (1990) *Restructuring: Place, Class and Gender*, London: Sage.

Bourdieu, P. (1984) *Distinction: A Social Critique of the Judgement of Taste*, London: Routledge and Kegan Paul.

Bowman, G. (1992) 'Fucking tourists: Sexual Relations and Tourism in Jerusalem's Old City', *Critique of Anthropology*, 9(2):77–93.

Brighton Borough Council (1938) *Brighton Official Handbook 1938/9*.

Brighton Borough Council (1951) *Brighton Official Handbook*.

Brighton Borough Council (1952) *Report of the Survey: County Borough of Brighton*.

Brighton Borough Council (1984) *Residents' Handbook*, Brighton: Home Publishing.

Brighton Borough Council (1986) *Brighton Borough Plan: Towards 2000*.

Brighton Borough Council (1987a) *Brighton Festival Times*.

Brighton Borough Council (1987b) *Newsline*.

Brighton and Hove Publicity Committee (1954) *Visitors' Handbook*.

Cooke, P. (ed.) (1989) *Localities: The Changing Face of Urban Britain*, London: Unwin Hyman.

Cooke, P. (1990) *Back to the Future: Modernity, Postmodernity and Locality*, London: Unwin Hyman.

Corner, J. and S. Harvey (1991) *Enterprise and Heritage: Crosscurrents of National Culture*, London: Routledge.

Cowan, R. (1987) 'What the tourist never sees', *Architect's Journal*, 8(7):42–3.

Cowen, H. (1990) 'Regency icons: marketing Cheltenham's built environment' in Harloe et al.

Department of the Environment/Urban and Economic Development Group (1994) *Vital and Viable Town Centres: Meeting the Challenge*, London: HMSO.

East Moulsecoomb Residents Association (1985) *EMRA Newsletter*.

Farleigh, A. (ed.) (1986) *A Regency Façade? Social Need and Voluntary Action in Brighton*, Brighton: Brighton Council for Voluntary Service.

Greene, G. (1975 edition) *Brighton Rock*, Harmondsworth: Penguin.

Harloe, M., C. Pickvance and J. Urry (1990) (eds) *Place, Policy and Politics: Do Localities Matter?* London: Unwin Hyman.

Harvey, D. (1993) 'From place to space and back again: reflections on the condition of post modernity' in J. Bird, B. Curtis, G. Putnam, G. Robertson and L. Tickner (eds) *Mapping the Futures: Local Cultures, Global Change*, London: Routledge.

Hewison, R. (1987) *The Heritage Industry: Britain in a Climate of Decline*, London: Methuen.

Kearns, G. and C. Philo (eds) (1993) *Selling Places: the City as Cultural Capital, Past and Present*, Oxford: Pergamon Press.

Lefebvre, H. (1991) *The Production of Space*, Oxford: Basil Blackwell.

Meethan, K.F. (1990) *Voluntary Action in Brighton Neighbourhood Associations*, Unpublished PhD thesis, University of Sussex.

Musgrave, C. (1970) *Life in Brighton*, London: Faber and Faber.

Robins, K. (1993) 'Prisoners of the city: whatever could a post modern city be? in E. Carter, J. Donald and J. Squires (eds) *Space and Place: Theories of Identity and Locality*, London: Lawrence and Wishart.

Rotenberg, R. and G. McDonogh (eds) (1993) *The Cultural Meaning of Urban Space*, Westport: Bergin and Harvey.

Queenspark Rates Book Group (1982) *Brighton on the Rocks: Monetarism and the Local State*.

Shields, R. (1990) *Places on the Margin*, London: Routledge.

Smith, N. and P. Williams (eds) (1986) *Gentrification of the City*, Boston: Allen and Unwin.

Urry, J. (1990) *The Tourist Gaze: Leisure and Travel in Contemporary Societies*, London: Sage.

Walton, J. (1983) *The English Sea-side Resort: A Social History 1750–1914*, Leicester: Leicester University Press.

Watson, G.L. and J.P. Kopachevsky (1994) 'Interpretations of tourism as a commodity', *Annals of Tourism Research*, 21(3):643–60.

Wright, P. (1985) *On living in an old Country: the National Past in Contemporary Britain*, London: Verso.

Zukin, S. (1990) 'Socio-spatial prototypes of a new organization of consumption: the role of real cultural capital,' *Sociology* 24(1):37–56.

11 Postcards — Greetings from Another World[1]

ELIZABETH EDWARDS

INTRODUCTION

The purpose of this chapter is to examine the role of modern tourist postcards of 'ethnographic' subjects in perpetuating notions of the exotic. There is nothing particularly original in this as such, but using it as a starting point, I hope to show that the exoticism manifested in these postcards is not merely the outpouring of vaguely defined cultural baggage or regurgitation of stereotype on the one hand or, on the other, insignificant ephemera. Rather, and more importantly, this exoticism both influences and is influenced by the central motivating structures in the touristic process itself, conspiring to create and sustain tourist desire and fantasy. Dependent on the production and, more importantly consumption, of such images is a multi-billion dollar industry; and as the availability of long-haul travel to 'exotic' locations increases so does the dependency on 'ethnographic' imagery to sell the product.

My argument is intended as exploratory, suggesting theoretical and cognitive approaches which might constitute the basis for further analyses. My remarks are based on a random sample of about 1500 modern postcard images, collected over the last two years as an on-going project which I have initiated to collect imagery of this nature in the visual collections of the Pitt Rivers Museum, University of Oxford. This sample is obviously tiny in the context of world production, but made, as it is, within the guiding framework of 'Traditional Culture as Tourist Commodity', some overall themes in imagery have already emerged.[2]

My argument here belongs firmly in the first of the three overlapping perspectives outlined by Selwyn at the beginning of this volume. My primary concern is with the contexts of the consumption of images at a meta-level rather than their production or individual consumption (although clearly the three are linked in a mutually sustaining relationship) for as has been argued, one of the keys to understanding tourist phenomena is the analysis of tourist representations and their consumption (Thurot and Thurot, 1983:173). Whereas there have been many representational and

The Tourist Image: Myths and Myth Making in Tourism. Edited by Tom Selwyn.
© 1996 John Wiley & Sons Ltd.

theoretical analyses of historical postcards (e.g. Alloula, 1986; Peterson, 1985; Corbey, 1989; Albers and James, 1990; Prochaska, 1990, 1991; Kreis, 1992) there are relatively few that examine modern imagery (e.g. Albers and James, 1983, 1988). Although I shall touch on the control of production of images as it relates to my particular hypothesis, I am not concerned here with the control of production and self-representation, some of which is home-produced neo-exoticism produced in response to Western demands and expectation (Mydin, 1992:251; Kulick and Willson 1992:148). These aspects would form a corollary to an extended form of this discussion. Nor am I concerned here with nationalist statements, expressions of ethnicity and identity. While all these factors are important facets in the analysis of postcard images, they are more useful within the detailed analysis of the production of representations of specific cultures, requiring as they do extended treatment beyond the scope of a single essay. Thus a generalized statement here would be dangerously reductionist. For this reason in the case of almost all the postcards considered in this discussion, the control of production is external to the subject either as culture or as a nation state and, as such, it might be argued, they have some cultural coherence. There is massive scope for culture- or nation-specific studies here, a vertical sampling, rather than the more horizontal approach under discussion. Finally I am not concerned with the grosser manifestations of stereotyping, for instance a card produced by Aerial Photography Services Inc.[3] of a Native American in gaudy war-bonnet standing beside a much reduced and equally gaudy 'Totem-pole',[4] or indeed pure fakery (for, in the postcard genre there is a very fine dividing line between the two).

I am concerned here instead with imagery which responds at a more subtle and more insidious level, the presentation and appropriation into touristic discourses of ethnographic reality which at a purely denotative level might indeed be described in objective terms as 'true' or 'real', that is it makes claims to represent accurately and to communicate experience or behaviour which has cultural relevance to the subject. It is the consumption of this imagery that is the more revealing of underlying structures of the contemporary 'exotic' rather than the overt stereotypes which so often attract attention. The content of the picture may appear documentary in quality, often captioned with 'ethnographic information' which suggests another level of the real, that of objective observed 'science', a verifiable, indeed, quantifiable authenticity as opposed to a perceived authenticity residing as much in myth and fantasy as in reality (see Selwyn, introduction to this volume). The process of consumption of postcard images themselves is on a metaphorical plane, external to the image itself and its referent (Albers and James, 1988:141).[5] In this transmission of the dominant concept of reality, so many elements in tourist expectation and experience are paralleled in the ontology of the photograph that photography does indeed seem the natural conduit and the natural icon for tourist experience.[6]

Drawing on theoretical perspectives on the nature of photography as a system of representation and its attendant social function and applying it to the theory and analysis of tourist desire and motivation, one begins to see the making of the symbolic structures of the image and the workings of the metaphor.

There is much variation and discussion as to what actually constitutes 'a tourist' and what motivates the said 'tourists' (e.g. Nash, 1981:462–3; Dann, 1981) and it would appear that motivation cannot be easily generalized in 'push and pull' models (such as that discussed by Dann 1981). I am dealing, in this instance, with cultural or ethnic tourism and its close relation, 'chic' or avant-garde tourism,[7] as opposed to recreational tourism. However, the categories of ethnic, historical, environmental and recreational tourism as outlined by Smith (1977:2–3) are not mutually exclusive. For instance the pleasure factor is not absent from ethnic and cultural tourism, nor ethnic from recreational, even if it is only a donkey ride up the local volcano. The motivations of cultural and ethnic tourism are in themselves an area of complex subjectivity, motivated by culturally determined, often self-referential, Western notions of the exotic combined in many cases with a genuine desire to 'know'. For tourism is a mass activity which may include private or individual pursuits. Indeed Allcock has recently argued that the theorizing of tourism would benefit from the inclusion of a model of 'implicit religion' which might allow for these subjectivities (Allcock, 1988:41). Manifested as a 'desire to know', the complex and often ambivalent construction of the 'exotic' has a long history in the writings of Western travellers (see for instance writings discussed by Alder, 1989; Mason, 1990 and Pratt, 1992). Lee and Compton have suggested (1992:733–4), drawing on psychology literature, that exploratory behaviour or the desire for it is fundamental to ethnic or cultural tourism, an overt response to a novel or different environment. Yet the motivations of that desire are not in themselves simple for as both Foucault and Lacan have suggested in very different ways, desire itself is a primordial element integrally connected with knowledge and power (Sturrock, 1979:89–91, 108, 135). Crapanzano has argued convincingly that it is identification of self which is the fundamental role of desire, for through that knowledge are posited the 'others' against or through which self can be individualized (Crapanzano, 1992:89–90). As we shall see, elements of all these arguments would appear to apply to the specifics of tourist experience.

THE IMAGE

Before we can proceed to an analysis of postcards themselves it is necessary to look briefly at the nature of the photograph in theoretical terms. The power of the still photograph lies in its spatio-temporal dislocation of nature, and the consequent decontextualization of those that exist within it, arrested in the flow of life and experience and transposed to other contexts. It can make the invisible visible, the unnoticed noticed, the complex simple and the simple complex (Sontag, 1979; Edwards, 1992a:6–8). Fragments come to stand for the whole, as an expression of apparent essences, what it is 'to be' something. They become symbolic structures, reifying culturally formed images as observed realities, rendering them 'objects'. In this process the signifier and the signified collapse into one another, the physical subject itself becomes indivisible from its symbolic or metaphorical meaning, the symbol becomes reality. Yet the relationship between signifier and signified is not fixed but arbitrary; thus the meaning of images becomes impermanent, free-floating, appropriated into the viewer's cultural discourse. The stillness and disconnectedness of the photograph allows the viewer to gaze, his or her control unchallenged, on the objectified subject. In this context the still image assumes the quality of the fetish both in the classic Marxist sense of concealing and perpetuating the social relations of its production and in the literal sense in that it is a value-loaded and pivotal embodiment of a set of transactions or encounters (Appudurai, 1986:53–4).[8]

Yet, paradoxically, it is the photograph itself which anchors images to the real world. The photographic image is stencilled from the physical world, the effect on chemicals of light reflected from an object. Thus there is a substantive relationship between the photograph and its referent which is analogical in bald terms, allowing a beguiling, naïve realism, which denies the mediation of creation and interpretation to the extent that photography allows us to believe. The act of photography or owning a photograph (postcard) authenticates and represents the *experience* of the possessor: it was there, I was there (Sontag, 1979:9).

THE EXOTIC AND THE TOURIST QUEST

The metaphorical or semiotic framework in which postcard imagery operates is, I would argue, clearly articulated if it is related to two influential theories of tourism: first, MacCannell's analysis of the quest for the authentic (1976) and, second, Graburn's hypothesis (1978) that tourism is akin to a sacred experience. While the perhaps exaggerated stance of both writers and the deeply structuralist and totalizing explanations of MacCannell have been criticized and modified over the years (e.g. Nash, 1984; Bruner, 1991),[9] the basic tenets of their arguments remain influential and they have a major contribution to make to the analysis of tourist postcards.

MacCannell argued that the tourist quest is a quest for the authentic.

Desire for the authentic is, he argued, integral to the structure of modern consciousness, an internal response to differentiation and alienation in modern society (1976:13–14). Graburn, following Turner's analysis of the 'pilgrimage' of the ritual process (Turner, 1969:166–9), argued that tourism is a form of ritual journey from the ordinary state to the spatially separated 'non-ordinary' for a finite period. It follows that knowledge and understanding gained by contact with the 'Other' during this period makes one a 'better' human being, having some sort of life-enhancing 'spiritual capital'.[10] Indeed, the *'rites de passage'* quality is emphasized in tourist brochures and other promotional literature, promising the 'journey of a lifetime', 'unique experience', 'never-to-be-forgotten', suggesting a transformed 'self' on return to the ordinary. This is commonly expressed by the notion the 'we can learn from them' (Cohen, 1989:36; Laxson, 1991; Bruner, 1991:239). In this context, the postcard, a fragment of 'sacred reality', assumes the character of a relic, a souvenir from the other side. Furthermore, a postcard sent home extends the experience of the non-ordinary to other viewers at the same time as marking the status gained by the sender through this transition into the non-ordinary. Susan Stewart writes perceptively on the postcard as souvenir, that it recaptures the external experience, domesticates it for the act of perpetual consumption as the focus for a narrative of the experience. Although the image is commercially produced, it was purchased within the context of the 'site'; this act of purchase, the act of surrendering it to a significant other and their reception of it validates the experience of the site in the tourist's external relations; it is self-affirming (Stewart, 1984:138). Thus the postcard becomes a multi-faceted icon of that tourist experience, a representation of the focus of devotion, a transition from a public to a private world and from the ordinary to the non-ordinary and back.

The nature of photography, which I summarized above, itself enhances this. Photography, in fragmenting both space and time, mirrors the tourist experience in which fragments are incorporated into a unified experience, an experience which, from beginning to end, revolves around images. The attraction of specific sites of tourism, be it the Maasaimara in East Africa or hill trekking in northern Thailand, and their ability to fulfil desires, is fed through the imagery of popular anthropology and travel literature such as *National Geographic* magazine, coffee-table books, postcards received, brochures, in-flight magazines, films, either fiction such as *Dances with Wolves* or documentary such as the *Disappearing World* series which stress the traditional (albeit under threat, political or environmental) (Singer and Woodhead, 1988; Pinney, 1989) and other outpourings of the mass-media.[11]

All such images, which appear as culturally authoritative statements 'about' cultures, embody, or are capable of being consumed, in terms of exotic and romantic notions of the 'Other' — yet that authority is drawn from what is purported to be anthropological truth.[12]

The desire for real experience is informed by internalized concepts of what constitutes 'Real' or 'Authentic' as applied to any specific culture, a perception which is invariably rooted in the past.[13] 'Real' Aboriginals make boomerangs, play didgeridoos and do dot paintings (Nadel-Klein, 1991:417; Taylor, 1988). Authenticity and thus desirability is expressed through a series of markers of differentness. Cohen (1989) has shown, for instance, how 'Remote', 'Primitive' and 'Unspoilt' are used almost universally as markers of tourist desirability. Indeed, notions of purity of culture and purity of nature are closely connected (I shall return to this point).

Timmer (1992)[14] has recorded how tourist expectations, and indeed what they 'see', are closely related to tourist literature on Papua New Guinea, especially that of Trans-Nuigini Tours, in a mutually sustaining relationship. Errington and Gewertz (1989) have shown that similar ideas of 'the primitive' and 'remote' are operating in tourist consumption in the Sepik River region of Papua New Guinea and Bruner (1991:239) has cited examples of East African peoples described variously as prehistoric and primitive, where the tourist will know that 'the civilized world is far behind'. In these one sees emerge an ideal of the primitive of long pedigree (see for example Smith, 1960; Honour, 1988; Bassani and Tedeschi, 1990:182; Wolf, 1992) in which the preoccupations of modern society are played out. Yet this is not without *frisson*, the threat of an encroaching modern world. The tourist believes he/she sees a timeless culture poised on the edge of change — 'to see it before it is too late' is a commonly expressed motive for exotic or cultural tourism.

These preoccupations are couched in a series of binary oppositions which are central to the metaphorical function of postcards — civilized/uncivilized, tame/savage, unnatural/natural, urban/rural, white/black, contained/unfettered, moral/licentious, fractured/harmonious, rational/irrational. The 'Other' is the antithesis of modern man or woman, humans in harmony with nature as natural man, with 'exotic' cultures shown as extensions of the natural world. This, it should be added, applies also to the traditional 'peasant' culture within industralized societies, peasant culture being perceived as rooted in the soil, the essence of place.[15] This notion of 'primitive man as an extension of nature' is clearly manifested, for instance, in a card dating from the 1970s in which, around the salutation 'Greetings from Australia' an elderly aboriginal is presented on a visual continuum with a koala bear and a kookaburra; in contrast, the bottom of the card is of sheep grazing in pastures, an example of nature contained. But such arrangements are not restricted to the cards themselves: the positioning of cards in shops (Nadel-Klein, 1991:419)[16] and pictures in travel brochures also present nature and traditional culture on a visual continuum. For instance British Airways *Worldwide 1992* brochure represented its 'Manyara Tour' in Tanzania, East Africa with three images

— a Maasai woman, a rhinoceros and a giraffe — across the top of the page, the first and last being given equal prominence. The captions read 'Masai villagers', 'Rhino', 'Masai Giraffe'. Although Masai is indeed, in zoological terms, a sub-species of giraffe, the arrangement of the photographs and their interaction with the text invites ambiguity and slippage. A similar construction and use of text accompanies the details of the 'Masai Tour' in Kenya (British Airways, 1992:130, 135).

It is these motifs which dominate the imagery of tourist postcards. All these markers operate in a timeless vacuum, atemporality becoming a unifying strategy in the creation of those other worlds. Both 'the sacred' and the 'photograph' are unfixed, outside time. For, like the sacred, still photographs stand diametrically opposed to the natural flow of life; indeed as Barthes (1984), Metz (1985) and others have argued, the photograph is a silent, immobile rigor mortis of reality — a symbolic death. This temporal ambiguity is of major significance for a great deal of tourist activity is directed at experiencing the past (Lowenthal, 1985; Urry, 1990:104–34), be it visiting National Trust houses or a self-referential encounter with the primitive. Indeed the act of 'viewing' both landscape and culture and of viewing their visual representations is heavily inflected and informed by associationalist 'pastness' (Bann, 1988:40); since the 18th century, when illustrated books began to proliferate, the past has become an increasingly visual experience (Lowenthal, 1985:257–8) to the extent that 'visualization' has become the predominant and distorting emphasis in patterning the past (Urry, 1990:112). While postcard imagery is informed in part by a desire for 'pastness', the atemporal nature of photography actually denies history in human terms; the past is thus not an historical past of past experience but merely an atemporal 'pastness' in opposition to 'now'. Rather than an active or empowering past, history collapses into nostalgia, an internalized, commodified longing, premised on the spectator's sense of historical decline, absence, loss of individual freedom and personal wholeness (Frow, 1991:135–6).[17]

Where the modern intrudes, it is often a conscious act on behalf of the image maker: for instance in the image of the Maasai man with a video-camera or wearing snorkling goggles,[18] the juxtaposed elements are not used as reflexive pointers, positioning the subject in the modern world and allowing the possibility of a plurality of identities which might identify the subjects as legitimate possessors of such technologies. Rather, the clash of signifiers in the image, heightened by the close photographic framing, serve to stress difference, not cultural engagement; for the meaning of the image still derives from the notion of the 'exotic' or 'primitive'.

There is a way, therefore, in which culture becomes dead through the act of photography (Metz, 1985:157–8), represented for tourist consumption by a moment that has vanished or perhaps never existed in terms of the subject's experience — a record of a constructed, inauthentic or pseudo-

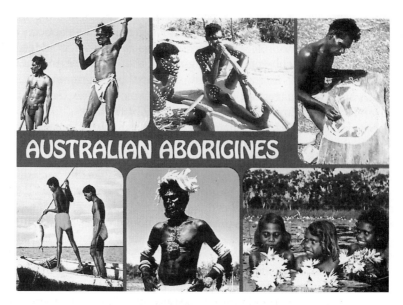

Figure 11.1 'Australian Aborigines'. *Source*: published by Nu-Color-Vu
Productions; purchased: Melbourne, 1992

event. Clifford's (1986:115) comment on the 'salvage paradigm' as a
'relentless placement of others in a present-becoming-past' assumes particular relevance when applied to postcards where culture is presented as a
spectacle to be gazed at rather than an active interaction with the world.
Thus photography reinforces monolithic and timeless visions of culture
extolled by tourist brochures and perceived as the desired authentic, as the
temporal dislocations of photography collapse the past and present into the
synchronic. 'There–then' becomes 'here–now' and indeed vice versa
(Barthes, 1977:44). This is exemplified by a postcard 'Australian Aborigines'
(Figure 11.1) produced by Nu-Color-Vu Productions which comprises a
grid-like arrangement of images showing Aboriginal people engaged in
stereotypical activities such as hunting, playing the didgeridoo and making
bark paintings (Edwards, 1992b). Individual technologies are not identified;
rather they are collapsed into generalized cultural markers of alterity. The
visual suggestion of the past is reinforced by the embalming nature of the
caption which states: 'Ancient traditions and crafts still thrive among
modern day Aborigines.' Authenticity of culture is presented as residing in
the past, an unchanging past without internal dynamic.

The long shelf-life of postcards and the increasing number of historical
images reissued as postcards alongside modern images would appear to
resist this idea. However such images are consumed within a semiotic
continuum. Indeed in terms of image content there is often little to tell

them apart. Hopi women still make pots, Turkana women still grind millet. Only the black and white as opposed to colour printing separates the past from the present. One should add that there is another genre of postcards — modern images, often soft focus, printed in black and white (or sepia) — which are deliberately nostalgic in nature. The oppositions which direct the consumption of images are not new. Whereas the specific points of departure may have shifted, from the dying race of the 19th century to the dying environment of the late 20th century (Ellen, 1986), the popular imagery of the 'primitive other' is remarkably tenacious. All semiotic structures I have suggested for modern postcard imagery can equally be identified in late 19th- and early 20th-century images: for instance, those supposedly sexually compliant women from Samoa (Nordstrom, 1991), primitive customs and dress in Southern Africa (Webb, 1992) or noble savages of North America (Kreis, 1992). The bare-breasted African 'village belle' of 19th-century photographs and early 20th-century postcards (for numerous examples and analysis see Corbey, 1989) has her modern counterpart in the sexually inviting 'Hi African Girl' produced in Nairobi in the 1980s (Figures 11.2 and 11.3).[19] Similarities cannot be dismissed merely as a visual correspondence or thematic correlation but seen rather as representing a similarly grounded consumption of culture and the articulation of continuing cultural fascinations over time.

Just as in the 19th century scientific anthropology gave weight to popular representations of variable veracity, so today many ethnographic postcards are presented as 'serious' ethnography, given the appearance of documentary realism[20] with an ethnographic caption (often accurate — one should not forget that accuracy is a perfectly viable option in tourist representations). Often the photographer is named, giving the suggestion of serious record photography, which of course it can be — for instance, anthropologist Maureen MacKenzie's images of Papua New Guinea[21] or, in the realms of travel photography, Alain Denis's photographs of Cameroon (1984)[22] or Roland and Sabrina Michaud's work in Afghanistan (1985a) and Central Asia (1985b, 1992).[23] Indeed the high quality of colour printing of many postcards and the fact that many of the images are 'signed' in one corner gives them the authenticity-enhancing aura and authority of serious travel photography,[24] with the suggestion of a claim to be 'art'.[25] But as the photographic subject becomes, as a postcard, a commodity to be possessed, one could equally argue that the ethnographic merely becomes a device through which gaze is legitimated, to persuade us that this is knowledge and understanding, not mere voyeurism — the passive and vicariously experienced spectacle which, as we have seen, photography offers. This point is well illustrated by a large-format postcard entitled 'Turkana girl wearing traditional beads and skirt', a photograph by Mirella Ricciardi, produced by Marketing and Publishing Ltd., Nairobi (Figure 11.4).[26] A heavily ornamented, bare-breasted young woman lies nonchalantly on a

Figure 11.2   Studio photograph of young Zulu women, *c.*1885–95. *Source*:
Purchased in the Cape by a soldier of the Middlesex Yeomanry, 1899–1902

sandbank, head resting in hand — a pose of classical reference. The soft
focus is enhanced by the textured card on which the image is printed, the
woman's body assuming a tactile quality, echoing the cicatrizations on her
abdomen. The ornament is ethnographically correct to be sure, but the
iconography and signification speak to the stereotype of the sexual
availability of black women: the opposition of savage/tame, unfettered/
contained, licentious/moral.

IMMEDIACY AND TRUTH

I want to look now at questions of immediacy, which are an important
locus of power in the photograph. Despite the barrier between image and
experience created by the camera, the easy immediacy of the photograph
has none the less always allowed us knowledge without experience

Figure 11.3 'Hi African Girl' (reverse). *Source*: Published by Sapra, Nairobi; purchased: Nairobi, 1990, 1992 and 1993

(Sontag, 1979:156). In the context of the postcard, the representational aspects of the object of tourist desire have, as we have seen, been internalized, and it is the *immediacy* of the image which predominates. As such, it suggests a direct contact with the desired object; postcards, because of the context of their consumption, allow us knowledge with perhaps the *suggestion* of experience.

Postcard responses can be divided into two interrelated categories which, it can be argued, inform in broad terms the two models I outlined earlier, Graburn's sacred journey and MacCannell's quest for the authentic. The first one can be identified as representing a generalized 'Exotic', which may be expressed in formalist terms, an aesthetic objectification where the subject is transformed into an art object for the viewer's consumption. Typical of this are the many 'Man in the Landscape' postcards whose imagery and associationalist meaning are derived from the ambivalent romantic images of landscape and the dangerous beauty of nature which have informed responses to landscape for the best part of 200 years but

Figure 11.4 'Turkana Girl wearing traditional beads and skirt'. *Source*: Photograph by Mirella Ricciardi, published by Marketing and Publishing Ltd. Nairobi; purchased Nairobi, 1990 and 1994

which have acquired new relevance in modern environmental concerns (Short, 1992:6–18). The presence of the 'exotic other' conceived, as we have seen, as 'natural man' signifies in this context the very 'naturalness' of that landscape — his/her place is integral to it, rather than suggesting power over it. Purity of nature, wilderness and purity of culture merge in a mutually sustaining 'authenticity' — a Samburu or Maasai girl wearing bead earrings in a Nairobi street is conceived as being less authentic than one with Mount Kilimanjaro in the background. There are many cards of the latter, but I have yet to locate any of the former.

The 'Exotic' is also expressed through specific items or actions of ethnographic veracity which act as cultural markers, which in turn function as metaphors. The fascination with dance, hunting, body paint, ritual and masquerade (all of which are the stock-in-trade of the postcard market) is derived from their being forms of behaviour which particularly inform primitivist or romantic responses. Coombes has commented, in the context of mid-century museum displays of ethnography, that 'art, religion, war and sex were the primary means by which the European could "know" the colonialised subject' (Coombes, 1994:113). It would appear that the touristic 'other' of the late 20th century is similarly constructed. Leading on from this, actions themselves become read as signifiers of the primitive just as items of material culture become cultural markers — the boomerang and the spear are eagerly embraced as confirming authenticity, things that are genuine, untouched, pristine, traditional (Handler, 1986:2).[27] The symbolic nature of objects and actions becomes exaggerated through their decontextualization rather like a kind of theatre, or even opera, functioning as an intense or heightened reality.[28] The subjects finally become symbols of themselves. At the same time the photographic frame contains the threat of the strange — its object distanced, safely diffused and contained within the viewer's terms of reference. Finally, as souvenir, this 'external experience is internalised; the beast is taken home' (Stewart, 1984:134).

The second strand of imagery is that of the quotidian. At first glance these images seem freer of the exotic constructs which so strongly inform the group we have just looked at. These photographs of everyday life show craftsmen at work, market scenes, bread making, baskets, pots and so forth. Yet by the same process, elements of the ordinary become exotic, nonordinary or even imbued with the essence or spirit of the desired, fetishized, even though their very ordinariness disguises this. The intensity of this perhaps relates to cultural responses to certain actions, as suggested earlier both in connection to the parameters of the 'authentic' and the markers of the 'primitive'; for instance, the many postcards showing Maasai bleeding cattle. Drinking raw cattle blood is a dietary staple of many pastoralist peoples, yet it is anathema to the cultures of most tourists.[29] Again ethnographic veracity is not necessarily the question, but I would argue that the most significant function of the 'quotidian' image is that of authenticating experience. This can operate at two levels: first, more prosaically, crafts authenticate 'traditional' aspects of production (lending authority to souvenirs purchased perhaps); objects thus produced and acquired are 'authentic' and stand opposed to the ordinary, the mass-produced items of modern society. A corollary is, of course, that although many of the craft productions offered to tourists can be readily bought (at a price) at home, the object accrues greater symbolic meaning and thus social value through being acquired in the state of the non-ordinary. As Appudurai has pointed out (1986:15), symbolic value and the social environment of commodity acquisition are integrally linked, articulated in the souvenir as the link between place, object, experience and narrative (Stewart, 1984:136). Indeed, shopping in local markets is one of the authentic experiences stressed by travel brochures, even at the recreational end of the market (Selwyn, 1992).

The second authenticating role is perhaps more significant in this argument. Postcards of the everyday suggest a level of intimacy of experience which appeals directly to the tourist's desire for the authentic. An example is found in a postcard from a series entitled 'African Life' produced by Art Publishers, Durban, Johannesburg and Cape Town, South Africa, which shows two women cooking (Figure 11.5). The caption reads: 'Maidens at an authentic Zulu Kraal, with its "fence" of broken branches; stir the village meal in large three-legged iron pots.' In this caption we see a number of touristic markers in operation — confirmation of authenticity, ethnographic detail and the suggestion of social wholeness (stirring the village meal).

Figure 11.5 'Maidens at an authentic Zulu kraal'. *Source*: Published by
Art Publishers, Durban; purchased Cape Town, 1993

Such postcards present some of the imponderabilia of daily life and serve
as traces of the authentic, distinguishing or making the experience of that
which is perhaps fleetingly glanced at by the tourist. It is these glimpses
and fragments which form the dense network of culture which might
satisfy the tourist notion of authenticity that is an integral part of tourist
expectation, the delineated essences, the 'ideal core of a sight' which
actually precedes the tourist's experience of them (Frow, 1991:124–5).

In this context such postcards inform MacCannell's model as applied in
contemporary situations. In this MacCannell, following Goffman, has
distinguished 'front' and 'back' realities in tourist experience. The former is
constructed as mere surface, performance, the inauthentic; the latter
penetrates 'behind the scenes', the reality of everyday existence, the
authentic. There are, of course, complex manifestations within this range,
movement from front to back corresponding with growing tourist understanding and the intensity of tourist demand for the authentic in a given
situation (MacCannell, 1976:105). Yet even the most 'authentic' experiences
must, as Crick has argued, be inauthentic, for the 'authentic' experience
suggests relationships which simply are not there because visitors cannot
share in the moral fabric of the visited, so that such experiences must
ultimately be vicarious (Crick, 1989:331). Furthermore, the very paradox of
the authentic is that as it is made, it becomes perceived as inauthentic; thus
authenticity becomes something 'other', over the horizon, ever moving

Figure 11.6 'Maasai Women'. *Source*: Photograph by Eric Harris; published by Kall Kwik, Mombasa; purchased Nairobi, 1990

out of reach (Frow, 1991:130). Yet, there remains a sustaining equation in the popular imagination between intimacy and truth. Significantly, this equation is also a guiding tenet of anthropological fieldwork and is a fundamental strand of similarity, as identified by Crick (1985), between anthropology and tourism (which he describes as classificatory kin). Images thus work at several levels to satisfy this touristic need. Postcards address this concern directly, for they allow us to believe in the experience of a 'back' reality. Like photographs of the tourist's own making, they are part of the guarantee of the 'correctness' of the immediacy experienced. John Taylor (1994) has argued convincingly that such images confirm the 'authenticity of response', protecting the tourist from the anxiety of having failed to recognize the desired object. Ethnographically realistic postcards in this context suggest 'this is how it really was', for photographs have an extraordinary power to subvert reality, becoming a substitute or even surrogate experience.

It is paradoxical that it is precisely within the context of the authenticating quotidian that one finds 'non-traditional', adopted or absorbed material culture intruding into the more traditional tourist imagery which we have discussed above: for instance, a postcard from Kenya showing a queue of Maasai women holding umbrellas and home-made tin billy cans (Figure 11.6)[30] or another from Australia showing two Aboriginal children

Figure 11.7 'Don't cry for me Melanesia', Kanganamun village, East Sepik, Papua New Guinea. *Source*: Photograph by Marsha Berman; published by Gordon and Gotch; purchased: village store Port Moresby region, 1991

in European clothing playing in the bush.[31] In this context such objects are markers of the authenticity of *encounter* not culture. Although they would at first glance appear similar to the Maasai with the video-camera etc. discussed above, they are signifiers of a very different order. The structuring of the image in formalist terms is very different, it is given a snapshot quality with its wider contextualizing framing stressing encounter, immediacy and realism rather than aestheticized visions of culture.

Their juxtaposition and co-existence with the more prevalent and traditional representations of the exotic point to the increasingly sophisticated and complex motivations and desires of post-modern tourism and to more complex representational structures and strategies. An interesting and powerful indication of this trend is found in a postcard produced from a photograph of Marsha Berman's, taken in Eastern Sepik, Papua New Guinea (Figure 11.7). It shows a young man walking through a clearing towards a village. The slogan on his T-shirt reads 'Don't Cry for Me Melanesia'. A sign within a sign, this image deliberately fractures the object of tourist desire in its traditional conception and confronts the tourists with their own agency in changing the Pacific. Furthermore, one might argue that the discomfort brought about by this image arises from the way in which it contradicts what we expect from a postcard as an object, suggesting the degree to which image content has become formally ritualized in some way. Moreover, postcards such as this have certain conceptual points in common with what John Taylor has termed oppositional photography within the tourist discourse (1994:240) which harness the dominant, and thus appropriate, modalities of tourism — in this Melanesian example, the postcard format itself — and use them to disturb and dislocate. The sadness inherent in the T-shirt logo might be dismissed as merely playing on tourist sentiment for the 'impure object of desire' were the tourist's own role in the situation not so strongly implicated.

One might then summarize that in the two broad groups of images, the first — the 'exotic' — addresses the abstract desire for the non-ordinary which has been characterized by Graburn as a 'rite de passage', while the second, the 'quotidian', enhances the notion of the authentic. However, no absolutely clear-cut division can be maintained, because, like all images in the public sphere, meaning is free-floating, operating several possible closures of meaning within a single image as it is bought, consumed and sent, eliciting different readings in different contexts. Furthermore, their structure and meaning are capable of fracture through a differently positioned, oppositional imagery which uses appropriate visual language but uses it to subvert. It will be interesting to chart the progress of this counter-language.

THE FAMILY OF MAN

Cutting across all this is another strand of meaning and consumption that we should consider briefly and which is related to the imagery of intimacy: this is the universalist vision, an apparently unmediated human response in which all peoples are bound together through the basic experiences of human existence. While this may be so (I shall leave this argument to the philosophers), we must look here at the appropriation of this idea into the discourse of tourist imagery. In this context it might be described as a version of romanticism. First of all, it might be argued, it diffuses some of the danger of the unknown and the strange inherent in the oppositions outlined earlier and transcends anxieties about self-identity or indeed self-authenticity in that through equivalence with others, the consumer is reassured of belonging. Such imagery might thus be described as having a confirming role. Second, and related to this, appealing to a common human bond, it contributes to the 'wholeness' which, as MacCannell argued, is central to the tourist quest, in allowing the tourist to identify with those forming the focus of their visit. This notion is not unconnected with some of the unarticulated mystifying techniques of the tourist industry and travel journalism which would suggest that tourism enhances the possibilities of global understanding and world peace (Crick, 1989:328–9). This naïvely

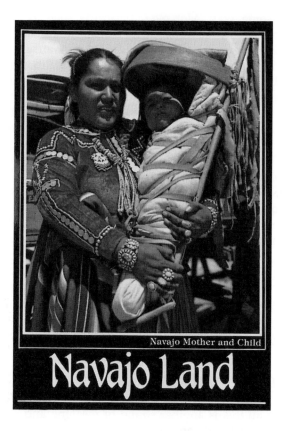

Figure 11.8 'Navajo Land'. *Source*: Published by Smith-Southwestern Inc;
purchased: Choma Valley Supermarket, New Mexico, 1991

romantic view finds its most ubiquitous visualization in portraits. The
smiling, welcoming faces of 'happy, friendly locals' in the travel brochures
are a common component of postcard imagery. They are pictures easily
related to at a human level which can operate both collectively and
individually; as Tagg has pointed out 'the portrait is . . . a sign whose
purpose is both the description of an individual and the inscription of
social identity' (Tagg, 1988:37). Thus the appeal lies at one level in both its
own individuality and in that of the consumer, for Handler has suggested
(1986:2) that the individual has a central place in the understanding of
reality and hence authenticity. One responds as one human being to
another. Madonna-like mothers and babies (a Navajo baby, the caption
tells us, 'seems quite happy [on its cradle board] and greets all strangers
with a smile' (Figure 11.8).[32] Other postcards show caring fathers, nuclear
families, young women offering food (often fruit),[33] the old men staring

Figure 11.9 'An elder of the Pitjantjatjara tribe'. *Source*: Photograph by Kerry Williams; published by Barker Souvenirs; purchased: 1992

thoughtfully into the distance (reflecting on the old way or the fount of ancient wisdom?) (Figure 11.9).

At first glance some of the intentionally unresolved contradictions which have run through this chapter might appear transcended by universalist consumption. However, another reading is also suggested. Possibly the subjects are desired only for their differentness and the viewer's encounter with that differentness — what appears to transcend the different in fact depends upon it for its very definition. Fascination (or desire) is itself couched in contradictions: so similar yet so different, so near yet so far. Perhaps such responses are a final absorption of images to give comfort and protection against the threat of the exotic, which, as Crapanzano outlined (1992:89–90), is a central feature of desire. In the apparent intimacy and immediacy the subject is still objectified, still unknown with 'no individuality, no presence, no status' (Clark, 1992:2–3). Immediacy is mistaken for intimacy; for as we have seen earlier, photography allows us to believe in such relationships. The fact that so many images can be appropriated into this willing mode of interpretation is magnificently exemplified by the Family of Man exhibition of 1955 (Steichen, 1955),[34] the most successful photographic exhibition of all time, where specific images were used, like postcards, in a public context, divorced from history and the culturally bound experiences of the people they portrayed. Like tourist experience, fragments cohere into apparent wholeness, standing for irreducible truth. In this context, images could only be read as metaphors within a universalist tradition, a metaphor of Western shape. Anchored by gnomic quotes from William Blake, the Bible and ancient Chinese proverbs etc., they 'create marvellous social fiction but a sad and specious history' (Kaufmann, 1982:198). Much the same can be said of postcards.

CONCLUSION

In this exploratory examination I have suggested the complex and sometimes contradictory nature of the ubiquitous ethnographic tourist postcard. It is its very ubiquity and apparently ephemeral nature which has meant that it has been largely overlooked. Yet there are, to my mind, a number of very pertinent reasons it merits attention of the kind I have focused on it here. First, the ethnographic postcard is part of a global currency of images which is the life-blood of the tourist industry. 'How does this work?' is not an unreasonable question for one working in visual anthropology to ask. Second, postcards provide one of the most widespread methods of disseminating images of other cultures in the modern world. They are a direct descendant of many of the images which, because they were printed on albumen papers in the 1880s, have themselves been fetishized and accorded the status of documents of anthropology in our archives and museums. Yet they have been created to inform in very similar ways.[35] As such, postcards are an important facet in the ongoing consideration of the politics of representation. As a museum curator I am acutely aware of the cultural baggage which is brought into my own and similar institutions by a visiting public, whose images of the world and other cultures are formed in part by the kind of exotic imagery perpetuated in tourist postcards. It is an imagery which it is our job to confront (Karp and Levine, 1991).

Perhaps the importance and power of traditional postcard imagery can be gauged by the resistance to its appropriating and stereotyping tendencies. In 1988 Aboriginal groups in Australia produced a postcard for the bicentenary (Nadel-Klein, 1991:422) which showed a young Aboriginal woman silhouetted against the Aboriginal flag — the legend across the bottom reads '200 years of postcards'.[36]

NOTES

1. This chapter has evolved out of two versions given at the Museum Ethnographers Group conference 'Museums, Anthropology and Tourism' at the University of Hull, March 1992 and at the ASA Decennial Conference in Oxford, July 1993. I am deeply grateful to Julia Harrison, Mike Hitchcock, Helene La Rue, Alison Devine Nordström, Roslyn Poignant and Tom Selwyn for their comments and friendly criticism of the various aspects and various drafts of this chapter.

2. I should like to thank all those colleagues, students, friends and relatives who send me a constant supply of images to supplement my own efforts — especially Johanna Agthe, Nick Edwards, Sara Joynes, Hélène La Rue, Linda Mowat, Roslyn Poignant, Max Quanchi and David Zeitlyn who provided much of the material discussed here.

3. My sample of this image was, interestingly, collected on the Cherokee Reservation, North Carolina (by Linda Mowat), suggesting that sensitivity in 'inauthentic' representation cannot be universalized and that other factors can be over-riding. Another card in the same series is captioned 'Chief Henry of the Cherokee Indian Tribe holds the title of "The Most Photographed Indian in the World"', suggesting that this is a measure of his 'reality'!

4. It is not merely the ethnographic detail of individual items of material culture which is incorrect in this image. The objects represent a conflation of very different Native American cultures. The feather war-bonnet, which has become *the* cultural marker for American 'Indians' was originally a mark of status among a number of groups from the Plains region, for instance the Blackfoot. The totem pole, on the other hand, originally functioned as clan insignia of ritual significance among peoples of the north-western Pacific coast of Canada such as the Haida and Kwakiutl.

5. For the purposes of this chapter the term 'photography' is used on occasion interchangeably with 'postcard'. The point is that a postcard is the means of transmission of a commercially produced and thus commercially directed and targeted form of travel photography and not photography taken by tourists. However in this connection it should be remembered that choice of subject, what is photographable in a given context, is derived from an imagery in which the postcard is formative (Chalfen, 1979:438, 443).

6. It has long been argued, correctly I think, that 'photography gives shape to travel'. For a résumé of these arguments see Urry (1990:136–40).

7. This 'chicness' has little to do with remoteness or a differently conceived 'authenticity' but with marketing, for instance as ecological or culturally sensitive combined with luxury. This is usually supported by governments anxious to attract wealthy punters.

8. For an elaboration of this argument on the fetish qualities of photography see Metz (1985).

9. See Selwyn's introduction to this volume for a résumé of these arguments.

10. Although I borrow the shape of this idea from Bourdieu (1984), it must be distinguished from 'cultural capital', where symbolic elements of differential access to certain types of knowledge are central, Bourdieu argues, to the struggles between classes to increase the volume and valuation of their 'knowledge' or 'cultural capital'. What I have termed 'spiritual capital' is clearly related to 'cultural capital'; Urry's discussion (1990:87–9) of 'cultural capital' in the context of tourism extends this line of argument.

11. Laxson's survey (1991) of educated American tourists to Pueblo sites came up

with the salutary suggestion that adventure fiction and general travel literature were the main sources drawn upon in the creation of imagery of the Pueblos, not 'serious' anthropology.

12. This truth may not be one recognized by modern practising anthropologists.

13. This notion would indeed appear to be a specifically Western or industrialized response. David MacDougall has recently suggested in his discussion of Indian tourists and photographers in Mussoorie, Uttar Pradesh, (1992) that Indian tourists desire to 'be' the authentic — photographed dressed in peasant or even film-star costume in an imagery derived from Indian cinema — rather than to be 'in touch' with the authentic as is central to Western touristic desire.

14. I am very grateful to Jaap Timmer, University of Amsterdam, for letting me see the relevant parts of his doctoral thesis in progress and allowing me to use some of his material here.

15. A full discussion of the images of peasant cultures found across Europe is unfortunately beyond the scope of this chapter. However, there is a vast output in this genre to be found in every tourist area in Europe, from peasants with truffle pigs in Dordogne, France, to wizened shepherds with Herdwick sheep in the English Lake District. A corollary to this is the representation of the rural as the idealized, cohesive everyday. John Taylor's excellent book *A Dream of England: Landscape Photography and the Tourist Imagination* (1994) came too late to be integrated fully in this chapter. While it deals with many of these specific issues as well as demonstrating a number of common concerns, it does not change my argument but rather strengthens it and suggests directions for further interrogation of the theme.

16. My own observations at many tourist sites would confirm this.

17. For an extended consideration of tourism and nostalgia see Frow (1991) and references therein.

18. Produced by Mount Kenya Sundries Ltd. Nairobi; photographer, Y.A. Bertrand.

19. Produced by Sapra, Nairobi.

20. I use this term very broadly, not in the Grierson sense of a politicized realism, although one can, of course, argue convincingly that tourist appropriation is in itself political.

21. See a series of postcards published by Web Books, Papua New Guinea.

22. See a series of postcards entitled 'Lumières d'Afrique' produced by Cinedia International in Paris for sale in Cameroon, many of which were published in a glossy volume, *Cameroun: Au-dela du regard* (1984). I am grateful to David Zeitlyn for tracking this down for me.

23. See a series of postcards produced by AGEP of Marseilles which was on sale in Kabul in the 1970s.

24. Significantly there appears to be a crude correlation, which requires further research to substantiate and quantify, between the quality of the card in terms of production and price and the claims of 'ethnographic authenticity'.

25. The cult of the photographer is certainly playing an increasing role in 'serious' tourist imagery. For instance, high-quality photographic postcards of Oxford produced by Chris Andrews and of the Lake District and Scotland by Colin Baxter are actually sold from stands surmounted by a large card bearing an enlargements of the *photographer's* signature. I have heard people ask for postcards by the photographer's name.

26. From a series of photographs by Mirella Ricciardi for her book *Vanishing Africa* (1971).

27. The tourist brochure designation 'Huli Wigmen' reported by Timmer (1992) overtly illustrates the conflation of a people and their 'cultural marker'.

28. One is reminded here of Werner Herzog's use of opera in ethnographic film, notably *Wootabe*, shown in 1992 in the BBC's *Under the Sun* series.
29. For example, two cards produced by Sapra, Nairobi; photographs by Y.A. Bertrand.
30. A photograph by Eric Harris produced in the Jambo Kenya series Kwik Kall, Mombassa, *c*. 1980.
31. Photograph by Michael Lees, published in the *Real Australia* series, a significant title in this context.
32. A card entitled 'Navajo Mother and Baby' produced by Smith-Southwestern Inc.
33. This imagery has long had sexual connotations from Eve onwards. See, for instance 17th-century Dutch painting (Schama, 1987:433).
34. And a follow-up volume of photographs by Ken Heyman, *The World's Family* (1982).
35. This is why I have initiated a project to collect modern postcard images as part of the visual collections at Pitt Rivers Museum.
36. Veronica Strang has reported a recent sighting of this postcard, not itself an icon of art, on the walls of the Powerhouse Museum, Sydney in March 1992.

REFERENCES

Adler, J. (1989) 'Origins of sightseeing', *Annals of Tourism Research*, 16, 7–29.

Albers, P. and W. James (1983) 'Tourism and the changing photographic image of the Great Lakes Indians', *Annals of Tourism Research*, 10(1), 123–48.

Albers, P. and W. James (1988) 'Travel photography; a methodological approach', *Annals of Tourism Research*, 15, 134–58.

Albers, P. and W. James (1990) 'Private and public images; a study of photographic contrasts in postcard pictures of the Great Basin Indians' *Visual Anthropology*, 3, 343–66.

Allcock, J.B. (1988) 'Tourism as sacred journey', *Lorsir et Societé*, 11(1), 33–48.

Alloula, M. (1986) *The Colonial Harem*, Minneapolis: University of Minnesota Press.

Appudurai, A. (1986) *The Social Life of Things*, Cambridge: Cambridge University Press.

Bann, S. (1988) 'Views of the past-reflections on the treatment of historical objects and museums of history (1750–1850)', in G. Fyfe and J. Law (eds), *Picturing Power*, London: Routledge, pp. 39–64.

Barthes, R. (1977) 'The photographic message' in *Image-Music-Text*, London: Fontana.

Barthes, R. (1984) *Mythologies*, London: Paladin.

Bassini, E. and L. Tedeschi (1990) 'The image of the Hottentot in the seventeenth and eighteenth centuries', *Journal of the History of Collections*, 2(2), 157–86.

Bourdieu, P. (1984) *Distinction: a Social Critique of the Judgement of Taste*, London: Routledge and Kegan Paul.

British Airways (1992) *Worldwide 1992* (holiday brochure).

Bruner, E. (1991) 'The transformation of self in tourism', *Annals of Tourism Research*, 18, 238–50.

Chalfen R. (1979) 'Photography's role in tourism: some unexplored relationships', *Annals of Tourism Research*, 6, 435–47.

Clark, G. (ed.) (1992) *The Portrait in Photography*, London: Reaktion Books.

Clifford, J. (1986) 'On ethnographic allegory' in J. Clifford and G.E. Marcus, *Writing Culture*, Berkeley: University of California Press, pp. 98–121.

Cohen, E. (1989) 'Primitive and remote', *Annals of Tourism Research*, 16(1).

Coombes, A.E. (1994) 'Blinded by "science": ethnography at the British Museum' in M. Pointon (ed.), *Art Apart: Art Institutions and Ideology Across England and North America*, Manchester: Manchester University Press.

Corbey, R. (1989) *Wildheid en beschaving: De Europese verbeelding van Afrika*, Baarn: Ambo.

Crapanzano, V. (1992) *Hermes Dilemma and Hamlet's Desire: On the Epistemology of Interpretation*, Cambridge, Mass.: Harvard University Press.

Crick, M. (1989) 'Representations of international tourism in the social sciences: sun, sex, sights, savings, and servility', *Annual Review of Anthropology*, 18, 307–44.

Dann, G. (1981) 'Tourism motivation', *Annals of Tourism Research*, 8(2), 187–219.

Denis, A. (1984) *Cameroun: Au delà du regard*, Paris: Edition Damalisque.

Edwards, E. (ed.) (1992a) *Anthropology and Photography 1860–1920*, Newhaven/London: Yale University Press.

Edwards, E. (1992b) 'The tourist icon: four Australian postcards', *Tourism in Focus*, 6, 4–5.

Ellen, R. (1986) 'What Black Elk left unsaid', *Anthropology Today*, 2(6), 8–12.

Errington, F. and D. Gewertz (1989) 'Tourism and anthropology in a post-modern world', *Oceania*, 60, 37–54.

Frow, J. (1991) 'Tourism and the semiotics of nostalgia', *October*, 57, 123–51.

Graburn, N. (1978) 'Tourism: the sacred journey' in V. Smith (ed.), *Hosts and Ghosts: the Anthropology of Tourism*, Oxford: Blackwell, 17–32.

Handler, R. (1986) 'Authenticity', *Anthropology Today*, 2(1), 2–4.

Honour, H. (1988) *The Image of the Black in Western Art*, Houston, Texas: Meril Foundation, Harvard University Press.

Karp, I. and S.D. Levine (1991) *Exhibiting Cultures*, Washington, DC: Smithsonian Press.

Kaufman, J.C.A. (1982) 'Photographs and history: flexible illustrations' in T.F. Barrow, S. Armitage and W.E. Tydeman (eds), *Reading into Photography: Selected Essays 1959–1980*, Albuquerque: University of New Mexico Press, 193–9.

Kreis, K.M. (1992) '"Indians" in old postcards', *European Review of Native American Studies*, 6(1), 39–48.

Kulick, D. and M.E. Willson (1992) 'Echoing images: the construction of savagery among Papua New Guinean villagers', *Visual Anthropology*, 5(2), 143–52.

Laxson, J. (1991) 'How "we" see "them": tourism and Native Americans', *Annals of Tourism Research*, 18, 365–91.

Lee, T.H. and J. Compton (1992) 'Measuring novelty-seeking in tourism', *Annals of Tourism Research*, 19, 732–51.

Lowenthal, D. (1985) *The Past is a Foreign Country*, Cambridge: Cambridge University Press.

MacDougall, D. (1992) 'Photo hierarchicus: signs and mirrors in Indian photography', *Visual Anthropology*, 5(2), 103–29.

Mason, P. (1990) *Deconstructing America*, London: Routledge.

Metz, C. (1985) 'Photography and fetish', reprinted in C. Squires (ed.) (1990), *The Critical Image*, London: Lawrence & Wishart.

Michaud, R. and S. Michaud (1985a) *Afghanistan*, London: Thames and Hudson.

Michaud, R. and S. Michaud (1985b) *Caravans to Tatary*, London: Thames and Hudson.

Michaud, R. and S. Michaud (1992) *Mirror of the Orient*, London: Thames and Hudson.

Mydin, I. (1992) 'Historical photographs — changing audiences' in E. Edwards (ed.), *Anthropology and Photography 1860–1920*, New Haven/London: Yale University Press, pp. 249–52.

Nadel-Klein, J. (1991) 'Picturing Aborigines: a review essay on "After Two Hundred Years"', *Cultural Anthropology*, 6(3), 414–23.

Nash, D. (1981) 'Tourism as an anthropological subject', *Current Anthropology*, 22(5), 461–81.

Nash, D. (1984) 'The ritualization of tourism: comment on Graburn's "The Anthropology of Tourism"', *Annals of Tourism Research*, 11(3), 503–6.

Nordström, A.D. (1991) 'Early photography in Samoa', *History of Photography*, 15(4), 272–86.

Peterson, N. (1985) 'The popular image' in I. and T. Donaldson (eds), *Seeing the First Australians*, Sydney: Allen and Unwin, 64–180.

Pinney, C. (1989) 'Appearing worlds', *Anthropology Today*, 5(3), 26–8.

Pratt, M.L. (1992) *Imperial Eyes*, London: Routledge.

Prochaska, D. (1990) 'The archive of Algeria imaginaire', *History and Anthropology*, 4, 373–420.

Prochaska, D. (1991) 'Fantasia of the Phototheque: French postcard views of colonial Senegal', *African Arts*, 24(2), 40–7.

Ricciardi, M. (1971) *Vanishing Africa*, London: Collins.

Schama, S. (1987) *The Embarrassment of Riches*, London: Collins.

Selwyn, T. (1992) 'Peter Pan in southeast Asia — views from the brochure' in M. Hitchcock, V.T. King and M.J.G. Parnwell (eds), *Tourism in Southeast Asia*, London: Routledge, 117–37.

Short, J. Rennie (1992) *Imagined Country*, London: Routledge.

Singer, A. and L. Woodhead (1988) *Disappearing World: Television and Anthropology*, London: Boxtree for Granada TV.

Smith, B. (1960) *European Vision of the South Pacific 1768–1850*, London: Oxford University Press.

Smith, V. (1977) 'Introduction', *Hosts and Guests: the Anthropology of Tourism*, Oxford: Blackwell.

Sontag, S. (1979) *On Photography*, Harmondsworth: Penguin.

Steichen, E. (1955) *The Family of Man*, New York: MOMA.

Stewart, S. (1984) *On Longing: Narratives of the Miniature, the Gigantic, the Souvenir, the Collection*, Baltimore: Johns Hopkins University Press.

Sturrock, J. (1979) *Structuralism and Since*, Oxford: Oxford University Press.

Tagg, J. (1988) *The Burden of Representation*, London: Routledge.

Taylor, J. (1994) *A Dream of England: Landscape Photography and the Tourist Imagination*, Manchester: Manchester University Press.

Taylor, P. (ed.) (1988) *After 200 Years*, Canberra: Aboriginal Studies Press.

Thurot, J. and G. Thurot (1983) 'The ideology of class and tourism: confronting the discourse of advertising', *Annals of Tourism Research*, 10(1), 173–89.

Timmer, J. (1992) 'Body Decoration, Tradition, Authenticity and Tourism: Altered Contexts in a Huli Society', unpublished paper given at the First European Colloquium on Pacific Studies, Nijmegen, December.

Turner, V. (1974) *Dramas, Fields, and Metaphors: Symbolic Action in Human Society*, Ithaca and London: Cornell University Press.

Urry, John (1990) *The Tourist Gaze: Leisure and Travel in Contemporary Societies*, London: Sage Publications.

Webb, V.L. (1992) 'Fact and fiction: nineteenth century photographs of Zulu', *African Arts*, 25(1), 50–9.

Wolf, W. (1992) 'Das sind die neu gefunden menschen oder volker', Europaische Indianerbilder des 16, bis 19, Jahrhunderts zwischen Entwurf und Projektion in P. Mesenholler (ed.), *Mundus Novus: Amerika oder die Entdeckung des Bekannten*, Essen: Klartext, 35–53.

12 The Museum of the Jewish Diaspora Tells a Story

DEBORAH GOLDEN

INTRODUCTION

A striking feature of Israeli life is the all-pervasive sense of the past. People appear to move in and out of a world of historical association, often going far back into ancient times, with the most extraordinary ease. Such backward-looking reference, however, cannot but be ambivalent. Zionism, like most national movements, maintains an uneasy relationship with the past from which it springs. On the one hand, it looks back for a legitimation of the present and guidelines to the future. On the other hand, it seeks to break with that same past. Israel is thus caught in a strange and contradictory relationship with Jewish history: it is, at one and the same time, a continuation of that past and its rejection.[1] One of the better places to examine this ambivalence is surely a museum where 'the past meets the present in the most organised and self-conscious fashion' (Grana, 1971:106).

The assumption that a visit to a museum may reveal as much about the preoccupations of its creators, as about whatever it has on display, underlies much of the current literature on museums, though studies differ as to just what those preoccupations may be. Some museums, particularly those devoted to ethnography and history, reveal a nostalgic yearning for what is seen to be the simple life of other times and other places. In this view museums, as one facet of tourism, manifest a response to and an attempt to assuage the fragmentary, disconcerting quality of modernity (Grana, 1971; Kavanagh, 1983; MacCannell, 1976; Horne, 1984). At the same time, such nostalgia is seen as constitutive of the very power of modernity, which asserts itself by seeking out the authentic elsewhere and bringing it back to be artificially preserved and paraded (MacCannell, 1976; Horne, 1984). Museums, as increasingly popular arenas of such displays, are the home ground on which modernity encounters its 'other' — either its own past or another culture (Grana, 1971; Stocking, 1985; Lumley, 1988). Some studies of historical museums link their propensity to nostalgia and portrayal of the past as conflict-free and depoliticized, not to some general anxiety about modern life but to the specific political requirements of those

The Tourist Image: Myths and Myth Making in Tourism. Edited by Tom Selwyn.
© 1996 John Wiley & Sons Ltd.

who wield power (Bennett, 1988; Wallace, 1981; Shanks and Tilley, 1987). Others focus on the fact that most museums are primarily dedicated to the collection and display of material objects. For some, this suggests that museums act as secular temples, or ancestral places, the focus of which, analogous to the religious relic, is the sacredness of the work of art or the authentic object (Grana, 1971; Horne, 1984; Gathercole, 1989). For others, the primacy of objects is seen as part and parcel of a particularly Western notion of identity whereby cultures, like individuals, construct themselves in and through the accumulation of possessions. In this view the process of constructing identity is intimately linked to ownership made possible by wealth (Clifford, 1988; Dominguez, 1986).

In spite of their differing emphases, all the above studies rest on the understanding that museums may reveal more about the particular context in which they are set up than about what is actually on display. In similar fashion, in 'listening' to the story of the Diaspora as told by the Nahum Goldmann Museum of the Jewish Diaspora, it is my intention to look at the way in which the Museum, through its presentation of a Jewish past, in actual fact addresses dilemmas of the Israeli present.

THE MUSEUM

Israel's 30th anniversary celebrations in May 1978 were the occasion of the official opening, by the Israeli president, of the new museum located in a purpose-built building on the Tel Aviv University campus.[2] The Museum — called in Hebrew *Beth Hatefutsoth* meaning the 'House of the Diaspora' — receives between 400 000 and 500 000 annual visitors, an estimated half of whom are Israeli and half tourists from abroad.[3] The majority of the visitors are Jewish[4] and, whether Israeli or foreign, they come to the Museum in an organized group of one form or another.[5] Although a visit by foreign dignitaries to the Museum is not compulsory, it is recommended by the Ministry of Foreign Affairs, particularly for dignitaries from countries in which the Jews formed or continue to form a significant proportion of the population.[6]

The Museum's central feature, on which this chapter will focus, is the permanent exhibition called 'The Story of the Diaspora'. It is designed according to themes: Family, Community, Faith, Culture, Among the Nations and Return which, together with the Entrance and a commemorative section called 'Remember', form an integral whole. A separate 'Chronosphere' provides an audio-visual chronological summary of the exhibition.

Throughout the three floors of the permanent exhibition are study areas which feature documentary films and computer programs providing information on Jewish communities throughout the world and on Jewish

Figure 12.1 General view of Beth Hatefutsoth, the Nahum Goldmann Museum of the Jewish Diaspora, Tel Aviv. (Beth Hatefutsoth Photo Archive with permission)

family names for which print-outs are available to take home. Visitors may also quiz themselves on general Jewish knowledge. The Jewish Family Genealogy Centre (*Dorot* — meaning generations), opened in 1985 and was established to record histories of Jewish families. Here again the latest computer technology enters family trees provided by visitors and seeks out links with other families. In another study area there are recordings of Jewish music available to the visitor for listening.

Against the backdrop of the permanent exhibition, the Museum encompasses a wide range of cultural and educational activities. Temporary exhibitions are held in the Museum foyer which usually display communities that have not received due representation in the permanent exhibition. Other cultural activities include lectures, symposia, films, musical evenings and study circles. There is also a photograph archive and a library.

Integral to the Museum is its education department which runs a variety of study days, workshops and seminars using the permanent exhibition as a resource. The Youth Wing caters for approximately 50 000 schoolchildren per year between the ages of 12 and 18. Though not compulsory, a visit to

Figure 12.2 The entrance to the permanent exhibition — enlarged replica from Titus Arch in Rome, showing the temple vessels being carried by Roman soldiers in a triumphal procession after the conquest of Jerusalem in 70 C.E. (Beth Hatefutsoth, permanent exhibition with permission)

the Museum is recommended by the Ministry of Education for school-children, and the aim of the Youth Wing is that every schoolchild will have visited the Museum at least once during their schooling. Visits are usually structured around a particular topic designed to coincide with the history being taught at school. The Youth Wing also runs outreach programmes in the form of study units that can be bought or borrowed by schools. A Seminar Department runs programmes on various aspects of Jewish identity in the Diaspora in 14 languages for 18 000 annual visitors from abroad, most of whom are Jewish students. Other groups consist of community leaders, rabbis, teachers, interfaith groups and German youth groups. There is also an increasing demand for seminars for adult Israelis including new immigrants and employees of industry, banks and the diplomatic corps. A special unit set up by the Israeli Defence Force runs seminars for tens of thousands of soldiers and officers.

Finally, a new wing currently under construction will be devoted to the subject of Jewish life over the last 200 years. This new wing, which did not form part of the original plan, is largely a response to criticisms that the existing exhibit inadequately reflects Jewish life in modern times, either in terms of the issues facing contemporary Jews or in terms of the neglect or under-representation of modern communities, particularly since a number of present-day major Jewish communities have only emerged over the last 200 years (Wigoder, 1988:19). It is clear that the addition of this new wing will change the meanings attributed to the present one and in this sense the Museum is as yet an unfinished story.

INTENTIONS

The idea of the museum was originally proposed by Dr Nahum Goldmann,[7] then president of the World Zionist Congress which accepted a resolution on the matter in 1959 and proceeded to raise the necessary finances among Jewish organizations in America.[8] Goldmann saw the primary purpose of the Museum as commemorative: 'Following the extermination under the Nazis of six million Jews, including the great majority of Central and Eastern European Jewry, and with the establish-ment of the State of Israel, the 2,500 year old chapter of the history of the Diaspora is, in a certain sense, drawing to a close.' Thus, the Museum was to 'create a living memorial of the Jewish Dispersion'. It was not, however, to function solely as a memorial but also to contribute towards 'forging the unity of the Jewish people now living in quite different and, in a number of respects, antagonistic spheres' (Goldmann, 1983:5).

For Goldmann, Israel and the Diaspora were mutually interdependent and the 'inability of both segments to understand each other, and a widening hiatus between them, would be disastrous for Jewish life, both in the State of Israel and in the Diaspora'. The Museum was to serve as a 'bridge' by giving Israeli youth an opportunity to 'comprehend the innate meaning of the greatness and creativity and, in its own fashion, the heroism of their Jewish ancestors' (ibid.).

The perception of a growing gap between young Israelis and the Diaspora underlies most statements of purpose of the Museum and the move in its emphasis from being commemorative to educational in intent. In the words of its first director the Museum was 'conceived of as a channel of communication . . . first and foremost, for the younger gener-ation of native-born Israelis who tend to have reservations and even scepticism towards the Diaspora world of their fathers; secondly, for the broad strata of present-day Diaspora Jewry whose attachment to Judaism is being continually weakened by assimilation; and finally for the Jewish and Israeli publics at large who seek a stronger affinity with their people's historic past' (Weinberg, 1980:5–6).

Furthermore, the Museum 'would help correct negative stereotype images of Jewish life in the Diaspora, and, through the visualisation of Jewish "roots", it would stimulate positive emotional reactions to the nation's past' (ibid.). Such negative stereotypes were further elaborated in an article on the role of the Museum in educating first-generation Israelis who 'cannot, have no desire to, identify with the image of the "Diaspora Jew" as they see him: strange and foreign in his own surroundings, cut off from the main-stream of culture, always persecuted and despised, constantly at the mercy of others, rootless and wheeling and dealing in order to survive' (Arbel, 1983:31–2).[9] Accordingly, the role of the Diaspora Museum was to 'break this vicious circle of alienation by creating a more balanced image of Jewish history' (ibid.).

As to how exactly to go about this, a number of proposals were raised. First, it was suggested that the original purpose of commemorating the communities destroyed in the Holocaust was too restricted. Since the establishment of the State of Israel, and the mass immigration this provoked, major Jewish communities in Arab countries had ceased to exist. It was decided that these too should be included in the Museum, a decision that may have been taken in the light of one of the Museum's aims to address itself to tensions between the Sephardi and Ashkenazi populations in Israel.[10] The original plan was that the Museum would be based on an ethnographic display of the life and culture of each of these communities. This approach was subsequently rejected because of fear that members of each community would come to see their own display without regard for the others. (This fear was to prove well-founded: nowadays the temporary exhibitions, designed to provide displays of specific communities not included in the permanent exhibition, are indeed visited in the main by members of that specific community.)[11] This would mean that the Museum, in terms of its attempt to promote a sense of unity — in its own understanding of the concept — would have failed. Furthermore, the Israel Museum in Jerusalem already had a large section devoted to Jewish ethnography. A chronological approach was also rejected since it was understood that such an approach would not do justice to the geographic dispersion of the Jews.

Finally, Abba Kovner, an Israeli 'poet, fighter and intellectual' as he was called in a tribute paid to him by the Museum after his death (Avner and Wigoder, 1988:13), suggested that the Museum be organized around a thematic structure, with each theme (sha'ar in Hebrew meaning gateway or 'portal' as Kovner preferred it to be translated) portraying a cardinal aspect of Jewish life.

Kovner[12] too expressed anxiety about the new generation of Jews both in Israel and abroad breaking with their past:

> And now, only a generation or two after the major portion of our nation was incinerated in Auschwitz, hundreds of thousands of Jews are turning away from their communities and quietly, unobtrusively disappearing, slipping into their alien surroundings painlessly and with no regretful farewells. At the

same time, one generation after the State of Israel was founded, the question arises there as to whether there is any Jewish meaning to the way of life of the second generation . . . It will indeed be a tragic irony of fate if a new *galut* [exile] emerges among the Jews living in the State of Israel — in their own land.

Thus, the Diaspora Museum was to serve as a 'contribution to the covenant . . . of the modern Jew with himself, with his own identity, the covenant of the Israeli with the Jewish people' (Kovner, 1988:7).

The thematic structure, in contrast to an ethnological approach, thus ensured that the story would be told as a whole rather than as separate stories of the various communities: 'Since the permanent exhibit is organised around themes, rather than chronologically or geographically, it focuses on what is common to the Jewish people as a whole and not on what is specific to individual communities' (Weinberg, 1988:24); and 'Had the planning team considered its prime task the underscoring and exposition of the essential differences that evolved in the Jewish communities under varying environmental conditions, they might have ruled out the thematic structure' (Weinberg, 1980:4).

In other words, from the viewpoint of the Museum's underlying conception, the heritage of particular communities was seen as fragmenting the collective identity. In fact, however, in what could be construed as an interesting challenge to this conception of unity, most complaints from the public about the Museum have been from people who did not feel that their specific communities had been adequately represented in the exhibition, if at all.[13]

The endeavour to present the entire story of Jewish life in the Diaspora also posed problems in terms of artifacts for display since, in the words of the Museum's director: 'No material relics which, even when assembled, could adequately reflect 2,500 years of Jewish life in the Diaspora . . . The Jews usually shared in the dominant material culture surrounding them; as a result, there remained very few material objects that were specifically Jewish — with the exception of religious or ceremonial articles . . . even these extant objects are not more than 300 years old' (Weinberg, 1980:5). It was therefore, decided to depart from traditional museum practice and base the exhibition almost entirely on reproductions.[14]

These reproductions, together with extensive use of audio-visual techniques — music, colour, light and shade, shapes and sounds — are designed to turn the exhibition into a place of lived 'experience'. The visitor is not to come to stare and wonder at ancient remnants of the past; rather, he or she is guided[15] through an exhibition that calls upon emotional involvement and identification: 'For the overwhelming majority of adult Jewish visitors, *Beth Hatefutsoth* is essentially an intense emotional experience' (Weinberg, 1988:20). And: 'In this respect *Beth Hatefutsoth* is a "warm" museum: most of its Jewish visitors respond in a strong emotional way. Individual differences notwithstanding, the emotional reactions of the visitors have on the whole a common denominator: their sense of identification with the past is vigorously awakened. In this respect, *Beth Hatefutsoth* has achieved one of its foremost educational goals' (Weinberg, 1980:11).[16]

It is this same desire to touch its audience emotionally that underlies the permanent exhibition's self-description as 'The Story of the Diaspora'. It offers itself, not as history but as a tale told by parent to child, or grandfather to grandson — it is cosy and comforting, with a beginning, middle and end, in which everything falls into place: 'To begin with I don't think it should be called a museum. It should be more like a grandfather taking his grandson for a walk through the exciting history of his forefathers' (Weisgal, first President of the Museum, quoted in Weinberg, 1988:22).[17]

THE STORY

How does the story begin? 'This is the story of a people which was scattered over all the world and yet remained a single family; a nation which time and again was doomed to destruction and yet, out of ruins, rose to new life.'[18] In its opening words, then, we are presented with two essential themes, each a dichotomy: unity and dispersion, life and death. The story, I propose, is an exploration of these themes and of the links between them. Whose story is it? Although most of the exhibition's texts were written by Abba Kovner and there is some use of quotations from traditional Jewish sources, only occasionally is the author of any particular text displayed, thus conveying a sense of a story that speaks for Jews at all times and in all places — not *a* story of the Diaspora, but *the* story.

The entrance to the exhibition, where we read the above words, takes us along a stone floor and through an opening in a stone wall. The stones — some dispersed, others forming the wall — recall both Jerusalem's natural landscape and the Western Wall there. These stones, both in terms of their inherent qualities and in their being of the land, evoke a sense of permanence and resistance to change.[19] And just as the stones were borrowed from the natural landscape to construct the Temple walls, so too their qualities lend to this human construction a sense of permanence and invulnerability to change.[20]

However, though the stones call to mind the Jerusalem landscape and the Western Wall, we the visitors are in fact *told* nothing at all — there is no explanatory label on the exhibit. Rather the very presence of the stones is deemed sufficient to evoke in us an understanding of their significance. The stones, to be communicative, rely on a world of tacit and assumed knowledge: like an axiom they cannot and must not be explained. These stones, unexplained as they are, provide the framework of the story: they are the stones from which we are exiled and the stones to which we will return.

Through the opening in the stone wall we are faced with the moment of exile. A large relief, based on the Arch of Titus in Rome, depicts Roman soldiers triumphantly parading the holy vessels taken from the Temple. The most prominent of these is the *menorah*, the seven-branched lampstand, that is both traditional Jewish symbol and national emblem of Israel[21] — a symbol that will recur throughout the exhibition. Accompanying the relief are the words 'Assyrians, Babylonians and Romans conquered the land and drove the Jews into exile but the Jewish nation persisted', words recalling the introduction to the story. Thus, though the Arch of Titus refers in actual fact to the destruction of the Second Temple in 70 AD, this specific occasion is symbolically used to represent all forced exiles, regardless of historic particularity.

The first theme, *Family*, is introduced by a multi-screen slide show entitled 'The Jewish Face: Portraits from the Four Corners of the World'. The photographs are many and diverse, and we are given to understand that their presentation is a denial of a Jewish physical stereotype.[22] But, continues the story, 'Behind the variety in these faces lies a common heritage: the Jewish family tradition and the Jewish way of life.' So we *are* to look for that which is common to all Jews — there is a common factor, though it is not racial but cultural.

This section, softly lit, cryptically labelled and accompanied by a woman's voice singing a lullaby alternately in Yiddish and Ladino,[23] presents two cycles: an individual's life cycle and the annual cycle of festivals and fasts that make up the Jewish calendar. The entire section can be seen as the presentation of the temporal order shared by Jews. In this sense, placed directly after the moment of exile, it conveys a direct response to the loss of land and the replacement of a spatial boundary by a temporal one.[24] Indeed, for Lewis, who discusses the Museum as an articulation of the Zionist vision, it is not one particular section but the entire exhibition that expresses the 'centrality of time in Zionist imagery'. Thus, 'Through diverse stimuli, the visitor learns how a people divided in social space preserved psychic unity through symbolic commitment to a common temporal vision, past and future' (Lewis, 1985:139).

We are first presented with the individual life cycle: circumcision ('the Jews practised circumcision in joy and in peril throughout the generations'); *Barmitzvah* ('the 13-year-old son is told: now you are morally responsible for your deeds'),[25] and marriage.

If we take a look at the exhibit presenting the Jewish marriage ceremony, we see that its mode of presentation is typical of the entire exhibition and expresses its central problem. The focal point of this exhibit is a white

Figure 12.3 Jewish wedding with the musicians (klezmerim) in background. Galicia, 19th century. Sculpture group. (Beth Hatefutsoth, permanent exhibition with permission)

plaster model intended to represent the essence of all Jewish weddings, the particular geographical and ethnic characteristics of which are muted (though a discreet label informs us that it is in fact a model of a 19th-century Eastern European Jewish wedding). In a glass case in front of the model are a number of authentic ritual objects. Alongside this, there are two colourful slide-shows, the one depicting illuminated ritual texts and drawings of weddings from the past and the other photographs of present-day weddings clearly identifiable with specific communities. Throughout the exhibition this recurring mode of presentation draws our attention to a polarity: that which is deemed as the unchanging essence on the one hand and those specific manifestations of this essential theme on the other.[26]

The second cycle to be presented in this section is the annual cycle of festivals and fasts that make up the Jewish calendar: 'A tree may be alone in the field, a man alone in the world, but no Jew is alone in his holy days'. Linking these two cycles, that of the home and that of the community, is the portrayal of the 'Jewish Home of Sabbath Eve'. Using the same mode of presentation as the marriage ceremony, the exhibit displays homes from different times and places in all of which the ritual objects remain the same.

The theme of the Sabbath recurs throughout the exhibition thus ascribing to it a constancy within changing surroundings.

Most of the festivals are presented by no more than the name of the festive day (in Hebrew, with an English transliteration and its English equivalent) alongside a pictorial image. Thus, for instance, the name of the festival *Sukkot* is placed alongside a black and white photograph of a father and a child praying against the background of a corn field. Only Passover and the Days of Awe (*Yom Kippur*) receive slightly more detailed treatment. Passover is presented in the same mode as that described for the Jewish wedding, while in the small darkened room set aside for the Days of Awe there is a picture of a group of men at prayer and a taped rendering of '*Kol Nidre*', the prayer sung on the eve of *Yom Kippur*.

If readers are asking themselves what these various festivals actually commemorate, then in a sense they are in the very same position as visitors to the Museum. This is because very little information is provided. Instead, the emphasis falls on images and the evocation of atmospheres. There are a number of points to be made about this experiential mode of presentation. First of all, as in the case of the stone-wall entrance to the exhibition, the absence of any explanation assumes a tacit understanding of the significance of the displays, thereby setting up a boundary between those who have been privy to these experiences and those who have not — in this case between Jews and non-Jews. The boundary is rigid precisely because, as is emphasized by the relative absence of words, experience can only be experienced; it cannot be explained or learned.[27]

Second, for those within the boundary, the absence of explanation allows for at least two possibilities: either an assumption on the part of those who conceived the exhibition, in view of their own deep immersion in Jewish tradition, of a greater knowledge on the part of its Jewish visitors than may be justified;[28] or, that by the very fact of being 'beyond words', the exhibits allow for an all-inclusiveness. For only minimal recognition — the vaguest memory of a lullaby or of a festival, a slight similarity between that photograph of an old man and the visitor's own grandfather — is needed for the visitor to sense that he or she belongs.[29]

This all-inclusiveness is perhaps best exemplified by an exhibit called simply 'Relationships'. The exhibit displays five photographs: a pair of clasped hands, an old man, an old couple, a grandmother with her daughter and her granddaughter, a grandfather and grandson. Alongside the photographs are the words: 'Phrases that became concepts: Honour thy father and mother; Show deference to the old; Cast me not off in my old age; Make thy books thy companions; A man shall help his fellow.' It is this same all-inclusiveness that allows for a blurring of past and present, religious and secular, Israeli and Jewish, Sephardi and Ashkenazi and indeed all political persuasions. Thus, for instance, in the exhibit called 'Commemorating Trial and Resistance', festivals whose import is clearly national–secular are placed alongside religious festivals as part of an uninterrupted and unproblematic continuum. Furthermore, according to the visitor's particular depth of knowledge and the nature of his or her attachment to Judaism, a photograph of a corn field may be seen, say, by a *kibbutznik* as emphasizing the agricultural significance of the festival or, by a Lubavicher *hassid*,[30] as only symbolic of its deeper religious significance.

But, as does the beginning of any story, this first theme of *Family* only receives its fuller meaning in relation to the others, and it is to the rest of the story that I now turn.

The central exhibit of the next theme, *Community*, is a white plaster miniature model of a Jewish community and its institutions. Although the model is based on figures from a 13th-century German Jewish community, once again the particular distinguishing features of time and place are rendered in neutral fashion. The model is a world in itself and the structure is almost entirely closed, open only at certain points to allow us visitors to peep inside, with that pleasurable childhood sensation of peering through the windows of a doll's house to see little people going about their activities. Here the scenes depict bringing up a case before the rabbinical law courts, attending the ritual bath, receiving food at the soup kitchen. We are witness to a self-sufficient world in which, we are told: 'All Jews are responsible for one another.' The second main exhibit in this section includes three documentary films about the Jewish communities in Salonika, the Eastern European *shtetl* and Fez, all three of which are no longer in existence. The significance of this choice of communities will become clearer later.

Leaving the shelter of the community, we come face to face with large letters engraved in the wall spelling out the imperative 'Remember' (*Zakhor*).[31] We are in the hall dedicated to the memory of 'Jewish Martyrs throughout the Ages'. The dimly lit hall is predominantly black, its focal point an imposing memorial column suspended from the high ceiling. The fact that the memorial column is suspended, rather than built up from the ground in the way of most memorials, gives the impression of an ordinance from the heavens, and in this sense echoes the biblical associ-ation of the divine imperative to remember. The column is composed of layer upon layer of black caging at the centre of which runs a thread of gold light. There is, in addition to the column, a large book entitled *Scrolls of Fire — A Nation Fighting for its Life — Fifty-Two Chapters of Jewish Martyrology*. The book, prefaced by the words of Menachem Mendel of Kotsk — 'There is nothing more whole than a broken Jewish heart', is opened at a new chapter — a poem and a painting — each week of the year. In chronological order, each poem describes a separate chapter of Jewish suffering, starting with the destruction of the First Temple in 58 BC and ending with one adjuring us to remember soldiers and civilians who have died 'for the freedom of Israel'. The poems and paintings are

Figure 12.4 Memorial column — an abstract metal construction
commemorating Jewish martyrology throughout the ages; in the centre a
permanent light rod. (Beth Hatefutsoth, permanent exhibition with
permission)

unsigned (although they are in fact by Abba Kovner and Dan Reisinger
respectively) and the absence of identifiable poet and painter attributes a
timeless quality to the book.[32]

On the wall, a plaque dedicated to the memory of those who died in the
Holocaust, reads:

> In the year 1933 of the Christian era, Adolf Hitler came to power in Germany.
> In his time, the Germans and their accomplices murdered six million Jews,
> among them a million and a half Jewish children. Imprisoned in Ghettos the
> victims fought desperately for their lives while the world stood by in silence.

The hall of commemoration is designed in such a way as to be central to
all the other sections. It provides access from the first floor to the next and
is visible from all three floors of the exhibition. The command to remember

accompanies us wherever we go. The deaths to be remembered are, on the one hand, distinctive and unique to particular historical circumstances as represented in the *Scrolls of Fire* and in the commemorative plaque. On the other hand, these personal fates are presented as manifestations of the collective destiny of the people as a whole, as represented by the memorial column.[33]

The next theme, *Faith*, is introduced by the statement: 'I have chosen the way of Faith. Belief in the one God and the sanctity of human life are the supreme values of the Jewish religion. The Torah and its commandments embrace man's total life experience. After the destruction of the Second Temple, the synagogue represented Jewish continuity.' The first display is a white model of a group of men in a synagogue awaiting a 10th man to join them so that they can begin the communal prayer. Against one wall, encased in glass, is an open Torah scroll accompanied by the words: 'A people embarked on a long journey with only a book as a guide.' But the central exhibit of the section consists of 18 small models of synagogues from various times and places. In its choice of the synagogue as the central expression of the notion of faith, the exhibition reinforces the emphasis on community organization of the previous section. It may be that this emphasis allows for a certain continuity between traditional and modern forms of community organization.[34] Furthermore, the fact that each synagogue reflects the architectural style of its surroundings — the synagogue in China looks like a pagoda, the Dutch one like a church — limits contacts with the non-Jewish world to matters of external form.

The next theme, *Culture*, is devoted to Jewish contributions to the arts and sciences. The first exhibit portrays a Jewish scribe engrossed in the task of copying out religious writings: 'The continuity of Jewish culture is anchored in the continuity of the Hebrew language.' Some exhibits indeed display those aspects of cultural activity whose sources of inspiration and subject matters are clearly rooted in Judaism. There are films on Jewish Art through the ages, an exhibit on the sacrifice of Isaac as a biblical motif in world art, displays on Jewish languages, the Jewish press and Jewish education. The theme also, perforce, makes manifest the influences of the wider world, not only in matters of form (as it did in the previous section) but also of content. We are therefore shown cultural achievement of different kinds whose link to Judaism lies only in the fact that the creators were themselves Jewish, including, for instance, a section on early contributions to science and art, and a slide-show on Jewish Nobel prize-winners. Although it is possible that Kafka and Freud, for instance, owed some of their insights to the fact that they were Jews, things Jewish are not what makes their work important.

Indeed, the increasing difficulty in making a clear statement about what is specifically Jewish about many of such achievements is manifest in the title of an exhibit that displays a sort of cultural family tree. Called 'One Culture

— Many Facets: the Growth of Pluralism in Modern Jewish Spiritual Life', it implies that no matter the diversity of cultural activity, this is all contained in some way under the same roof. We may ask, however, how many 'facets' can be contained within one culture before it becomes two or three or indeed as many cultures as the 'facets' themselves?

We are introduced to the next theme, entitled *Among the Nations*, by an ever-revolving circle of words that reads 'I will not die'. This section, chronological in format, takes the visitor through selected stations of Jewish settlement in the Diaspora, from the community in Alexandria in the 1st century through to the settlement in the United States in the 19th, each station displaying in great detail its particular mode of economic, legal, organizational, religious and cultural life, its relations with other Jewish and non-Jewish communities.[35]

The conflicts within and between Jewish communities that are mentioned convey no sense of rupture or upheaval, nor the fierceness of antagonisms. The response to the rise of the Hasidic movement in 18th-century Poland, for instance, is described thus: 'Many of the traditional leaders were apprehensive of the new movement. The Vilna *Gaon* headed its opponents'. Instead, the locus of irreconcilable and indeed fatal conflict is transferred to relations between the Jews and the surrounding non-Jewish world: 'The story of the interaction between Jews and their changing environments is a continuous drama of settlement and expulsion, disaster and recovery.' Although the stations attempt to portray the complexity of interaction between the Jews and their surroundings, the message conveyed time and time again is that the Jews remained ultimately vulnerable. The clearest illustration of this may be found in the station showing Jewish life in Spain during the Middle Ages. It is shown, first, as a time of unprecedented material, social and cultural flowering for the Jews. A pictorial mural illustrates this 'Golden Age' — a synthesis of Jewish and non-Jewish life — by means of the personal biographies of Hisdai Ibn Shaprut, 'physician, statesman and adviser to the Caliph of Cordova . . . admired by his own people as judge and protector', and Samuel Ha-Nagid, 'diplomat and military commander, scholar and poet, spokesman for the Jews of his country'. But if we look further, an additional picture depicts: 'The assassination of his son and heir Joseph Ha-Nagid, who was involved in court intrigues, foreshadows the approaching outbreaks against the Jews of Granada.' We are shown the gradual taking over of Spain by Christians and their interference in the life of the Jews, culminating in their forced conversion and ultimate expulsion from Spain in 1492. A display entitled 'Eclipse', which shows and describes the signing of the documents decreeing the Jews' expulsion, reads: 'with a stroke of a pen, a 1,000 years of Jewish life in Spain came to an end'. In this very statement, the exhibition appears to question the worth of those thousand years. Look, we are told, all that glory came to nothing!

Figure 12.5 The Menorah at the end of the 'Gate of Return', symbolizing
the return to Zion. In the background, a map of the holy sites of Eretz,
Israel with Jerusalem in the centre. (Beth Hatefutsoth, permanent
exhibition with permission)

And as if to underscore the point, the last exhibit in this section is
entitled 'Crossroads', which poses a number of dilemmas with which Jews
have been confronted since the Emancipation. The visitor, called upon to
press the button of his or her choice, is faced with a description of the
implications of the decisions.[36] The final dilemma, entitled 'Towards the
Year 2,000' presents a Tunisian Jew with the choice of integrating into her
'country of residence' or immigrating to Israel. On choosing the latter, and
pressing the appropriate button, we are told: 'This is not a station anymore:
this is home.'

'Next Year in Jerusalem', the ancient prayer, introduces us to the next and
final theme called *Return* which, like the Entrance to the exhibition and the
theme of *Family*, is heavily imbued in cryptically captioned imagery. First,
we meet 12 portraits of contemporary Israelis whose life stories are intended
to exemplify the modern rendering of the biblical prophecy 'Thy children
shall return to their own borders' — the ingathering of the exiles and return
of the 12 tribes. Next, through an ascending and winding passage, designed
in such a way as to give the sense of a ship at sea, and to the sounds of
ancient Jewish melodies and Israeli folk-songs, alternating slides depict

Jerusalem as a city of spiritual vision on the one hand and political Zionism on the other. Throughout, this mingling of past and present portrays Israel as born of the past — a realization of ancient prophecy.

The theme, and the story, come to their completion with the words 'Wherever I go, I am going to the Land of Israel', attributed to Rabbi Nachman of Braslav.[37] The final image is that of a large *menorah* carved into the wall — the *menorah* we first saw being carried out of the Temple by the Romans — behind which is a picture of heavenly Jerusalem. It is the exiled *menorah* returned home. On leaving the exhibition we read: 'To remember the past; To live the present; To trust the future.'

THE MORAL OF THE STORY

Is that the end of the story? Certainly one of the ways in which the Diaspora Museum wishes us to perceive the exhibition is as a journey, in time and space, on which we are fellow travellers. What is the nature of the journey? It is a journey from a time and place presented as familiar and safe to one strange and dangerous, and back again. The exhibition takes us from the most personal realm — place of birth, family, community — in which meaning is private, sensuous and assumed – into the wide world among the nations — the meaning of which cannot be assumed but must be explained in much explicit detail — and back again. It is a journey from a world deemed permanent and invulnerable to one deemed contingent and transitory and back again. The entire exhibition is, in a sense, a generalized version of one of the particular stories told in the theme *Among the Nations*. It is the story of not one particular community, but magnified and made to encompass an entire people — that 'single family' which, in spite of endless variations, lives out a single fate, adheres to an unchanging core. The Jews, we are told, wherever, whenever, are ultimately vulnerable outside of their home. Do not stray too far, is the implicit warning, for fear of punishment.

In this sense the story is a cautionary tale — a story told by grandfather to grandchild *at home* about dangerous places elsewhere. Home is a safe place from which stories about dangerous places are told, their danger contained in a story, in a museum, in Israel.[38] So that if the Museum might at first appear almost anti-nostalgic in its portrayal of the past as fraught with danger, its message could be said to be nostalgic in the original meaning of the term: that people far from home die of homesickness (Starobinski, 1966). Paradoxically, this warning is actually underlined by the portrayal of the periods of flourishing in the Diaspora such as that enjoyed by Spanish Jewry; for they are held up as a terrible illusion, and surrendering to this illusion will bring suffering, if not upon ourselves, then worse, upon our children.

It is in this context that we may interpret the absence of authentic artifacts which, notwithstanding the original intentions of and constraints upon the creators of the museum,[39] could be understood as saying something about the inauthenticity of the life that is on display. To paraphrase MacCannell's chapter on the framing of tourist experience called 'Staged Authenticity' (1976), I would suggest that the Museum is an exercise in 'staged inauthenticity'. In this interpretation the absence of authentic articles is actually a statement about the transitory nature of life in the Diaspora. If, as Walter Benjamin suggests, 'the presence of the original is the prerequisite to the concept of authenticity' (Benjamin, 1982:222), then the absence of the original may be a way of saying that there is or will be nothing real left of the Diaspora — that the Diaspora, like the reproductions, is inauthentic. This contrast between the inauthentic Diaspora and authentic Israel is echoed in a story related at the end of a descriptive article about the Museum that appeared in a major daily newspaper:

> There's a cafeteria at the Museum where we went to have lunch. Next to us sat a fat man, dressed in a funny striped suit. He is Angus, his wife is called Suzy and they're from Maryland in the United States. The man looked at the menu and asked us what couscous is. I told him that couscous is a Tunisian dish. He asked me whether they serve this Tunisian dish as a reminder of dishes eaten in the Diaspora. He thought that the cafeteria was some sort of extension of the exhibition he had just seen. I told him that life starts where the exhibition leaves off. They sell couscous because people are hungry and want to eat and anyway there is no more Diaspora in Israel. People from Poland eat couscous and people from Morocco eat gefilte fish, it's simply a matter of hunger, and not a matter of an exhibition (Holler, 1988).

Indeed, the Museum's self-conscious pride in its own technical brilliance — in 'taking, as it were, the dust off ancient history' (Weinberg, 1988:24) — is part and parcel of the Museum's message that the past — the Diaspora — has been surpassed by the present — Israel. Thus, the Museum not only commemorates the past but also commemorates itself commemorating.

Eisen (1986), writing about concepts of home and exile in Jewish thought and their implications for contemporary relations between Israel and the Diaspora, particularly the United States, suggests that the Museum is evidence of a relatively recent sense of security among Israelis that the past is indeed past:

> Where else but in a museum, after all, can one move from Alexandria and Rome to Baghdad and Pumbedita, and on to Cordova, Worms, Vilna and Fez, with no sense of dislocation whatever, utterly confident that the past is past and we who visit it at our leisure are not? In the Diaspora Museum one descends the stairs from these reminders of Jewish exile, leaves relative darkness for the light, and returns to the living story of modern Zion — the consummation of all one has seen. Outside, past the postcards and the

cafeteria, the light is bright, as only reality can be. 'Remember where you stand', the Museum advises. 'Only the Land around you, and the sea in the near distance, are real. The rest is not. If you come from a diaspora of the present, know that, sooner than you think, your community too will be a part of our past, a room in our museum' (Eisen, 1986:147).

In this reading, then, the return to Israel is really and truly a happy ending and the story might end there, if it could.

But perhaps, rather than a story with a beginning, middle and end, it is more like one of those children's nursery rhymes which, having come to an end, return to the beginning only to start all over again. For in laying emphasis on the stones at the beginning and the end of the story whereby the Diaspora is no more than an exile against which notions of home are carved out — 'an historical aberration that was frequently punished by death', as one visitor to the Museum put it (Yapp, 1988:52) — then the Museum is in danger of losing 2500 years of Jewish history and thereby undermining the very reason for its establishment. For, as was manifest in the various declarations of intent, the Museum saw its role as presenting the Diaspora, particularly to the young generation of Israelis, not as shameful but as a source of pride and identification — as a means of infusing their life as Israelis with Jewish content (however so defined). Thus we may recall Kovner's fear of a new exile in Israel whereby the state has become an end in itself: 'Perhaps in modern times we have confused means and ends; perhaps that which was necessary for survival in the past has now turned into the purpose of life itself' (Kovner, 1988:13).[40] Furthermore, precisely because the Museum aspires to locate a heritage that is common to all Jews, everywhere, it cannot posit an ending to the story that would exclude the majority of today's Jewish population who continue to live in the Diaspora.[41] By virtue of its very own aspirations, the Museum cannot unequivocally embrace its own ending to the story in the form of return to Israel.

The ambivalence conveyed by the story is, in part, due to the fact that it has two audiences. On the one hand, the story is asking those Jews living in the Diaspora to come home. For these the Museum is a museum with all its connotations of a storage place for relics no longer part of the living world; indeed it is a burial place — not only for those who died in the Diaspora but for the Diaspora itself.[42] On the other hand, the story is asking Israelis to look to the Diaspora for their Jewishness — though not to the extent that they might choose to live there. The difficulty is that again, in terms of the Museum's own project, such a bifurcation into two audiences is untenable. For in that case the Museum, rather than acting as a 'bridge' (to recall Goldmann's term) between Israel and the Diaspora, is merely emphasizing the gap. It is perhaps for this reason that the exhibition returns again and again to the image of the family tree since this allows for both rootedness and dispersion at one and the same time.

The problem, therefore, that the Museum sets itself is to seek out a 'common heritage' applicable to both audiences — those in Israel and those in the Diaspora or, in other words, to pinpoint that which is common to all Jews at all times and in all places. Interestingly, one of Kovner's suggestions to bring the exhibition to a close was to set up a mirror in which the visitor would see him or herself reflected, since 'the Jewish people . . . are they not then the authentic exhibit of our museum?' (Ben-Gal, 1988:28). The proposal — both in being raised and ultimately rejected — is indicative of a problem unresolved. For such an ending would have suggested the very minimal definition of Jewishness which the Museum, in its quest for a 'common heritage' *behind* the variety of Jewish faces, seeks to surpass.

The difficulty of solving the problem formulated in such a way is again apparent in the exhibition's mode of presentation of a neutral essence together with its historically specific manifestations. For, though the Museum seems to suggest that life lies in that invulnerable, unchanging, stone-like essence while death lies in historical circumstance and change, this suggestion does not allow for the fact that such an essence is dependent for its very life on its numerous and varied historical manifestations. There is, after all, no such thing as *the* Jewish wedding, a strange, white neutral ceremony, but only Jewish weddings of particular times and particular places. But again, to give undue weight to the particular would undermine the Museum's very quest for a collective identity over and above its various manifestations.

What of the 'common heritage' that is to be found in the portrayal of the family at home celebrating the Sabbath? Within this view, it is precisely those few, authentic ritual objects that provide the key to the common heritage as do the synagogues whose content remains intact while only the external form changes. However, in view of the Museum's reaching out towards an all-inclusiveness, an identification between a common heritage and an adherence to Jewish religious law is not one that the Museum can accept, either descriptively or normatively. So that here again this resolution, like the return to Israel, though present as a possibility, cannot be embraced unequivocally.

So where then is that elusive heritage? I would suggest that because it is so difficult to pinpoint what is common to the lives of Jews, then it is to their deaths that the Museum looks. In spite of the Museum's vivid portrayal of life in the Diaspora, it is a story underpinned by death. In this story, life itself is born of death: the thread of light at the centre of the all-pervasive memorial column is apparent to the eye only through the surrounding black caging: the introductory words to the *Scrolls of Fire* read: 'There is nothing more whole than a broken Jewish heart.' Furthermore, the custom whereby a new chapter of the *Scrolls of Fire* is revealed each week is analogous to the weekly reading of the biblical portion. We seem to be told that the memory of the dead is to accompany us through the exhibition as do the biblical readings through the year, and that this memory is a source of life as is the Bible. Death unites Jews of all times and places, in Israel and the Diaspora, says the Museum.

But here again the Museum cannot rest content with this ending to the story for, in explicit opposition to the portrayal of Jewish history as filled with suffering and death, the Museum was set up to celebrate a Jewish past of vibrancy and life.[43] So, like the child's incessant rhyme, the story begins again.

NOTES

I would like to thank the members of staff of *Beth Hatefutsoth* who kindly gave me their time.

1. For a systematic attempt to trace the links between contemporary Israeli political culture and traditional Judaism, see Leibman and Don-Yehiya (1983).
2. In view of the Museum's status as a national institution, during its planning stages there was much vociferous protest on the part of a number of dignitaries against the proposal to locate it in Tel Aviv rather than Jerusalem, including the threatened resignation by the then Mayor of Jerusalem (reported in *Haaretz* 1 November 1960).
3. By way of comparison, *Yad Vashem*, the central museum and monument to the memory of the Holocaust (to which there is no entrance fee), receives more annual visitors than any other site in Israel — an estimated 1 123 000 per year. The Israel Museum in Jerusalem receives between 700 000–900 000 annual visitors.
4. The last survey carried out by the Israeli Ministry of Tourism to include the Diaspora Museum was in 1979–80 when 24 percent of tourists coming into Israel by air visited the Museum. Of these, 78 percent were Jews and 19 percent non-Jews. In that same year, 36 percent of these tourists visited the Israel Museum, out of whom 51 percent were Jews and 48 percent non-Jews.
5. To the best of my knowledge, no survey has been carried out with regard to the socio-economic background of its visitors. The Museum's public relations officer told me that since most Israelis come to the Museum within the framework of organized trips arranged through their work-place, community centres or local union, on the whole they are 'not from the professional middle-classes'. Although the 'elite' (her term) visited the Museum when it first opened, they now tend to attend special occasions only such as openings of exhibitions. This data may be contrasted with Merriman's findings (1989:166) that most visitors to museums in Britain are the 'better-educated and well-off'.
6. According to diplomatic protocol set out by the ministry of Foreign Affairs, *Yad Vashem* is the only site in Israel to which every foreign dignitary, visiting Israel for the first time in an official capacity, is taken.
7. Nahum Goldmann, son of a writer and Hebrew teacher, was born in 1895 in Lithuania. When still a child his family moved to Germany where he spent the rest of his childhood. Goldmann's early career as a Zionist was chiefly as a publicist and writer. He was forced to leave Germany in the early 1930s and after the war settled in New York where he was active in the organization of

the World Jewish Congress of which he eventually became president. During the period of the British Mandate in Palestine, Goldmann played a decisive role in the diplomatic activities designed to bring about the immediate establishment of a Jewish state. Following the declaration of the state, he declined an invitation to join the new government in Israel, preferring to continue his work in the Diaspora. Goldmann was largely responsible for initiating the controversial negotiations with the Federal Republic of Germany on the payment of reparations to Israel. He was frequently critical of the Israeli leadership, particularly of what he regarded as their inflexible policy towards the Arabs. Furthermore, although he recognized the centrality of Israel in contemporary Jewish life, he nevertheless rejected the 'somewhat naive Zionist idea that a normal life is possible only in a homeland and that Diaspora life is in some way abnormal.' He firmly insisted on the necessity (and on the reality) of the Diaspora, not only as a source of material and spiritual support for Israel, but as the embodiment of those quintessentially Jewish 'spiritual values' that had ensured Jewish survival throughout its dispersions and would continue to do so in the future. Political Zionism, in securing a territorial centre for Jews, was a necessary but not sufficient condition for the continued survival of the Jewish people except in the merely nominal sense. For Goldmann, power, in the sense of military might, was short-lived; Jews, on the contrary, have always 'survived through ideas' (1977:139).

8. The original cost of the Museum was $11 million, the bulk of which was raised among *Landsmanshaften* (Jewish organizations based on common origin in Eastern Europe) in New York. At present, the Museum's yearly budget comprises: self-generated income derived from admission fees, sales, concessions and payments by institutions for services rendered; subsidies from the Israeli government and other institutions including the World Jewish Congress, Tel Aviv University and Tel Aviv Municipality; and private donations.

9. This stereotype (strikingly close to an anti-semitic portrait of the Jew) is part and parcel of the 'negation of the Diaspora' which, though a feature of Zionist ideology generally, has been differentially emphasized at different periods and by different political persuasions. See, among others, Leibman and Don-Yehiya, 1983.

10. This was told to me by Geoffrey Wigoder, an historian on the original planning team of the Museum. I have been unable to find any reference to such a purpose in the Museum's publications, although the need to take account of the contribution of the 'Jewish communities of Moslem countries' to the 'national heritage' is mentioned in regard to the new wing currently under construction (Shmueli, 1988:11).

11. This was told to me by the Museum's Public Relations Officer.

12. Abba Kovner was born in 1918 and grew up in Vilna in a traditional Jewish family. As a young man he was active in the left-wing Zionist youth movement Hashomer Hatzair. He was a leader of the Vilna Ghetto uprising against the Nazis and subsequently of the partisan fighters in the forest around Vilna. He then became a leading activist in the smuggling of illegal immigrants into Palestine. During the Israeli War of Independence he served as an officer in a prestigious infantry unit. He settled on Kibbutz Ein Hahoresh where he lived until his death in 1987. On his death he was laid in state in the front courtyard of the Diaspora Museum where his coffin was draped in the red flag of the left-wing of the Labour movement. He was known primarily as a poet of the Holocaust and was the winner of a number of prestigious literary prizes including, in 1970, the Israel Prize. Ironically, within the context of the call to

resistance in 1941, it was Kovner himself who, making use of the biblical phrase, proclaimed: 'Let us not be led like sheep to the slaughter.' This same phrase was subsequently to become a common derogatory term for the passivity of Diaspora Jews in the face of adversity — precisely the sort of stereotype that the Diaspora Museum saw its purpose as dispelling. Mintz (1984:261), discussing Kovner's poem 'Hamafte' ah Tsalal' (The Key Sank), first published in 1950, about the enclosure and destruction of the ghetto, has described his stance towards the victims as one of 'sardonic unforgivingness'. It is perhaps pertinent to note Goldmann on the same topic: 'I have often said to Israelis that I am not sure whether a Jew who went to Auschwitz saying the *shema* [daily prayer], or a Jew who refused to deny his faith and stayed in the Ghetto was any less heroic than the soldiers who marched with the armies singing war songs' (1977:36).

13. See, for instance, among many such complaints, *Davar*, 3 February 1980 and *Maariv*, 4 February 1980 on the neglect of the Romanian community; *Haaretz*, 29 April 1979 on the neglect of the Hungarians; Geoffrey Wigoder in the *Jewish Chronicle*, 20 July 1979 answering a complaint on behalf of the Museum from a British Jew; and *Bemaaracha*, April 1988 on the under-representation of Sephardi Jewry. To the best of my knowledge there have been no surveys on audience response to the Museum.

14. In view of the fact that the Museum contained so few authentic articles, when it was first opened there was some debate as to whether to categorize it as a museum at all. The controversy was settled in 1979 when the European Council of Museums selected it as the Museum of the Year. Since then the Museum has received a number of national and international awards for tourism including the Silver Otter Award, 1981, from the British Association of Travel Writers; the Speaker of Knesset Prize in 1984 (for the Museum's exhibition on Ethiopian Jewry); and the Tourism Institute of the Year Award in 1985. The Museum is one of Kenneth Hudson's 39 'museums of influence' (1987).

15. Due to the fact that on the whole visitors come to the Museum in groups, most are indeed guided through the Museum by an official guide. In the context of the Museum's educational activities, the importance of the guide is specifically noted: 'The function of the guide in the Youth Wing is to mediate and help convey the conceptual message of the exhibits to the pupil' (Arbel, 1983:35).

16. Jeshajahu Weinberg, prior to becoming first director of the Museum, was Director of Tel Aviv's municipal theatre. He himself used the analogy between the type of emotional identification he wishes the Museum to evoke among its visitors and that evoked by going to the theatre or cinema (Weinberg, 1980:12). For the intentional arousal of 'experience' at another type of Israeli museum, see Katriel (1993).

17. See Shamgar-Handelman and Handelman (1986) for an analysis of the intentional arousal of emotion so as to evoke collective sentiments in holiday celebrations in Israeli kindergartens. That the Museum sees its role as arousing the appropriate emotions reinforces the sense that it views its adult visitors as children.

18. Unless otherwise indicated, all quotations are taken directly from the permanent exhibition.

19. See Eliade (1959:155–6) on the power of stones to reveal 'the nature of an *absolute* existence, beyond time, invulnerable to becoming'. Within the Israeli context, Zerubavel (1994:85) notes that the fact that Masada, erected on a massive rock in the desert, has 'nature as its monument' serves to reinforce the temporal continuum between the ancient site and contemporary Israel.

20. See Handelman and Katz (1990) for a discussion of the symbolism of the Wall within the context of the Israel Remembrance Day Ceremony. See also Webber (1981) and Aronoff (1981), both of whom regard the Wall as a key symbol, together with *Yad Vashem*, of Israeli 'civil religion.'

21. According to tradition, the *menorah* was a feature of the Tabernacle in the desert and later of the Temple at Jerusalem. A similar article is used at *Channukah*, a festival associated with Jewish resistance against foreign domination. The *menorah* was adopted as Israel's national emblem in 1949. For a detailed description and analysis of the adoption of the *menorah* as state symbol, see Handelman and Shamgar-Handelman (1990); see also Aronoff, 1981 and Leibman and Don-Yehiya (1983:108–9).

22. See Kovner (1988:8) for an explicit statement of this message; and also Shamir (1981:6) in a book written for schoolteachers using the Museum as a resource for teaching history.

23. The languages of the Ashkenazi and Sephardi Diaspora Jews respectively.

24. See Zerubavel (1982) in the chapter entitled 'Sacred Time and Profane Time' for a discussion of time as an important, sanctifiable dimension of the universe among Jews.

25. For an analysis of the exhibition as systematically excluding and marginalizing women, see Yizraeli (1989). Her interest in the Museum is as a metaphor for Israeli political life from which women are on the whole absent, and she does not otherwise criticize the Museum's underlying conception.

26. That this mode of presentation is intentional is made clear by Shamir (1981:7): 'The white models symbolise the unchanging element of this festival (and the same principle is at work in other exhibits). The colour white is intended to prevent reference to ethnographic and folkloristic aspects and to emphasise the symbolic significance.'

27. For a discussion of the experiential mode as crucial to the formation of English nationalism, see Wright (1985) and in particular the essays, 'Trafficking in history' and 'Coming back to the shores of Albion: The secret England of Mary Butts (1830–1937)'.

28. A suggestion raised in conversation by the director of the Seminar Department.

29. This recognition, minimal but powerful, is attested to in a letter written by an American visitor to the Museum on his return home: 'The lullaby, a Yiddish song I had heard only a few times before, like the faces, reached deep inside me in an instant. We went back to *Beth Hatefutsoth* two more times in our short month in Israel, and that elusive melody has come to symbolise all I saw, all I experienced in that extraordinary place — the sweet lilting tune and the words expressing all the mother's love, the joy of life, and at the same time, deep sadness and pain, the struggle for life of the shtetl Jews that is my father and mother, their fathers and mothers' (Salzman, 1981).

30. This pair — the *kibbutznik* and the Lubavicher *hassid* — was proposed to me in conversation by the director of the Seminar Department as indicative of the Museum's wide appeal. The director of public relations also suggested that the Museum's success lay in its holding a 'key' to everyone.

31. For a discussion of the command to remember as an integral part of Jewish collective consciousness and the supplanting of traditional vehicles of Jewish memory in modern times by history, see Yerushalmi (1982).

32. The book no doubt deserves its own detailed analysis. See Mintz (1984:259–63) for a discussion of Kovner's writing.

33. This collapsing of particular historical catastrophes into a general fate (also manifest in the way the various exiles at the beginning of the exhibition are

treated) has a precedent in rabbinical tradition (see Yerushalmi, 1982). It would be interesting to see to what extent the Museum is an extension of traditional Jewish ways of viewing history. Certainly in its emphasis on remembering as essential for continuity into the future, the Museum echoes a deep tradition. Katriel (1994), writing on Israeli pioneering settlement museums, identifies a similar strategy whereby particular historical events are subsumed under an archetypical narrative of Zionist redemption.

34. In 1981, for example, there was a proposal to use the Museum as part of a group task set for boys of *Bar-Mitzvah* age on the kibbutz. The task was entitled, 'The Kibbutz as a Jewish Form of Organization.' (See an article entitled 'Jewish — not religious — renewal: secular *kibbutzim* grapple with the question of how to mark the *Bar-Mitzvah* occasion' reported in *Jerusalem Post*, 28 September 1981).

35. The stations include Alexandria, Babylonia, Byzantium, Spain, Ashkenaz, Italy, Ottoman Empire, Holland, Poland–Lithuania, Yemen and the United States.

36. The dilemmas are: (a) 'The French Revolution' which, referring to the equality granted to the Jews by the National Assembly, poses the choice between 'abandoning your Jewish heritage' or 'remaining a faithful Jew'; (b) 'Liberalism' refers to the dilemma of a mid-19th-century Viennese banker who must choose between 'total assimilation' and 'reform Judaism'; (c) 'Reaction', which refers to the outbreak of pogroms in Russia in 1881, poses the choice between emigrating to America or to Zion; (d) 'Radicalism' refers to Eastern Europe in 1920 when two radical movements for social change beckon: 'world revolution' or 'Jewish Socialism'; (e) 'Crisis of Democracy' refers to the rise of the Nazis and offers the choice to 'fight the Nazis democratically' or to become a 'militant activist'; (f) 'Europe or Israel' ('struggle for national survival') or elsewhere ('concern for personal rehabilitation'); and finally, (g) 'Towards the Year 2000' which sets up the choice between integrating in 'your country of residence' or 'immigrating to Israel'.

37. The phrase in its original context referred to the Land of Israel in a purely spiritual sense. In the context of the Museum it may be interpreted spiritually, politically or both.

38. Within the Israeli context, see Bruner and Gorfain (1984:68) for a discussion of the 'authoritative telling' of the story of Masada by which the power of the state is both expressed and created. In their view, *Yad Vashem*, the Museum of the Diaspora and Masada constitute 'metonymic sites of a guided tour [that] stand in a dialogic relationship to each other in that they create a multivocal discourse about the fate and alternatives available to Jews in different historical eras and cultural contexts'.

39. The Museum historian suggested that the absence of original artifacts reflects Judaism's negation of idols:

> Using reconstructions deprives the object being displayed of the reverent stature granted it by the classical museum. It is, in fact, reduced to a mere tool in a setting which hints at the permanent beyond the transient. As a result, the absence of authenticity, which may have been interpreted as a weakness . . . [is] the principal means for successfully conveying the Jewish message that man shall not bow down before his own handiwork; i.e. the negation of idolatry in all forms (Ben-Gal, 1988:28).

40. Zerubavel (1994:86) views the establishment of the museum as one indicator of Israelis' increasing willingness to acknowledge their Diaspora roots.

41. It may be that the construction of the new wing reflects an acknowledgment of

the Diaspora as a more permanent feature of the Jewish world than might have been hoped for in the original Zionist vision.

42. Handelman and Shamgar-Handelman (1991:4) discuss the creation of links between nation and land in Israel through the symbolic elaboration of national memorials. They argue that these links are least problematic in the case of the military cemetery because of the actual presence of the sacrificial dead and most problematic in the case of the Holocaust memorial which commemorates those who lived and died elsewhere. Hence it is the latter memorial that requires the greatest degree of symbolic elaboration in order to 'reconstitute the absent sacrifice and embed its presence in the land'. Though not included in their list of places of commemoration, it would be argued that the Museum of the Diaspora shares some of the same difficulties as the Holocaust Memorial.

43. Thus Weinberg has explicitly contrasted *Beth Hatefutsoth* with Israel's museum and monument to those who died in the Holocaust: 'Yad Vashem is devoted to Jewish death whereas Beth Hatefutsoth is devoted to Jewish life' (quoted in *Washington Jewish Week*, 28 July 1988; see also Weinberg, 1988:22). Wigoder (1983:20) and Arbel (1983:21–31) are also on record making a similar contrast.

REFERENCES

Arbel, R. (1983) 'Beth Hatefutsoth and the "Sabra"' in G. Wigoder (ed.), *Beth Hatefutsoth — The First Years.*

Aronoff, M.J. (1981) 'Civil religion in Israel', *RAIN*, 44, June, 2–6.

Avner, Y. and G. Wigoder (eds) (1988) *Beth Hatefutsoth: the First Ten Years*, Tel Aviv: Beth Hatefutsoth.

Ben-Gal, E. (1988) 'Museology and Judaism: thought on the planning of Beth Hatefutsoth' in Y. Avner and G. Wigoder (eds), *Beth Hatefutsoth: the First Ten Years.*

Benjamin, W. (1982) 'The work of art in the age of mechanical reproduction' in *Illuminations*, London: Fontana.

Bennett, T. (1988) 'Museums and "the people"' in R. Lumley (ed.), The Museum Time Machine, New York: Comedia.

Bruner, E.M. and N. Gorfain (1984) 'Dialogic narration and the paradoxes of Masada' in E.M. Bruner (ed.), *Text Play and Story: the Construction and Reconstruction of Self and Society*, 1983 Proceedings of the American Ethnological Society.

Clifford, J. (1988) 'On collecting art and culture' in *The Predicament of Culture: Twentieth Century Ethnography, Literature and Art*, Harvard University Press.

Dominguez, V.R. (1986) 'The marketing of heritage' (review article), *American Ethnologist*, 13(3), 546–55.

Eisen, A.M. (1986) *Galut: Modern Jewish Reflection on Homelessness and Homecoming*, Bloomington: Indiana University Press.

Gathercole, P. (1989) 'The fetishism of artifacts' in S. Pearce (ed.), Museum Studies in Material Culture.

Goldmann, N. (1977) *Community of Fate: Jews in the Modern World*, Jerusalem: Israeli Universities Press.

Goldmann, N.(1983) 'A bridge between Israel and the Diaspora' in G. Wigoder (ed.), *Beth Hatefutsoth — The First Years.*

Grana, C. (1971) 'The private lives of public museums: can art be democratic?' in *Fact and Symbol: Essays in the Sociology of Art and Literature*, Oxford University Press.

Handelman, D. and L. Shamgar-Handelman (1990) 'Shaping time: the choice of the national emblem of Israel' in E. Ohunki-Tierney (eds), *Culture Through Time: Anthropological Approaches to History*, Stanford: Stanford University Press.

Handelman, D. and L. Shamgar-Handelman (1991) 'The presence of the dead; memorials of national death in Israel', *Suomen Antropologi*, 4, 3–17.

Holler, M. (1988) 'In the footsteps of lost communities', *Maariv*, 3 June (in Hebrew).

Horne, K. (1984) *The Great Museum: the Re-presentation of History*, London and Sydney: Pluto Press.

Hudson, K. (1987) *Museums of Influence*, Cambridge: Cambridge University Press.

Katriel, T. (1993) 'Remaking place: cultural production in an Israeli pioneer settlement museum', *History and Memory*, 5(2), 104–35.

Katriel, T. (1994) 'Sites of memory: discourses of the past in Israeli pioneering settlement museums', *Quarterly Journal of Speech*, 80, 1–20.

Kavanagh, G. (1983) 'History and the museum: the nostalgia business', *Museums Journal*, 83 (2–3), September/December, 139–41.

Kovner, A. (1988) 'To Beth Hatefutsoth on its inauguration' in Y. Avner and G. Wigoder (eds), *Beth Hatefutsoth — the First Ten Years*.

Leibman, C.S. and E. Don-Yehiya (1983) *Civil Religion in Israel: Traditional Judaism and Political Culture in the Jewish State*, Berkeley: University of California Press.

Leibman, C.S. and E. Don-Yehiya (1984) 'The dilemma of reconciling traditional culture and political needs: civil religion in Israel' in *Religion and Politics in Israel*, Bloomington: Indiana University Press.

Lewis, A. (1985) 'Phantom ethnicity: "Oriental Jews" in Israeli society' in A. Weingrod (ed.), *After the Ingathering; Studies in Israeli Ethnicity*, New York: Gordon & Breach.

Lumley, R. (1988) *The Museum Time Machine: Putting Cultures on Display*, London and New York: Routledge; Comedia.

MacCannell, D. (1976) *The Tourist: a New Theory of the Leisure Class*, New York: Schocken.

Merriman, N. (1989) 'The social basis of museum and heritage visiting' in S.M. Pearce (ed.), *Museum Studies of Material Culture*.

Mintz, A. (1984) *Hurban: Response to Catastrophe in Hebrew Literature*, New York: Columbia University Press.

Pearce, S.M. (ed.) (1982) *Museum Studies in Material Culture*, Leicester: Leicester University Press.

Salzman, N. (1981) 'Beth Hatefutsoth in Tel Aviv', *Jewish Currents*, May.

Shamgar-Handelman, L. and D. Handelman (1986) 'Holiday celebrations in Israeli kindergartens: relationships between representations of collectivity and family in the nation-state' in M. Aronoff (ed.), *The Frailty of Authority*, New Brunswick and Oxford: Transaction Books.

Shamir, I. (1981) *The Study of History through Beth Hatefutsoth*, Tel Aviv: Everyman's University Press (in Hebrew).

Shanks, M. and C. Tilley (1987) 'Presenting the past; towards a redemptive aesthetic for the museum', in M. Shanks and C. Tilley (eds), *Reconstructing Archaeology*, Cambridge University Press.

Shmueli, E. (1988) 'Beth Hatefutsoth' in Y. Avner and G. Wigoder (eds), *Beth Hatefutsoth: the First Ten Years*.

Starobinski, J. (1966) 'The idea of nostalgia', *Diogenes*, 54, 81–103.

Stocking, G. (ed.) (1985) *Objects and Others: Essays on Museums and Material Culture*, Wisconsin University Press.

Wallace, M. (1981) 'Visiting the past; history museums in the United States', *Radical History Review*, 25, 63–96.

Webber, M. (1981) 'Resacralisation of the Holy City; the capture of Jerusalem in 1967', *RAIN*, 47, 6–10.

Weinberg, J. (1980) *A Different Kind of Museum*, Tel Aviv: Beth Hatefutsoth.

Weinberg, J. (1988) 'Aspects of Uniqueness' in Y. Avner and G. Wigoder (eds), *Beth Hatefutsoth: the First Ten Years*.

Wigoder, G. (1983) Beth Hatefutsoth — the First Years, Tel Aviv: Beth Hatefutsoth.

Wigoder, G. (1988) 'The first decade' in Y. Avner and G. Wigoder (eds), *Beth Hatefutsoth: the First Ten Years*.

Yapp, M. (1988) 'Gentiles and other wounded spirits: Israel's friends and relations', *Encounter*, February, 52–6.

Yerushalmi, Y.H. (1982) *Zakhor: Jewish History and Jewish Memory*, Washington University Press.

Yizraeli, D. (1989) 'The Golda Meir effect', *Politikia*, 29 July, 44–7 (in Hebrew).

Zerubavel, E. (1982) *Hidden Rhythms: Schedules and Calendars in Social Life*, Chicago: University of Chicago Press.

Zerubavel, Y. (1994) 'The death of memory and the memory of death: Masada and the Holocaust as historical metaphors', *Representations*, 45, 72–100.

Bibliography

Adams, K. (1984) 'Come to Tana Toraja, land of the heavenly kings. Travel agents as brokers in ethnicity', *Annals of Tourism Research*, 11, 460–85.

Adler, J. (1989) 'Origins of sightseeing', *Annals of Tourism Research*, 16, 7–29.

Albers, P. and W. James (1983) 'Tourism and the changing photographic image of the Great Lakes Indians', *Annals of Tourism Research*, 10(1), 123–48.

Albers, P. and W. James (1988) 'Travel photography: a methodological approach', *Annals of Tourism Research*, 15, 134–58.

Albers, P. and W. James (1990) 'Private and public images; a study of photographic contrasts in postcard pictures of the Great Basin Indians' *Visual Anthropology*, 3, 343–66.

Allcock, J.B. (1988) 'Tourism as sacred journey', *Lorsir et Société*, 11(1), 33–48.

Alloula, M. (1986) *The Colonial Harem*, Minneapolis: University of Minnesota Press.

Anderson, B. (1983) *Imagined Communities: Reflections on the Origin and Spread of Nationalism*, London: Verso.

Andrew, C. (1977) An Investigation into Holiday Brochure Design, unpublished MSc thesis, University of Surrey.

Appudurai, A. (1986) *The Social Life of Things*, Cambridge: Cambridge University Press.

Arbel, R. (1983) 'Beth Hatefutsoth and the "Sabra"' in G. Wigoder (ed.), *Beth Hatefutsoth — The First Years*.

Aronoff, M.J. (1981) 'Civil religion in Israel', *RAIN*, 44, June, 2–6.

Ashbee, C.R. (1908) *Craftsmanship in Competitive Industry*, Campden and London: Essex House Press.

Ashkenazi, Michael (1983) Festival Change and Continuity in a Japanese Town, unpublished PhD thesis, Faculty of the Graduate School of Yale University.

Ashworth, G.J. and J.E. Tunbridge (1990) *The Tourist — Historic City*, London: Belhaven Press.

Ashworth, G.J. and H. Voogd (1990) *Selling the City: Marketing Approaches in Public Sector Urban Planning*, London: Belhaven Press.

Ashworth, G.J. and P.J. Larkham (eds) (1994) *Building a New Heritage: Tourism, Culture and Identity in the New Europe*, London: Routledge.

Avner, Y. and G. Wigoder (eds) (1988) *Beth Hatefutsoth: the First Ten Years*, Tel Aviv: Beth Hatefutsoth.

Aziz, H. (1995) 'Understanding attacks on tourists in Egypt', *Tourism Management*, 16(2), 91–7.

Bagguley, P., J. Mark-Lawson, D. Shapiro, J. Urry, S. Walby and A. Wardle (1990) *Restructuring: Place, Class and Gender*, London: Sage.

Bann, S. (1988) '"Views of the past" — reflections on the treatment of historical objects and museums of history (1750–1850)', in G. Fyfe and J. Law (eds) *Picturing Power* 39–64, London: Routledge.

Barthes, R. (1977) 'The photographic message' in *Image-Music-Text*, London: Fontana.

Barthes, R. (1982) *Image-Music-Text*, London: Fontana.

Barthes, R. (1983) *The Eiffel Tower*, New York: Hill and Wang.

Barthes, R. (1984) *Mythologies*, London: Paladin.

Bartokowski, F. (1995) *Travelers, Immigrants, Inmates*, University of Minnesota Press.

Bassini, E. and L. Tedeschi (1990) 'The image of the Hottentot in the seventeenth and eighteenth centuries', *Journal of the History of Collections*, 2(2), 157–86.

Baudrillard, J. (1968) *Le Système des Objets*, Paris: Gallimard.

Baudrillard, J. (1975) *The Mirror of Production*, St Louis: Telos Press.

Baudrillard, J. (1983) *Simulations*, New York: Semiotext, Foreign Agent Press.

Baudrillard, J. (1988) *Selected Writings*, Cambridge: Polity.

Ben-Gal, E. (1988) 'Museology and Judaism: thought on the planning of Beth Hatefutsoth' in Y. Avner and G. Wigoder (eds), *Beth Hatefutsoth: the First Ten Years*.

Benjamin, W. (1982) 'The work of art in the age of mechanical reproduction' in *Illuminations*, London: Fontana.

Bennett, T. (1988) 'Museums and "the people"' in R. Lumley (ed.), *The Museum Time Machine*, New York: Comedia.

Berger, J. (1983) *Ways of Seeing*, London: BBC and Penguin.

Berger, Peter, L., Briggite Berger and Hansfried Kellner (1973) *The Homeless Mind: Modernisation and Consciousness*, Harmondsworth: Penguin.

Bharati, Agehananda (1978) 'Actual and ideal Himalayas: Hindu views of the mountains' in James F. Fisher (ed.), *Himalayan Anthropology*, Paris and the Hague: Mouton.

Bishop, Peter (1990) *The Myth of Shangri-la*, Berkeley: University of California Press.

Bishtha, Mīnbahādur (1983) 'Yasarī Eutā Rāshtra Bānchne Bahānā Garcha' (Thus a nation pretends to live) in Tāranath Sharmā (ed.): *Samsāmayik Sājhā Kavitā*, Kathmandu: Sājhā Prakāshan.

Black, A. (1990) 'In the eyes of the beholder? The cultural effects of tourism in Malta', *Problems of Tourism*, University of Warsaw 13(3/4).

Black, A. (1996) 'Negotiating the tourist gaze: the example from Malta' in J. Boissevain (ed.), *Coping with Tourists. European Reactions to Mass Tourism*, Oxford: Berghahn Books.

Boissevain, Jeremy (1965) *Saints and Fireworks, Religion and Politics in Rural Malta*, London: Athlone Press.

Boissevain, Jeremy (1978) 'Of men and marbles: notes towards a reconsideration of factionalism' in M. Silverman and R.F. Salisbury (eds), *A House Divided? Anthropological Studies of Factionalism*, : Memorial University of Newfoundland, pp. 99–110.

Boissevain, Jeremy (1981) 'Ritual escalation in Malta', mimeo, Institute of Development Studies, University of Sussex.

Boissevain, Jeremy (1984) 'Ritual escalation in Malta' in E.R. Wolf (ed.), *Religion, Power, and Protest in Local Communities*, New York: Mouton, pp. 163–83.

Boissevain, Jeremy (1988) 'Festa Partiti and the British: exploding a myth' in V. Malia-Milanes (ed.), *The British Colonial Experience 1800–1964: the Impact on Maltese Society*, Malta: Mireva Publications, 215–29.

Boissevain, Jeremy (1991) 'Ritual, play and identity: changing patterns of celebration in Maltese villages', *Journal of Mediterranean Studies*, 1, 87–100.

Boissevain, Jeremy (1992) 'Introduction' in J. Boissevain (ed.), *Revitalizing European Rituals*, London: Routledge.

Boissevain, Jeremy (ed.) (1996) *Coping with Tourists: European Reactions to Mass Tourism*, Oxford: Berghahn.

Boorstin, D.J. (1964) *The Image: a Guide to Pseudo-events in America*, New York: Harper and Row.

Booth, Alan (1985) *The Roads to Sata*, New York, Tokyo: Weatherhill.

Bouquet, M. (1985) *Family, Servants and Visitors, The Farm Household in Nineteenth and Twentieth Century Devon*, Norwich: Geo Books.

Bouquet, M. (1986) '"You cannot be a Brahmin in the English countryside", The partitioning of status and its representation within the farm family in Devon', in A.P. Cohen (ed.): 22–39.

Bouquet, M. (1987) 'Bed, breakfast and an evening meal: commensality in nineteenth and twentieth century Hartland', in M. Bouquet and M. Winter (eds.): *Who From Their Labours Rest? Conflict and Practice in Rural Tourism*, Aldershot: Avebury, pp. 93–104.

Bourdieu, P. (1977) *Outline of a Theory of Practice*, Cambridge: Cambridge University Press.

Bourdieu, P. (1984) *Distinction: a Social Critique of the Judgement of Taste*, London: Routledge and Kegan Paul.

Bowman, G. (1992) 'Fucking tourists: sexual relations and tourism in Jerusalem's Old City', *Critique of Anthropology*, 9, 2, 77–93.

Bowman, G. (1992) 'The politics of tour guiding: Israeli and Palestinian guides in Israel and the Occupied Territories', in D. Harrison (ed.), *Tourism and the Less Developed Countries*, London: Belhaven Press, pp. 121–34.

Brandes, S. (1980) *Metaphors of Masculinity: Sex and Status in Andalusian Folklore*, Philadelphia: University of Pennsylvania Press.

Brewer, Jeffrey P. (1984) 'Tourism and ethnic stereotypes, variations in a Mexican town', *Annals of Tourism Research*, 11, 487–501.

Bridge, G. (1992) Review of Fainstein, S., Gord, I. and Harloe, M.: Divided Cities, Oxford: Blackwell, *Times Higher Education Supplement*, 13 November.

Brighton and Hove Publicity Committee (1951) *Visitors Handbook*.

Brighton and Hove Publicity Committee (1954) *Visitors' Handbook*.

Brighton Borough Council (1938) *Brighton Official Handbook 1938/9*.

Brighton Borough Council (1951) *Brighton Official Handbook*.

Brighton Borough Council (1952) *Report of the Survey: County Borough of Brighton*.

Brighton Borough Council (1984) *Residents' Handbook*, Brighton: Home Publishing.

Brighton Borough Council (1986) *Brighton Borough Plan: Towards 2000*.

Brighton Borough Council (1987) *Brighton Festival Times*.

Brighton Borough Council (1987) *Newsline*.

British Airways (1992) *Worldwide 1992* (holiday brochure).

Britton, R. (1980) 'Let us handle everything: the travel industry and the manipulation of the travel experience', *USA Today*, May, 45–7.

Britton, R. (1983) *Tourism and Underdevelopment in Fiji*, Canberra: ANU Press.

Brown, D.J.J. (1988) 'Unity in opposition in the New Guinea Highlands', *Social Analysis*, 23, 89–109.

Brown, D.J.J. (1992) 'Spiralling connubia in the Highlands of Papua New Guinea', *Man* (N, S) 27, 821–42.

Bruner, E.M. and N. Gorfain (1984) 'Dialogic narration and the paradoxes of Masada' in E.M. Bruner (ed.), *Text Play and Story: the Construction and Reconstruction of Self and Society*, 1983 Proceedings of the American Ethnological Society.

Bruner, E.M. (1989) 'Cannibals, tourists and ethnographers', *Cultural Anthropology*, 4(4).

Bruner, E. (1991) 'The transformation of self in tourism', *Annals of Tourism Research*, 18, 238–50.

Buck, R. (1977) 'The ubiquitous tourist brochure, explorations in its intended and unintended use', *Annals of Tourism Research*, 4, 195–207.

Buck, R. (1978) 'Boundary maintenance revisited: tourist experience in an old order Amish community revisited', *Rural Sociology*, 43(2), 221–34.

Buck, R. (1979) 'Bloodless theater: images of the old order Amish in tourism literature', *Pennsylvania Mennonite Heritage*, 2(3), 2–11.

Callinicos, A. (1989) *Against Postmodernism*, Cambridge: Polity.

Candler, Edmond (1905) *The Unveiling of Lhasa*, Thomas Nelson: London.

Chalfen R. (1979) 'Photography's role in tourism: some unexplored relationships', *Annals of Tourism Research*, 6, 435–47.

Chalfen, R. (1979) 'Comment on Uzzell', *Annals of Tourism Research*, 12, 123–6.

Clark, G. (ed.) (1992) *The Portrait in Photography*, London: Reaktion Books.

Clifford, J. (1986) 'On ethnographic allegory' in J. Clifford and G.E. Marcus, *Writing Culture*, Berkeley: University of California Press, pp. 98–121.

Clifford, J. (1988) 'On collecting art and culture' in *The Predicament of Culture: Twentieth Century Ethnography, Literature and Art*, Harvard University Press.

Club 18–30, Summer 1984 brochure.

Club Méditerranée 1987 brochure.

Cohen, A.P. (ed.) (1986) *Symbolising Boundaries, Identity and Diversity in British Cultures*, Manchester: Manchester University Press.

Cohen, E. (1971) 'Arab boys and tourist girls in a mixed Jewish Arab community,' *International Journal of Comparative Sociology*, XII, 4:217–33.

Cohen, E. (1972) 'Towards a sociology of international tourism', *Social Research*, 39(1).

Cohen, E. (1973) 'Nomads from affluence: notes on the phenomenon of drifter-tourism', *International Journal of Comparative Sociology*, 14(1–2), 89–103.

Cohen, E. (1979) 'A phenomenology of tourist experiences', *Sociology*, 13, 179–201.

Cohen, E. (1979) 'Rethinking the sociology of tourism', *Annals of Tourism Research*, 6(1): 18–35.

Cohen, E. (1979) 'A phenomenology of tourist experiences', *Sociology*, 13(2): 179–201.

Cohen, E. (1983) 'Ethnicity and legitimation in contemporary Israel'. *Jerusalem Quarterly*: 28.

Cohen, E. (1986) 'Lovelorn farangs: the correspondence between foreign men and Thai girls,' *Anthropological Quarterly*, LIX, 3:115–27.

Cohen, E. (1988) 'Authenticity and commoditization in tourism', *Annals of Tourism Research*, 15, 371–86.

Cohen, E. (1988) 'Traditions in the qualitative sociology of tourism', *Annals of Tourism Research*, 16, 30–61.

Cohen, E. (1989) 'Primitive and remote: hill tribe trekking in Thailand,' *Annals of Tourism Research*, 16: 30–61.

Cohen, E. (1993) 'The study of touristic images of native people. Mitigating the stereotype of the stereotype' in D. Pearce and R, Butler (eds), *Tourism Research. Critiques and Challenges*, London: Routledge, pp. 36–69.

Cohen, Eric and Robert L. Cooper (1986) 'Language and tourism', *Annals of Tourism Research*, 13, 553–63.

Collins English Dictionary (1982) London and Glasgow: Collins (6th edition).

Cooke, P. (ed.) (1989) *Localities: The Changing Face of Urban Britain*, London: Unwin Hyman.

Cooke, P. (1990) *Back to the Future: Modernity, Postmodernity and Locality*, London: Unwin Hyman.

Coombes, A.E. (1994) 'Blinded by "science": ethnography at the British Museum' in M. Pointon (ed.), *Art Apart: Art Institutions and Ideology Across England and North America*, Manchester: Manchester University Press.

Corbey, R. (1989) *Wildheid en beschaving: De Europese verbeelding van Afrika*, Baarn: Ambo.

Corner, J. and S. Harvey (1991) *Enterprise and Heritage: Crosscurrents of National Culture*, London: Routledge.

Cosmos, Summer Sun 1984 brochure.

Cowan, R. (1987) 'What the tourist never sees', *Architect's Journal*, 8(7):42–3.

Cowen, H. (1990) 'Regency icons: marketing Cheltenham's built environment' in Harloe et al.

Crapanzano, V. (1992) *Hermes Dilemma and Hamlet's Desire: On the Epistemology of Interpretation*, Cambridge, Mass.: Harvard University Press.

Crick, M. (1985) '"Tracing" the anthropological self: quizzical reflections on fieldwork, tourism and the ludic', *Social Analysis*, 17, 71–92.

Crick, M. (1988) 'Sun, sex, sights, savings and servility: representations of international tourism in the social sciences', *Criticism, Heresy and Interpretation* I(1), 37–76.

Crick, M. (1989) 'Representations of sun, sex, sights, savings and servility: international tourism in the social sciences', *Annual Review of Anthropology*, 18, 307–344.

Dann, G. (1976) 'The holiday was simply fantastic', *Revue de Tourisme*, 3, 19–23.

Dann, G. (1977) 'Anomie, ego-enhancement and tourism', *Annals of Tourism Research*, 4, 184–94.

Dann, G. (1981) 'Tourism motivation', *Annals of Tourism Research*, 8(2), 187–219.

Dann, G. (1985) 'The tourist as child. Some reflections', *Cahiers du Tourisme*, Série C, no. 135.

Dann, G. (1988) 'Images of Cyprus projected by tour operators', *Problems of Tourism*, XI(3), 43–70.

Dann, G. (1993) 'Advertising in tourism and travel: tourism brochures' in M. Khan, M. Olsen and T. Var (eds), *VNR's Encyclopedia of Hospitality and Tourism*, New York: Van Nostrand Reinhold, pp. 893–901.

Dann, G. and J. Cole, (1976) 'The tourist in Barbados: stranger and friend', *Caribbean Issues*, 2(1), 3–13.

de Kadt, E. (1979) *Tourism: Passport to Development?*, Oxford: Oxford University Press.

de Kadt, E. (1990) 'Making the alternative sustainable: lessons from development for tourism', working paper, Institute for Development Studies, University of Sussex.

Denis, A. (1984) *Cameroun: Au delà du regard*, Paris: Edition Damalisque.

Department of the Environment/Urban and Economic Development Group (1994) *Vital and Viable Town Centres: Meeting the Challenge*, London: HMSO.

Dominguez, V.R. (1986) 'The marketing of heritage' (review article), *American Ethnologist*, 13(3), 546–55.

Douglas, Mary (1970) *Purity and Danger*, Harmondsworth: Penguin Books.

Droog, Marjolijn (1991) 'En dan wordt je weer gewoon mens' Het opleven van feesten in een Oostenrijke dorp, unpublished MA thesis, Department of Anthropology, University of Amsterdam.

Durkheim, E. (1965[1915]) *The Elementary Forms of the Religious Life*, London: Free Press.

East Moulsecoomb Residents Association (1985) *EMRA Newsletter*.

Eco, U. (1986) *Faith in Fakes*, London: Secker and Warburg.

Eco, U. (1987) *Travels in Hyper-Reality*, London: Pan Books.

Edwards, E. (1992) 'The tourist icon: four Australian postcards', *Tourism in Focus*, 6, 4–5.

Edwards, E. (ed.) (1992) *Anthropology and Photography 1860–1920*, Newhaven/London: Yale University Press.

Eisen, A.M. (1986) *Galut: Modern Jewish Reflection on Homelessness and Homecoming*, Bloomington: Indiana University Press.

Eisenstadt, S.N. (1985) *The Transformation of Israeli Society*, London: Weidenfeld and Nicolson.

Ellen, R. (1986) 'What Black Elk left unsaid', *Anthropology Today*, 2(6), 8–12.

Erisman, (1983) 'Tourism and cultural dependence in the West Indies', *Annals of Tourism Research*, 10(3).

Errington, F. and D. Gewertz (1989) 'Tourism and anthropology in a post-modern world', *Oceania*, 60, 37–54.

Faraway Holidays 1983 brochure.

Farleigh, A. (ed.) (1986) *A Regency Façade? Social Need and Voluntary Action in Brighton*, Brighton: Brighton Council for Voluntary Service.

Fees, Craig (ed.) (1986) *A Child in Arcadia: The Chipping Campden Boyhood of H.T. Osborn 1902–1907)*, Chipping Campden: Campden and District Historical and Archaeological Society,

Fees, Craig (1988) Christmas Mumming in a North Cotswold Town: With Special Reference to Tourism, Urbanisation and Immigration-Related Social Change, PhD thesis, Institute of Dialect and Folk Life Studies, University of Leeds.

Fees, Craig (1988) 'Maypole dance in the twentieth century: further studies of a north Cotswold town', *Traditional Dance* 5/6, 97–134.

Fiefer, M. (1985) *Going Places*, London: Macmillan.

Fine, E. and J. Speer, (1985) 'Tour guide performances and sight sacralisation', *Annals of Tourism Research*, 12, 73–95.

Fisher, James (1986) 'Sherpas and tourists', *Contributions to Nepalese Studies*, 14(1), Kathmandu.

Flair, Summer 1984 brochure.

Frank, Dietmar (1978) *Dreamland Nepal*, New Delhi: S. Chand and Co.

Frow, J. (1991) 'Tourism and the semiotics of nostalgia', *October*, 57, 123–51.

Gathercole, P. (1989) 'The fetishism of artifacts' in S. Pearce (ed.), *Museum Studies in Material Culture*, Leicester: Leicester University Press.

Geertz, C. (1979) 'Suq: the bazaar economy in Sefrou' in C. Geertz, H. Geertz and L. Rosen (eds), *Meaning and Order in Moroccan Society: Three Essays in Cultural Analysis*, Cambridge: Cambridge University Press, pp. 123–276.

Gellner, E. (1974) *Legitimation of Belief*, London: Cambridge University Press.

Gellner, E. (1983) *Nations and Nationalism*, Oxford: Blackwell.

Girard, R. (1965) '"Triangular" desire' in R. Girard (ed.), *Deceit, Desire and the Novel: Self and Other in Literary Structure*, Baltimore: Johns Hopkins Press, pp. 1–52.

Go Greece 1995 brochure.

Goffman, E. (1959) *The Presentation of Self in Everyday Life*, New York: Doubleday.

Goldmann, N. (1969) *Memories*, Wiedenfeld & Nicolson.

Goldmann, N. (1977) *Community of Fate: Jews in the Modern World*, Jerusalem: Israeli Universities Press.

Goldmann, N. (1977) '75 years of Zionism' in *Community of Fate*.

Goldmann, N. (1977) 'The Jewish spirit of Israel and the Diaspora' in *Community of Fate*.

Goldmann, N. (1983) 'A Bridge between Israel and the Diaspora' in G. Wigoder (ed.), *Beth Hatefutsoth — The First Years*.

Goodman, Roger (1987) A Study of the Kikokushijo Phenomenon: Returnee Schoolchildren in Contemporary Japan, unpublished PhD thesis, Faculty of Social Anthropology and Geography, University of Oxford.

Gottlieb, A. (1982) 'Americans' vacations', *Annals of Tourism Research*, 9, 165–87.

Graburn, N. (1977) 'Tourism: the sacred journey' in V. Smith (ed.), *Hosts and Guests: the Anthropology of Tourism*, Philadelphia: University of Pennsylvania Press.

Graburn, N. (1983) 'The anthropology of tourism', *Annals of Tourism Research* 10(1): 9–33.

Graburn, Nelson H.H. (1983) To Pray, Pay and Play: the Cultural Structure of Japanese Domestic Tourism, *Les Cahiers du Tourisme*, serie no 26, Centre des Haute Etudes Touristiques, Université de Droit, d'Economie et des Sciences, Aix-en-Provence: Centre des Hautes Etudes Touristiques.

Grana, C. (1971) 'The private lives of public museums: can art be democratic?' in *Fact and Symbol: Essays in the Sociology of Art and Literature*, Oxford University Press.

Greenblatt, S. (1991) 'Resonance and wonder', in I. Karp and S.D. Levine (eds) *Exhibiting Cultures*, 42–56, Washington: Smithsonian Institution Press.

Greene, G. (1975 edition) *Brighton Rock*, Harmondsworth: Penguin.

Greenwood, D. (1989[1977]) 'Culture by the pound: an anthropological perspective on tourism as cultural commoditisation' in V. Smith (ed.), *Hosts and Guests: the Anthropology of Tourism*, Philadelphia: University of Pennsylvania Press.

Gritti, J. (1967) 'Les contenus culturels du Guide Bleu: monuments et sites a voir', *Communications*, 10, 51–64.

Hale, S. (1988) 'Sugar mummies and their prey', *The Observer*, 30 October: 35.

Hall, C.M. (1992) 'Sex Tourism in South-east Asia' in D. Harrison (ed.), *Tourism in the Less Developed Countries*, London: Belhaven Press, pp. 64–74.

Halliwell, Leslie (1985) *Halliwell's Film Guide*, London: Granada.

Handelman, Don (1977) 'Play and ritual: complementary frames of meta-communication' in A.J. Chapman and H. Foot (eds), *It's a Funny Thing, Humour*, London: Pergamon Press.

Handelman, Don (1987) 'Play' in Mircea Eliade (ed.), *The Encyclopedia of Religion*, Vol. 2, New York: William Pith, 363–8.

Handelman, D. and Shamgar, L. (1990) 'Shaping time: the choice of the national emblem of Israel' in E. Ohunki-Tierney (ed.), *Culture Through Time: Anthropological Approaches to History*, Stanford: Stanford University Press.

Handelman, D. and L. Shamgar-Handelman (1991) 'The presence of the dead; memorials of national death in Israel', *Suomen Antropologi*, 4, 3–17.

Handler, R. (1985) 'On having a culture: nationalism and the preservation of Quebec's patrimoine', in G. Stocking (ed.), *Objects and Others: Essays on Museums and Material Culture*, Wisconsin University Press.

Handler, R. (1986) 'Authenticity', *Anthropology Today*, 2(1), 2–4.

Harloe, M., C. Pickvance and J. Urry (1990) (eds) *Place, Policy and Politics: Do Localities Matter?* London: Unwin Hyman.

Harrison, D. (1992) *Tourism and the Less Developed Countries*, London: Belhaven Press.

Harrison, D. (1992) 'International tourism and the less developed countries: the background' in D. Harrison (ed.), *Tourism and the Less Developed Countries*, London: Belhaven Press, pp. 1–18.

Harvey, Andrew (1984) A Journey in Ladakh, Paladin Books: London.

Harvey, D. (1993) 'From place to space and back again: reflections on the condition of post modernity' in J. Bird, B. Curtis, G. Putnam, G. Robertson and L. Tickner (eds) *Mapping the Futures: Local Cultures, Global Change*, London: Routledge.

Hatch, Elvin (1985) 'Culture' in Adam Kuper and Jessica Kuper (eds), *The Social Science Encyclopedia*, London: Routledge and Kegan Paul, 178–9.

Heidegger, Martin (1977) *The Question Concerning Technology and Other Essays*, trans. William Lovitt, New York: Harper Torchbooks.

Heidegger, Martin (1978) *Being and Time*, trans. John Macquarrie and Edward Robinson, Oxford: Blackwell.

Heidegger, Martin (1985) *History of the Concept of Time*, trans. Theodore Kisiel, Bloomington: Indiana University Press.

Hendry, Joy (1984) 'Shoes, the early learning of an important distinction in Japanese society', in Gordon Daniels (ed.), *Europe Interprets Japan*, Tenterden, Kent: Paul Norbury Publications.

Herzfeld, M. (1985) *The Poetics of Manhood: Contest and Identity in a Cretan Mountain Village*, Princeton: Princeton University Press.

Hewison, R. (1987) *The Heritage Industry: Britain in a Climate of Decline*, London: Methuen.

Hilton, James (1947) *Lost Horizon*, London: Pan Books (1st Edition 1933).

Hobsbawm, E. and Ranger, T. (eds) (1983) *The Invention of Tradition*, Cambridge: Cambridge University Press.

Holler, M. (1988) 'In the footsteps of lost communities', *Maariv*, 3 June (in Hebrew).

Honour, H. (1988) *The Image of the Black in Western Art*, Houston, Texas: Meril Foundation, Harvard University Press.

Hori, Ichiro (1963) 'Mysterious visitors from the harvest to the new year' in Richard Dorson (ed.), *Studies in Japanese Folklore*, Bloomington: Indiana University Press.

Horne, K. (1984) *The Great Museum: the Re-presentation of History*, London and Sydney: Pluto Press.

Hudson, K. (1987) *Museums of Influence*, Cambridge: Cambridge University Press.

Hutt, Michael (1984) 'Neon lights and vedic caves: European influences on the Nepali writer', *South Asia Research*, 4(2).

Hutt, Michael (1991) *Himalayan Voices, an Introduction to Modern Nepali Literature*, Berkeley: University of California Press.

Hutton, W. (1994) *The State We're In: Why Britain is in Crisis and How to Overcome it*, London: Jonathan Cape.

Inspirations India 1995 brochure.

Intasun, Summer 1984 brochure.

Intourist, *Magnolia Holidays* 1984 brochure.

Jackson, A. (1987) 'Reflections on ethnography at home and the ASA' in A. Jackson (ed.): 1–15.

Jackson, A. (ed.) (1987) *Anthropology at Home*, ASA, Monograph 25, London: Tavistock.

Jameson, F. (1985) 'Post-modernism and consumer society' in H. Foster (ed.), *Post-modern Culture*, London: Pluto.

Kabbani, R. (1986) *Europe's Myths of the Orient*, London: Macmillan.

Karch, C. and G. Dann, (1981) 'Close encounters of the Third World', *Human Relations*, 34(4), 249–68.

Karp, I. and S.D. Levine (1991) *Exhibiting Cultures*, Washington, DC: Smithsonian Press.

Katriel, T. (1993) 'Remaking place: cultural production in an Israeli pioneer settlement museum', *History and Memory*, 5(2), 104–35.

Katriel, T. (1994) 'Sites of memory: discourses of the past in Israeli pioneering settlement museums', *Quarterly Journal of Speech*, 80, 1–20.

Katz, S. (1985) 'The Israeli teacher-guide', *Annals of Tourism Research*, 12, 49–72.

Katznelson-Shazar, R. (ed.) (1975[1932]) *The Plough Woman*, New York: Herzl Press.

Kaufman, J.C.A. (1982) 'Photographs and history: flexible illustrations' in T.F.

Barrow, S. Armitage and W.E. Tydeman (eds), *Reading into Photography: Selected Essays 1959–1980*, Albuquerque: University of New Mexico Press, 193–9.

Kavanagh, G. (1983) 'History and the museum: the nostalgia business', *Museums Journal*, 83 (2–3), September/December, 139–41.

Kearns, G. and C. Philo (eds) (1993) *Selling Places: the City as Cultural Capital, Past and Present*, Oxford: Pergamon Press.

Kedourie, E. (1960) *Nationalism*, London: Hutchinson.

Kenna, M. (1993) 'Return migrants and tourist development; an example from the Cyclades', *Journal of Modern Greek Studies*, 11, 75–81.

Kent, N. (1983) *Hawaii: Islands Under the Influence*, New York: Monthly Review Press.

Khuri, F. (1968) 'The etiquette of bargaining in the Middle East', *American Anthropologist*, LXX:698–706.

Kim Moon, Ok-Pyo, (1986) 'Is the Ie disappearing in rural Japan? The impact of tourism on a traditional Japanese village', in Joy Hendry et al. (eds) *Interpreting Japanese Society*, Oxford: JASO.

Koster, Adrianus, Yme Kuiper and Jojada Verrips (eds) (1983) *Feest en ritueel in Europa, antropologische essays*, Amsterdam: VU boekhandel/Uitgeverij.

Kovner, A. (1988) 'To Beth Hatefutsoth on its inauguration' in Y. Avner and G. Wigoder (eds), *Beth Hatefutsoth — the First Ten Years*.

Kreis, K.M. (1992) '"Indians" in old postcards', *European Review of Native American Studies*, 6(1), 39–48.

Kulick, D. and M.E. Willson (1992) 'Echoing images: the construction of savagery among Papua New Guinean villagers', *Visual Anthropology*, 5(2), 143–52.

Kuoni Worldwide 1986 brochure.

Lash, S. (1990) *Sociology of Postmodernism*, London: Routledge.

Lash, S. and Urry, J. (1987) *The End of Organised Capitalism*, Cambridge: Polity Press.

Laurent, A. (1967) 'Le thème du soleil dans la publicité des organismes des vacances', *Communications*, 10, 35–50.

Laxson, J. (1991) 'How "we" see "them": tourism and Native Americans', *Annals of Tourism Research*, 18, 365–91.

Lāmichhāne, Shankar (1975) *Godhuli Samsar*, Kathmandu: Ratna.

Lāmichhāne, Shankar (1979) 'Ardhamudit Nayan ra Dubna Lāgeko Ghām' (The half-closed eyes and the setting sun) in Bhairav Aryāl (ed.), *Sajha Katha*, Kathmandu: Sajha Prakasan, 3rd edition.

Lee, T.-H. and J. Compton (1992) 'Measuring novelty-seeking in tourism', *Annals of Tourism Research*, 19, 732–51.

Lefebvre, H. (1991) *The Production of Space*, Oxford: Basil Blackwell.

Leibman, C.S. and E. Don-Yehiya (1983) *Civil Religion in Israel: Traditional Judaism and Political Culture in the Jewish State*, Berkeley: University of California Press.

Leibman, C.S. and E. Don-Yehiya (1984) 'The dilemma of reconciling traditional culture and political needs: civil religion in Israel' in *Religion and Politics in Israel*, Bloomington: Indiana University Press.

Leibman, C.S. and Don-Yehiya, (1984) *Religion and Politics in Israel*, Bloomington University Press.

Levi-Strauss, C. (1958) *Anthropologie Structurale*, Paris: Plon.

Levi-Strauss, C. (1967) *Totemism*, London: Penguin Books.

Levi-Strauss, C. (1986[1964]) *The Raw and the Cooked*, Harmondsworth: Penguin.

Levi-Strauss, C. (1987[1983]) *The View from Afar*, Harmondsworth: Penguin.

Levine, Donald N. (1979) 'Simmel at a distance: on the history and systematics of the sociology of the stranger' in William A. Shack and Elliot P. Skinner (eds), *Strangers in African Societies*.

Lewis, A. (1985) 'Phantom ethnicity: "Oriental Jews" in Israeli society' in A. Weingrod (ed.), *After the Ingathering; Studies in Israeli Ethnicity*, New York: Gordon & Breach.

Lowenthal, D. (1975) 'Past time, present place: landscape and memory', *The Geographical Review*, no. 1, January: 1–36.

Lowenthal, D. (1985) *The Past is a Foreign Country*, Cambridge: Cambridge University Press.

Lumley, R. (1988) *The Museum Time Machine: Putting Cultures on Display*, London and New York: Routledge; Comedia.

MacCannell, D. (1976) *The Tourist: a New Theory of the Leisure Class*, New York: Schocken.

MacCannell, D. (1989) 'Introduction' to special edition on Semiotics of Tourism, *Annals of Tourism Research*, 16(1).

MacCannell, D. (1992) *Empty Meeting Grounds*, London: Routledge.

MacDougall, D. (1992) 'Photo hierarchicus: signs and mirrors in Indian photography', *Visual Anthropology*, 5(2), 103–29.

Manning, Frank E. (1983) 'Cosmos and chaos: celebrating the modern world' in Frank E. Manning (ed.), *The Celebration of Society: Perspectives on Contemporary Cultural Performances*, Bowling Green, Ohio: Bowling Green University Press.

Martinez, D.P. (1990) 'Tourism and the Ama, the search for a real Japan' in Eyal Ben-Ari, Brian Moeran and James Valentine (eds), *Unwrapping Japan*, Manchester: Manchester University Press..

Mason, P. (1990) *Deconstructing America*, London: Routledge.

Mauss, M. (1967) *The Gift*, London: Routledge.

Mayo, E. and L. Jarvis (1981) *The Psychology of Leisure Travel, Effective Marketing and Selling of Travel Services*, Boston: CBI.

McDonald, M. (1987a) 'The politics of fieldwork in Brittany', in A. Jackson (ed.): 120–138.

McDonald, M. (1987b) 'Tourism: chasing culture and tradition in Britanny', in M. Bouquet and M. Winter (eds): 120–134.

McKean, Philip Frick (1989[1977]) 'Towards a theoretical analysis of tourism: economic dualism and cultural involution in Bali' in V. Smith (ed.), *Hosts and Guests, the Anthropology of Tourism*, Philadelphia: University of Pennsylvania Press, 119–38.

Meethan, K.F. (1990) Voluntary Action in Brighton Neighbourhood Associations, Unpublished PhD thesis, University of Sussex.

Meleghy, Tamas, Max Preglau and Alois Tafertshafer (1985) 'Tourism development and value change', *Annals of Tourism Research*, 12, 181–99.

Mellinger, W. (1994) 'Toward a critical analysis of tourism representations', *Annals of Tourism Research*, 21, 756–79.

Mendosa, Eugene L. (1983) 'Tourism and income strategies in Nazare, Portugal', *Annals of Tourism Research*, 10, 213–38.

Merriman, N. (1989) 'The social basis of museum and heritage visiting' in S.M. Pearce (ed.), *Museum Studies of Material Culture*.

Metz, C. (1985) 'Photography and fetish', reprinted in C. Squires (ed.) (1990), *The Critical Image*, London: Lawrence & Wishart.

Michaud, R. and S. Michaud (1985) *Afghanistan*, London: Thames and Hudson.

Michaud, R. and S. Michaud (1985) *Caravans to Tatary*, London: Thames and Hudson.

Michaud, R. and S. Michaud (1992) *Mirror of the Orient*, London: Thames and Hudson.

Minces, J. (1982) *The House of Obedience: Women in Arab Society*, London: Zed Press.

Mintz, A. (1984) *Hurban: Response to Catastrophe in Hebrew Literature*, New York: Columbia University Press.

Moeran, B. (1983) 'The language of Japanese tourism', *Annals of Tourism Research*, 10(1), 93–108.

Moscardo, G. and P. Pearce (1986) 'Historic theme parks: an Australian experience in authenticity', *Annals of Tourism Research*, 13, 467–79.

Musgrave, C. (1970) *Life in Brighton*, London: Faber and Faber.

Mydin, I. (1992) 'Historical photographs — changing audiences' in E. Edwards (ed.), *Anthropology and Photography 1860–1920*, New Haven/London: Yale University Press, pp. 249–52.

Nadel-Klein, J. (1991) 'Picturing Aborigines: a review essay on "After Two Hundred Years"', *Cultural Anthropology*, 6(3), 414–23.

Nash, D. (1970) *A Community in Limbo, an Anthropological Study of an American Community Abroad*, Bloomington: Indiana University Press.

Nash, D. (1977) 'Tourism as a form of imperialism' in V. Smith (ed.), *Hosts and Guests: the Anthropology of Tourism*, Oxford: Basil Blackwell, pp. 33–47.

Nash, D. (1981) 'Tourism as an anthropological subject', *Current Anthropology*, 22(5), 461–81.

Nash, D. (1984) 'The ritualization of tourism: comment on Graburn's "The Anthropology of Tourism"', *Annals of Tourism Research*, 11(3), 503–6.

Nolan, S. and M. Nolan (1978) 'Variations in travel behaviour and the cultural impact on tourism' in V. Smith (ed.), *Tourism and Behavior*, Studies in Third World Societies, No. 5, Williamsburg: College of William and Mary. pp. 1–15.

Nordström, A.D. (1991) 'Early photography in Samoa', *History of Photography*, 15(4), 272–86.

Nunez, T. (1977) 'Touristic studies in anthropological perspective', in V.L. Smith (ed.): 207–16.

O'Rourke, D. (1987) *Cannibal Tours* (film) Canberra: O'Rourke and Associates.

Odermatt, Peter (1991) Over de nuraghen en wat verder over de zee kwam! Een onderzoek naar het tourisme in Sardinë, unpublished MA thesis, Department of Anthropology, University of Amsterdam.

Ogura, Manabu (1963) 'Drifted deities in the Noto Peninsula' in Richard Dorson (ed.), *Studies in Japanese Folklore*, Bloomington: Indiana University Press.

Ong, A. (1985) 'Industrialisation and prostitution in southeast Asia', *Southeast Asia Chronicle*, LXXXXVI:2–6.

Ono, Sokyo in collaboration with William P. Woodward (1962) *Shinto, the Kami Way*, Tokyo: Charles E. Tuttle.

Pahl, R. (1984) *Divisions of Labour*, Oxford: Blackwell.

Papson, S. (1981) 'Spuriousness and tourism', *Annals of Tourism Research*, 8, 220–35.

Passariello, Phyllis (1983) 'Never on Sunday? Mexican tourists at the beach', *Annals of Tourism Research*, 10, 109–22.

Peacock, J. (1986) *The Anthropological Lens: Harsh Light, Soft Focus*, Cambridge: Cambridge University Press.

Peake, R. (1989) 'Swahili stratification and tourism in Malindi Old Town, Kenya', *Africa*, 59(2).

Pearce, P. (1989) *The Social Psychology of Tourist Behaviour*, Oxford: Pergamon.

Pearce, S.M. (ed.) (1982) *Museum Studies in Material Culture*, Leicester: Leicester University Press.

Pegasus, Caribbean Sun 1985 brochure.

Peltours 1983 brochure.

Peterson, N. (1985) 'The popular image' in I. and T. Donaldson (eds), *Seeing the First Australians*, Sydney: Allen and Unwin, 64–180.

Pfaffenberger, B. (1983) 'Serious pilgrims and frivolous tourists', *Annals of Tourism Research*, 10, 57–74.

Pi-Sunyer, Oriol (1977) 'Through native eyes: tourists and tourism in a Catalan maritime community' in V. Smith (ed.), *Host and Guests: the Anthropology of Tourism*, Oxford: Blackwell.

Picard, M. (1992) 'Cultural tourism in Bali: national integration and regional differentiation' in M. Hitchcock, T. King, and M. Parnwell (eds), *Tourism in South-East Asia*, London: Routledge.

Picone, Mary J. (1984) Rites and Symbols of Death in Japan, unpublished PhD thesis, Faculty of Social Anthropology and Geography, University of Oxford.

Pinney, C. (1989) 'Appearing worlds', *Anthropology Today*, 5(3), 26–8.

Plath, David W. (1964) *The After Hours, Modern Japan and the Search for Enjoyment*, Berkeley: University of California Press.

Popper, K.R. (1972) 'The bucket and the searchlight: two theories of knowledge' *Objective Knowledge: An Evolutionary Approach*, Oxford: Clarendon Press, 341–61.

Popper, K.R. (1976) *Conjectures and Refutations* (6th impression), London: Routledge and Kegan Paul.

Popper, K.R. (1977) *The Logic of Scientific Discovery* (9th impression), London: Hutchinson.

Poundstretcher 1986 brochure.

Pradhan, Parashu (1984) *Pratinidhi Kathaharu*, Kathmandu: Om Prakash Agraval.

Pratt, M.L. (1992) *Imperial Eyes*, London: Routledge.

Prochaska, D. (1990) 'The archive of Algeria imaginaire', *History and Anthropology*, 4, 373–420.

Prochaska, D. (1991) 'Fantasia of the Phototheque: French postcard views of colonial Senelgal', *African Arts*, 24(2), 40–7.

Puijk, Roel (1996) 'Dealing with fish and tourists. A case study from Northern Norway in J. Boissevain (ed.), *Coping With Tourists: European Reactions to Mass Tourism*, Oxford: Berghahn Books.

Pulsipher, G. *Media Production Marketing*.

Queen Spark Rates Book Group (1982) *Brighton on the Rocks: Monetarism and the Local State*, Queen Spark, Brighton.

RGB (1992) Royal Government of Bhutan, Department of Education, *Eighth Quarterly Policy Guidelines and Instructions*, Thimphu, March.

Ricciardi, M. (1971) *Vanishing Africa*, London: Collins.

Robins, K. (1993) 'Prisoners of the city: whatever could a post modern city be? in E. Carter, J. Donald and J. Squires (eds) *Space and Place: Theories of Identity and Locality*, London: Lawrence and Wishart.

Rosenow, J. and G. Pulsipher (1979) *Tourism — the Good, the Bad and the Ugly*, Lincoln, Neb.: Media Production Marketing

Rotenberg, R. and G. McDonogh (eds) (1993) *The Cultural Meaning of Urban Space*, Westport: Bergin and Harvey.

Saga Worldwide 1983 brochure.

Said, Edward, W. (1985[1978]) *Orientalism*, London: Peregrine Books.

Salzman, N. (1981) 'Beth Hatefutsoth in Tel Aviv', *Jewish Currents*, May.

Schama, S. (1987) *The Embarrassment of Riches*, London: Collins.

Scott, J.C. (1990) *Domination and the Arts of Resistance: Hidden Transcripts*, New Haven: Yale University Press.

Segalen, M. (1987) Review, Cohen, A.P. (ed.) 1986 *Symbolising Boundaries* in *Sociologia Ruralis*, XXVII, 4, 341–3.

Selwyn, T. (1993) 'Peter Pan in South-East Asia. Views from the brochures' in M.

Hitchcock, V. King and M. Parnwell (eds), *Tourism in South-East Asia*, London: Routledge, pp. 117–37.

Selwyn, T. (1994) 'The anthropology of tourism: reflections on the state of the art' in A.V. Seaton et al. (eds), *Tourism: the State of the Art*, Chichester: John Wiley.

Selwyn, T. (1995) 'Landscapes of liberation and imprisonment: towards an anthropology of the Israeli landscape' in E. Hirsch and M. O'Hanlon (eds), *The Anthropology of the Landscape*, Oxford: Oxford University Press.

Serchan, Bhupi (1983[1969]) *Ghumne Mechmathi Andho Manche* (A blind man on a revolving chair), Kathmandu: Sajha Prakasan, 4th edition.

Shack, William A. and Elliott P. Skinner (eds) (1979) *Strangers in African Societies*, Berkeley and Los Angeles: University of California Press.

Shamgar-Handelman, L. and D. Handelman (1986) 'Holiday celebrations in Israeli kindergartens: relationships between representations of collectivity and family in the nation-state' in M. Aronoff (ed.), *The Frailty of Authority*, New Brunswick and Oxford: Transaction Books.

Shamir, I. (1981) *The Study of History through Beth Hatefutsoth*, Tel Aviv: Everyman's University Press (in Hebrew).

Shanks, M. and C. Tilley (1987) 'Presenting the past; towards a redemptive aesthetic for the museum', in M. Shanks and C. Tilley (eds), *Reconstructing Archaeology*, Cambridge University Press.

Sharma, Ratnadev (1971) 'Ma Pani Euta Anautho Manche' (I too am a remarkable man), *Madhupark*, 4(7) Kathmandu.

Sharma, Taranath (ed.) (1983) *Samasamayik Sajha Kavita*, Kathmandu: Sajha Prakashan

Shepherd, Richard (1990) 'Happy tourist, unhappy traveller', *Himal*, Sept.–Oct.

Shields, R. (1990) *Places on the Margin*, London: Routledge.

Shmueli, E. (1988) 'Beth Hatefutsoth' in Y. Avner and G. Wigoder (eds), *Beth Hatefutsoth: the First Ten Years*.

Short, J. Rennie (1992) *Imagined Country*, London: Routledge.

Simmel, Georg (1950) 'The Stranger' in *The Sociology of Georg Simmel*, trans. and edited by K.H. Wolff, New York: Free Press.

Simply Caribbean 1994–95 brochure.

Sinclair, D. (1995) Tourism in Guyana: a Semiotic Analysis, unpublished MPhil thesis, University of the West Indies, Barbados.

Singer, A. and L. Woodhead (1988) *Disappearing World: Television and Anthropology*, London: Boxtree for Granada TV.

Smith, A.D. (1986) *The Ethnic Origin of Nations*, Oxford: Blackwell.

Smith, A.D. (1991) *National Identity*, London: Penguin

Smith, B. (1960) *European Vision of the South Pacific 1768–1850*, London: Oxford University Press.

Smith, N. and P. Williams (eds) (1986) *Gentrification of the City*, Boston: Allen and Unwin.

Smith, V.L. (ed.) (1977) (revised 1989) *Hosts and Guests, the Anthropology of Tourism*, Philadelphia: University of Pennsylvania Press.

Smith, V. (1977) 'Introduction', *Hosts and Guests: the Anthropology of Tourism*, Oxford: Blackwell.

Smith, V. (1988) 'Geographical implications of "drifter" tourism: Borocay, Philippines' in *Symposium on Tourism*, International Geographical Union, 13–20 August, Christchurch, New Zealand.

Sontag, S. (1979) *On Photography*, Harmondsworth: Penguin.

Speedbird Worldwide 1986 brochure.

Starobinski, J. (1966) 'The idea of nostalgia', *Diogenes*, 54, 81–103.

Steichen, E. (1955) *The Family of Man*, New York: MOMA.

Stewart, S. (1984) *On Longing: Narratives of the Miniature, the Gigantic, the Souvenir, the Collection*, Baltimore: Johns Hopkins University Press.

Stocking, G. (ed.) (1985) *Objects and Others: Essays on Museums and Material Culture*, Wisconsin University Press.

Stott, Margaret (1979) 'Tourism in Mykonos: some social and cultural responses', *Mediterranean Studies*, 1, 72–90.

Strathern, M. (1987) 'The limits of auto-anthropology', in A. Jackson (ed.): 16–37.

Strathern, M. (1987) 'Historical events and the interpretation of images', presented at the Symposium on 'Culture and History in the Pacific', Academy of Finland, 1987, published in the *Transactions of the Finnish Anthropological Society*, Helsinki, edited by J. Siikala.

Stringer, P. (1984) 'Studies in the socio-environmental psychology of tourism', *Annals of Tourism Research*, 11, 147–66.

Sturrock, J. (1979) *Structuralism and Since*, Oxford: Oxford University Press.

Subedi, Abhi (ed.) (1982) *Pachhis Varshaka Nepali Kavita*, Kathmandu: Royal Nepal Academy.

Tagg, J. (1988) *The Burden of Representation*, London: Routledge.

Tamari, S. (1989) 'The revolt of the petite bourgeoisie', paper read at Georgetown University, Washington, DC, 26 April.

Tamari, S. (1991) 'The Palestinian movement in transition: historical reversals and the uprising', *Journal of Palestine Studies*, XX, 2:57–70.

Taylor, J. (1994) *A Dream of England: Landscape Photography and the Tourist Imagination*, Manchester: Manchester University Press.

Taylor, P. (ed.) (1988) *After 200 Years*, Canberra: Aboriginal Studies Press.

The International Herald and Tribune, 11 May 1983.

Thurot, J. and G. Thurot (1983) 'The ideology of class and tourism: confronting the discourse of advertising', *Annals of Tourism Research*, 10(1), 173–89.

Timmer, J. (1992) 'Body Decoration, Tradition, Authenticity and Tourism: Altered Contexts in a Huli Society', unpublished paper given at the First European Colloquium on Pacific Studies, Nijmegen, December.

Tokushima, Tomao (1980) 'Tourism within, from and to Japan', *International Social Science Journal*, 32, 128–50.

Toutain, Pierre (1986) *Nepal*, London: Merehurst Press.

Truong, T.-d. (1990) *Sex, Money and Morality: Prostitution and Tourism in Southeast Asia*, London: Zed Books.

Turner, L. (1976) 'The international division of leisure: tourism and the Third World', *Annals of Tourism Research*, 4, 12–24.

Turner, V. (1974) *Dramas, Fields, and Metaphors: Symbolic Action in Human Society*, Ithaca and London: Cornell University Press.

Turner, Victor (ed.) (1982) *Celebration: Studies in Festivity and Ritual*, Washington DC: Smithsonian Institution Press.

Urry, J. (1990) *The Tourist Gaze: Leisure and Travel in Contemporary Societies*, London: Sage.

Uzzell, D. (1984) 'An alternative structuralist approach to the psychology of marketing', *Annals of Tourism Research*, 11: 79–99.

van den Berghe, P. (1980) 'Tourism as ethnic relations: a case study of Cuzeo, Peru', *Ethnic and Racial Studies*, 3(4), 375–91.

van den Berghe, P. (1994) *The Quest for the Other*, Seattle and London: University of Washington.

Vassallo, Mario (1979) *From Lordship to Stewardship: Religion and Social Change in Malta*, The Hague: Mouton.

Vassallo, Mario (1981) 'Pageantry and secularisation — the Malta case' *Melita Theologica*, 32, 50–8.

Vogt, J. (1976) 'Wandering: youth and travel behaviour', *Annals of Tourism Research*, 4, 25–41.

Wagner, R. (1986) *Symbols that Stand for Themselves*, Chicago: University of Chicago Press.

Wallace, M. (1981) 'Visiting the past; history museums in the United States', *Radical History Review*, 25, 63–96.

Walton, J. (1983) *The English Sea-side Resort: A Social History 1750–1914*, Leicester: Leicester University Press.

Watson, G.L. and J.P. Kopachevsky (1994) 'Interpretations of tourism as a commodity', *Annals of Tourism Research*, 21(3):643–60.

Webb, V.-L. (1992) 'Fact and fiction: nineteenth century photographs of Zulu', *African Arts*, 25(1), 50–9.

Webber, J. (1981) 'Resacralisation of the Holy City; the capture of Jerusalem in 1967', *RAIN*, 47, 6–10.

Weber-Kellerman, Ingeborg (1985) *Saure Wochen Frohe Feste. Fest und Alltag in der Sparache der Bräuche*, Munich and Luzern: Bucher.

Weinberg, J. (1980) *A Different Kind of Museum*, Tel Aviv: Beth Hatefutsoth.

Weinberg, J. (1988) 'Aspects of Uniqueness' in Y. Avner and G. Wigoder (eds), *Beth Hatefutsoth: the First Ten Years*.

Weiner, M.J. (1981) *English Culture and the Decline of the Industrial Spirit*, Cambridge: Cambridge University Press.

Werdmolder, H. (1979) 'Karnaval anders bezien. Een studie naar het organisatorische aspect van het karnaval te Venlo', *Volkskundig Bulletin*, 5, 1–20.

Whitfield, Christopher (1958) *A History of Chipping Campden*, Eton, Windsor: Shakespeare Head Press.

Wigoder, G. (1983) Beth Hatefutsoth — the First Years, Tel Aviv: Beth Hatefutsoth.

Wigoder, G. (1988) 'The first decade' in Y. Avner and G. Wigoder (eds), *Beth Hatefutsoth: the First Ten Years*.

Williamson, J. (1983) *Decoding Advertisements. Ideology and Meaning in Advertising*, London: Marion Boyars.

Wolf, W. (1992) 'Das sind die neu gefunden menschen oder volker', Europaische Indianerbilder des 16, bis 19, Jahrhunderts zwischen Entwurf und Projektion in P. Mesenholler (ed.), *Mundus Novus: Amerika oder die Entdeckung des Bekannten*, Essen: Klartext, 35–53.

Wright, P. (1985) *On Living in an Old Country: the National Past in Contemporary Britain*, London: Verso.

Xuereb, Paul (1979) 'Review' of Mario Vassallo, *From Lordship to Stewardship: Religion and Social Change in Malta*, Sunday Times (Malta), 16 September, 10.

Yamaguchi, Masao (1977) 'Kingship theatricality and marginal reality in Japan' in R.K. Jain (ed.), *Text and Context, the Social Anthropology of Tradition*, Philadelphia: Institute for the Study of Social Issues.

Yamaguchi, Masao (1987) 'The dual structure of Japanese emperorship', *Current Anthropology*, 28(4) (supplement), 5–11.

Yapp, M. (1988) 'Gentiles and other wounded spirits: Israel's friends and relations', *Encounter*, February, 52–6.

Yerushalmi, Y.H. (1982) *Zakhor: Jewish History and Jewish Memory*, Washington University Press.

Yizraeli, D. (1989) 'The Golda Meir effect', *Politikia*, 29 July, 44–7 (in Hebrew).

Yoshida, Teigo (1981) 'Stranger as God, the place of the outsider in Japanese folk religion', *Ethnology*, 202, 87–99.

Zerubavel, E. (1982) *Hidden Rhythms: Schedules and Calendars in Social Life*, Chicago: University of Chicago Press.

Zerubavel, Y. (1994) 'The death of memory and the memory of death: Masada and the Holocaust as historical metaphors', *Representations*, 45, 72–100.

Zinovieff, S. (1991) 'Hunters and hunted: *Kamaki* and the ambiguities of sexual predation in a Greek town' in P. Loizos and E. Papataxiarchis (eds), *Contested Identities: Gender and Kinship in Modern Greece*, Princeton: Princeton University Press, pp. 203–20.

Zukin, S. (1990) 'Socio-spatial prototypes of a new organization of consumption: the role of real cultural capital,' *Sociology* 24(1):37–56.

Index